[The summarye of the chronicles of Englande ... abridged and continued, vnto 1573] (1579)

John Stow

[The summarye of the chronicles of Englande ... abridged and continued, vnto 1573]

Summarie of Englyshe chronicles.
Stow, John, 1525?-1605.
An abridgment of "A summarie of Englyshe chronicles" (STC 23319-23325.2).
Title and imprint from STC.
Dedication signed: Iohn Stovve.
Signatures: pi *A6 **2 A-2G 2H6+.
Imperfect; lacks leaves U4,5 and all after 2H6.
[524+] p.
[London : T. Marshe, [1573]]
STC (2nd ed.) / 23325.6
English
Reproduction of the original in the Bodleian Library

Early English Books Online (EEBO) Editions

Imagine holding history in your hands.

Now you can. Digitally preserved and previously accessible only through libraries as Early English Books Online, this rare material is now available in single print editions. Thousands of books written between 1475 and 1700 and ranging from religion to astronomy, medicine to music, can be delivered to your doorstep in individual volumes of high-quality historical reproductions.

We have been compiling these historic treasures for more than 70 years. Long before such a thing as "digital" even existed, ProQuest founder Eugene Power began the noble task of preserving the British Museum's collection on microfilm. He then sought out other rare and endangered titles, providing unparalleled access to these works and collaborating with the world's top academic institutions to make them widely available for the first time. This project furthers that original vision.

These texts have now made the full journey -- from their original printing-press versions available only in rare-book rooms to online library access to new single volumes made possible by the partnership between artifact preservation and modern printing technology. A portion of the proceeds from every book sold supports the libraries and institutions that made this collection possible, and that still work to preserve these invaluable treasures passed down through time.

This is history, traveling through time since the dawn of printing to your own personal library.

Initial Proquest EEBO Print Editions collections include:

Early Literature

This comprehensive collection begins with the famous Elizabethan Era that saw such literary giants as Chaucer, Shakespeare and Marlowe, as well as the introduction of the sonnet. Traveling through Jacobean and Restoration literature, the highlight of this series is the Pollard and Redgrave 1475-1640 selection of the rarest works from the English Renaissance.

Early Documents of World History

This collection combines early English perspectives on world history with documentation of Parliament records, royal decrees and military documents that reveal the delicate balance of Church and State in early English government. For social historians, almanacs and calendars offer insight into daily life of common citizens. This exhaustively complete series presents a thorough picture of history through the English Civil War.

Historical Almanacs

Historically, almanacs served a variety of purposes from the more practical, such as planting and harvesting crops and plotting nautical routes, to predicting the future through the movements of the stars. This collection provides a wide range of consecutive years of "almanacks" and calendars that depict a vast array of everyday life as it was several hundred years ago.

Early History of Astronomy & Space

Humankind has studied the skies for centuries, seeking to find our place in the universe. Some of the most important discoveries in the field of astronomy were made in these texts recorded by ancient stargazers, but almost as impactful were the perspectives of those who considered their discoveries to be heresy. Any independent astronomer will find this an invaluable collection of titles arguing the truth of the cosmic system.

Early History of Industry & Science

Acting as a kind of historical Wall Street, this collection of industry manuals and records explores the thriving industries of construction; textile, especially wool and linen; salt; livestock; and many more.

Early English Wit, Poetry & Satire

The power of literary device was never more in its prime than during this period of history, where a wide array of political and religious satire mocked the status quo and poetry called humankind to transcend the rigors of daily life through love, God or principle. This series comments on historical patterns of the human condition that are still visible today.

Early English Drama & Theatre

This collection needs no introduction, combining the works of some of the greatest canonical writers of all time, including many plays composed for royalty such as Queen Elizabeth I and King Edward VI. In addition, this series includes history and criticism of drama, as well as examinations of technique.

Early History of Travel & Geography

Offering a fascinating view into the perception of the world during the sixteenth and seventeenth centuries, this collection includes accounts of Columbus's discovery of the Americas and encompasses most of the Age of Discovery, during which Europeans and their descendants intensively explored and mapped the world. This series is a wealth of information from some the most groundbreaking explorers.

Early Fables & Fairy Tales

This series includes many translations, some illustrated, of some of the most well-known mythologies of today, including Aesop's Fables and English fairy tales, as well as many Greek, Latin and even Oriental parables and criticism and interpretation on the subject.

Early Documents of Language & Linguistics

The evolution of English and foreign languages is documented in these original texts studying and recording early philology from the study of a variety of languages including Greek, Latin and Chinese, as well as multilingual volumes, to current slang and obscure words. Translations from Latin, Hebrew and Aramaic, grammar treatises and even dictionaries and guides to translation make this collection rich in cultures from around the world.

Early History of the Law

With extensive collections of land tenure and business law "forms" in Great Britain, this is a comprehensive resource for all kinds of early English legal precedents from feudal to constitutional law, Jewish and Jesuit law, laws about public finance to food supply and forestry, and even "immoral conditions." An abundance of law dictionaries, philosophy and history and criticism completes this series.

Early History of Kings, Queens and Royalty

This collection includes debates on the divine right of kings, royal statutes and proclamations, and political ballads and songs as related to a number of English kings and queens, with notable concentrations on foreign rulers King Louis IX and King Louis XIV of France, and King Philip II of Spain. Writings on ancient rulers and royal tradition focus on Scottish and Roman kings, Cleopatra and the Biblical kings Nebuchadnezzar and Solomon.

Early History of Love, Marriage & Sex

Human relationships intrigued and baffled thinkers and writers well before the postmodern age of psychology and self-help. Now readers can access the insights and intricacies of Anglo-Saxon interactions in sex and love, marriage and politics, and the truth that lies somewhere in between action and thought.

Early History of Medicine, Health & Disease

This series includes fascinating studies on the human brain from as early as the 16th century, as well as early studies on the physiological effects of tobacco use. Anatomy texts, medical treatises and wound treatment are also discussed, revealing the exponential development of medical theory and practice over more than two hundred years.

Early History of Logic, Science and Math

The "hard sciences" developed exponentially during the 16th and 17th centuries, both relying upon centuries of tradition and adding to the foundation of modern application, as is evidenced by this extensive collection. This is a rich collection of practical mathematics as applied to business, carpentry and geography as well as explorations of mathematical instruments and arithmetic; logic and logicians such as Aristotle and Socrates; and a number of scientific disciplines from natural history to physics.

Early History of Military, War and Weaponry

Any professional or amateur student of war will thrill at the untold riches in this collection of war theory and practice in the early Western World. The Age of Discovery and Enlightenment was also a time of great political and religious unrest, revealed in accounts of conflicts such as the Wars of the Roses.

Early History of Food

This collection combines the commercial aspects of food handling, preservation and supply to the more specific aspects of canning and preserving, meat carving, brewing beer and even candy-making with fruits and flowers, with a large resource of cookery and recipe books. Not to be forgotten is a "the great eater of Kent," a study in food habits.

Early History of Religion

From the beginning of recorded history we have looked to the heavens for inspiration and guidance. In these early religious documents, sermons, and pamphlets, we see the spiritual impact on the lives of both royalty and the commoner. We also get insights into a clergy that was growing ever more powerful as a political force. This is one of the world's largest collections of religious works of this type, revealing much about our interpretation of the modern church and spirituality.

Early Social Customs

Social customs, human interaction and leisure are the driving force of any culture. These unique and quirky works give us a glimpse of interesting aspects of day-to-day life as it existed in an earlier time. With books on games, sports, traditions, festivals, and hobbies it is one of the most fascinating collections in the series.

The BiblioLife Network

This project was made possible in part by the BiblioLife Network (BLN), a project aimed at addressing some of the huge challenges facing book preservationists around the world. The BLN includes libraries, library networks, archives, subject matter experts, online communities and library service providers. We believe every book ever published should be available as a high-quality print reproduction; printed on-demand anywhere in the world. This insures the ongoing accessibility of the content and helps generate sustainable revenue for the libraries and organizations that work to preserve these important materials.
The following book is in the "public domain" and represents an authentic reproduction of the text as printed by the original publisher. While we have attempted to accurately maintain the integrity of the original work, there are sometimes problems with the original work or the micro-film from which the books were digitized. This can result in minor errors in reproduction. Possible imperfections include missing and blurred pages, poor pictures, markings and other reproduction issues beyond our control. Because this work is culturally important, we have made it available as part of our commitment to protecting, preserving, and promoting the world's literature.

GUIDE TO FOLD-OUTS MAPS and OVERSIZED IMAGES

The book you are reading was digitized from microfilm captured over the past thirty to forty years. Years after the creation of the original microfilm, the book was converted to digital files and made available in an online database.
In an online database, page images do not need to conform to the size restrictions found in a printed book. When converting these images back into a printed bound book, the page sizes are standardized in ways that maintain the detail of the original. For large images, such as fold-out maps, the original page image is split into two or more pages

Guidelines used to determine how to split the page image follows:

- Some images are split vertically; large images require vertical and horizontal splits.
- For horizontal splits, the content is split left to right.
- For vertical splits, the content is split from top to bottom.
- For both vertical and horizontal splits, the image is processed from top left to bottom right.

F. Douce

Francis Douce.

Hearne reprinted the curious preface in p. 607 of his Robert of Gloucester.

Suum cuiqz.
Tho. Hearne
Aug. 21. 1723.
Ex dono amiciss.
doctissimiqz viri
Thomæ Bakeri, S.T.B.
Cantabrigiensis.

This Book, upon account of the Preface, is a very great Curiosity, wch Preface confirms my Conjecture about John Stowe, in my Discourse upon Mr. Murray's Fragmts in my Appendix to Heming's Chartulary.

January hath xxxi. dayes.

iii	A	Circumcision of Christ.	1
	b	Octa. of saynt Stephen	2
xi	c	Octa. of Saint John	3
	d	Octa. of Innocents	4
xix	e	Deposition of S. Edward	5
viii	f	Epiphanie Domini	6
	g	Transla. Wilielmi	7
xvi	A	Lucian priest.	8
v	b	Lewes confessor	9
	c	Paule the first Heremite	10
xiii	d	Sol in Aquarius.	11
ii	e	Richard marter	12
	f	Hillarius.	13
x	g	Felicis	14
xviii	A	Archadius marter	15
vii	b	S. Mauritius.	16
	c	Saint Anthonie	17
xv	d	Prisce virgin	18
iiii	e	Wolstan bishop	19
	f	Fabian and Sebastyan	20
xii	g	Agnes virgyn	21
	A	Vincent marter	22
i	b	Emerentiane	23
	c	Timothe bishop	24
ix	d	Conversyon of S. Paule.	25
	e	Policarpe bishop	26
xvii	f	Julian confessor.	27
vi	g	Valleri bishop	28
	A	Theodore priest.	29
xiiii	b	Basilius bishop.	30
iii	c	Saturne & victor.	31

	d	Briget virgin Fast.	1
xi	e	Purification of Marye.	2
xix	f	Blase bishop.	3
viii	g	Gilbert confessor.	4
	A	Agathe virgin.	5
xvi.	b	Amandus bishop & conf.	6
v	c	Augali bishop.	7
	d	Paule bishop	8
xiii.	e	Apolline virgin.	9
ii	f	Sol in Pisces	10
	g	Desyderius bishop	11
x	A	Dorothe virgin.	12
	b	Wolfrane bishop	13
xviii	c	Valentine marter	14
vii.	d	Faustine Jouine.	15
	e	Julian virgin	16
xv	f	Policronius bishop	17
iiii	g	Symon bishop:	18
	A	Sabin and Julian mar.	19
xii	b	Myldred virgin.	20
i	c	xxxix. marters	21
	d	Cathedra Petri.	22
ix	e	Fast.	23
	f	Mathias Apostle.	24
xvii	g	Alexander bishop	25
vi	A	Eusebius priest	26
	b	Augustine.	27
xiiii	c	Oswalde bishop.	28

Marche hath xxxi. dayes.

iii	d	Dau.d bishop.	1
	e	Chadde confessor	2
xi	f	Maurice confessor	3
	g	Adrian bishop.	4
xix	A	Foce & Eusebii	5
viii	b	Victor & victorin	6
	c	Perpetue & Felix	7
xvi	d	Deposi. of Felix	8
v	e	Quadragenta mar.	9
	f	Aggeus prophete	10
	g	Gorgonius mar: Sol in Aryes	11
xiii	A	Gregorius bishop.	12
ii	b	Theodore mar	13
x	c	Longine mar.	14
	d	Cyriaci marter.	15
xviii	e	Hylarius bishop.	16
vii	f	Patrick & Gertrudis	17
	g	Edward king & confessor	18
xv	A	Joseph the husband of Mary.	19
iiii	b	Cuthbert bishop	20
	c	Benedic abb	21
xii	d	Aphrodosius bysh	22
i	e	Theodore virgin	23
	f	Pygmenus. Fast	24
ix	g	Annunciation of Mary	25
	A	Castor mar.	26
xvii	b	Eulalia virgin	27
vi	c	Victor mar	28
	d	Augenii mar	29
xiiii	e	Quirine mar	30
iii	f	Adelmus bishop	31

Aprill hath xxx. dayes.

	g	Theodore virgin	1
xi	A	Mary Egyptiace	2
	b	Rychard byshop	3
xix	c	Ambrosius	4
viii	d	Martyanus mar	5
xvi	e	Syxtus byshop	6
v	f	Egesyppus	7
	g	Euphemii vyrgyn	8
xiii	A	Perpetuus bishoppe	9
ii	b	vii. vyrgyns	10
	c	Marcus marter	11
x	d	Sol in Tauro.	12
	e	Oswald Archbyshop	13
xviii	f	Guthlacye	14
vii	g	Olyke	15
	A	Isydore	16
xv	b	Anicete	17
iiii	c	Eleupherius bishop	18
	d	Alphege	19
xii	e	Tiburtius	20
i	f	Sother virgin	21
	g	Symon bishop	22
ix	A	S. George mar.	23
	b	Lucretia.	24
xvii	c	Marke Euangelist.	25
vi	d	Anastasii	26
	e	Vitalis marter	27
xiiii	f	Petri Mediolanensis	28
iii	g	Clete bishop,	29
	A	Depo. Erkenwald. Fast.	30

May hath xxxi. dayes.

xi	b	Philip and Iacob.
	c	Athanasii bishop
xix	d	Inuent of the Crosse
viii	e	Floriani mar.
	f	Godard,
xvi	g	John Portlatine.
v	A	John of Beuerley
	b	Apparitio Mich.
xiii	c	Gengulfi marter
ii	d	Gordian and Epimachy
	e	Anthony mar.
x	f	Sol in Gemini.
	g	Boniface martyr
xviii	A	Sophia virgin
vii	b	Seruacii confessor
	c	Transl. of S. Bernard
xv	d	Dioscoride marter
iiii	e	Dunston bishop
	f	Bernardine
xii	g	Helene Quene
i	A	Juliane virgin
	b	Urbane marter
ix	c	Translation Francisci.
	d	Desideri mar.
xvii	e	Adelme byshop
vi	f	Augustin of Englande
	g	Bede priest
xiiii	A	Germaine bishop
iii	b	Nicodeme
	c	Coronation mart.
xi	d	Marcell martyr.

June hath xxx. dayes.

	e	Nichodeme	1
xix	f	Erasmus byshop	2
viii	g	Basill	3
xvi	A	Petroci confessor	4
v	b	Boniface bishop	5
	c	Melon bishop	6
xiii	d	Translatio Wolstan	7
ii	e	Wilhelmi confessor.	8
	f	Transl. Edmond.	9
x	g	Iue confessor	10
	A	Barnabe apostle	11
viii	b	Sol in Cancro	12
vii	c	Anthony	13
	d	Basil bishop and confessor	14
xv	e	Vite & Modeste	15
iiii	f	Trans. Richard	15
	g	Botulphe	17
xii	A	Marci & Marciliani	18
i	b	Geruasie	19
	c	Transla. Edward	20
ix	d	Walburge virgin	21
	e	Albon martyr	22
xvii	f	Etheldred Fast.	23
vi	g	Nati. Iohn Baptist.	24
	A	Transla. Helene.	25
xiiii	b	Iohn and Paule	26
iii	c	Achasius confessor	27
	d	Leo bishop Fast	28
xi	e	Peter and Paule.	29
	f	Commemo. of Paule	30

Julye hath xxxi. dayes.

xix	g	Octa. John Baptiste	1
viii	A	Visitation of our Lady	2
	b	Transl. of S. Thomas	3
xvi	c	Translation of S. Martin	4
v	d	Zoe Virgin and marter	5
	e	Octa Peter and Paule	6
xiii	f	Dog dayes begin	7
ii	g	Deposition of Grimbalde	8
	A	Cirilli bishop	9
x	b	Seuen brethren	10
	c	Transl. of S. Benet	11
xviii.	d	Nabor and Felix.	12
vii	e	Priuate Sol. in Leo.	13
	f	Transl. of S. Thomas	14
xv	g	Transl. of S. Swythen	15
iiii	A	Transl. of S. Osmond.	16
	b	Kenelme king	17
xii	c	Arnolphe bishop.	18
i	d	Rufine and Justine.	19
	e	Margaret	20
ix	f	Praxede virgin	21
	g	Mary Magdalen	22
xvii	A	Appollinaris	23
vi	b	Christian virgin. Fast.	24
	c	Iames Apostle.	25
xiiii	d	Saint Anne	26
iii	e	vii. Slepers.	27
	f	Sampson bishop	28
xi	g	Martha.	29
xix	A	Abdon & Sennes marters.	30
	b	Germain bishop	31

August hath xxxi. dayes.

viii	c	Lammas day.	1
xvi	d	Stephen	2
v	e	Stephanus bisshop	3
	f	Iustini cõfessor	4
xiii	g	Affra vyrgin	5
ii	A	Transfiguracion	6
	b	The feast of Iesu	7
x	c	Sixtalte	8
	d	Romayne	9
xviii	e	S.Laurence day	10
vii	f	Tiburtyne marter.	11
	g	Clare vyrgin	12
xv	A	Rochus	13
iiii	b	Sol in Virgo	14
	c	Assumptyon of Mary	15
xii	d		16
i	e	Octa, of S.Laurence	17
	f	Agapeth mar	18
ix	g	Magnus marter.	19
	A	Lewes. confessor	20
xvii	b	Bernard	21
vi	c	Octassumptyon of Mary,	22
	d	Tymothe Fast	23
xiiii	e	Bartholomew Apostell	24
iii	f	Ludouici kyng	25
	g	Seuerene byshop	26
xi	A	Dogdayes ende	27
xix	b	August byshop	28
	c	Decolation of S.Iohn	29
viii	d	Felix	30
	e	Cuthburge vyrgyn	31

September hath xxx. dayes.

xvi	f	Egidius abbot	1
v	g	Antonini mar.	2
	A	Gregory byshop	3
xiii	b	Transl. of Cuthbert	4
ii	c	Bartin abbot	5
	d	Eugenius	6
x	e	Edigon	7
	f	Natiuity of Mary	8
xviii	g	Prothus	9
vii	A	Syluius byshop	10
	b	Jacobus priest	11
xv	c	Maurelius bishop.	12
iiii	d	Amantii marter	13
	e	Holy Roode day	14
xii	f	Sol in Libra	15
i	g	Edyth virgin	16
	A	Vyctoryn byshop	17
ix	b	January mar	18
	c	Lambert	19
xvii	d	Eustace Fast	20
vi	e	S. Mathevve Apostel	21
	f	Tecle virgyn	22
xiiii	g	Mauritius confessor	23
iii	A	Andochi mar.	24
	b	Firmin marter	25
xi	c	Cyprian and Justyne	26
xix	d	Seueryne byshop	27
	e	Cosme and Damian	28
viii	f	Michael Archangel.	29
	g	Hierom priest.	30

October hath xxxi. dayes.

xvi	A	Remigius bishop	1
v	b	Leodegarii	2
xiii	c	Candidi marter	3
ii	d	Fraunces confessor.	4
	e	S. Fayth virgin	5
x	f	Marci & Marcelliani.	6
	g	Pelagie virgin	7
xviii	A	Nicasius confessor.	8
vii	b	Dionise.	9
	c	Welfriede virgin	10
xv	d	Transl. of S. Edward	11
iiii	e	Calixtus bishop	12
	f	Wolfrane bishop	13
xii	g	Sol in Scorpio.	14
i	A	Galli confessor	15
	b	Maximini marter	16
ix	c	Etheldred virgin	17
	d	S. Luke Euangelist.	18
xvii	e	Quirine marter	19
vi	f	Austrebert martyr	20
	g	xi. M. virgins	21
xiiii	A	Mary Salome	22
iii	b	Romany Archbishop	23
	c	Chrysspine	24
xi	d	Euaristus	25
xix	e	Ursula virgin	26
	f	Maglorius bi[illegible] fast.	27
viii	g	Simon and Iude Apostles	28
	A	[illegible]	29
xvi	b	Ibacuk prophete	30
	c	Quirinus martir	31

November hath xxx. dayes.

	d	All sainctes day	1
b	e	All soules day	2
xiii	f	Wenefryde virgyn	3
	g	Amancius	4
ii	A	Lete priest	5
	b	Leonard	6
x	c	Willibrode bishop	7
xviii	d	Quatuor coronato.	8
	e	Theodore mar.	9
vii	f	Martin byshop	10
xv	g	Marten	11
	A	Sol in Sagittarius	12
iiii	b	Bryce	13
	c	Transl. Erkenwald	14
	d	Macute	15
xii	e	Deposi. Edmond	16
	f	Init. Reg. Elyzabeth.	17
i	g	Octa. Martini	18
ix	A	Elyzabeth	19
	b	Edmond king	20
xvii	c	Present. of our Lady	21
vi	d	Cicilie virgyn	22
	e	Clement bishop	23
xiiii	f	Grisogoni marter	24
iii	g	Katherine virgyn	25
	A	Peter bishop	26
xi	b	Vitales and agricole	27
	c	Ruffinus	28
xix	d	Saturnine Fast	29
viii	e	Andrew Apostel.	30

December hath xxxi. dayes

xvi	f	Crisanti & Darie marters		1
v	g	Libiani		2
	A	Deposition Osmund		3
xiii	b	Barbara virgin		4
	c	Saba abbot		5
ii	d	Nicolas bishop		6
v	e	Octa. Andrewe		7
	f	Concep. Mary		8
xviii	g	Cyprian abbot		9
vii	A	Eulalie		10
	b	Anteppa.	Sol in Capri.	11
v	c	Paule byshop		12
iiii	d	Lucy vyrgyn		13
	e	Necasii		14
xii	f	Valery		15
	g	O sapientia		16
i	A	Lazarus byshop		17
ix	b	Gracian bishop		18
	c	Venesey virgyn		19
xvii	d	July mart.	Fast.	20
vi	e	Thomas Apostle.		21
	f	30. marters		22
xiiii	g	Victor virgyn		23
iii	A	40. Virgyns.	Fast	24
	b	Christmas daye		25
xi	c	S. Stephen marter		26
	d	S. Iohn Euangelist.		27
xix	e	Innocentes daye.		28
viii	f			29
	g	Trans. of S. James.		30
xvi	A	Siluester bishop.		31

Craſt Trinitatis.	Quind. Trinitat.
Octabis. Trinitat.	Tres Trinitat.

¶ Michaelmas Terme beginneth the ix. day of October, if it be not sonday, and endeth the 28 of Nouember, and hath viii. Returnes, that is to saye:

Octabis Micha.	Craſt. Anima.
Quind Michael.	Craſt Martini.
Tres Michael.	Octa. Martini.
Menſe Michael.	Quind. Martini.

☞ Note also that the Eſchequer openeth eyghte dayes before anye Terme beginne, excepte Trinitye Terme, which openeth but foure dayes before.

And now followeth the Lawe dayes in the Court of Charches, & audience of Canterbury, with other Eccleſiaſtical and Ciuill lawes throughe the whole yeare.

These dayes are not chaũged except they light on a sonday or holy day, and euery day is called a Lawdaye, vnleſſe it be sonday or holye daye.

Michaelmas Terme.

Fides.
Edvvardi
Luke Eua.
Simond & Iude.
Animarum
Martini.
Edmondi regis.
Katherine.
Andre.
Conceptionis.

IIt is to be noted that the firste day followinge euerye of these feastes noted in euery terme, ý Courte of the arches is kept in Bowe Churche in the forenone. And the same first day in the after noone is the Admirall Courte for Cyuill causes kepte in Southwarke.

2 The secōd day following euerey of the said feastes, the Court of audience of Caunterbury is kept in the cōsistory in Powles in ý forenone. And the same day in ý after noone in the same place, is the prerogatiue court of Cāterbury kept.

3 The thirde daye after any such feast in the forenone, the consistory Court of the bishop of London is kept in Powles Church in the cōsistorye, and ý same third day in ý after none is ý Court of Delegats and of ý Queenes highnes cōmissioners vpon appeales kept in the same place.

Hillarye

Hillarye Terme.

NOte ỹ the 4. first dayes of this Terme be certain and vnchaunged. The other are altered for the course of the yeare, and are sometime kepte and sometime omitted. For if it soo happen that one of those feastes fall on the Wednesdaye common=lye called Ashwednesdaye, after ỹ day of Blase, so that the same law day after Ashwednesday cānot be kept, because the lawday of tho=ther feast doth light on ỹ same day: then the second law day after Ash=wednesday shalbe kept, and the o=ther omitted. And if the law daye after that wednesday be the nexte day after the feast of S. Blase, thē shal al & euerye these Court daies bee obserued in order, as maye bee kept conueniently.

And marke that although ỹ Ashe=wednesday be put ỹ seuenth in or=der, yet it hath no certayne place, but is chaunged as the course of Easter.

Hillarij.
VVulstani
Pauli conuersi.
Blasii.
Scolastice.
Valentini.
Cinerum.
Mathie.
Cedde.
Perpetue & Felici.
Gregorij.
Annunciationis.

Quind. Pasche. Alphegi. Marci Euang. Inuentio S. Crucis. Gordian. Dunstani. Ascentionis

IN this terme, the first sitting is alway kept ye monday being ye xv. day after Easter, & so forth after the feastes here noted which shall next followe by the course of the yeare after Easter. And the like space beinge kepte betwene other feastes.

The rest of the lawe dayes are kepte, to the thirde of the Ascention, whiche is the last daye of this Terme.

And if it happen yt the feast of Ascention of our Lord do come before any of the feastes aforesaid, then they are omitted that yeare.

As it happened in the yere 1567. the dayes of Gordian and Dunstan are omitted, because the feaste of the Ascention chaunced to fall before them. And likewise, if anye of those dayes come before the xv. of Easter those dayes are omitted.

Trinitye Terme.

Note that the law dayes of this Terme are altered by meane of Whitsontide, and the first sittinge is kepte alwayes the first Law day after the feast of the holye Trinitye, and the second session is kepte the first Lawe day after Corpus Christi except Corpus Christi daye fal on some daye here named: which chaunceth somtime, and then ye ofter day is kept, and after that seconde session, accompt 4. dayes or ther about, and then locke which is the nexte feast daye, and the first Lawday after ye saide feast shalbe the third session. The other Lawedayes followe in order, but somany of them are kept as for the time of the yeare shalbe though meete.

Trinitatis.
Corp^o Christi.
Bonifacii.
Barnabe.
Butolphe.
Iohannis.
Pauli.
Thome.
Swithini.
Margarete
Anne.

And note generally that euerye day is called a Lawday that is not sonday or holy daye, and that if the feast daye beinge knowne of anye Court day in any Terme, the first

 or se-

or seconde daye followynge bee Sondaye, then the Courte daye is kept the day after the said holy daye or feast.

❧

To the righte honourable, Lionel Ducket, Lord Maior of the Cittye of London, the righte worshifull Aldermen his brethren, and the Commoners of the same Cittye, Iohn Stowe Cittizen wysheth longe health and Felicitye.

AMongest other Bookes, (righte honourable and vvorshipful) vvhich are in this oure learned age published in great nombers, there are fevve, eyther for the honesty of the matters, or commodity vvhich they bring to the Cōmon vvealth or for the pleasantnes of the study and reading, to be preferred before the Chronicles and Histories. VVhat examples of men deseruing immortalitye, of exploites vvorthye

*A. iiii. great

great renovvne, of vertuous liuing, of the posterity to be embraced. Of vvise handling of vvaightye affayres dilligently to be marked, and aptlye to be applyed. VVhat encouragemente of nobilitye to noble feates, vvhat discouragement of vnnaturall subiectes from vvicked treasons, pernitious rebellions, and dampnable doctrines. To conclude, vvhat persvvasions to honestye, godlines, and vertue, of all sort, vvhat disvvasions from the contrarye, is not plentifullye in them to be founde: so that it is as harde a matter for the readers of Chronicles in my fansye, to passe vvithout some colors of VVisedom, inuitaments to Vertue, and lothing of noughty factes, as it is for a vvelfauoured man to vvalke vppe and dovvne in the hot parchinge Sũne,

and

and not to be therewith Sunneburned. They therfore which wyth lõg study, earnest good will, and to their great costes and charges, haue broughte hidden Histories from dustye darcknes, to the sight of the worlde, and haue bene dilligent obseruers of commõ wealthes, and noted for the posteritye, the fleetinge manners of the people, and accidentes of the tymes: deserue at the least thankes for their paines, and to be misreported of none, seinge they haue laboured for all. I write not this to complaine of some mens ingratitude towardes mee (althoughe iustlye I mighte) but to shovve the commodities which ensue of the readinge of Historyes, that seinge they are so great and so manye, al menne would (as they oughte) imploye their dili-

gence

gence in the honest fruitful, and delectable perusinge of the same, and so to accompte of the Authors, as of men carefull for their countrey, and to confesse if neede require, by vvhō they haue taken profite. It is novve eight yeares, since I (seinge the confuse order of oure late Englishe Chronicles, and the ignoraunt handlinge of auncient affayres, leauing mine ovvne peculiar gaines, consecrated my selfe to the searche of our famous Englishe Antiquities, vvhat I haue done in theym before time, the former editions of my Summarye of Chronicles may vvell testify, but hovve farre (be it spoken vvithout arrogancye) I haue laboured for the truth, more thenne some others, the late edition vvill euidentlye declare, vvherin that I differ from the inordinate, and vnſkilfull collectiōs of other men, it is no maruaile, ſeing that I do not fullye agree vvith my ſelfe. This hath beene laide to my charge, and many great vvords made of it, by him vvho vvith more honeſty might haue holden his peace: for that himſelfe (ſince I begā to vvrite) hath alvvayes followved me in matter, but not in truth. But to returne let it be conſidered that there is nothinge perfect at the firſt, and that it is incident to mankinde to erre and ſlip ſometime, but onlye the pointe of phantaſticall fooles to perſeuer and cōtinue in their errors. VVherfore ſeing that the peruſinge of auncient Recordes, and beſt approued hiſtories of all times, do not onelye moue mee, but of their authoritye driue mee to acknovvledge both

mine

mine and other mens errors, and in acknovvledginge to correct them: I truſte to obtaine thus muche at your honour and vvorſhippes hands, that at the leaſt you vvill call to remembraunce a moſte gentle and vvyſe Lavv of the politike Perſians: vvher in it vvas enacted that a man accuſed to be in their Lavves a treſpaſſer and foūd giltie of the crime, ſhould not ſtraight vvaye be condempned, but after a dilligente enquirye and ſearche of his vvhole life and cōuerſation, if the nomber of his laudable factes did counteruaile the contrary, he vvas full quite of the treſpaſſe. The ſame Lavve doe I vviſhe youre honoure and vvorſhips, and all the Readers of my late Summarye of Chronicles to put in vre, that if the errors be not ſo plentifull, as Hiſto-

ryes

ries trulye alledged, your honour & worshippes vvill beare vvith them. For this I promise, and meane God willing to perfourme, that thoughe I by followinge some late vvriters of Histories, haue somevvhat some-thinge stumbled: Yet so to trye all matters vvorthye of immortalitye by the certayne touchstone of the auncient and best allovved Histo-riographers that neither anye body by mee shalbe deceiued, nor I for-ced to craue further pardonne if I do offende. And thus muche to your honour and vvor-ships at this time.

Your most humble

John Stovve.

¶ To the Reader.

Callyng to memorye (gentle Reader) with what dilligence (to my great cost and charges) I haue trauayled in my late Summary of ye Chronicles: As also ye vnhonest dealings of some body towardes mee (wherof I haue long since sufficientlye written and exhibited to the learned and honourable) I perswaded with my selfe to haue surceased frō this kinde of trauel, wherin another hath vsed to reape the fruits of my labours.* But now for diuers causes thereto mouinge mee, I haue once againe brieflye ran ouer this small abridgement, placing the yeares of our Lord, the yeres of ye Kings, wyth ye Shyriffes and Maiors of London in a farre more perfect and plain order, then heretofore hath bene published.

*Setting (as it were) his marke on another mās vessell.

Touching Ri. Grafton his slanderous Epistle though the same wyth other his abusing of me, was answeared by the learned & honourable, & by theym forbidden to be reprinted: he hath since ye time in his second impression placed his former lying Preface, wherin hee hath these woordes.* Gentle Reader, this one thinge offendeth me so much, that I am inforced to purge my selfe therof, and I howe my

*In the first page the 16 17.18.19 & 20. lines.

my simple and plaine dealing therein. One Iohn Stow of whō I wil say none euill. &c. hath published a Booke * and therin hath charged mee bittarlye, but chiefelye with two thinges. The one, that I haue made E. Halles Chronicle my Chronicle, but not withoute mangelinge, and (as hee saith) withoute anye ingenious and plaine declaration thereof. The other thinge that hee chargeth me withall, is that a Chronicle of Hardings which he hath, doth much differ from the Chronicle, which vnder the sayd Hardinges name was printed by mee, as though I had falcifyed Hardings Chronicle &c. For answeare I say *the offence by me committed, requireth no such forced purgation. I haue not so bitterlye charged him, as he hath plainly accused himselfe in those thinges to haue offended.* My wordes be these. Some bodye (without any ingenious and plaine declaratiō therof, hath published, but not without māgling, master Halles bokefor his owne. I name not Grafton. This is the firste. The second is thus. Iohn Hardinge &c. exhibited a Chronicle of Englande, with a Mappe or description of Scotland, to king Henrye the sixt, which Chronicle doth almost altogether differ from that which vnder his name was imprinted by Ri. Graftō.

*In the seconde page the 1. and 2. lines. The 4. 5. & 6. &c.

(I leaue his simple and plaine dealing to the iudgemente of others.

* In commending mine authors.)

* I saye not that I haue such a Chro

After

nicle of I. Hardings.

* After this in ẏ same preface he braggeth to haue a Chronicle of Iohn Hardings writtē in the latine tōgue, which hee assureth himselfe I neuer sawe, and doubteth whether I understand. If hee haue any such booke, it is like he would alledge it, as he hath done manye other Authors, whereof I am better assured, he hath neuer seene so muche as the outside of theyr bookes. * If ther be no such Chronicle of Iohn Hardings, as he braggeth on, it is like I haue not seene it, & must needes be hard to understande it. Then he saith my latter Summary differeth cleane from my first. To this I aunswere, I haue not chaunged eyther worde or title, but haue corrected my first Booke, as I haue founde better Authours. But hee himselfe hath made his last abridgementes, not onelye cleane contrary to his first, but the two abridgementes contrarye the one to the other, and euerye one contrary to his mere Historye. For his true alleaging of Authors let men iudge, of those which are common in our vulgar tongue, as Policronicon, Ro. Fabiā, Ed. Hall, Doctour Cooper. Note those Authors in their yeres, and peraduenture ye shal finde no such matter. Trye and then trust.

* Ri. Graftō neuer sawe Robert de Auesberye, Tho. Walsingham H. of Leicester Regester of Berye and many other which hee alledgeth, for that hee findeth thē alledged in my Summarye.

This Preface is left out of ye last Editio & perhaps (as Grafton's was) by order.

A description of Englande, Scotlande, Wales and Cornewall.

Ritaine vvhich by two names is called Eglād and Scotland, is an Iland in the Ocean sea, situat righte ouer against the Regiō of Gallia: (now called Fraūce) One parte of which Ile Englishmen do inhabite, an other part Scottes, the third part Welshmen, and the fourth part Cornishmē. Al they eyther in language, conditions or lawes, doe differ amonge theymselues.

Englande (soe called of Englishmen whiche did wynne the same is the greatest parte, whiche is deuided into xxxix. Counties, which we cal Shyres. Wher of ten, that is to saye, Kent, Sussex, Surreye, Southampton, Barkshire, Wyltshyre, Somersetshyre, Deuonshyre and Cornewall: do containe the first part of that Islande, which part bendeth towarde the Thirty nine Counties or shyres.

South

South, standing betwene the Thames and the sea.

From thence to the ryuer of Trente, whiche passeth throughe the myddes of Englande, be. xvi. shires, wherof the first. vi. (standing Eastward) are Essex, Middelsex, Herfordshire, Suffolke, Northfolke, and Cambridgeshire, the other ten whiche stande more in the middle of the countrey are these. Bedforde, Huntington, Buckingham, Oxforde, Northampton, Rutlande, Leycester, Notingham, Warwyke and Lyncolne. After these, there bee syxe whiche border westwarde vpon Wales, as Glocester, Herefordе, Worcester, Salop, Staffordе, and Chester. About the middle of the Region lye Darbyshyre, Yorkeshyre, Lancashyre, and Cumberlande. On the left hande toward the west, is Westmerland. Against the same is the Bishoprike of Durham, and Northumberlande, which boundeth vpon the north in the marches of Scotland. The shyres be deuided into. xxi. Byshopryks, whiche by a Greeke worde, bee called Dioceses. Of whiche Dioses, the Archbishop of Cantorbury, hath Kent. Rochestar hath a part of Ket. London hath Essex, Midlesex, a part of Herford. Chichester hath Sussex. Wynchester

Twoo and twenty byshops in Englande. iiij. in Wales.

chester hath Hampshire, Surrey, & the Ile of Wight. Salisbury hath Barkshyre and Wiltshire. Exetor, hath Deuonshire, & Cornwale. Bath and Welles, hath Somersetshire. Worcester hath Worcestershire, and part of Warwickeshire. Glocestar hath Glochestarshire. Hereford hath part of Shropshire, and Herefordshire. Couetrie, & Lichfeld hath Staffordshire, and thother part of Warwickshire. Lyncoln hath Lincoln, Leicester, Huntington, Bedford, Buckingham, and the residue of Hertfordshire. Ely hath Cambridgeshire, and the Ile of Ely. Norwiche hathe Suffolke and Northfolke. Oxforde hath Oxfordshire. Petarborough hath Northamptonshire and Rutlād. Bristowe hath Dorsetshire. And this is the Prouince of the Archebishop of Canterbury, which is the primate of England, with Wales. The archebishop of Yorke, hath Yorkeshyre, Notinghamshyre, and a piece of Lancasshyre. The byshop of Durham, hath the byshoprike so commonly called, and Northumberland. Chestar hath Cheshire Darbyshire, & a pece of Lancashire. Carleile, cōtaineth Cūberlande & Westmerlād. And this is the prouince of Tharchbyshop of Yorke, which is an other prienate of England, and was of long time also prymate of all Scotland: but these Dioceses take their names of the cities where those Seas be placed. The chiefe wherof, is London, wher in the begynning was the Archbyshops Sea: but afterwardes transposed to Canterburye, a Citie in Kent, placed in a soyle amiable and pleasaunt. London standeth in Middlesex, on the Northsyde of the Thames. That most excellent and goodly ryuer, begynneth a lytle aboue a vyllage called Wynchelcombe in Oxfordshyre still increasynge, and passeth fyrst by the Uniuersitie of Oxford, and so with a merueylous quiet course by London, & then breketh into the French Ocea͞ by main tydes, whyche twise in xxiiij houres space doth ebbe and flow more then xl. myles, to the great comoditie of trauailers, by whych all kyndes of marchandise be easely conueyghed to London, pryncipall store and staple for all commodities within this Realme. Upon same ryuer is placed a stone bridge,

London bridge.

worke very rare & marueylous, whiche bridge hath xx. Arches made of foure squared stone, of height lx foote, and of breadth .xxx. foote, distant one from another xx. foote, compacte and ioyned to

gethe

gether, with vaults and Sellers. Vpō both sides be houses builded, that it semeth rather a continuall strete, then a bridge. The Oceā sea doth bound Englande the first parte of Brytayne, Easte and Southe, Wales and Cornewall, west. The ryuer of Twede deuideth England, & Scotlād North. The lēgth of the Ilande begynneth at Portesmouth in the South part, and endeth at Twede in the North, contayninge 3?0. myles. This Realme aboue other is most fruitfull on this syde Humbre: for beyond, it is fuller of mountaynes. And although to the beholders of that countreye a far of, it maye seeme plaine, yet it is ful of many hilles, and those for the most part bare of trees: the valleis wherof be very delectable, inhabited for the moste parte by noble men, who accordynge to auncient and olde order, desyre not to dwel in Citties, but nere vnto valleis and Riuers in seuerall villages: for auoydinge of vehement windes, because that Ilande naturally is stormye.

Humber hath his beginning a litle on this side Yorke, and by and by runneth Southward, & then holdeth his course Eastward, and so into the mayne Sea, greatly increased by the Riuers of Dune and Trent. Trent beginneth a little frō Stafford, running through Darbyshire and Leicestershire, passing by Lichfeld and Notingham on the right hande, and Dane on the left: so that both those riuers doe make an Ilande, whiche is called Auxolme, and then ioyning together on this syde Kingston vpon Hul, a goodly marchant towne, they fall into Humbre: by whiche Riuer they may arriue out of Fraunce, Germany and Denmarke. Englande is fruitefull of beastes and aboundeth with cattel, whereby thinhabitants be rather for the moste Graziers, then Ploughmen, because they giue themselues more to feedyng, then to tyllage. So that almoste the thyrde parte of the countree is employed to cattell, Deare red and fallow, goates (whereof there be store in the Northpartes, and Conies, for euery where there is iolye mayntenaunce of those kindes of beastes: because it is full of great wooddes, whereof there ryseth pastime of hunting greatly exercised, specially by the nobilitie & Gentlemen: (there be more parkes in England then in all Europe besydes.)

Description of Scotland.

SCOTLANDE, an other parte of Britaine, began sometime at the hyll called Grampius, stretching to the farthest

coaste

coaste Northwarde, but after the ouerthrowe of the Pictes, it began at the Riuer Twede, and so meeting at the Riuer of Tyne, the fortune of warres altering the same, as it doth all other thinges. Therfore the length of Scotlande from Tweede to the furthest coast, is esteemed to be. 480. miles: But as Scotland is lōger then Englād, so it is narrower & endeth like a wedge. For the mountaine Grampius, is ill fauoured and craggie, pearcing through the bowels of Scotland from the coast of the Germain sea, that is to saye from the mouth of the riuer of Dee, to the bondes of Irelande, euen to the lake of Lomunde, which lieth betwene that coūtrey and the same hill. The Riuer of Tweede which springeth out of a litle hil, not farre beyonde Foxborough is mingled with the Germaine Ocean, ioyning Southwarde with that countrey which is called the Marches, being the bonds betwene England and Scotland: The sayd Ryuer of Tweede seperateth the Marches from Northumberlande, the furthest countrey of England, hauing prospect to the Germaine Sea, the chief town wherof is Barwick, now in possession of the English, in old time called Ordolucarum. The Westerne limit of Scotland, whilom was Cumberland, which the Ryuer of Solue deuideth frõ the valley of Annandia. Betwen these two Regiõs the Cheuiot hilles appeare. Nere to the Marches, Pictlande bordereth, now termed Laudone, bounding upon the East, a very hilly countrey barren almost of anye trees. The most famous townes of the same be Dunbare, Hadington, Lethe, Northberwicke, & Edingborough, ẏ kinges seate, where also is the Castell of Maidens, a very strong and defensible place. The same citie ẏ Riuer of Forthea (commonly called the Frithe) doeth water and passe by: which being carryed into the Germain Ocean, maketh great armes or meres, commonly called the Scotysh sea: Wherein besydes other, is the Ileland of S. Columbe, by name called Aemonia. The same Ryuer agayne deuydeth from Laudone, a Countrye adioynynge (aboundante of all thinges) called the Fife, in which countrye are many Townes, as Donfernule, Cupre, but ẏ notable towne of S. Andrewe, speciallye famous for the Unyuersity, and beutifyed with ẏ Seat of the Archebishoppe and primate of all Scotlande. On the other syde towards the Irishe syde Northward, is Nidisdalia, is lia, soe called of the Ryuer that passeth thereby, where be the strong townes of Douglasse & Donfreie. Upon the South adioyneth Gallouidia, more aboundante of fodder for cattel, the͂ of Wheat. where is the Towne of Candida Casa, and the auncient temple of S. Ninian, adourned also with an Episcopal Sea. In those partes besides the Towne of Victona, is a lake of a wonderfull nature, because ye one syde in winter doth freese, and thoother not. By that standeth the Countrie of Haricta, once renowned wyth the towne Haricton whereof perchaunce it toke the name. Aboue Haricta towardes the West, is Elgoina, bordering uppon the Ocean wherin is ye lake Lomunde, which is very brode and large, contayning many Ilands situate at ye foote of the mountaine Grampius, eighte myles from the castell of Dombritom besides the Ryuer of Bodotria, now named Leuinus, entring into ye Riuer of Glota. But a good space on this syde Grampius, ryseth the ryuer of Taus, the greatest in al Scotland, taking his name of a Lake from whence it springeth, which falling by Atholia & Calydonia, passeth by many places, but chiefly by Perthum now called S. Iohns towne: and lastly by Deidonum, in time

past

past called Alectum, and there breaketh into the Germain sea, and at the mouth forceth greate estuaces or armes of the sea. Against Taus is Angusie, whyche by meanes of that riuer is fertile and prosperous, and is deuided from Fife, To ÿ same vpon the North adioyneth Atholia, not the barronest Countrie, as well for water as for plenty of soile. On thother side Argatelia showeth it selfe, which beinge ful of Lakes, yeldeth greater plenty of fodder then fruit, whose vttermost boundes stretche so farre, as Ireland is not distant past xvi. miles, about which the promontorie or forland, called Nãdes hedde standeth. That Coast whilom the Silures amply did inhabite. Betwen this and Elgonia, Westwarde lyeth the Countrye of Sterlynge, see called by a towne there. Here the Forrest of Calydonia began on the left syde, which with ent stretcheth far and brood.

This forrest somtimes bredde whyte Bulles, lõg mained like Lyons, which were so wylde as they could not be tamed, but because the fleshe was pleasant and deinty to the mouthe, the hole race of them almost is extinguished.

Ther likewise is the castel of Calydone, situate by Taus called Doucheldine. Frõ a litle

[l]ittle hil of ẏ Foreſt riſeth Glota, which [b]y brode chanell falleth into the Iriſhe [O]cean. For ſtaied in a maner by the ban= [k]es of the mountaine Grampius, it ſlyd= [d]eth into the Sea by great tydes, ſo as [t]he Romains thoughte it to be an other [I]land. Of that riuer the Dale was cal= [l]ed Glorcuale, which the countrey that ry= [u]er runneth by, and in the ſame is the [C]itie of Glaico, a goodly Uniuerſitie. A= [g]aine towardes the Eaſte is ioyned the [C]ountrie of Anguſie & Mernia, vpon the [S]ea coaſte, whereein Fordune by ſituation [i]s very ſtronge, and for the reliques of [S]ainte Palladius the Scottiſhe Apoſtle [f]amous.

Of the ſame ſyde of Scotlande, is the [C]ountree of Marria, garniſhed with a [C]itie called Aberdone, ſtanding betwene the two ryuers of Dona and Dea, with a Schole alſo adorned. Then followeth Moronia, which the two notable Riuers doe compaſſe aboute, called Nea & Spea. At the mouth of this laſt ryuer, ſtandeth the Towne of Elgis: Aboute the bankes whereof, bee huge woddes repleniſhed with all ſortes of wylde beaſtes. There is a lake alſo called Spina, ſtored wyth plenty of Swannes. But in the midle parte ſtandeth the broade countreye of

Roſſia.

Rossia, stretching to the uttermost angle euen to both the Seas, and the further it goeth Eastward, the better it is inhabited. In the same is a bosome of the Sea, now and then so conuenient for saylers as commonlye it is called the porte of Helth, (or the hauen of safetye,) and the towne Thana. The bredth of the Ilande is very short, for falling into the forme of a wedge is scant xxx. myle ouer, which defended with three promontories like towers, repelleth the greate waues and surges of the Sea: and enuironned with two goulfs, which those promontoryes do inclose, the entries be quiet & calme, and the waters peaceable. The straight of that land is at this daye called Cathanese, coastynge uppon the Sea Deucalidon. Thus much of the particulers of Scotland. But the same is in euery place full of good hauens and nauigable entries, Lakes, with mershes, fluddes, fountaynes, very ful of fyshe, and mountaynes, upon the toppes wherof be pleasaunt playnes, yelding greate store of grasse, and plentye of fodder for Cattel, woddes likewyse full of wylde beastes. That part of the land is well susteyned wyth commodities, and therfore the people hard to be vanquished at

anye

my time by reason the woddes and marshes beat land, for refuge and hungre ers fed wyth veneson and fyshe. Aboute Scotlande in the Irishe Seas, are xl. Ilandes, Many of these in length at least are xxx. myles, but in breadth not aboue xii. Amonges them is Iona beautifyed wyth the Tombes of the Scottysh kinges. The Ilanders generally speake Irish, whych declareth them to take their originall of the Irishe nation. Beyonde Scotlā: toward the North, be the Isles of Orcades: whych bee xxx. in numbre, some lying in the Deucalidon sea, & some in the Germanine Occane, the principall of whych Ilandes is Pamonia, because it is a Bishops sea, and is vnder the gouernement of Scotlande. The Ilanders vse the Gothes speche whych argueth them to procede from the Germaines. They be talle of stature, but verye healthy and lustie of body and mind, liuing very long, although their chiefest foode is fishe, for the land almost continually beset with cold, in many places is not able to beare corne, generally almost without tree or bush. Besides the Orchades standeth Thule, which they cal Ila. From that Ilād not aboue one daies sayling, is the frosen Sea. In which sea standeth

standeth Islande, in whiche Ilande our marchauntes repaire for fishing once euery yere in the Sommer. And because it is the furthest Ilande towardes the North, there be some that doe suppose it to be Thule. And thus muche haue I to sey of the site of Scotland. Now of the nature and manners of the people. The Scottes whiche inhabite in the Southerne partes, be wel nurtured and liue in good ciuilitie, & the most ciuile vse the Englishe speeche. And for that wood there is geason and skant, their commune fewel is of a blacke stone, which they digge out of the earth. The other part, Northren, and ful of mountaines, a very rude and homely kind of people doth inhabete, which are called the Red shankes, or wylde Scottes. They be clothed with a mantell and shirt saffroned, after the Irishe manner, goyng naked to their shynnes. Their weapons are bowes and dartes, with a very broad sworde and a dagger sharpe onely at the one side. All speake Irishe, fedinge on fishe, milke, chese, and fleshe, hauinge a great nombre of Cattell. The Scottes differ from the Englishe in lawes and customes, because they vse ÿ ciuile law as all other Countries do. The Englishe

haue

haue their owne lawes and edictes. In certaine other conditions, they be not farre vnlike, but their language is one their habite and complexion like, one corage in batteyle, and in the nobilitie one desire and pregnancie in huntinge. The Country houses be narrow coue-red with strawe & rede, wherin the peo-ple and beastes do lodge together. Their townes besydes Sainete Johns towne are vnwalled, whiche is to be ascribed to their hardines, fixing al their succour and helpe alway, in the valiaũce of their body. The Scottes are very wyse as their learning declareth. For to what so euer arte they doe applie them selues, they easely profite in the same. But the idle and slouthfull: and suche chieflye as shunne & auoyde labour liue in great pouertie, and yet wyll not sticke to bost of their nobility and gentrie, as though it were more semely for the honest to lacke, then commõly by exercise of some honest arte, to get their liuing: and thus muche of Scotlande.

WALES the thirde parte of Britain lyeth vpon the left hande: whiche like a Promontary or Forlande, or an Ile (as it were on euery side is compassed with the mayne sea: except it be on the Easte Description of Wales.

part with the riuer of Seuerne: which deuideth Wales from England. Although some late writers affirme Herford to be a bond betwene Wales and Englande, and say that Wales beginneth at Chepstoole, where the riuer Veye, augmented with an other riuer called Lugge, passig by Herforde, doth runne into the Sea, which riuer riseth in the middle of Wales out of that hil ẏ Sabrine doth. For euen to ẏ place there goeth a great arme of the Sea, which passinge through the lande Westward: on the right hand leaueth Cornewal, and on the left Wales. Therefore Wales is extended from the towne of Chepitol, where it beginneth almoste by a straighte line a litle aboue Shrewsbury, euen to Westchester Northward. Into ẏ part, so many of the Britaynes as remayned aliue after ẏ slaughter & losse of their countrey, at ẏ length being driuē to their shiftes, did repaire (as auncient writinges report) where partly through refuge of the mountaynes, & partly of the woddes & marshes they remayned in safetye; whiche parte they enioye euen to this day. That lād afterwardes the Englishmenne did call Wales: & the Britaynes ẏ inhabitantes of the same Walshmen: for amonges ẏ

This arme of the sea as I iudge, is nowe called Aust, where is a passage betwen the village of Aust and Chepstol.

Germai

Germaynes, Walshman signifyeth a stranger, an alien, an outborne or strang mā that is such a one as hath contrary language frō theirs, for Wal in their tōgue is called a stranger borne, as an Italiā or Frenchman, which differ in speache from the Germaine.

Man signifyeth Homo: which is a man in Englishe. Therfore Englishmen, a people of Germanye, after they had won Britaine, called the Britaines which escaped after the destruction of their cōtry (after their countreye maner) Walshmen: because they had an other tōgue or speech besides theirs, and the land which they inhabited Wales, which name afterwardes both to the people & country did remaine. By this meanes the Britaynes with their kingdome lost their name.

The country soyle towardes the Sea coast, and in other places in the valleis and playnes is most fertile, which yeldeth both to man and beast, great plentye of fruit and grasse: but in other places for the most part it is barraine and lesse fruitful, because it lacketh tillage, for which cause husbandmenne do liue hardlye, eatinge Oten cakes and drinking milke mixt with water, and soure whaye. There be manye townes and

Foure bishoppes in Wales.

strong castels, and foure bishopprikes, if the bishopprike of Hereford be counted in England, as the late writers declare. The first bishopprike is Meneuc, soe called of Meneua, whiche at this daye they call S. Dauids, a Cittye verye auncient, situate uppon the Sea coast, and boundeth Westward towards Irelande. Another is Landaffe, the thirde Bangor, and the fourth saint Asaph, whiche be under Tharchbishop of Canterburie. The Walshmen haue a Language from the Englishmē, which as they say, that fetche their Pedigree from the Troyans, doth partly sounde of the Troyan antiquitye, and partly of the Grekes. But how soeuer it is, the Walshemen do not pronounce their speach so pleasantly & gentlye as the Englishmen doe, because they speake more in the throt, and contrarywyse the Englishmen, rightly following the Latines, do expresse theyr voyce somwhat within the lips, which to the hearers semeth pleasant & swete And thus much of Wales.

Description of Cornewall.

Cornewal beginneth on ẏ syde which standeth toward Spaine Westward: Toward the East, it is of bredth fourescore and ten myles extendinge a litle beyōd S. Germaynes, which is a very famous

villags

village situated on the righte hande vpō the sea coast, where the greatest breadth of that coūtry is but xx. myles: for this parcell of land on the right hand is cōpassed with the coaste of the mayne sea: and on the lefte hand wyth that arme of ẏ sea, which (as before is declared) parteth the land, & runneth vp to Chepstol, wher the coūtry is in forme of a horne: For at the first it is narrowe, and then groweth broder a little beyond the said towne of Saint Germaine. Eastwarde it bordereth vpon England, West, South and Northe, the mayne sea is rounde about it: It is a very barraine soyle, yelding fruit more through trauaile of the tillars and husbandmen, then throughe the goodnes of the ground, but there is greater plentye of Leade and tinne: in ẏ mining and digging wherof doth specially consist the liuinge and sustentation of thinhabitantes. Their tongue is far dissonant from Englysh, but is muche lyke to the Walshe tongue, because they haue manye wordes commune to bothe tongues, yet this difference there is betwene them, when the Welshman speaketh the Cornishman rather vnderstandeth many wordes spoken by the Walshemā, thē the whole tale he telleth, whereby it is manifest, that those three people do understand one an other in like maner as the Southerne Scottes do perceiue and understand the Northren. But it is a thing very rare and maruelous, that in one Iland there should be such variety of speaches. Cornewal is in the Diocesse of Excetour, which was ones worthye to bee counted the fourth part of the Ilande, as well for the contrarietye of language, as for the first inhabitantes thereof, as is before sayde. After wardes the Normans which constituted a kingdome of all those three partes, reckened Cornewall to be one of the countres or shyres of the coūtry. Thus muche of the particuler description of Britaine, ẏ the whole body of the Realm (by the members) may be ẏ better knowen to some peraduenture that neuer heard the same afore.

The forme of the Iland is Triquetra, hauinge three corners, or three sydes: Two wherof, that is to saye: The corner toward the East, & thother toward the West (both extending Northwardes) are the longest.

The thyrd syde which is the Southsyde, is farre shorter then thother, for ẏ Ilād is greater of length thē of bredth.

And

And as in the other two partes is contayned the length, euen so in the last, ye breadth. In which place the breadth beginneth, and so continuinge from the South part to the North, it is but narrowe. The firste and righte corner of which Ilande Eastwarde is in Kent, at Douer and Sandwitch. From whence to Calleis or Bulloigne in Fraunce, is the distance of xxx. myles. From this Angle which is againste Fraunce to the thirde Angle, which is in the Northe in Scotlande, the mayne whereof boundeth vpō Germanye, but no land seene, and there the Iland is like vnto a Wedge, euē at the very Angle of the lande in Scotland. The length wherof is 7. hundreth myles. Againe, the length from this corner at Douer in Kente, to the vttermoste part of Cornewal, being S. Michels mouē, (which is the West part or west Angle) is supposed to be 300. myles.

From this left Angle being the West part and thuttermost part of Cornewall, which hath a prospect towarde Spayne, in which part also standeth Irelande, situated betweene Britayne and Spayne, to the North Angle, in the furthest part of Scotland, in which part the Iland doth ende, ye lengthes 800. miles, in which part there bee verye good hauens, and safe harborowghes for shippes. & apte passage into Irelande, beinge not paste one day sayling, but the shorter passage is from Wales to Waterford a towne in Ireland vpon the sea coast, muche lyke to that passage betwene Douer and Calice, or some what more: but the shortest passage of al, is out of Scotlande. Fro this last angle to Hampton: which is a towne vpon the sea coast, with a hauē so called towarde the South, & therfore called Southampton) betwene the Angles of Kent and Cornewall, they doe measure by a straighte lyne the whole length of the Iland. and do saye that it contayneth 800. myles, as the breadthe from Menevia, or saincte Dauids to Yarmouth, whiche is the vttermost part of the Iland towardes the East: doth containe 200. myles: for the bredth of ỷ Iland is in the Southpart, which part is the front and beginning of the Land, & endeth narrow, or as it were in a straight So the circuit or compasse of the Iland is xviii. C. miles, whiche is 200. lesse then Cæsar doth accompt.

Thus much touching the Diuision of England with the forme and situation of the same.

OF BRVTE THAT first gouerned this Land, with the yeares before Christe his byrth, vvhen euerye kinge began their reignes, till Cimbilinus, and then followeth the yeares from CHRIST his byrthe.

BRute the sonne of Siluius, 1108.
the sonne of Ascanius, the sonne of Æneas. After a longe and werye iourneye out of Italy with his Troyans, passynge throughe Fraunce, buylded the Citye of Towres, and the arriued in this Isle which was called Albion, at a place now called Tottnes in Deuonshyre, the yeare of ye world 2855. the yeare before Christes natiuitye 1108. wherein he first began his raigne, and named it Britaine, or rather Brutaine after his name. Hee buylded the Citye of newe Troye, now called London, he stablisht therein the Troyan Lawes, and deuided the whole Ilande amonge his three sonnes. Unto his eldest sonne named Locrine, he gaue the middle part of

Troyan Lawes.

of Britaine, now called Englande, with the superioritye of all this Ile. Unto Camber he gaue Wales, and to Albanact, Scotlande, he deceased when he had raigned 24. yeares, and was buried at new Troye.

1084. LOcrine chased the Hunnes, which inuaded this Realme: and pursued thẽ so sharpelye, that manye of theym with their kinge named Humber, was drowned in a riuer, which til this day is named Humber. This king Locrine had to wyfe Guendolin, daughter of Corineus duke of Cornewall, by whom he had a sonne named Madan, he also kept as paramour, the beautiful Ladye Estrilde, by whõ he had a daughter named Sabrine. And after the death of Corineus, hee put from him the saide Guendolin and wedded Estrilde, but Guendolin repaired to Cornewall, where shee gathered a greate power, and foughte with kinge Locrine and slue him, when he had raigned .xx. yeares, hee was buried at newe Troye. She drowned the Ladye Estrilde, with her daughter Sabrine in a riuer, that after the yonge maydens name is called Seuerne.

How Humber toke that name.

Seuerne.

1064. GVẽdolin wife to Locrine (for so much as Madan her sonne was to youg to gouerne)

gouerne) was made ruler of the whole Isle of Britaine, which she wel & discretelye ruled xv. yeares, and then lefte the same to her sonne Madan. Gueadoline a Queene raigned.

MAdan used greate tirannye amonge his Britaines: and being at his disport of huntinge, was deuoured by wild wolues, whē he had raigned xl. yeres. 1049 The kings deuoured by wolues.

MEmpricius ŷ sonne of Madan, beinge kinge, by treason slue his brother Manlius. Hee fell in slouth, and so to lecherie, takinge the wiues & doughters of his subiectes: and lastlye hee forsoke his wife and concubines, and fel to the sinne of Sodomie with beastes. And going on hunting, was destroyed of wild wolues: when he had raigned twentye yeares. 1009. One brother traytetrously slayeth the other.

EBranke the sonne of Mempricius, had xxi. wiues, of whom he receiued xx sonnes, and xxx. daughters, which were sente by their father to Alba Siluius, the fourth king of Albanoies in Italye, to be maryed to the Albanes. Assaracus the seconde sonne of Ebranke, with the rest of his yonger brethren, by the ayde of Alba Siluius, conquered all Germany. Of these brethren had Germanie the name, à Germanis fratribus, ŷ had subdued it. Ebrank was founder of Alclud in Scotlande, 989. Germanye toke the name of Ebranke his sonnes, who conquered the same. Dunbritain. Edēbrough.

which

Bamburghe and Yorke builded. which is Dunbritaine, hee made the Castel of Maidens, now called Edenbrough. He made also the Castel of Bamburghe, he builded Yorke Citie, & was ther buried, when he had raigned lx. yeares.

929. BRutus the eldest sonne of Ebranke, who for his lusty courage was surnamed Greneshielde, raigned xii. yeeres and was buried at Yorke.

917. Chester builded. LEill the sonne of Brute Greneshielde, a louer of peace, builded Carleile now called Chester, but since by the Romaynes the same was reedifyed, when a Legion of knightes was sent thether, and by them named the Citye of Legions. Leil in the ende of his raigne fell to slouth and lust of the body, by meane wherof ciuil strife was raysed, and not in his dayes ended, he raigned 25. yeres and was buryed at Carleil, alias Chester.

892. Canterbury Winchester and Shaftesbury builte. RVdhudebras the sonne of Leil, builded Canterburye, Winchester, and Shaftsburye, wherein hee builded Temples, and placed Flamines. He raigned xxix. yeares.

863. Stamford an Vniuersitye. BLadud the sonne of Rudhudibras, whoe had long studyed at Athens, broughte with hym 4. Philosophers, to keepe schole in Britaine: for the which he builded Stamforde, and made it an Vniuersitye,

flye. He builded Bathe, wyth the whot bathes, and practised the arte of Necromancye, he decked himselfe in fethers, and presumed to flye, but by falling on the Tẽple of Apollo, he brake his neck, when he had raigned twentye yeares.

Bathe with the whote bathes buil. The king attempteth to flye.

LEire sonne of Bladude, succeded his father. He builded Cair Lair, now called Leicester. Hee had thre daughters, Gonorell, Ragan, and Cordelle. Which Cordelle for her wysedom and vertue towardes her father, succeded him in the kingdom. Whẽ he had raigned xl yeres, he deceysed, & was buryed at Leicester.

844. Leister builded.

COrdila the yongest daughter of Leire, succedyng her father, was sore vexed by her two nephues, Morgan of Albanie, and Conedagus of Camber and Cornewal, who at the length toke and cast her in prison, where she beinge in dispeire of recoueringe her estate, slue her selfe, when shee had raigned fiue yeares, and was buryed at Leicester.

805. Cordila a Queene raigned.

MOrgan ye eldest sonne of Dame Gonorel, claymed Britain, & warred on his nephew Conidagus yt was kig of Cãber, but Conedagus met with Morgan in Wales, & there slue him: which place is called Glamorgã til this day. Whẽ Conedagus was king of al Britain; he builded a temple

800. Howe Glamorganshire toke that name.

S. Johns towne builded. Bangor builded.

temple of Mars at Perche, that nowe is S. Johns towne in Scotlād, he builded an other of Mineruae in Wales, which now is called Bangor. The third he made of Mercurie in Cornewall, he raigned xxiii. yeares, and was buried at newe Troye.

7 6 6. Bloude rayned.

Riuallo sonne of Conidagus, succeded his father, in whose tyme it rayned bloud three dayes, after which tempest ensued a greate multitude of venemous flyes, which slue much people. And thē a great mortality in this lād, which caused almost desolation of the same. This Riuallo raigned xlvi. yeares, and was buried at Yorke.

Rome builded.

Rome was builded in Italy by Remus and Romulus 356. yeares after Brute arriued in this Land.

7 2 2. Gurgustius, sonne of Riuallo a common dronkarde, whereof folowed all other vices, raigned xxxviii. yeares, & was buried at Yorke.

6 8 4. Sicilius, brother of Gurgustius, of whom is lefte but little memorye: raigned xlix. yeares, and was buried at Bathe.

6 3 6. Iago or Lago, cosen of Gurgustius, raigned xxv. yeares, and was buryed at Yorke.

Game of Chesse deuised.

The game of Chesse, was deuised by Excerses the Philosopher, other wyse named Philometre, to reproue and correct the

the

the cruell minde of a famous tyraunte called Enilmerodach kynge of Babilon, aboute the yeare before Christ his birth 614.

Kinimacus raigned .liiii. yeares, and was buried at Yorke. 612.

Gorbodug raigned lxiii. yeares, and was buryed at new Troye. 559.

Ferrex with his brother Porrex, ruled fiue yeares, but it was not longe ere they fell at ciuill discorde for the soueraigne dominion in which Ferrex was slaine. And Porrex afterwardes by hys mother was killed in his bedde. 496.

The brother slue the brother, and the mother murdred her owne sonne, Brutus line extinguished.

Thus cruelly was the bloud & house of Brute destroyed, when this Realme by the space of 616. yeares, had bene gouerned by that lynage. And also this Realme was deuided with ciuil warres, for lacke of one soueraigne gouernoure, which continued by the space of li. yeares, untill Dunwallo.

Mulmutius Dunwallo, yͤ sonne of Gloten, Duke of Cornwal, reduced this Realme into one Monarchie, being before by ciuile warres and discention, seuered into diuers Dominiōs. He was the first that ware a crowne of Golde: He constituted good lawes, which lōg after, were called Mulmutius Lawes. 446

First kinge that ware a crowne of golde.

He builded Blackewell Hall.

The second lawes, were Mulmutius Lawes.

Hee gaue priuileges vnto Temples, & ploughes, and began to make the foure notable wayes in Britaine. In London called then new Troy, he builded a temple, which some suppose to be Blackwel Hall, which was called Templum pacis. Finallye when hee had brought this Realme to quietnes, raigninge herein xl. yeres, he dyed honourably, leauing after him two valiant sonnes, Belinus & Brennus. He was buried at newe Troye in the Temple of Peace.

461.

BElinus and Brennus, sonnes of Mulmucius, deuided this whole Isle betwen theym. Unto Beline the elder brother, was appoynted England, Wales & Cornewall. Unto the other the North part beyonde Humber. This Brennus desirous of glorye and Dominion, raysed war agaynst Beline. But in conclusion by the meanes of their mother they were accorded, and Brennus being geuen wholy to the studye of warres, lefte his countrey to the gouernaunce of his brother, and went into Fraunce, where in ẏ prouince of Lions for his excellent qualities, hee was greatly esteemed of Siguinus kinge of the countrey, whose daughter hee maryed. And of the Galles was made soueraigne Captaine, whan they made theym

The yonger brother persecuteth the elder.

theyr voyage to Rome. Beline in the meane time both in ciuil iustice and also in Religion, greatlye increased hys Realme. He finished the foure wayes begonne by his father. He made tributorye to him Denmarke. In London he made the Hauen which at this daye is called Belines gate. He builded the Tower of London. After hee had raigned wyth his brother, and alone, xxvi. yeres, he dyed, and his ashes in a vessell, was set on a high Pinacle ouer Belines gate. he builded Caerufke vpon the riuer Vske, which since by a Legion of ye Romaynes there placed, was named Kaerlegion, and now Carlion.

Foure notable wayes.

Belines gate builded.

Tower of Londō first builded.

Carlion builded.

G Vrgiūtus the sonne of Beline, subdued Denmarke, compelling them to continue their tribute, and in his returne home met with a fleete of Spaniardes, whiche were seekinge for habitations, because their countreye was soe populous, and not able to sustaine theym, to whom the king graunted the Ile of Ireland to hold the same of hym. He raigned xix. yeres, & was buryed at Carlion. In his tyme Cambridge was builded. 375.

Ireland inhabited.

Cambridge builded.

G Vinthelinus sonne of Gurguntius, a Prince sobre and quiet, who had to wife a notable womā named Marcia, of 356.

excellent

Marcian lawes the third. cellent learning and knowledge. She deuised certayne lawes, whiche were named Marcian lawes. She raigned .xv. yeares, and was buried at newe Troy.

3 3 0 Cecilius, the sonne of Guintheline, raigned .vii. yeres (as the Scottes write) in the first yeare of his raigne, a people of Almain called Pictes, arriued here in Brittayne, and possessed those parties, whiche nowe be the marches of Englād and Scotlande. Cecilius was buried at Carlion

The Pictes first inhabited the marches.

3 2 3 Kimarus, a wylde yong man, liuinge after his own lust, reigned but thre yeares, and was slayne as he was hunting of wilde beastes.

3 2 1 Elanius, called also Danius, was kyng ix. yeares.

3 1 1 Morindus, the bastard sonne of Danius, raigned viii. yeares, hee foughte with a king who came out of Germany, and slewe him with all his power. Moreouer out of the Irishe seas in his tyme came a wonderful monster, which destroyed muche people. Whereof the king hearing, woulde of his valiaunte courage needes fight with it, by whome he was cleane deuoured.

The king deuoured.

3 0 3 Gorbomannus, eldest sonne of Morindus renued the temples of his Gods, gouernise.

uerned his people in peace and wealth, hee builded Grantham in Lincolneshyre. He raigned xi. yere. Grantham builded.

ARchigallo brother to Gorbomannus, was in conditions vnlike to hys brother, for he deposed the noble men, & exalted the vnnoble. He extorted from men their goodes to enriche his treasurye: for which cause by the states of the Realme, hee was depriued of his royall dignitye, when hee had raigned fiue yeares. 292.

The kinge depriued.

ELidurus the thirde sonne of Morindus, gouerned his people iustly. As hee was hunting by chaunce, hee met wyth his brother Archigallo, whom moste louinglye hee embraced, and founde the meanes to reconcyle him to his Lordes, and then resigned to him his royal dignitye, when he had raigned fiue yeres. 285.

ARchigallo thus restored to his royall estate, ruled the people iustly x. yeares, and lyeth buryed at Yorke. 282.

ELidurus after the death of his brother Archigallo, for his pitie and iustice, was agayne chosen kinge. Hee raigned not passing two yeares, but his yonger brotherne, Vigenius and Peredurus, raysed warre agaynste him: toke him prisoner, and caste him into ye Tower of London, 272.

The yonger bretherne persecuteth the elder.

 don,

don where shee remayned duringe this raigne.

270. Vigenius and Peredurus, after the taking of their brother, raigned together vii. yeares. Vigenius then died, and Peredurus raigned alone ii. yeares. Hee builded the towne of Pickering.

The towne of Pickeringe builded.

261. Elidurus ỳ third time was made king, who continued his raigne honourablye, but being brused with age & troubles, he finished his life, when hee had raigned 4. yeares, and was buryed at Carlisle.

258. Gorbonian raigned ten yeares.

248. Morgan guided the Realme peaceable xiiii. yeres.

234. Emerianus his brother, tyrannously raigned 7. yeares, and was deposed.

227. Iuall was chosen king for his iustice, which gouerned peaceable xx. yeres.

207. Rimo gouerned this land peaceablye 16. yeares.

197. Geruntius raigned twenty yeares;

187. Cathlus raigned ten yeares, he hon by all oppressiones of the poore.

167. Coillus succeded who quietlye gouerned xx. yeares.

147. Porex a vertuous and gentle prince raigned v. yeares.

136. Chirinnus, through his dronkennes raigned but one yeare.

Fulgen his sonne raigned 2. yeares. 135.
Eldred raigned but one yere. 133.
Androgius, raigned likewyse one yere. 132.
Varianus geuen to the lustes of the fleshe, raigned three yeares. 13[illegible].
Eliud raigned v. yeares, who was a gret Astronomer. 128.
Dedantius raigned v. yeares. 12[illegible].
Detonius raigned in the lande two yeres. 120.
Gurginius raigned iii. yeres. 118.
Merianus was king two yeares. 115.
Bladunus gouerned this land two yeres. 11[illegible].
Capenus raigned .iii. yeares. 111.
Ouinus ruled this lande ii. yeares. 108.
Silius raigned in this land ii. yeres. 106.
Bledgabredus raigned x. yeares, & gaue himselfe to Musicke. 104.
Archimalus was king .ii. yeares. 94.
Eldelus raigned iiii yeares. In his time were seene Globes of fyre burninge out of the ayre. 92.
Rohanns was king two yeres. 88.
Redargius raigned king iii. yeares. 86.
Samulius raigned king ii. yeeares. 83.
Penisellus was king three yeares. 81.
Pirthus ruled this land ii. yeares. 78.
Caporus was king two yeares. 76.
Dinellus the sonne of Caporus, a vertuous and Prince, gouerned [illegible] yeares. 74.

70. Ile of Elye
Heli his sonne, raigned not one yere. Of him ye Ile of Elye toke his name: for yt hee there builded a goodlye Pallace and was there buryed.

69. Lud repayred newe Troye, and named it London.
Lud the eldest sonne of Hely, amended his Lawes, and toke awaye all vsages that were noughte. He repayred the Cittye thenne called new Troye, wyth fayre buildinges and walles, & named it Luddon. He builded on the West part thereof, a stronge gate, which vnto this time is called Ludgate. He raigned xi. yeares, and was buried nere to the same Ludgate, in a Temple, which hee there builded. He left two sonnes, Androgius and Theomancius, who being not of age to gouern, their vncle Cassibelan obtayned the Crowne.

58. Iulius Cæsar his first voyage into Englande.
Cassebilanus after the death of his brother Lud, ruled xix. yeares. In the viii. yere of his raigne, Iulius Cæsar comminge vnto that parte where Callaice Bologne nowe stande, he determined to make warre into Britaine, which vntill that time remayned vnknowen to the Romaynes. This quarell was because in the warres of Fraunce he perceyued Frenchmen to haue much succour & aide from thence. Wherfore hauing prepared lxxx. shippes, hee sayled into Britain

wher

where at the first being weryed with an
ard & sharpe batayle. And after with
daine tempests his nauye almoste de-
royed: he returned agayn into Fraunce,
ere to winter his men. The nexte
Springe whiche was the yeare before
Christ .l. His nauye beinge newe rig-
ed and encreased, he passed the Seas
gaine with a greater armye. But w hy-
s he went towards his enemyes on
nde, his shippes lying at anker, were
gaine by tempest almost lost: for eyther
ey were driuen on the Sandes, where
ey stacke fast, or els through beatinge
ne an other with force of the tempeste,
ey were destroyed. So that xl. were
ost, the other with muche labour were
ued. Vpon lande also his horsmen at
e first encounter were vanquished, &
abienus the Tribune slaine. At ẏ second
onflicte not without great daunger of
is men, he put the Brytaynes to flight,
rom thence he went to ẏ riuer of Tha-
es, on the further syde wherof Cassi-
ilanus with a great multitude of people
as keeping the bankes, who had set al
e said bankes of the riuer, and almost
ll the shalowe places vnder the water
with sharpe stakes, euery one of thē as
ig as a mās thigh, bounde about with

The second voyage of Julius Cæsar into England.

lead, and drawen so fast into the bottome of the riuer, that they cã neuer be remoued. Cassibilanus and his Brytaynes not being able to resist the violence & force of the Romaynes, hid themselues in wodes, and with sodaine eruptions oftentimes inuaded them: but in the meane tyme their strongest Cittye now called London, submitted it selfe to Cæsar, deliuering vnto him hostages: which example also the other Citties followed, whereby Cassibilanus after manye losses was constrayned to giue pledges, and to agree that Britaine should become tributarye to the Romaynes. Then Cæsar like a conquerour, with a great nomber of prisonners sayled into Fraunce, and so to Rome, where shortlye after he was by the Senate slaine with bodkins.

Englande tributarye to the Romaynes.

Cæsar conquering the worlde, was slaine with bodkins.

The Castels of Douer, Caterbury, Rochester, and the tower of Lõdõ builded.

Iuliu. Cæsar builded in this lande the Castels of Douer, of Cantorbury, Rochester, and the Tower of London, the Castel and towne of Cæsarsburye, now called Salisburye. Hee also edifyed Cæsars Chester, now called Chichester, and the Castell of Excester. &c.

Salisburye, Chichester, and Excester builded.

Touchinge the barbarousnes of the Britaynes at that time, theyr coyne was of brasse, or els ringes of Iron, sysed at a certain waight of mony: they thought

A discriptiõ of the Brytaynes

a heinous thing to tast of a Hare, a Hen
a Goose: they clothed themselues in
ether, they dyed theymselues with
Woade, which settinge a blewishe cou-
loure vpon them, made them more ter-
ible to beholde in battaile, they ware
heir heare longe, and shaued all partes
f their bodies sauing the head & vpper
ippe: they had ten or xii. wyues a peece,
ommō with themselues, specially bro-
hers with brothers, and parents with
heir children, but the issue that came of
hem was accoumpted his that first maryed the mother.

Theomantius the sonne of Lud, and ne-phewe to Cassibelane, raigned quiet-lye xxiii. yeares, he was buried at London. 37.

Cimbalinus the sonne of Theomantius, raigned xxxv. yeares, and was buri-ed at London. In the xiii. yeare of his raigne, CHRIST our Sauiour was borne. 38.

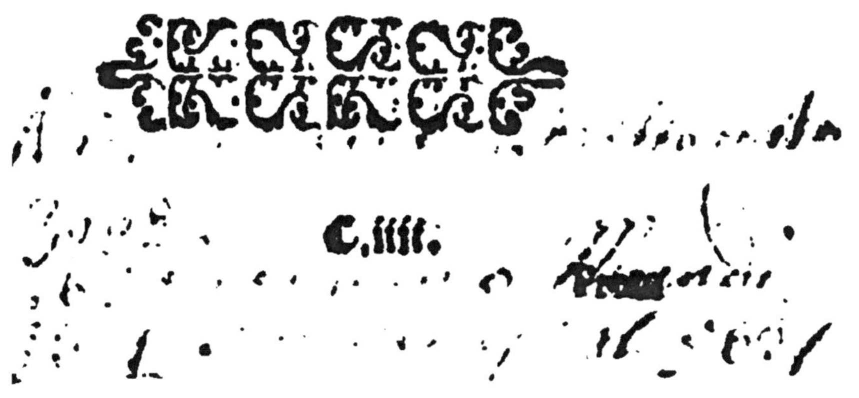

From this place followinge, the yeres from Christ his birth, are placed in the Margent.

Anno Christi. 1. When Cæsar Augustus the second Emperour by ẏ wil of GOD had stablyshed peace throughe the world, our redeemer Iesus Christ, verye God and man, was borne in the xlii. yeare of the raigne of Augustus, he beganne to preache the xv. yeare of Tiberius, and suffered his passion the xviii. yeare of the same Tiberius.

61. GViderius the first sonne of Cimbaline, was ordayned king. This man was valeaunt, hardye, wealthye, and trusted much in his strength. He denyed to pay tribute to the Romaynes, he raigned. 23 yeares.

44. Southampton how it toke that name. ARuiragus the yongest sonne of Cimbaline, was ordayned kinge of Britaine. He slue Hamon neare to a Hauen of the sea, and threwe him gobbet meale therin. Wherefore it is now called Southhampton.

Claudius the 4. Emperour, sailed into this Iland which no man before Iulius Cæsar durst come unto, and there without anye battayle or bloudshed the most part

part of this Ilande yelded unto hym in a smal time: hee also subdued unto the Empyre, the Iles of Arcadie, and those which lye in the Ocean sea beyond Britaine. Claudius toke kinge Aruiragus to his grace, and gaue hym his doughter in mariage named Genissa. This Claudius builded Gloucester.

Sainte Peter, by the tyrannye of Nero, was crucifyed at Rome, after the byrthe of Christ xlviii. yeres. And S. Paule was there beheaded with the sworde.

The yeare after Christes incarnation lxiii. came into Britaine (sent by S. Philip the Apostle) Ioseph of Aramathie, and xi. other Christians, who builded them a Chappel in the Ile of Aualon, & after was ther buryed, which place beinge since encreased and newly builded by diuers Princes, was named Glastenburye. Aruiragus raigned xxviii. yeares, and was buryed at Glocester.

First Christians in Britaine.

73

MArius the sonne of Aruiragus, an excellent wise man, rained liii. yeres.

Vespasian who was Emperoure after Nero, was sent into Britayn, he subdued to the Romaine Empyre the Ile of Wight.

Rodricke kinge of the Pictes, accompanyed with the Scottes, inuaded Britayne.

taine, and spoyled the countrye with swoorde & fyre, unto whom Marius with his knightes gaue a sharpe battayle, wherein Rodrike was slaine, wyth a greet nomber of his souldiors. To them which remayned, Marius gaue inhabitaunce in the furthest part of Scotlād. And forasmuch as the Britaynes disdained to geue their daughters to them in mariage, they acquainted them with the Irishmen, and maryed their doughters, & grew in processe of time to a gret people. This Marius repayred & fortifyed the City of Caerleō now called Chester.

124. COilus the sonne of Marius, brought up in Italye among the Romaynes, paid the tribute trulye. He builded Colchester, raigned lv. yeares, hee was buryed at Yorke.

Colchester builded.

179. LVcius the sonne of Coilus, whoe in all his actes folowed the steppes of his forefathers, was of all men loued and dreaded. He sent his two Embassadours Eluanus and Meduuinus. ii. learned men in the Scriptures, wyth his louinge letters to Eleutherius bishoppe of Rome, desiring him to sende some deuoute and learned men, by whose instruction both he and his people mighte be taughte the fayth and Religion of Christe: wherof

Britaine receyued the fayth.

Eleu-

...utherius beinge verye glad, baptised ...se two messengers, makinge Eluanus ...ishop, and Meduuinus a teacher, and ...t also with them into Britaine two fa... ...us clarkes Faganus and Deruuianus: ...y whose diligence Lucius and his peo... ..., were instructed and baptised in the ...th of Christ. At this time xxviii. te... ...s of Flamines, were made Cathedrall ...urches, and bishoppes placed as Fla... ...es before h id bene, London, Yorke, & ...lion, were Archbishoppes.

London, Yorke, and Carliō, thre Archbishoppes.

...hean first Archbishop of London in ... time of Lucius: builded the Church ...S. Peter on Cornehill in London, by the ...e of Ciran chiefe butler to king Luci... Also Eluanus builded the librarye in ... same Church, and conuerted manye ... the Droydes to the Christen faith. Lu...s raigned xii. yeares, and was buried ...Glocester. After whose death, for so ...ch as of him remayned no heyre, the ...raynes fel at great discord, which con...ued xv. yeares.

Thean first Archbishop of London.

Eluanus the secōd Archbishop of London.

...uerus beinge a cruel man, gouerned ...he Romaynes stoutely, and hauing o... ...come his ciuill warres, he was dri... ...n into Britaine, wher with great and ...uous battailles wining part there... ...he did seperate it from the rest of the

205.

Iland,

Ilande, with a Rampier of earthe and turues, as it were a wall highe aboue the earthe, for that there remayneth before the Rampier a ditche, oute of the which the turues were taken. It began at Tine, and reached to the Scottish sea, which is yet called the Scottishe banke. This Seuerus gouerned Britayne viii. yeares, and was buryed at Yorke.

Scottishe bancke.

213. BAssianus Caracalla, succeded his father in the Empyre. Of nature hee was cruell and fierce, able to endure al peines and laboures in warfare. He raygned xiii. yeares, after whom of longe time was no kinge in Britaine, but the same was only gouerned by the Emperours of Rome.

280. CArassius a Britayne of low birth, but valiant and hardy in martial dedes, purchased of the Emperour, the keping of the coastes of Britayne: by meanes whereof he drew to him many knightes of his countreye, and addressed deadlye warre against the Romaynes, & toke on him the gouernmente of Britaine in the tyme of Dioclesian. Till that time this land was in good quietnes by the space of lxxvi. yeares.

292. ALectus a Duke of Rome, slue the said Carassius, when he had raygned viii. yeres

eares, and thenne Alectus gouerned the Britaynes, vsinge among them much tiranny. Wherfore they intending vtterly to expel the Romaines, moued Asclepiodatus to take on hym the kingdome: whoe gathered a greate power, & made sharpe war vppon the Romaynes, vntil at length Alectus was slaine, when hee had gouerned Britaine iii. yeares. Saint Albon suffered martyrdome vnder Dioclesian and Maximilian in the yere of our Lord 293. the 20. day of June.

Alectus slaine.

Asclepiodatus beseyged the City of London with a stronge siege, wherein was Liuius Gallus, ỹ Romaine Captaine: and ere it were long, by violence entered the Citty, and slue Gallus neare vnto a broke, into which broke he threwe hein, by reason whereof, it was called Gallus broke: and nowe Walbroke. After whiche victorye, throughe greate discention, Asclepiodatus was slaine. 295.

Walbroke in London.

Asclepiodatus slaine.

Coill toke on him the kingdom, & gouerned the same one yeare. 301.

Constantius a Duke of Rome, was sent into Britaine to recouer the tribute: after whose arriual kinge Coil shortlye dyed. Wherefore the Britaynes to haue more surety of peace, willed this Duke 302.

to

to take to wyfe Helena the doughter of Coill, which was a wonderfull fayre mayden, and therewyth well learned. This Constantius when hee had recouered the tribute, returned to Rome as chiefe ruler of Britayne, he was buryed at Yorke.

307. Constantine the sonne of Constantius, succeded, aswell in the kingdome of Britayne, as in the gouernaunce of other Realmes, that were subiect afore to his father. This Constantine was a right noble and valiant Prince, and sonne of Helena, a woman of great sanctimonye. Hee was surnamed the greate Constantine, and had the fayth of Christ in such reuerence, that alwayes most studiously he endeuoured to augment the same. In witnes of his beliefe, hee caused a booke of the Gospel to be caried before him, and made the Bible to bee copied out, and sent into all partes of the Empyre. Of this man the kings of Britaine had first the priuiledge to weare close crownes. He raigned xxxi. yeres.

Kings ware close crownes.

Helena the mother of Constantine, compast the Cittye of London, and the towne of Colcheiler wyth walles. She did repayre the Cittye of Hierusalem.

S. Helene an English woman.

Octauius whom Constantine made Lieue-

ant in Britaine rebelled, & endeuous
d to expel the Romaynes. Wherof whē
onstantine had knowledge, hee sente a-
ist hym a Duke named Traherne, with
egions of souldiours, after whose ar-
iual was fought a fierce battaile, nere
Winchester. In whych Traherne was
onstrayned to flye towarde Scotlande:
whom Octauius folowed, and in Westmerlande gaue to him the second battel,
n which Octauius was chased, and driuen to forsake the land.

Octauius repayring his army, came a- 314.
gaine into Britaine, but in the meane
time an Earle, which fauoured his par
tye, by treason murdered the forenamed
Traherne. And then Octauius raigned at
the least liiii. yeares.

Maximus sonne of Leonine, and cosine 379.
germaine to Constantine the greate,
was made king of Britaine. This man
was mightye of his handes: but for þ
he pursued the Christians, hee was called Maximus the tyraunte. Maximus raig- Litle Bri-
ned viii. yeres. He sayled into Armeri- taine con-
ca, nowe called little Britaine, and sub- quered.
dued þ countreye, gaue it to Conon Meri-
doke, to hold for euer of þ kings of gret
Britaine. Maximus was cōstrained of the
souldiours to take on him þ Imperiall
Crowne,

Crowne: and therfore beinge in Fraūce, passed further into the landes of the Empyre, and subdued a great part of Fraūce and all Germanye. Gratian the Emperour of him was put to flight at Paris, and slaine at Lions.

Vrsula of Englande.

Vrsula, with the eleuen thousand Virgens, which were sent into litle Britain to be maried to the aforesaid Conon and his knightes, were slaine of the barbarous people being on the sea.

391.

GRatian that was sent into Britaine of Maximus, to defende the lande from Barbariens, toke on him the kingdome, and exercised all tyranny vpon the people: for which cause hee was abhorred of the Britaines, and by them slaine whē he had raigned foure yeres. The Britaines were inuaded againe of the Pictes & Scottes, which notwithstanding the foresayd wall that was made by the Romaines, spoyled the country verye sore, so ẏ they were driuen to seke for new helpe at the Romaynes: who sente to them a companye of souldiours, which againe chased the Pictes, and made a wall of stoone of the thicknes of viii. foote, and in heighte xii. foote. Which thynge when they had done, comforting the Britaynes, and admonishing them hereafter

to

trust to their owne manhode, they re-
rned to Rome. The Scottes and Pictes
gayn entered Brytaine, spoiling the coū-
cy, and chasing the commons so cruel-
y, that they were altogether cōfortles.
In this necessitie they sent for Ætius the
Romaine Captaine, beyng then in Frāce,
ut they had no comfort at his hand. And
therfore were forced to sende to Aldroenus king of little Brytaine, to desyre aide
and comfort: whiche they obtayned, in
condition, that if they atchieued the victory, Constantine his brother should be
made kinge of Brytaine: Whiche thinge
being graunted, the sayd Constantine gathered a company of souldiours. And
when he had manfully vanquished their
enemies, according to promise, he was
ordeined kyng.

Scottes and Pictes inuade this realme, the Romains refuse to defende the same: but rather lose their tribute

Here endeth the dominion and tribute of the Romaines ouer this lande, whiche had continued. 483. yeares.

435

Constantine, brother of Aldroenus, after he had chased and ouercome the Pictes and Scottes, was crowned king of great Brytaine, and guided the lande x. yeares in quietnes. A certaine Picte watchinge his tyme, by secret meanes traiterously slue the kyng in his chamber.

The king slaine by a Picte.

D Constan-

445 Constantius his eldest sonne, which for his soft spirite was made Monke at Winchester, by the meanes of Vortiger, was taken out of the cloyster, and made kinge, under whose name the forsayde Vortiger ruled all the land, & used great tyranny. And Constantius was slayne of certayne Pictes, whome Vortiger had ordayned for a garde to his bodye. Wherof when Vortiger had knowledge, he made semblaunt of great sorrowe and heauines: and caused the sayd Pictes to be put to death, thoughe hee in deede were the chiefe causer of their treason. So this Constantius raigned but two yeares. And Aurelius and Vther, the kynges yonger brethren fled into litle Britaine.

A monke made king

The kinge traiterously slayne.

447 Vortiger was by force ordeined kyng, which was neither a mā of his hāds nor good in counsayle, but subiecte to auarice, and pryde, so lecherous, that hee defiled his owne daughter, and gatte on her a sonne. In his time was so greate plentie of corne and fruite, that the lyke had not bene sene many yeares before. Whiche plentie was cause of idlenes, gluttony, lechery, & other vices: so that through their incontinent and riotous liuing, ensued so great pestilence & mortalitie, that the liuing scantly suffised to bury

Plenty of corne and Grayne.

Pestilence.

rey the dead. Also the Scottes and Pictes hauing knowledge of the death of their knightes whiche were slayne by Vortiger, for murdering of the king, inuaded and spoyled the lande of Britaine. Vortiger prouoked by the multitude that tried out against him, concluded that all, bothe Englishemen & Saxons, that were able to beare armes and had no dwelling place, shoulde be sent for out of Germany, and that the Barren marish groūd should be geuen them to dwel in. Which councel being well liked, embassadors were sent into Germany, where they founde the Germaines so ioyfull of theyr requeste, that with al speede in thre long shippes with a faire winde, they came into Brytaine. At that tyme, and all other tyme after, there came out of Germany three sortes of people Englishemen, Saxōs and Iuits. Hingist and Horsus, twoo brethren were their captains, the Ile of Thanet was deliuered them to inhabite in. By their manhode in many battailes, he vanquished the Pictes, & other enemies: and therefore had thē in great loue & fauour. Hēgist one of ÿ Saxōs, foūd meanes ÿ Vortiger maried his daughter Rowan, a mayden of wonderfull beauty and pleasauntnes, but a miscreant and Pagane.

The Scottes and Pictes spoyled this lande.

Saxons sent for into Britayne.

First Saxons entring this Realme.

For her sake, the king was deuorced frō his lawfull wyfe, by whom he had thre sonnes. For whiche dede well nere all the Brytons forsoke him, and the Saxones, daily encreased both in fauour, multitude and authoritie.

Vortiger diuorced.

Saint Germaine came into Britaine, to reduce them from the heresie of Pelagius.

Pelagius heresy.

The Britaines consideringe the daily repaire of the Saxones into this realme, shewed to their king, the ieopardie that might ensue, and aduertised hem to auoyde the daunger, and expell them out of the realme: but Vortiger, by reason of his wife, bore suche fauour to the Saxons that he would in no wise heare the coūcell of his subiectes. Wherefore they depriued him of his royall dignitie, when he had raigned. vij. yeare, & ordeyned to their king, his eldest sonne Vortimerus.

Vortiger depriued.

454 VOrtimer being made king, in all haste pursued the Saxones, and by his marciall knighthoode, vanquished them in foure great battailes, untill at length he was poysoned by meane of Rowen his stepmother, after he had raygned syxe yeares.

The kyng poysoned.

460 VOrtiger obtayned agayne the kyngedome. Shortly after Hengistus (which was

was chased of Vortimer, into the Isle of Thanet, entered the lande with a number of Saxones, but when he heard of the great assemble of the Brytons, he treated for peace, whiche was concluded. Not longe after, the Saxons slue on the playne of Sarisbury. iiii. C. lx. Barons & Earles, and toke the king prysoner, and constrained him to graunt unto them Kent, Sussex, Suffolke, and Norfolke. Then Hengist began his dominion ouer Kent, sending for moe Saxons, to inhabite the Prouinces, and shortly after made warre upon the Britaines, and so chased them, that hee kepte his kingdome of Kent in peace & warre. xxiiii. yeares.

Barons slain

First kingdome of the Saxons.

Aurelie surnamed Ambrose, and Uther, the brethren of Constantius kinge of Britaine, whiche was slayne by the treason of Vortiger, landed with a nauye of shippes at Totnes, and by the help of Britaines, whiche gathered to them, made warre upon Vortiger, and burned him in his castell in Wales, when he had secondly raigned syxe yeares.

Vortiger burned.

AVrelius Ambrose, was ordeined kynge of Britaine, whiche immediatly hasted him with an armie towardes Yorke, against Octa sonne of Hengist, who with his Saxons kept the citie, where he disco-

466

 uered

sited, and toke prysoner the sayd Octa.

The seconde kingdom of the Saxons. A Saxon named Hella, with his thre sonnes, and a company of Saxons, landed in the South part of Britaine, slewe the Britons, and chased many of them into desertes and woodes, & subdued the countreyes of Southery, Somerset, Deuonshire, and Cornewall, whiche after was called the Kingdome of South Saxons.

Portsmouth. A Saxon named Porthe, landed with his twoo sonnes, at an hauen in Southhampton shire. After whom the hauen is named Portsmouth.

The thirde kingdom of the Saxons. The kingdome of the East Saxons conteyning Norfolke, and Suffolke, began in Britaine under a Duke named Vffa.

498 Vther, surnamed Pendragon, was crouned kinge of Britaine. Hee was enamoured upon the dukes wife of Cornewall, and to obtayne his unlawful lust, made warre upon her husband Garelus, and slue him in battaile, he was buried at Stonehing.

516 Arthur, the sonne of Vther, gouerned the land. xxvi. yeares, hauing continuall warre with the Saxons. Of this Arthur be wrytten many thinges of small credence, he was in dede a noble & victorious prince. And fought. xii. notable battayles against the Saxons. But hee might

might not clearelye voyde them out of the lande.

Frosard saith Arthur builded the castle of Wyndsor, and there founded the order of the round Table. Wyndsor castell buylt.

The kingdome of the west Saxons began in Britain, vnder a Saxō called Cerdicus. They lāded first at Yernouth. This lordship conteined Wiltshire, Somersetshire, Barkeshire, Dorsetshire, and other. The fourth kingdom of Saxons.

Arthur whē he had set his land in some quietnes, betoke the rule thereof to his nephew Mordred, and with a chosen armye sayled into Fraunce. This Mordred, in the absence of Arthur, by treason was crowned kyng. Of whiche when relation came to Arthur, with all haste hee made backe to Britaine, where hee was mette of Mordred, which gaue vnto him other strong battayles. And lastlye, in a battayle foughten besides Glastenbury, Mordred was slayne, and Arthur wounded vnto the death, and he was buried at Glastenburie. Mordred vsurped. Mordred slayne, and Arthur also.

543 Constantine, kinsman to Arthur, was ordeyned kyng of Britayne, betwixt him and the twoo sonnes of Mordred, was foughten sundrye battayles. In the whyche lastlye the twoo brethren were slayne.

Gildas the wyse. Gildas the wise a Britayne, flourished in this tyme.

Aurelius Conanus a Britaine, raysed warre against Constantine: and after sore fight, slue him in the fielde, when he had raigned three yeares he was buried at Stonehing.

545 AUrelius Conanus, was crowned kyng, he was noble, hardy, and liberal: but he cherished suche as loued discention within his realme, and gaue light credence to them, whiche accused other. He imprisoned his vncle, which was right heire to the crown, he raigned. xxx. yeres.

The. v. and vi. kingdoms of the Saxōs. The kingdome of Northumberlande, began first vnder a Saxone, named Ida. This prouince was firste deuided into twoo kingdomes. The one was called Deyra, whiche contained the land from Humber to Tyne: The other Brenicia, whiche included the Countrey frō Tyne to the Scottishe Sea. After this the Britaines decreased daily in lordshippe and rule, and drewe them towarde Wales, so that the countrey about Chester, was the chiefe of their lordship.

578 VOrtiporus, the sonne of Conanus, was ordayned king of Britayne, he was a victorious Prince: and in diuers battayles discomfited the Saxones, he raigned

ned foure yeares.

Malgo, gouerned the Britaines v. yeres, he was the comeliest man then lyuing, and therwith indued with knightly manhode, but he delited in the foule sinne of Sodomie. 582

Ethelbert, king of the Saxons in Kent, gaue battayle to Ceaulinus, kynge of the West Saxons, in whiche fight were slain two dukes of Ethelbertes, and him selfe with his people chased. This was the firste warre betwene the Saxons, within this realme.

The firste warre betwene the Saxons in this realme.

Careticus began to rule the Britanes. This man was odible both to God & to his subiectes. The Saxons being accompanied with Gurmundus kyng of Ireland, made warre vppon Careticus, in suche wyse that he was fayne to take the toun of Cicester, where they assaulted him so sore that he with his men fled from thēce into Wales: when he had raigned thre yeres. Gurmūdus builded Gurmunchester. 586

Gurmund chester.

Ethelfridus gouerned the North Saxons, who made such continuall warre vppon the Britaines, and chased them so sore that it is thought he slewe moe of them then all the other Saxon kinges. By this crueltie the fayth of Christe was almost 588

vtterly

The Saxons had the whole possession of this Realme.

vtterly extinguished among the Britains manye of them were chased oute of the Iland, the rest remained in Wales, and the Saxones obtayned the whole dominion of this Ilande: sauing a parte of Scotlande.

S. Augustine came into Englande.

In Anno Domini. 596. S. Gregory sent Augustine, Melitus Iustus, and Iohn, with other learned men to preache the Christe faith to the Angles: whiche were first receiued of Ethelbert kyng of Kent, whom they conuerted with diuers of his people. This Ethelbert first began to build S. Augustines in Cantorbury, Saint Paules in London, and Saint Andrewes in Rochester. The yeare of our Lorde 604. Sibertus king of East Saxons, buylded Westminster, the which because it was an vnfruitfull and thorny piece of grounde, it was called in the Saxons tongue Therneye, the Ile of Thornes.

S. Austins at Cantorbury, S. Paules in London. S. Andrewe in Rochester. Westmister buylded.

613

Cadwanc, Duke of Northwales, was made soueraigne of the Britaines, who gaue strong battaile to Ethelfride kynge of Northumberlande, and so discomfited the saide Ethelfride, that he was forced to intreate for peace: After whiche concorde made, they continued all their life tyme louing frendes, he raigned. xxii. yeares.

About

About this tyme began the kingdome of Mercia, or middle England vnder Penda: which Lordship conteined Huntingtonshire, & other, At that time raigned in diuers partes of this land. vii kinges. Sibertus among the East Saxons, Redwallus, king of east angles, now called North folke, and Suffolke, Ethelbert king of Kent, Ethelwolphus of Sussex. Ringilus & Quincellinus of West Saxones Penda of Mercia. Edwine of Northumberlād, which Edwine was baptised of Paulinus, & after him, many of his people. This Paulinus buylded the great churche at Lincolne. In those daies suche was the peace, and tranquilitie throughout all Britaine, which way soeuer king Edwines dominion lay, that weake woman might haue walked with her new borne babe ouer all the Ilande without any damage. Moreouer for the refreshing of wayfaring men, he ordayned cups of iron & brasse, to be fastened by such cleare fountaines as did runne by ẏ wates side. He began the cathedrall church of Yorke, & pointed there a Byshop see for Pauline.

The seuenth kingdome of the Saxōs

Lyncolne

Yorke.

635

Cadwaline the sonne of Cadwane, began his raigne ouer the Britaines, He was valiaunt and mighty, and warred strongly vppon the Saxones, and made

Penda

Penda king of Mercia, tributarie to hym; he raigned 48. yeares, and was buried at Londō in S. Martins church by Ludgate.

Cambridge repayred.

Sigebert, king of East angles, caused good learning pitifully decayed to bee taught, and erected Scholes in diuers partes of his dominion. The vniuersitie of Cambridge was by him repayred. In the yeare of our Lord 673. Atheldrith the Queene, began to buylde the Monasterie at Ely.

Ely.

Malmesbury

Meldulphe began the abbey of Malmesbury.

Peda, the sonne of Penda, was founder of Medeshamstede, nowe called Peterborowe.

Kenwalcus king of West Saxons, buylded the bishops see of Winchester, and made Agelbert the firste byshop of the see. And after him was one named Wine of whome the Citie tooke the name of Wynchester.

Peterborow
Winchester.

Benet the monke, and maister of the reuerend Beda, was famous in Britaine. This Benet brought first the craft of glasing into this lande.

Glasing brought first into Englād.

Cissa begun the abbey of Abington, & Erkenwalde bishop of London, buylded the abbeis of Chertsey in Southerie, and of Barking in Essex, Anno. 677.

Abington
Chertsey and Berking.

Ceād-

Eadwalladar, was ordained kynge of Brytaines, and ruled three yeares. Hee ewe Lothaire, kyng of Kent and Athel- olde king of South Saxons, and then slaking his kingly authoritie, he wēt Rome there to be Christened, who af- r became a monke, and was buried at ome. He was the laste king of Britain. 685

The king be came a Monke.

his lande after his tyme was called nglia, and the inhabitauntes therof An- les, or Englishemen, the Britaines were alled Walshemen, which name was ge- en them by the Englishmen or Saxons, who used to call all men Walshemen at be straungers unto them. This hap- ened after the Conquest of Cæsar. 735. eares. From the entring of the Saxons, nder their leaders Hengist and Horsus, n the time of Vortiger, 236, or nere there bout.

The Ilande called vni- uersally Englande.

Thus endeth the reigne of the Britons: nd nowe followeth the reigne of the Sax- ons, chiefly of the West Saxons, because (in rocesse of tyme) they subdued the other kynges, and brought it agayn into one mo- narchie.

[Ne raigned among the West Saxons, a noble man of great power and wyse- dome, and therewith valiant and hardy. 687

In

in feates of Armes very expert: he maintained suche warre against the Kentishe Saxons, that he constrained them to intreate of peace, geuing him for the same great giftes. This Ine was the sonne of Kenrede, the sonne of Ceadwolde, brother to Keadwold, & sonne to Chenlinge, sonne of Kenri, sonne of Cerdic, the first kinge of the West Saxons. This man builded the colledge of Welles, he also builded Glastenbury, and paide the Peter pence first to Rome. When he had gouerned the west Saxons by the space of .xxxvii. yeeres, by the earnest labour of his wife Ethelreda whiche was Abbesse of Barking in Essex, gaue vp his royall power, and went to Rome.

The college of Welles, and Glastenbury newlye builded.

Kingdome forsaken.

Edilwalde sonne of Scisa, king of the South Saxons, gaue to bishop Wilfride the Ile of Selsee, wherin the said Wilfride builded a monasterie, and became the first byshop of the Prouince. In the Ilande were 300. bondmen and women, whom he did not only deliuer by Christening them, from the bondage of the Deuill, but also he geuinge them their freedome, did loose them from the yoke of the bondage of man.

Selsee.

726 Ethelarde was kinge of the west Saxons, in whose tyme the reuerend Beda

was

s famous, and wrote his booke cal-
Anglica historia, to Ceaulphe kyng of
rthumberlande. This holy man Beda, Beda decea-
his learning & godly life, was renou sed.
d in all the worlde, he ended his last
about the the yeare of Christ. 734. in
lyfe he compiled, lxxviii. bookes.
gwinus bishop of Winchester, builded
eshame. Ethelarde reigned fourtene Eouesham.
res.
Ethred was kynge of West Saxones. 740
This man made warre vpon Ethel-
lde of Mercia. He raigned xvi. yeares.
elwalde builded Crowland. Crowland.
gebert kyng of West Saxones, was ty- 757.
annous towardes his subiectes, he
aunged auncient lawes and customes,
er his owne pleasure. And because a
tayne noble man, some deale sharp-
aduertised hym to chaunge his man-
rs, he caused the same persone to bee
t cruelly to death. But for so much as
continued in his malice, he was de-
ued of al kingly authoritie, and last-
as a persone desolate, wandring in a
ode, was slayne of a swyneherde, he The kyng
gned not one yeare. slayne.
enulphus, of the linage and bloude of
Cerdicus, appeased certaine murmurs 757.
d grudges y were, among y people for

the

the deposing of his predecessor Sigebert. But as he haunted a woman, which he kept at Merton, he was slayne by one Clio, the kinsman of Sigebert, late kyng. When he had raigned 29. yeares, he was buried at Winchester.

Kenulfus slayne.

786

BRithricus, of the bloude of Cerdicus, knightly ruled his lande the space of xvii. yeares he maried Ethelburge, the daughter of Offa, kinge of Mercia, by whose power he expelled Egbert, that was an under kyng in the Lordeship of west Saxons. In his time it rayned bloud which falling on mens clothes, appeared lyke crosses.

It rayned bloud.

S. Albons buylded.

Offa, king of Mercia, builded Saynt Albons, he chased the Britaines into Wales and made a famous dike betwene Wales and the utter boundes of Mercia, which is nowe called Offa dyke

The Danes first entred this land.

The kyng poysoned.

Anno 800. The Danes first arrived in the Ile called Portland, but by the strẽgth and puissaunce of Brithricus, and other kynges of the Saxons, they were driven backe, and compelled to voyde the lãd: Brithricus, was poysoned by his wyfe Ethelburga. For which deede, the nobles ordeined, that from thẽceforth the kings wiues shuld not be called queenes, nor suffered to sit with thẽ in places of estate.

Kenulfe

Kenulfe kyng of Mercia, buylded Winchecombe at the dedication whereof in the presence of .xiii. byshops, and tenne Dukes, he delivered Egbertus kynge of Kent, whome he had taken prysoner. Moreouer, his liberalitie was suche, y euery man departed with full purses. Winc

80.

Egbrithous the Saxon, obtayned the gouernement of the West Saxons, he tamed the Welshemen, vanquished Bernulphus, kinge of middle Englande, and subdued to his obeysaunce the Kentishe Saxons, East Saxons, and Northumbers, & raigned ouer the more part of England, xxxvii. yeres, and vii. monethes, & was buried at Winchester.

839

Adhelnulphus, the sonne of Egbrithius, began his reigne ouer the more parte of Englande, in this tyme there came a great army of the Danes, with 350. ships into the mouthe of Thames, and so to London and spoiled it, and put to flight Begrthculfe kyng of the Mercies, with all his armye, whiche came to bidde hym battayle. Adhelnulphus kyng of the West Saxons, and his sonne Adhelwalde with all his army, came against the forsayde Danes, and in a place then called Aclea, they fought a fierce and cruell battayle, wherein the moste parte of the Pagans

London spoiled.

E was

was venquished, so þ before that time was never hearde that so many were slayne in one daye.

Adhelstane, the sonne of Adhelnulfus, & Calchere the Earle, slue a great army of Normans in Kent, in a place called Sandwiche, and toke nyne of their shippes, the other fled.

Adhelnulfus, did make the tenth parte of his kingdome free from all tribute and service to the king, and offered it to the holy Trinitie, he went to Rome, and toke his sonne Alfred with him. In the meane season his sonne Ethelwald rebelling, usurped the kingdome, so that when Adhelnulfus returned, he was contented to devide the kingdome. He raigned [illegible] yeares, and was buried at Storching.

857 Ethelwalde after his father raigned [illegible] yeares and a halfe, who reigned with his father had likewise raigned two yeare and a halfe. After his fathers disease, against the worthines of Christianitie, yea and contrary to the custome of all Pagans, he presumed to his fathers mariage bed, and with great infamie maried Iudith the French kings daughter, he was buried at Shireburne.

860 Athelbrict, brother to Ethelwalde, tooke under his dominion Kent, Southerie and

and Southsex. In this tyme the Paganes spoyled the Citie of Winchester, who when they returned with a great praye towardes their shippes, Osrike Earle of Hampton and his folke, and Adhelnulphus Earle, with Barkeshire, met them valiauntly, where the Paganes were slayne on euery corner. Athelbricht raigned tyue yeares, and lyeth at Shireburne.

Etheldred brother to Adhelbricht, receyued the kyngdome of the West Saxons. In his tyme a great nauy of Danes entred this lande with whom Etheldred had many battayles. 866

Hingwar and Hubba attempting firste to ouercome the Prouince of the Northumbers, raged ouer all the same, and made greate spoyles, whome none of that Prouince myght withstande, Hingwar hauing gotten a praye, left Hubba, and with a great nauy he sayled from the North, to the East part of England, where they slewe bothe men, women, and children, commaunding that neyther the chastitie of Matrones or Virgines shoulde bee regarded.

This wicked Hingwar, tooke Edmonde the King of that Prouince, in a village then called Egilisdum, neare to a woode bearing the same name, where this holy

Edmōd king of that kyngdome.

Edmond being constant in the faythe of Christe, was firste (by the commaundement of Hingnar) beaten with battes, then scourged with whippes, he stil calling on the name of Jesus, his aduersaries in a great rage shotte at him, til his body was full of shaftes, and lastly they stroke of his head.

When king Etheldrede had reigned sr. yeares, he died, and was buried at Winburne, by the counceil of Elfled his wife, he builded the monasterie of Saint Peter at Glocester.

Women disfigured themselues. Anno 870. at Colingham abbey, Ebbe Abbesse, cut of her nose and vpper lippe, and perswaded all her sisters to doe the lyke, that they being odible to the Danes, mought the better kepe their virginitie, in despite whereof the Danes burned the Abbey with the nunnes.

872 Alfrede the fourthe sonne of Æthelwolphe, receyued the gouernement of the whole realme, and with a very smal number fought a sharpe battaile against the whole army of the Paganes at Wiltõ.

Alfrede beinge chased of the Danes, was forced to hide him with a certayne Cowherd in Somersetshire. Where on a tyme as the Cowherdes wife prepared to bake breade, the king sate by the fyre prepa-

eparinge his bowes and shaftes, the
ife being a sharpe woman, threw aside
e Kinges bowes and shaftes, and sayd,
ou fellowe, why doost thou not turne
e bread, whiche thou seest burne, thou
te glad to eate it or it bee halfe baked.
This woman thought not that it had
ne king Ælfrede, who had made so ma-
battayles against the Paganes, & got-
n so many victories. For God dyd not
nely vouchsafe to geue hym victory
er his enemies, but also to be vexe-
ed of them, to the end he should know
ere is one God of all, to whome all
nees should bow, in whose handes the
rtes of Kings be, who deposeth mighty
men from their seates, and doth exalt
e humble and meeke. This Ælfrede restored, and honourablye repayred the citie of London (after it hadde bene amongest other cities destroied with fires and the people killed vp) and made it habitable againe, committing the custody thereof to his sonne in lawe Æthered, Earle of the Mercies, vnto which King, all Englyshemen, Mercies, Kentishe-men, South, and West Saxones, submitted them selues.

London newly buylded and made inhabitable.

Ælfrede commaunded to builde two Monasteries, one of mõkes of Ætheling.

 ise

Salisbury. the other at Sceaphtes burghe for Nunnes, he ordayned the hundredes, and tenthes, which men cal Centuries, and Cupinges, he sent for Grimbalde to come into Engsland, that by his aduise he might erect the study of good learninge, which at that tyme was almoste cleane decayed.

Iohannes Scotus, a man of sharpe wyt, and muche eloquence, was sent for into Englande, the king vsing the company of these men, learned liberall sciences, in so much that neuer mã was of a sharper vnderstanding, or more elegant in interpreting and expoundinge. He translated into Englishe Orosius, Gregories Pastorals, Beda de gestis Anglorum, Boetius de consolatione philosophie, and a booke of his owne called Enchiridion. He began to traslate the Psalter. He deuided the 24 howers of the daye and night into three partes: he spent viii. houres in writing reading, and prayeng, viii. houres in prouision and tending of his body, and viii. houres in hearing and dispatchinge the matters of his subiectes. He rayned xxix. yeres, & was buried at Winchester.

EDward, the eldest sonne of Ælfred, was annoynted king. He buylded a citie on the north side at Herefórde, betwixte the riuers Memeran Beneficiam, & Ligã, an other

other at Witham, an other at Hereford
the southside of the ryuer Ligean. He
so buylded a towne by the ryuer of
ercia, and named it Thilwal, and repai-
d the towne of Manchester, after all
hiche dedes by him done, he deceased
Fatingdon, and was buried at Winche-
r in the new churche, which he his fa-
er Ælfrede had builded, when he had
igned xxiiij. yeares.

Delstane, after Edward his father, was
crowned at Kingston. His coronatio
as celebrated in the market place vpo
tage erected on hie, that he might bee
ne the better of the multitude. Hee
ought this land to one monarchie: for
expelled vtterly the Danes, & quieted
e Welshemen, and caused them to paye
nto hym yearely for a trybute, twenty
ounde of golde. 300. pounde in syluer.
d 2500. head of Neate, with houndes
d haukes to a certayne number. And
ter that he had by battaile conquered
cotlande: hee made one Constantine
nge of Scottes vnder hym. This
ng did raigne fiftene yeares, and lieth
Malmesburye. In king Adelstanes
ayes, Gwy Earle of Warwike, slew Col
ond the Danish Giaunt in Hide meade
ighe vnto Winchester.

924

King crowned at Kingston.

Gwy of Warwike.

Edmund

940 Edmunde brother to Adelstane, tooke on him the gouernaunce of this realme. He was a man disposed of nature to noblenes and iustice. He raigned vi. yeres, and was buried at Glastenbury.

948 Eldred succeded Edmond his brother, for his sonnes Edwine, and Edgar, were thought to younge to take on them so great a charge. He tooke on hym but as a protectour, but afterwardes he was crowned at Kingston. He quieted & kept in due obeysaunce the Northumbers and Scottes, and exiled the Danes. He raigned nyne yeares, and was buried at Wynchester.

955 Edwine succeded his uncle Eldred, in the kyngdome, he was crowned at Kingston. In the selfe day of his coronation, he sodainly withdrew himself from his lordes, & in the sight of certain persons, rauished his own kenswoman the wife of a noble man of his realme, & after ward slue her husband, that he might haue the unlawfull use of her beautie. For whiche acte, and for banishing Dunstane, he became odible to his subiectes. And of the Northumbers & people of middle England, that rose against him, was depriued whē he had reigned iiii. yeres. He was buried in Winchester.

e king deposed.

Edgar

Dgar the peaceable, brother to Edwine was crowned at Bathe. Hee was for s manifolde vertues greatly renou- ed, so excellent in iustice, and sharpe n correctiō of vices, as well in his ma- strates, as other subiectes: that neuer efore his dayes was used lesse fellony y robbers, or extortion or brybery by lse officers. He chastised also the great egligence, couetousnes, & vicious li- ing of the Clergy, he reformed and rought them to a better order. Of sta- re he was but little, yet of mynde va- liaunt and hardy, and verye experte in arciall pollicie. Hauing restored and elve founded xlvii monasteries which fore his tyme had bene destroyed, and tending to continue that his intent til e number of 50. were accomplished. e confirmed the monasterie of Worce- er, which Oswalde thē byshop of Wor- cester, by the kings cōsent, had enlarged madeit ÿ cathedral church of ÿ Shire. Alwin Alderman, kinsman to kyng Ed- ar, founded Ramsey: king Edgar confir- ing the same. Edgar being at Chester, ntred the riuer of Dee, toke the rule of e helme, and caused viii. kynges to owe hym unto S. Johns churche, and om thence unto his pallaice, in token that

959 The king crowned at Bathe.

Worcester minster.

Ramsey founded.

Eight kings rowed king Edgar.

that he was Lorde and king of so many prouinces. He raigned xvi yeares, and was buried at Glastenbury.

975 The kynge crowned at Kingstone. The kyng murdred by his stepmother.

EDwarde the sonne of Edgar, was crowned at Kingston. While he was huntinge in a forest (by chaunce) lost hys company, and rode alone to refreshe him selfe at the castle of Corsse, whereby the counsayle of his stepmother Elphrede, he was trayterously murthered, as he satte on his horse, when he had raigned thre yeares. He was buried at Shafteibury.

978 The yonger brother vniustly getting his elder brothers patrimony, doth not log enioy the same with quietnes.

AEtheldrede, the sonne of Edgar was crowned at Kingstō. But because he came to the kingdome by killinge his brother, he could neuer get the good wil of the people. of this arose ciuill warres and discordes, as well of the nobles as of the common sorte, wherof the Danes tooke newe occasion, and Swayne kynge of Denmarke, being their captaine, they inuaded Englande, and after diuers ouerthrowes geuen to the men of this Ilande, they possessed the same, and put kyng Etheldred to flight, constraining him to liue in exele among the Normans.

Not long after Swanus departed this life, & left Canutus his sonne, successor in the kingdome. Ethelred hearinge Swanus was dead, returned with

rede with Edmonde his sonne, and mo-
d warre against Canutus, whoe fyn-
ing him selfe not able to matche with
m, went into Denmarke. Etheldrede be-
ng thus restored, shewed great cruelty
pon the Danes that remayned, sparinge
either yong nor old. Canutus being ve-
y desirous to reuenge the same, came
to Eng. ande against Etheldred raging
ith fire and swoorde. Etheldred in the
eane season died, when he had raigned
8. yeares, and was buried in the north
le of Paules church. In the yere of our
ord 994. King Ætheldred did erect the
ishopprike of Excester. He builded Taui- Bishop sea
oke in Deuonshire, whiche was begon at Excetor.
y Earle Orgarus. In this kinges raigne A great fire
great part of the citie of London was in London.
wasted with fyre.

Edmond the sonne of Etheldred, succe- 1016
ded in the kingdome, who was surna- Edmond
med Ironside: and whiles betwene hym Ironside.
and Canutus, striuing for ŷ empire many
bloudy battails were fought, & neither
of thē could attein any victory, ŷ kings
thēselues attēpted to fight hād to hand, England de-
in which cōbate after long & doubtfull uided.
fight, they both being weried fel to a co-
uenāt, ŷ the one half of ŷ kingdō should
be vnder Canutus, & the other half vnder
Edmond,

Edmond, who not longe after was slayne by the treason of one Edricke of Straton. This Edricke was not long vnrewarded, for himselfe making vaunt thereof vnto Canutus sayde: Thus haue I done for the loue of thee. To whome he aunswered saying: and thou shalt die, as well thou art worthy, because thou art gilty of treason against God and me, in that thou hast slayne thy owne lorde and king, & straghtwayes he caused Edricke to be tormented to death with firebrondes and lynkes, and then his feete beynge bounde together, to be drawen through the streates of the Citie of London, and cast into a ditche called Houndes ditche, for that the citezens there cast their dead dogges, and suche other filthe.

Treason rewarded.

Hunsditche.

These princes raigned together one yeare, and this Edmonde was buried at Glastenbury.

1018 CAnutus the Dane, chalenged all England to him selfe, and slue the brother of Edmond. But because he had no heire that lawfully might succede him, he procured to haue geuen hym in mariage Emma the wydowe of king Etheldrede, who at that tyme was with Edward, and Allured her sonnes in exile with Duke Richard, in Normandie. Emma the Queene

conclu-

ncluded mariage with the Dane, upon Mariage on condition.
ndition, that the kingdome of Eng-
nd should remaine unto the children
at were begotten of her, if any of them
remaine aliue: by reason of this ma-
age, shortly after she did beare Canutus
onne of his owne name. By this affi-
tie and alliaunce, the Danes become of
more strength and power.
Canutus subdued the Scottes, whereby Canutus kig of four kingdomes.
was king of foure kingdomes, Eng-
de, Scotlande, Denmarke, and Norwaye.
founded a newe S. Edmonds bury, re-
ring the donatiō which Edmond king S. Edmonds bury.
ȳ West Saxons had geuen. Hee raigned
yeares & was buried at Winchester.
Arold vsing the force of the Danes that 1035
dwelt in Englande, inuaded the re-
ne whiles his brother Hardicanutus,
uerned in Denmarke, And not beyng
mindfull by whose helpe and ayde he
ne to the kingdome, rewarded the
nes with great power and dignitie,
t the Englishemen he displaced and Harold a Tyraunt.
ndled them as bondmen and slaues, &
d so muche displeasure vnto his mo-
r in law Emma, that he did constraine Emma and her children banished.
e to flie. He tormented to death Alu-
ed the sonne of Emma, whiche shee had
king Etheldred. He raigned thre yeres

and

Harold dead without issue. and was buried at Westminster, & after at S. Clements without temple barre.

1041 HArdicanutus, the lawfull begotten sonne of Canutus and Emme, fetched his mother out of exile. And in reuenge of displeasure that was done to her, and of the murther of his brother Allured, he

Canutus reuenged on his brother. commaunded the carkas of Harold to bee digged out of the earth, and to be throwē into the ryuer of Thames, where by a fysher it was taken vp and secretly buried in the Danes churchyarde at London, which is Saint Clementes without Tēple barre, as is aforesaid. Shortly after, he sent for Edward the sonne of Etheldred, his brother of ỹ mothers side, to come into Englande, and embraced him with all loue and fauour, and delt much more gently with the Englishe men then did kyng Harold. He raygned three yeare, and was buryed at Wynchester.

The rule of the Danes ouer the English men ceased when Hardicanutus was dead.

43 EDwarde the sonne of Etheldred, was crowned at Winchester. This Edward for his excellent holines, is vntill this daye called Saint Edward, who so sone as he had gotten his fathers kingdome, of his

his owne free will released the tribute of 40000. pounde, called Dane gelt, whiche the englishe people euen from the very beginning of the raigne of ye Danes was compelled to paye to their kynges euery yeare. He was also the chiefe author and cause, that the law which we call the Cōmon law, was first braught vp. He toke to wife Edgitha the daughter of Earle Godwine, who because shee brought him forth no chyldren, neither was there anye hope that shee shoulde beare any, when he did se that many did gape after the kingdome, he began to be carefull for one that shoulde iustlye succede hym. And therfore he sent for home into Englande his nephewe Edwarde, the sonne of kinge Edmonde his brother, who by reason of his long absence out of the countrey, was commōly called the outlawe. This is that Edward the sonne of king Edmond, surnamed Ironside, whiche remained aliue, whome Canutus when he had gotten Englande, had sent into Swethen, with his brother. He knowinge the aduise of his vncle, came againe into Englande, & brought with him Agatha his wife, and Edgare, Margarete, and Christiana, hys chyldren, while at Panonia, in hope of the kingdō: where

Danegelt.

The cōmō lawe.

Edgitha was barren.

where he liued but a while. Thus S. Edward being disappointed bothe of his nephue and his heire. For that Edwarde the outlawe, was bothe by nerenesse of bloud, and by lawfull succession right heire vnto the kingdome, without delay pronounced Edgare the outlawes sonne, and his great nephewe to be heire of the kingdome, and gaue hym a surname Adeling, but because this Edgare was but young of yeares and within age, by his Testamẽt he made Harolde the sonne of Godwine Regent, vntyll the younge Edgar shoulde bee of age to receiue the kyngdome. And that then he shoulde be made kyng, whiche thinge Harold with a solempne othe, promised to see so performed. Notwithstandinge, he immediatly after the death of Edward, refused the name of Regent, and pronounced him selfe king, whiche thing shortly after brought destruction, both to himselfe and to all englande. This Edward reigned. xxiii. yeares vi. monethes and odde dayes. He was buried in Westminster, whiche he had newly buylded.

1066 Harold, as afore is sayd, by force vsurping the kingdome, that he might in some behalfe seme to make the yong Edgar amendes for the wrong he had done him, gaue

ue him the Earledom of Oxford. But
n þ meane season England began to be
ossed & turmoyled wyth warres with=
n and withoute, for the disheritinge of
right heyre, is alwayes wonte to be
he beginning of ciuil warres. And first
f all Tostus inuiyng the prosperitye of
is brother, stirred vp troubles within
he Realme: for he ioyning himselfe to
arolde the kinge of Norwaye, assaulted
England in warlike sorte both by sea &
and. Whose attempte whiles Harolde
f Englande prepared to withstande
William Duke of Normandye, who not=
withstanding, he was a bastard, was a
inne to S. Edward in the third & fourth
gree of consanguinitye, seinge a con=
enient time and occasiõ offered to take
he kingdom in, gathered a great nauy,
nd came into Englande with a verye
well appointed armye, alledginge that
y al right and title, it was due to him
y the gift of king Edwarde his kinse=
nan, and also by the couenaunte þ was
nade, and by othe establisshed betwixte
Harolde and him. Harolde notwithstã=
dinge he was bare of men, by reason of
he battaile that he fought against Tostus
and the men of Norwaye, yet hearing of
Williams comming, went straight wayes

William conquerer cosen to K. Edwarde.

 against

against him. And bothe armyes being broughte into arraye, the battayle was fought, wherein great slaughter of Englisshmen was made, and the Normās gate the victorye. Kinge Herolde was smitten throughe the braynes wyth an arrowe, when hee had raigned ix. monethes, and was buryed in the Priorye of Waltham, whych hee had builded. Thus Harolde beyng depriued both of his life and kingdom, receyued due punisshment for his periurye.

This battaile was fought at Hastings in Sussex, vppon the xiiii. day of October (by the agrement of all, both Latin Frenche, and Englishe writers of time) in the yeare of our Lord. 1066.

Thus endeth the raigne of the Saxōs ouer this Realme, who were first sent for by Vortiger, aboute the yeare of our Lorde. 450 and had nowe continued sometime in warres wyth Britaynes, then with the Danes, nowe with the Normans, as is aforeshewed by the space of sixe hundred yeares.

Yet

thousand sixe and sixtie yeare
it was, as we do read,
When that a Comet did appeare,
and Englishmen laye dead.
From Normandy Duke William then,
to Englandeward did saile,
And conquered Harold and his men,
and brought this land to baile.

WILLIAM
conquerour.

WILLIAM DVKE OF Normandy, surnamed Conquerour, bastarde sonne of Robert the sixte Duke of ye Duchie: and nephewe vnto king Edward, began his dominion ouer this Realme of Englande the xiiii. daye of October, in the yeare of our Lorde 1066. After the battaile at Hastinges, comming to London he was receiued of the Clergye & people, and crowned on Christmas daye. Which daye by the Historiographers of that time, was accompted the first of the yeare following, and so called 1067. Anno Regni. 1. 1067.

But after the accompt of Englād now obserued, the yere beginneth not till the 25. of March following.

The Englishmen that escaped in the battaile at Hastinges, did there endeuour to make the yonge Edgar king, to whom moste iustlye it did appertaine, but fearing the power of William, they left of, so that Edgar mistrustinge his estate in Englande, toke shipping with his mother Agatha, and his sisters, intending to go home againe into his coūtry but being driuen with contrarye windes, arriued in Scotlande, where hee w well receiued of kinge Malcolme, w being sorye that Edgar was so expel oute of his kingdome, toke this yong man into his allegiaunce, with all Englishmen that were fled with hi and toke Margaret the sister of Edgar his wyfe.

This yeare through the great sute labour of William then bishop of l don, Kinge William the Conque graunted the Charter and liberties t same William Bishop, and Godfrey beinge Portgreue, and all the Bu of the same Citye of London, in large forme as they enioyed the same the time of S. Edward before ẏ con n rewarde wherof, the same Cittizens ue fixed on his graue beig in ÿ midle ỽ greet West ile of S. Paules Church in ondon, this Epitaphe following.

O William a man famous in wisedowe and holines of life, who first with S. Edard the king and confessour, being famiiar, of late preferred to be bishop of Lon-n, and not longe after for his prudencye d sincere fidelitie, admitted to be of coūaile with the most victorious Prince Wil-am king of Englād of that name the first, ho obtained of the same great and large riuiledges to this famous Cittie, The Se-te and Cittizens of London to him ha-inge well deserued, haue made this: Hee ontinued bishoppe xx. yeares, and dyed in the yeare of Christ his natiuitye. 1070.

Epitaphe of William bishop of London.

THese Marble Monumentes to thee,
thy Cittizens assigne,
Rewardes, (O father) farre vnfitte,
to those desertes of thine.
Thee vnto them a faithfull frende,
thy London people founde,
And to this towne of no small waight,
a staye both sure and sound.
Theyr liberties restorde to them,
by meanes of thee haue beene.

 Their

Their publique weale by meanes of thee,
large giftes hath felt and seene.
Thy riches, stocke, and beautye braue,
one houre it hath opprest,
Yet these thy vertues and good deedes,
with vs for euer rest.

KInge William besieged the Cittye of Oxford, which rebelled agaynst him, and with small busines subdued ẏ same, he afterwardes went to Yorke & destroyed it vtterlye, and slue the Cittizens with fyre and sworde. Anno. 2.

1068. KIng William gaue to Earle Robert, the countye of Northumberlande, against whom ẏ men of the countrye did arise and slue him, and 900. of his men: And kinge William came vppon them ẏ did that deede, and slue them euery one. Anno. 3.

This Robert was none of K. Williams kinne.

1069. AGelricus bishop of Durham, being accused of treason, was taken and imprisoned at Westminster. And his brother Egelwine beeing made bishop there in August was banished. The sonn of Swannus & his brother Osburne, ca oute of Denmarke with 300. sayle in Englande, to driue oute kinge William Also Edgar Etheling, the sonne of Edwar and the Earle Waltherus, and many o ther makinge a league ioyned their p wers togeather, & came to Yorke, wh in short space they wanne both the Citye and Castell, and slue manye Thousandes of the people. But when ÿ winter was past, king William came uppon them with a greate power, and slue the most part, the rest he put to flighte: And then Edgar Etheling submitting himselfe to king William, obtayned his mercye.

Anno. 4.

King William bereued all the Monasteries and abbeyes in Englande of their gold and siluer, and appropriated the saide Monasteries and abbeyes to himselfe. He also brought vnder knightes seruice all those ÿ helde Baronies, and had them free from all secular bondage, appointinge them howe manye souldiours they should send him, & his successors in time of warre. An. 5. 1070.

EDwine Earle of Mercia, Mercarus Erle of Northumberlande, and Sward, with Egelwine bishop of Durham, and manye other, both of the Clergye and Laietye, keeping ÿ woddes, at the last came into the Ile of Elye, & Hereward being their Captaine, they sore afflicted that countrey, but king William with a great power besieging the Ile, they all, sauing Hereward, submitted them to the kinge, who comitted some to perpetual prisō, 1071.

Manye noble men fled to the Ile of Elye.

 some

some he put to death, the other hee raunsomed, but Hereward by stronge hande brought his men out of the Ile, and so longe as he lived he wrought notable treasons against the Kinge. Anno. 6.

1072. Scotlande subdued. KIng William with a great power invaded Scotlande, where hee forced Malcolme to do him homage. Egelwine bishop of Durham dyed in prisō at Westminster. In a counsaile holdē at Windsor, the Primacye of the Church of Canterburye, over the Church of Yorke was examined, where by the authoritye of olde writinges, it was proued that the Church of Yorke oughte to be subiecte.

Yorke subiect to Canterburye.

Anno. 7.

1073. Normandye rebelled. KIng William with a great power of Englishmen, went into Normandye, which rebelled and subdued the same, spoylinge the Cittyes, townes, vineyardes and corne. &c. Anno. 8.

1074. Maryed priestes. POpe Gregorye the seuenth, in a synode excommunicated all committers of Simonye, and remoued all maried priestes from executinge of deuine seruice, forbiddinge the laye people to heare the same, whereof arose great troubles in England.

Radulph president of the East English, by the counsell of the Earles Welcheofus and

and Roger, trauailed to expell kinge William out of his kingdom, they sent the kinge of Denmarke, desyringe his de: and hauinge confederet with the Welshemen, euery one in his iurisdiction robbed the kinges townes. Kinge William came sodainlye out of Normandie, on the Earles aforesayde, committing them to prison, and banished many out of the Realme. The Welshmen here caused to haue their eyes put out, some be banished, and some to be hanged. This beinge done, Knute the sonne of Swane, and Hacon the Earle came out of Denmarke wyth 200. sayle of menne of warre, but when they hearde that their autors wer ouercom, they turned back into Flaunders.

Conspiracy.

Knute a Dane landed in England.

Anno. 9.

Kyng William commaunded Welcheos sus Earle of Northumberlande, to be heated in Winchester. Then kinge William sayled into Britayne, and besieged the Castel of Dolens, where he preuayled not, but made peace wyth the Frenche kinge. Walther bishop of Durham, bought of king William ye Earledome of Northumberlande, wherein hee vsed such crueltye to the inhabitantes, that lastly they slue him, & an hundred of

1075.

Execution at Winchester.

Bishop of Durham slaine.

of his men, by the riuer of Tine.

Anno. 10.

1076. Great frost. The earth was hard frosen, from the first of Nouember, till the middest of Aprill. An. 11

1077. Blasing star. Vpon Palmesonday about none, appeared a blasing starre neare vnto ye Sunne. Anno 12.

1078. Lanfranke Archebishop of Canterburye dedicated the Church of Becca.

Anno. 13.

1079. King Williã with a great power subdued Wales. Trustin Abbot of Glastenburye, committed a filthye acte in his Church, for hee caused three monkes to be slaine (which were layed vnder the alter) and xviii. men to bee wounded, ye bloud of them ranne from the Alter vpon the steppes, and from the steppes alonge the pauement. Anno. 14.

Murther at the high Alter.

1080. Gret wind. This yeare was a greate winde on Christmas daye. Anno. 15.

1081. Earthquake. There was a great Earthquake and roaring out of the earth, the sixte Aprill. Anno. 16.

1082. Bermondsye. Alwyn Childe, a Cittizen of London, founder of the Monasterye of saint Sauiour at Bermondsey, by lycence of the kyng, gaue vnto those Monkes diuerse rentes in the Cittye of London.

Anno. 17

Inge William caused inquirye to be made, howe manye acres of grounde ere sufficiente for one ploughe by the are, how manye beastes to the tilling one hyde, howe manye Citties, Castels, Fearms, Graunges, Townes, rivers, marishes & woddes, what rente ey paid by yere, & how many Knights souldiours were in euery countye of e Realme, all which was put in writing, and remayneth at Westminster in e kinges treasurye. After wardes hee me fiue shillinges of siluer of euerye lough, that is of euery hyde of ground roughout this Realme. An. 18. 1083.

A greate taxe.

Inge William take homage and othe of allegeaunce of all Englande, and torting a great summe of money, sayd into Normandy. Anno. 19. 1084.

Exaction.

he Normans accomplished theyr pleasure in this lande, so y^t it was a proch to be called an Englishman, e more the people spake of equitie, ore wrong was done. The iusticers ere the authors of al unrighteousnes, ho so euer did take a Deere or a Goat, d his eyes pute oute. For the space of ore then xxx. myles, good profitable ne ground, was turned into a chase wilde beastes. In building of 1085.

The name of an Englisheman, odious in England.

Castels

Castels, this king exceeded all his predecessoures, hee builded twoe at Yorke, one at Notingham, an other at Lincolne.

Lincolne. Reming bishop of Dorchester, remoued his sea to Lincolne, wher he builded a newe Churche to be his seate.

Anno. 20.

1086. A greate floud. There was a great water floude, so that the hilles were consumed & made softe, and with their fall ouerwhelmed many villages. Kinge William builded twoe abbeies in Englande, one at

Battaile abbeye and Selbe builded. Hastinge called the Abbeye of battaile, where the battaile was fought betwene him and Harolde, the other at Selbe, hee builded the thyrd in Normandy at Cane.

Anno. 21.

1087. Thre bishops. The kinge made his thre Chaplaines bishops, Maurice of London, William of Norwich, and Robert of Chester.

Bones of Gawen. In a prouince of Wales called Ros, was founde the Sepulcher of Gawen, (who was sisters sonne of Arthur king of the Britaynes) beinge in lengthe xiiii. foote.

Kinge William lyinge at Roane in Normandy, Philip king of Fraunce said that he kept his Chamber as women do in childbedde, and nourished his fatte bellye, but when he is Churched I will offer a Thousand candels wyth him.

King

King Williã hearinge of these stormes, in the moneth of August, wente wyth a great armye into Fraunce, and spoyled all thinges sparing nothing, last of all hee burned the Cittye of Meaux, with our Ladyes Churche, and two Anchors that were enclosed in the same Church, whiche perswaded themselues that they ought not to forsake theyr house in such extremitye, whereat the king reioysing, chered the menne to feede the fyre, and came himselfe so neare, þ with the heate therof and of his harnesse, he gate a disease to the encrease of his sicknes. Also it came to passe that the kings horse leapinge ouer a ditche, did brest the inner partes of the king, wyth þ paine whereof he was sore afflicted, and returned to Roane where he ended his life, the 9. day of September, in the yeare of oure Lord. 1087. when he had raigned xx. yeares and xi. monethes lackinge fiue dayes, and was buried at Cane in Normandye. Hee had manye children by Queene Matild, to wit, Robert to whom he gaue Normandye: Richard who dyed yonge: Williã to whõ he gaue Englãd: Henrye to whom hee gaue hys mothers possessyons & treasures. And v. doughters, Cicili abbes of Cane; Constance

K. William gate a disease that shortned his life.

K. William dyeth.

Hee had ix. children.

maryed

maryed to Alane Earle of Britaine, Adela wyfe to Stephen Earle of Bloyes, Margaret and Ellenor.

VVILLIAM RVfus, or VVilliam the redde, for that he was red coloured.

Anno Regni. 1.

VVilliam Rufus, the seconde sonne (at that tyme lyuing) of William Conquerour, began his reigne ouer the Realme of Englande, the ninthe day of September, in ẏ yere of our Lord. 1087. He was crowned [at] Westminster the first of October. [He] was variable, inconstante, couetous [and] cruell. He burdened his people [with] vnreasonable taxes. He pilled the [ric]he and opprest ẏ poore. And what he [got], he wastfully spent in gret bank[et]ting and sumptuous apparell. He would neyther eate, drinke, or wear anye thinge, but that it cost vnmea[sura]bly deere. And for an example (whiche is to bee noted in these oure dayes) a morninge his Chamberlaine bring[inge] him a newe payre of hosen, he deman[ded] what they coste, the Chamberlai[ne] aunswerid thre shillings: At whiche

The best payre of hose for the kinge cost

e king being wrath, sayde: away beg- but iii. shil
er ÿ thou arte, bringe mee a payre of a linges.
marke. Then his Chamberlaine set a
aire ÿ were muche worse, & saide they
st a marke, where with the king was
el pleased.

Almost all the nobles of the Realme, 1088.
trary to their oth, raised war against
ing Williã, & would haue had Roberte
s eldest brother to be King. But King
illiã by fayre wordes pacifying som of
e principal, besieged the residue in the
astell of Rochester, where hee wyth
uch laboure ouercame thẽ. This yere A great
great earthquake ouerturned manye earthquake
uses & Churches in Englãd. An. 2

This yere died Lãfranke Archbishop 1089.
of Canterbury, who among his wor-
s of charitye, builded two hospitals
ithoute the Citye of Canterburye, the
e of S Iohn, the other at Herbaldowne,
d gaue them sufficiente yerely rents. Hospitalls of
King William kept in his handes the S. Iohn and
hurches & Monasteries of all Eng- Harbal-
nde, after ÿ the pastours were deade, downe buil-
aking great spoile thereof, and letting ded.
em out to his men. Anno. 3.

King William makinge war against 1090.
his brother Robert Duke of Normã-
e, made great spoyles in his brothers
countrye.

countrye, but at length a greement was made wyth condition, that if one of the dyed wythoute issue, the other shoulde succeede in the inheritaunce. In the meane season, Malcolmus kynge of the Scottes, did homage to the kinge of Englande.

Conditions of peace.

K. Of Scots did homage

A great tempest fel on S. Lukes daye, specialiye in Winchcombe, where a gret part of the steple was ouerthrowe. And in London the winde ouerturned six hundred houses, and the roofe of Bowe Church in Cheape, wher wyth some persones was slayne. The rafters, was caryed awaye, and foure of them of 26. foote in lengthe, were with suche violence petched in the ground, y^t scantly foure foote did remayne aboue ye groũd.

Tempest at Winchcõbe in London 600. houses ouerturned with the roofe of Bowe Church.

Anno. 4.

1091. New Castel

King William went into Northũberlande, and repayred such Castels as the Scots by theyr warres had impayred, and builded the new Castell upon Tine, &c.

Sarisbury.

Osmonde bishop of Sarisbury, founded the Cathedrall Church there.

Anno. 5.

1092. Great frost.

IN Englande fell wonderful aboundaunce of rayne, and after ensued a great frost, that horses and cartes passed commonly ouer greate ryuers, when it thawed the Ise brake downe many greet bridges.

K. William lying sicke, promised to amend his wicked lawes. He gaue the Archbishopricke of Canterbury vnto Anselme, & to Robert Blote, he gaue the bishopricke of Lincolne. But when the kinge was amended of his healthe, he was sorye that he had not sold the bishopricke of Lincolne. The same yere Malcolmus King of Scottes comming into Englande, was mette withal, and sodainlye slaine with his sonne and heyre also, by Robert Mowbray Earle of Northumberland. This yere John bishop of Welles by greasinge the kinges handes, transposed his byshops sea to Bathe.

Anselme Archbishop of Canterbury.

K. of Scots with his sonne slaine.

William warren Earle of Surreye and Gondred his wyfe, founded the Priorye of Lewes in Sussex. Anno. 6.

King William builded the Citye of Carlile, which was destroyed by the Danes 200. yeares before, and out of the South partes of Englande, he sent men to inhabite there. This yeare a fyerye flake was seene in the ayre, from the South to the North, in the kalendes of August, and there folowed a greate famine, and after so greate a mortalitye, that

1093.

Carlile builded.

Fire Empressions.

Famine and mortalitye.

that the quicke were scantly able to burye the dead.

Anno.7.

1094. THe bishoprike of Thetford, was tra
slated to Norwich, by Herbert Losinge
Northumberlande spoiled. This yere king Willia sent his brother
Henrye into Northu(m)berland with a great
power to vexe the countrye, which he
spoyled: the Earle was taken, and ma-
K. William inuaded Wales. ny were disherited, some had their eyes
put out &c. The Kyng with a great po-
wer entred Wales, but beinge not able
to followe the Welshemen amonge the
hilles, he builded two Castels in ŷ borders, and returned. An.8.

1095. Goinge to Hierusalem. GReat preparation was made by the
Christians to go against the infidel
at Hierusalem, Peter the Heremite bei
their first leader, & after Godfrey of Bo
loigne. Anno.9.

1096. Normandy layd to gage ROber Duke of Normandy, laid Nor
mandye to gage, to his brother kin
William, for x. thousand pounds of sil
uer, and then toke his iourney towar
Hierusalem, Anno 10.

1097. Nice and Antioche won by the Christians. DUke Godfreye, Duke Beamond, an
Robert Duke of Normandye besie
ged the Citye of Nice, & toke the same
they toke also the Citye of Antioche.
Anno.11.

KInge William was in Normandye, and gaue himselfe to warres ther, so with exactions & tributes he did not onelye shaue, but also flea the people of Englande, Anno.12. 1098.

Great exactions.

THis yeare the Christians tooke the Citty of Hierusalem, and placed ther a king and a Patriarche. K. William kepte his Courte at Westminster in the newe hall, and heard men say it was to bigge: he aunswered and said, this hall is not bigge enough by the one halfe, & but a Chamber in comparison of that he was about to make. As king William was a huntinge in the new Forest, word was brought him that his people was besieged in Cenomania, hee forthwith toke shipping, though he were vehementlye persuaded to the contrarye, for there was at that time a greate tempest, to whom hee aunsweared, I neuer heard that any King was drowned. At this tyme he gate more honour, then euer hee did in al his life, for hee chased his enemyes, and returned againe into England with victory. This yere in Sommer, blood sprang out of the earth at Finchamitede in Barkeshire. Anno. 13

1099. Westminster hall builded.

Wet at Westminster.

KInge William the morrow after Lamas daye, went a hunting in the new 1100.

William Rufus death.

forrest, where Walter Tyrell shooting at a Deere, did unawares hit the kinge that hee fell downe starke deade, and neuer spake word. His men (and specially his knightes) gate them awaye, but some of them came backe againe, and layde his bodye (whiche was all to wrapped in bloud) upon a colliers Carte, which one silly leane beast did drawe, and an husbandman was constrayned to bringe ý body unto the Cittye. Hee was buryed the morrowe after his death at Winchester, at whose buryal menne coulde not weepe for ioy. He raigned xii. yeares & xi. monethes lackinge viii. dayes. Hee gaue unto the Monks, called Monachi de Charitate, in Southwarke the great newe Church of Saint Sauiour of Bermondsey, and also Bermondsey it selfe with all the appurtenaunces. He also founded a goodlye Hospitall in the Citye of Yorke, called S. Leonardes, for the sustentacion and finding of ý poore as wel brethren as sisters, which be manifoldlye encreased by him and his heyres, kinges of England.

Bermondsey and S. Leonards builded.

Hen

HENRY
Beauclarke.

HENRY ẏ brother of William Rufus and the first of that name, for his learnig called Beauclarke, began his Dominion over this Realme of Englande, the first day of August, in the yere of oure Lord. 1100. He was crowned at Westminster on the v. day of August. He maried Maulde the doughter of Malcolme king of Scottes, of whom he begat William and a doughter named Maulde. At the beginning of his raigne, he restored the state of the Clergy, asswaged the greeuous payments, reduced againe S. Edwards lawes. He made a measure of a yarde, by the length of his arme.

Anno Reg. ni. 1.

Iordan Bisset Baron, ẏ sonne of Raffe the sonne of Brian Bisset, founded ẏ house of S. Iohn of Hierusalem, nere unto London by Smithfielde. The same Iordan Bisset gaue unto Roberte the Chapleyne xiiii. Acres of groũd lying in the fielde next adioynynge unto Clarkes well, to build thereuppon what house of Religion the sayd Roberte woulde. Hee also

S. Iohns Hospital by Smithfielde.

Clarken well.

[illegible] the peece of grounde [illegible] adioyning, to builde [illegible] mall. &c.

Anno. 2.

Robert Duke of Normandye the kinges eldest brother, which was nowe
returned from Hierusalem, made warre
upon his brother Henry for the crowne
of England. But by mediation a peace
was made on this condition, that Henry
should pay three thousande markes yerely to Duke Robert, and if the one dyed
without issue, the longer liuer shoulde
inherite. Anno. 3.

The Cathedrall Church in the Citie
of N[illegible] was founded by Herbert
bishop of N[illegible]. This yere the Priory [illegible] of S. Bartholmew in Smithfielde [illegible] founded by a
[illegible] named Rever,
[illegible] was at this day a layfold
[illegible] and filthy the place whe-
[illegible] were put
to execution. Anno. 4.

Robert Duke of Normandy came
into England, though the subtility
of Kinge Henry his brother, released
him the tribute of thre Thousand markes of siluer. An. 5.

The yonger brother [illegible]

It was not long ere great malice was
kindled betwene the two brethren

Robe-

Robert and Henry, wherevppon deadlye warre ensued. The same yeare appeared in the South about the Sonne, circles, and a blasinge starre. Robert de Fitzham builded Teukesburye, and there was buryed. Teukesbury

Anno. 6.

KIng Henry continued in Normandye, makinge stronge warre vppon his brother Robert. Eudo Dapifere, or sewer to king Henry, founded the Monasterye of S. John in Colchester. Simon Earle of Northampton, founded the Monasterye of S. Andrew in Northampton.

1105. S. Johns in Colchester. S. Andrewe in Northampton.

Anno. 7.

ROBert Duke of Normandy, came to his brother at Northampton, as frend he desired him to beare brotherly loue towarde him, but K. Henry feelinge his conscience marked with an whot yron, accusing him because he had so vnmeetly vsurped the title of the kingdome, which pertained to his elder brother, & fearing men more then God, he reconciled the nobles of the Realme vnto him by fayre promises, & then ÿ Duke returning into Normandye, the king followed with a greate power, where betweene them was manye sore battailes foughte, but at the last the valiant man

1106. The elder brother seeketh frendship at the yonger brothers hand, but findeth violence.

Roberte Duke of Normandye was takē.

Two moones at once. Uppon Maundie thursdaye, there was seene two full Moones, one in the East, and another in the West. Anno. 8.

1107. When King Henry had disposed & set in order Normandie according to his pleasure, hee returned into England and brought with him his brother Robert, and William of Morton and put them in perpetual prison. But shortlye

The younger brother put the elder brothers eyes out and kept him in prison. after Duke Robert deceyuing his keepers, sought to escape, but he was takē in the field, and when it was tolde the King his brother, hee commaunded to kepe him darke, and to put out his eyes, which being done, frō that houre unto the daye of his death, hee pyned away in sorrowe and griefe of minde.

This yeare dyed Maurice Bishop of London, who is named to bee founder of S. Paules Church in London, because he newly buylded the same. The Priorye of Christes Church in London was founded by [illegible] Norman. Anno. 9.

Christes Church.

1108. Richard le Beaumes, was elected bishop of London. Anno. 10.

1109. Henry Emperour of Rome, required to have Maude the Kinges daughter unto him in marriage, which was graunted, and the king toke three shellinges of

A taske

[illegible]very kynde of [illegible]. The kinge [illegible]
[illegible]nd the [illegible] [illegible]
[illegible], and [illegible]

[illegible]

[illegible] Henrye [illegible]
[illegible]
[illegible]e to Roberte [illegible]
[illegible] Earle of Gloucester [illegible]
[illegible]lded the Castell of Bristowe, and [illegible] [illegible]
[illegible]eye of S. James in [illegible] [illegible] Cy-
[illegible] same Cittye, where his bo[illegible] [illegible]ed, [illegible]
[illegible]ryed. And his sonne Earle William [illegible] Kensham.
[illegible]ganne the abbeye of Kensham.

Anno. 12.

[K]inge Henrye went into Normandy [illegible]
to make warre against the Earle of [An]gewe, which kept Cinomania against [the] kinges will, and with fyre & sworde [he] spoyled his whole countrye.

Anno. 13.

[T]his yere was a great mortalitye of men. 1112. Mortalitye.

Anno. 14.

[T]he king subdued the Welshemen. 1113.

Anno. 15.

[T]he fourth of Aprel, the river of Thames was dryed up, and two myles [int]o the Sea was also dryed up by the [spa]ce of two dayes. There was manye [gre]at stormes, & a blasing starre appeared [in] the month of May. 1114. Thames dryed up.

An. 16.

King

1116. KIng Henry hauing gret warres with Lewes King of Fraunce, the Realme of England was sore vexed with exacions. Anno 18.

1117. IN March was exceeding lightning, and in December thunder, and haile, the Moone both times was turned into bloud. Anno.19.

1118. THis yere dyed Mauld Quene of England, & was buried at Westminster. She builded an Hospital nere unto London without Holborne, which now is ÿ Parishe Church of S. Giles in the field. Matildis hospital.

This yere begã the order of ÿ knightes of the Temple. Anno 20. Knightes of the temple.

1119. MAnye sore battailes were foughte in Fraunce & Normandy, betwene K. Henry of England, & Lodowike ÿ Frēch Kinge, in the end wherof K. Henry had the victorye. Anno.21.

1120. KIng Henry hauing tamed the Frenchmen, & pacifyed Normandye, sailed ouer into Englande, in which voyage W. Duke of Normandye, and Richard ÿ sones of K. Henry & Mary his doughter, Ric. Erle of Chester, & hys wife, with many noble men & womē, to the nōber of 160, persons were drowned. 22. The kinges children drowned.

8181. KIng Henry maryed the Duke of Lovans doughter. Anno, 26.

Cardinall came into England, who inueying against priestes Concubines, was himselfe detected of whoredome. The King caused al the coyners of England to haue their priuy mēbers cut of, & also their right hand, because they had corrupted the coigne. 1125. Corners punished.

Anno.27

Henry the Emperour dyed, and Maulde the Empresse came into England, & dwelt with the Queene in her Chāber, because shee was suspected of her husbands death, the King her father loued her wel, because hee had none other heyre. 1126. Maulde the Empresse.

Anno.28.

Richard bishop of Londō being dead, Gilbert succeeded in his place, this Richarde bishop of London, founded S.Osythe in Essex. 1127. S.Osithes in Essex.

Anno 29. 1128.

King Henry went with a warlike armye into Fraunce, because Lodowicke the French King, defended the Earle of Flaunders the Kinges nephew and enemye.

Anno.30

King Henry helde a greate counsel at London, wherein it was graunted him to haue the correction of the Clergye, which came to an euil purpose, for the King toke infinit sommes of money of of priests, and suffered them to do what they would. Anno 31.

[illegible] THis yeare Kinge Henrye gaue his daughter ÿ Empresse, vnto Geffreye Plantagenet Earle of Angewe. Anno 32.

[illegible] KInge Henrye made [illegible] at [illegible] Castle. Kinge Henryes daughter the Empresse, did beare vnto Geffreye Plantagenet, a sonne, and named him Henry, which when the King knewe, he called his nobles together, and ordeyned that his daughter and ÿ heyres of her body, should succede him in the kingdome.

London burnt. A great part of London was burnt with fyre, which began at Gilbert Beckets house.

Hospitall of S. Crosse. Henrye Blois bishoppe of Winchester founded the Hospitall of S. Crosse neare vnto Winchester. Anno 34.

1133. Earthquake. THere was greate darkenes in England, & Earthquakes. Anno 35.

1134. R. Shortehose dyed in prison. MAulde the Empresse brought forth a sonne named Geffrey, for ioy wherof Kinge Henrye went ouer into Normandie. The same yeare dyed in prison Roberte Shorthose eldest sonne to W. Conqueroure, & brother to K. Henrye, he was buried at Gloucester. Anno 36

1135. KIng Henry remayning in Normandie vpon a day when he came from his hunting, did eate Lampries, whereof he tok[e]

by

's death. Other write he toke his death by a fall of his horse. He deceased ye first day of December, when he had reigned 35. yeres 4. monethes. He builded Reading, Chester, Windsor, and Woodstocke, and to the nomber of 25. strong holds. The kinges body laye a great while at Roan vnburyed, his bowels, braynes, and eyes was buryed there, the reste of his body powdred with salte, & wrapped in Bulles hydes because of ye stech, which poysoned them that stoode about him, was buried at Reading. The Phisitiõ who had ben hired with great reward to cleaue his head to take oute the braine, with the stenche thereof dyed. K. Henry dyed. Reding builded.

STEPHEN
Earle of Bologne.

STEPHEN Erle of Bologne, the sonne of the Earle of Bloys and Adela, William conquerours daughter, nephew to King Henry the first, tooke on him ye gouernance of this Realme of England the second day of December, in the yere of our Lorde 1135. Anno Reg. 1.

1135. He was Crowned at Westminster
on S. Stephens daye. This was a noble
man and hardy, of passing comly fauor
and personage, in all Princely vertues
he excelled: as in marshal pollicy, gentlenes, and liberality towards all men.
For although he had continuall warre,
yet on he neuer burden his commons
with exactions. Hee made warres a-
1136. gainst David of Scotlande, because hee
refused to do him homage, for Northumberland and Huntingdon, which he held
by his wife. But at the length Stephen
agreed with David Kinge of Scots, after that hee had won from him certaine
townes and Castels, and gaue to Henry
the sonne of David, the Earledome of
S. Paules Churche brent. Huntingdon. S. Paules Churche in
London, was burnt. Anno. 2.

Stephen passed ouer into Normandye,
1137. against Geffreye Earle of Angewe the
husband of Maulde the Empresse, which
was righte heyre to the Crowne, and
when he had quieted that prouince, hee
made Eustace his sonne duke of Normi-
dye, & ioyned frendship with Lewes
of Fraunce. Anno. 3.

1138. Great trouble was in Englande, in-
somuch as diuers of the Nobles maintained Maulde the Empresse against Stephen,

.u. David King of Scottes inuaded
rthumberland, wher by meane of Tru-
n bisshoppe of Yorke, the Scottes had
ouerthrow, and were slaine in great
nber. Anno. 4.

Jng Stephen went into Scotlande, 1139.
where by fire and swoꝛd he compel-
David King of Scots to agree with
, and to geue in hostage, Henry his
ne, with whom K. Stephen returned
o Englande, and then made warres
inst the nobles which fauoured the
e of Maude the Empresse. The same
e Maude ẏ Empresse came into Eng
de with Roberte Earle of Gloucester
brother, & arriued at Arundel, wher
y were ioyfully receiued by William
Albeneto. Erle Robert with x. knigh
, and as many Archers on hoꝛsback
d through ẏ middest of the Realme
Walingford and so to Gloucester, and
led thoſe countryes. Anno. 5.

Maulde the Empresse.

Jnge Stephen besieged the Citie of 1140.
Lincolne agaynſte Ranulphe Earle of
ster, but Robert Earle of Gloucester
e with a great power & rescued the
e, chased ẏ kinges armye, and toke
a prisoner on Candelmas daye, and
ughte him to Maulde the Empresse,
o sente him to the Castel of Bristowe,
this

K. Stephen taken prisoner.

this being done, the Empresse was almost of all Englishmen taken to be their Ladye, saving onlye of the Kentishmen who kept King Stephens wife Lady. By the great power of Londoners, who had assaulted vppon the Empresse, was taken Robert Earle of Glocester, whereupon shortly after both the King and the Earle was delivered by exchaunge, in this civil battaile, the Citye of Winchester was destroyed. Galfridus de Mandevile Earle of Essex, fortifyed the Tower of London. This Galfride was founder of the Abbey of Walden. Anno. 6.

Walden.

1141. KInge Stephen hearinge that the Empresse was at Oxforde in the Castle wyth a small companye, hee gathered a great armye and besieged the Empresse continually, but the Empresse perceyving she was voyde of all helpe, with a womanishe subtiltie, clothing her selfe and her companions in white, by the night wente over the Thames a foote, which then was frosen over, and was hidde with snowe, and that night she went to the castell of Wallingforde, and the Castell of Oxford was yelded to the King. 7.

The Empresse escaped.

1142. KInge Stephen tooke William de Mandevile at S. Albons, and compelled him to delivere the Tower of London.

castels of Walden and Plessis, when
s Williā was destitute of his fathers
sessions, he inuaded the abbey of Ram
, draue out the Monkes, and set Ros
s in that place. Anno. 8.

Ing Stephen continued in warres a- 1143
gainst the nobles of this Realme, and
yne besieged Lincolne, but was dri-
from thence by Ranulphe Earle of
ster Anno. 9.

Ing Stephen chased the Earle of Glou- 1144
cester, and many other of his enemies
n the buylding of Farendune Castle,
toke it into his owne hand. The Je-
s crucified a childe vpon Easter day
Norwiche. Anno. 10.

Ing Stephen tooke Ranulphe Earle of
Chester, who came peaceably vnto him 1145
kept him in prison till he had deli-
ed the Castell of Lincolne, and other
els. And thē the King was solemnely
owned at Lincolne. Anno. 11.

Blasing starre appeared in the West 1146
many dayes. Anno. 12. A Comete.

uid king of Scottes, gaue order of 1147
nighthoode vnto Henry the eldest
ne of Geffrey Plantagenet, Duke of
rmandy. Anno. 13.

ffrey Plantagenet, Duke of Normandy, gaue Normandy to his sonne Hēry 1148

on his mothers behalfe. Anno. 14.

This yeare died Geffrey Plantagenet, Earle of Anjou, and husband to Mauld the Empresse, and then was Henry her sonne made Earle of Anjou: and Duke of Normandy. This yeare was a great frost that men wente ouer the Thames on foote. Anno. 15.

Henry Duke of Normandy, maried Alianore, whom the French king Lodowike had diuorced from hym. Mauld the wife of king Stephen died, and was buried at Feuersham. Anno. 16.

Eustace king Stephens sonne, died sodainly, and was buried at Feuersham.

Henry Duke of Normandy, with a great army arriued in Englande, and at the first wanne the castell of Walmesbury, and shortly after many other townes and Castels. Betweene hym and King Stephen were foughten many battayles, but Duke Henries busines prospered. Anno. 17.

Peace was agreed betwene Mauld the Empresse, her sonne Henry, and king Stephen, vpon thys conditiō, that Stephen during his life, shoulde holde kyngdom of Englande, and Henry in the meane tyme to be proclaimed heyre apparaunt. Thus the warres which

con-

ned 17. yeres, to the a quiet end Anno. 1154
Henry Duke of Normandy, sayled into Normandy, and by little and little ga-thered into his owne handes al the lord-shippes that his father had geuen hym. King Stephen departed this worlde the xxv. day of October, when he had reig-ned xviii. yeares x. monethes and dyuers dayes. He founded the abbaie of Cogge-shall in Essex, of Forness in Lancashire, and Feuersham in Kent, where he being Feuersham. was buried.

HENRY THE seconde.

HENRY the seconde of that Anno reg. 1. name, the sonne of Geffrey Plantagenet, and Maude the Empresse, daughter of king Henry the first, began his reigne ouer this realme of Englande, the xxv. day of October in the yeare of our lorde 1154. He was crow-ned at Westminster the xix. day of Decem-ber. He was somwhat red of face, short of body, & therwith fat. Of speache rea-sonable, wel learned, noble in chiualry, of courageous hearte, wyse in coun-sel, liberall to straungers, but harde to his familiars, unstedfast of promise, geuen somedeale to pleasure, and an open breaker of wedloche.

1155 King Henry sent solempne messengers to Pope Adrian, that he might haue licence to enter Irelande by force of armes to subdue the same, and reduce those rude people to Christianitie and humanitie, whiche the Pope willingly graunted, and gaue him priuiledge beginning thus. Adrian byshop, seruaunt of the seruauntes of God, to his deare beloued sonne in Christe, the moste noble kyng of England, health, &c. Anno. 2.

1156 King Henry went ouer into Normandy, and with long siege tooke diuers castels. Anno. 3.

1157 The kinge made a great armye into Wales, where he felled their woodes he fortified the castle of Rutland, reedified the castle of Basingwerke, and subdued the Welshemen. Anno. 4.

1158 Upon Christmas daye kynge Henry ware his crowne at Winchester, and neuer weare it after. Anno. 5.

1159 Huntington. King henry confirmed the donations whiche Mauld the Queene had before geuen to the Monastery in Huntingdon Anno 6.

1160 Kinge Henrys maried Margarete the French

enche kynges daughter beinge but
thre yeares olde, unto his sonne Henry
beyng but seuen yeare olde. Anno.9.
Kyng Henry caused al his subiectes to
sweare fidelitie to his sonne Henry 1152
concerning his enheritaunce. Thomas
the kynges Chauncellour toke the othe
first, sauing his fidelitie to king Henry
the father. This Thomas was elected Thomas Becket.
Archebyshop of Caunterbury.

This yeare came into England xxx. Germains, as wel men as wome, their heade and ruler being one Gerardus, they denied the sacramentes of baptisme, matrimonie, and the Eucharist, they beyng apprehended, the Bishops gaue sentence against them, and the king gaue commaundement that they should be marked with a hote Iron and whipped, and that no man should helpe them with house roume or any other succour, they toke their punishement very gladly. Their capitayne going before them singing, blessed are ye when men do hate you. They were marked in the forehead with an hote Iron, & their captayne was marked both in the forehead and the chinne, & being whipped and thrust out in the wynter tyme, they died with colde. Anno.9.

1163 A combate. Robert de Mountford, fought hande to hand with Henry of Essex, concerning treason to the King, and had the victory of him, for whiche cause the saide Henry ran in great infamy and was also disherited, but through the kinges pardon, he became a Monke at Reading. The same yeare Malcolme the Scottish kyng, and Rese the Prince of Southwales, dyd homage to king Henry and his sonne. This yeare London bridge was first begon to be made of timber by one Peter of Colechurch. Anno.10.

1164 Parliament at Claringdon. A Councell was holden at Claringdon, in presence of the Kyng, the Archbyshops, byshops, lordes, barons &c. whiche was recognised, and by al these other confirmed many ordinaunces. Thomas archbishop of Caunterbury being sworne to the same, shortly after sore repented and fledde the realme. Anno.11.

1165 Erthquake. A Great earthquake the xxvi. daye Jan. in Ely, Northfolke & Southfolke so y it overthrew the y Rode upon their feete, and made the bels to toll. An.12.

1166 Quene Elianor brought forth a sonne named John. Anno.13.

1167 This yeare fell a discorde betwene the Frenche kyng and the king of Englande. Anno.14.

Cert

Conan Earle of little Britayne, dyed, and lefte to his heyre a daughter named Constance, whiche hee had by the kyng of Scottes sister, which Constance king Henry maried to his sonne Geffrey. Anno. 14. 1168

Robert de Bosçue seconde Earle of Leycester, founded the monasterye of Leycester of chanons regular, and Eton of Nunnes, was founded by Amicia his wyfe. Anno. 15. 1169 [illegible]

King Henry caused Henry his eldest sonne to be crowned, as he thought to the great quietnes both of him selfe and of the realme, but it proued to the contrary. Thomas by mediation of Alexander byshop of Rome, and Lewys the Frenche kyng, was restored to his byshopriike. And not long after, by fower knightes named William Tracie, Reignold Fitzurse, Hugh Morvill, and Richard Brito was he slayne at Caunterbury. Anno. 17. 1170

King Henry entred into Irelande with a warlike power, where the archebishops & bishops receiued him for their king, and did sweare fealtie vnto him, the like did many princes of that countrey. Anno. 18. 1171

A voyage into Irelande.

On Christmas day at night were hard great and terrible thonders, both in 1172

England, Fraunce, and Ireland. Kyng Henry sent ambassadours to Alexander byshop of Rome, to purge him selfe of the death of Thomas Becket. Anno.10.

1173 King Henry the younger, tooke parte with the Frenche kyng his wiues father, Rychard Duke of Aquitayne, and Geffrey Earle of Britaine, did chuse rather to take their brothers parte, then their fathers. On euery side was made conspiracies, robberies and burninges, yea his sonnes persecuted him, euen to the death. Anno.20.

1174 King Henry the elder retourned into England, and subdued his Rebelles. The citie of Leicester was by the kinges commaundement vtterlye burned, the walles & castel rased, the inhabitauntes sparpled into other Cities and the Earle imprisoned. The fift daye of September Christes churche in Cantorburye, by a miserable fyre was for the better part brent, with certayne houses of office in the court. Anno.21.

Leicester burned.

Christes churche in Canterbury brent.

1175 King Henry the sonne with his brethren and other, were reconciled to kyng Henry the father. The kynge of Scottes became the kyng of Englandes liege man, and did homage.

Anno.22.

The

The kinges of Englande bothe father and sonne, went together with great deuotion to visite the tombe of Thomas late archebyshop of Caunterbury, and from thence throughout all Englande, accomplishing in deede the peace which they had promised. Not long after, the kyng layde flatte with the grounde the castels of Huntington, Walton, Grobie, Stutbury, Hay, Trell, and many other, in reuenge of the harme that y Lordes therof had done to him.

Many castels destroyed.

The kyng called a conuocation of the Clargy at London, in the which conuocation, when the Popes legat was set, & the archebyshop of Cantorbury on hys right hande, as Primate of Englande. The archebyshop of Yorke, disdayninge to sytte on the lyft hande, whereby hee should seme to giue place to the archbyshop of Cantorbury: came and swapte him downe to haue thruste his tayle betwixt the legate and the archebishop of Cantorbury, the archebyshop of Cantorbury being lothe to remoue, the other set his buttocke in his lappe, but he had vnnethe touched the archebishop of Cantorbury with his bum, when the byshops and other of the clergy and leyte, stept to him, pulled him, and threw him

A presumptuous archebishop of Yorke, well rewarded.

to the

to the grounde, and when they began to laye on him with fistes and battes, the byshop of Cantorbury yelding good for euell, sought to saue him. The archbyshop of Yorke with his rent cope, gotte vp and away straight to the Kyng with a great complaint, but when the truthe of the matter by examination was knowen, he was well laughed at for his remedye. Anno 23.

1177 King Henry when he had disposed all thinges in this realme as he would, he sayled into Normandy, where he and Lodowike kyng of Fraunce entred into amitie, promising by othe together to go to Hierusalem. Anno. 24.

1178 Richard de Lucie, the kynges Justiciar, layde the foundation of Westwoode, or Lelenose in Rochestar diocese An. 25.

1179 King Henry the yonger went ouer sea and spent three yeares in skirmishing against the Frenchemen. Anno. 27.

1181 The olde coyne in Englande was altered, and newe brought in place. The Coyners were raunsomed for corrupting the olde money. Anno. 28.

1182 Robert Harding, a Burgess of Bristowe to whom king Henry gaue the Baronie of Barkeley, buylded S. Augustines Bristowe. Anno. 29.

S. Austins at Bristowe.

Ky

King Henry did his indeuour to cause his two sonnes, Geffrey of Britain, and Richard duke of Aquitaine, to do homage unto Hēry his eldest sonne, Geffrey dyd it willingly, but Richard refused, wherewith king Henry ye father being wroth, commaunded king Henry the yonger, to do what laye in him to tame the pride of his brother Richard. The younge kyng gathered a great army, entending to fyght with his brother, but hys lyfe was cutte of as it had bene a weauers threde. He was buried at Roane. An 30. — 1183

One brother persecuting an other, God cutteth of the persecutour.

Baldwyne byshop of Worcester was elected archebyshop of Caunterbury. — 1184

Anno. 31

Heraclius Patriarche of Hierusalem, came to kyng Henry, desiring him of ayde agaynst the Turkes, which was denied. The newe temple in the West parte of London, was dedicated by the sayde Heraclius. — 1185

The newe temple in Lōdon dedicated.

Mauld daughter to kynge Henry the first, Empresse, and wyfe unto Henry the Emperour, and mother of king Hēry the second, died, of whom was made this Epitaphe.

Mauld the Empresse deceased.

The daughter, spouse, and parent eke,
of Henry lieth here:
Great of parentage, higher by mariage,
most high by childe birth deare,

Epitaphe.

Anno. 32.

1186 A Terrible earthquake throughout the worlde, in Englande many buildinges were ouerthrowen. The mother church of Chichester and al the whole city was burnt the xx of October. Anno 34.

An earthquake. Chichester burnt.

1188 Kyng Henry of England, and Philip kyng of Fraunce, with many other toke vpon them the crosse, to go to Hierusalem, but by meanes of a discorde that fell betwene the two kynges, they departed one from another. The towne of Beuerley was burnt. Anno. 35.

Beuerley burnt.

1189 Richarde Earle of Poitowe made warre against kyng Henry his father, and takyng part with the Frenche king, wan from him diuers cities, townes, and castels, namely the citie of Canomannia. For sorowe wherof the first daye of July in the yeare of our Lorde 1189. Kynge Henry ended his life, when he had raigned xxxiiii. yeares, ix. monethes, and xii daies, he lieth buried at Founteuerard. His sonne Geffrey Earle of Britaine, was buried three yeares before him, who left a sonne named Arthur, and a daughter named Elianour.

Richard

RICHARDE with the Lyons harte.

Richarde the first, for his valiauntnes, surnamed Cuer de lion, with a lions harte, being the second sonne of Henry the seconde, began his raigne the sixte daye of July, and in the yeare of our Lorde 1189. he was bigge of stature, and had a mery countenaunce. Hee commaunded that no Jewes nor women should be at his coronation, for feare of enchauntementes, for breakyng of whiche cōmaundement, many Jewes were slayne. Anno. 1. Iewes slayne.

The king set at libertie Elianor his mother, which long before at the commaundement of his father her husbande, had bene kept in close pryson. But after her enlargement, the realme was much governed by her. Elianor released. Kyng Richarde gave over the Castels of Berwyke and Rokesburghe, to the Scottishe Kinge for the sum of x.M. li. He also sold to þ bishop of Durham, his owne province, for a great piece of money, and created him Earle of the

A fabule de-uise.

of the same. He fayning to haue lost hys Signet, caused a newe to be made, and to be proclaimed, that whosoeuer would safely keepe and enioy the things which before tyme they had enrouled, shoulde come to the newe seale. He gaue his brother John the Prouinces of Notingham, Deuonshire, and Cornewall, and created him Earle of Lācaster. In this time were many robbers and outlawes in Englād amongest the which Robert Hoode and little John, continued in woodes, despoyling and robbing the goodes of the ryche. The sayde Robert entertayned an hundred tall men, and good archers, with suche spoyles as he got. Uppon whome foure hundred, were they neuer so strong, durste not geue the onsette. Poore mens goodes he spared, aboundauntly relieuing thē with that which he gotte from abbeyes, and the houses of ryche carles.

Robert hood and other outlawes.

The citizens of London, obtayned to bee gouerned by Baylifes, where as before tyme they were gouerned by Portgreues. The chiefe magistrate or Ruler of the Citie of London, in the tyme of holye kynge Edwarde, was named:

The names of the chiefe magistrates of the Citie of London, since kynge Edward the confessor, Before the Conquest which were not changed yerely, but cōtinued during their lyues.

Wolgga- } Portgreue.

In the tyme of William Conquerour, William Rufus.

frey de } Port- } Recelde } Pro-
num } greue. } Pare } uost.

In the tyme of kyng Henry the first.

he } Port } Leofia- } Prouost.
ne } greue } nus. }

After them.

ricus } Port- } Ro.Bar- } Prouost.
cii. } greue } querell. }

In tyme of kyng Stephen.

ert } Port- } Andrewe } Prouost.
ter } greue. } Buchuint }

In the tyme of Henry the seconde.

fitz } Portgreue.
ter }

After hym.

fitz } Portgreue.
ily. }

After hym.

lphe } Portgreue.
el. }

The first Baylifes.

Henry Cornehyll }
Richard Reinery. } Baylifes.

1190 King Richard betooke the guidyng of this lande to the bishop of Ely, Chaũcellour of England, & sayled into Normandy: and when he had apointed good gouernours ouer that coũtrey, he went to meete the Frenche King, and hauinge made sure league one with an other, they went towarde Hierusalem.

Jewes were robbed, and slewe them selues.

The Jewes at Lincolne, Stamforde, Fayre and Lynne, were robbed & spoiled. And at Yorke, to the number of 500. besides women and children, entred a Tower of the Castle, the people assaylinge the same, the Jewes cute the throtes of their wyues and children, and cast their bodies ouer the walles vnto the Christiãs headdes, the rest that were not thus slain, they locked vp in the kinges lodging, & set the house on fyre and burnt both the house and them selues.

A ditche about the Tower of Lõdõ

William bishop of Ely, causing a depe ditche to bee made about the Tower of London, had thought that he could haue caused the riuer of Thames to go round about it, but he bestowed great coste in vayne. Anno, 2.

John

John Herlion } Bayliffes.
Roger Duke. }

King Richard in his iourney towardes Hierusalem, subdued the Isle of Cypres, and then ioyning his puisance with the Frenche kinges in Asia, conquered Acon, where there grewe betwene kyng Richard and Philip the French king a greuous displeasure: for whiche cause Philip shortly departed thence. And comming into Fraunce, inuaded the countrey of Normandy. And John brother of king Richarde, tooke on him the kingdome of Englande. Kyng Richard restored to the Christiās the citie of Ioppa. This yeare was founde at Glastenbury the bones of kyng Arthur. 1191

Arthurs bones founde,

William Hauarde } Anno. 2.
John Buckmote } Bayliffes.

WIlliam bishop of Ely, withstoode John the kinges brother: but the sayde John stoode stiffely in his errour, and sayde he wist not if his brother Rychard were aliue or not. To whome the Bishop aunswered, if king Richard be yet liuing, it were vntruthe to take frō him the crowne. If he be dead, Arthur the elder brothers sonne, must enioy the same: 1193

Nicolas Duke ⎫ Anno. 4.
Peter Newlay ⎭ Baylifes.

1193 King Richard hauing knowledge that Philip of Fraunce inuaded Normandie and that John his brother had made himselfe king of Englande, made peace with the Turkes for thre yeres, & with a small cōpany returning homeward by Thrace was taken prysoner by the Duke of Ostriches men, who broughte hym to Henry the Emperour, and he kept hym in pryson a yeare and fiue monethes.

K. Richard taken prisoner.

Roger Duke ⎫ Anno. 5.
Richard fitz Alyn ⎭ Baylifes.

1194 VVilliam bishoppe of Ely, was by strength banished the lande. The kynges frendes entreated this matter cō‑cernyng the kynges raunsome, whiche was set at 100000. pounde, wherupon commaundement was directed from ŷ kynges Justices, that al the byshoppes, Prelates, Earles, Barones, Abbayes, & Priories, should bringe in the fourthe part of their reuenues for the kings rāsome, and besides this they brought of their good will, their golden and siluer chalices, to performe this dede of charitie. John the kynges brother when hee heard of the imprisonment of his brother, made great warre within the land, and

The kynges raunsome.

o take by strength the castels of Windsore, Notingham, and others. King Richarde was deliuered, and arriued at Sandwiche the Sondaye next after the feaste of S. George. He called a counsel at Winchester: where he deposed his brother John, and crowned himselfe againe king of Englande, then hee called into his handes all suche thinges as he had before geuen or solde by patentes or otherwyse, by which meanes he gathered a summe of money, & sayled into France where shortly after a peace was concluded betwene the twoo kynges for one yere. John which had taken parte against his brother, by meanes of Elianor his mother, was reconcyled.

K. Rychard delyuered.

K. Rychard again crowned,

fitz Isabell. } Anno 6.
fitz Arnold. } Bayliffes.

King Richarde sent messengers to the Pope, complaynyng vpon the Duke of Austriche for misusing of him and hys people as they came by distresse of weather through his countrey. The Pope excommunicated ÿ Duke of Austriche, & commaunded him to release ÿ couenauntes ÿ he constrained the king to make, but ÿ duke contemned the Popes authoritie.

1195

bert Besant } Anno 7.
te le Iosue } Bayliffes.

1196 WIlliam with the bearde, moued the common people to seeke libertie and freedome, and not to be subiecte to the ryche and mighty, by which meanes he drew to him many great companies, whereof the kyng being warned, commaunded him to cease from those attempted, but the people styll folowed him: and he made to them certayne Orations openly. Hee was after taken in Bowe church in Cheape, but not withoute sheading of bloude: for hee was forced by fyre and smoke to forsake the church. When he was taken, hee with nyne of his adherentes, were hanged.

William for- [illegible] fire [illegible] [illegible].

Gerarde de Anteloche } Anno reg. 8.
Robert Durant. } Bayliffes.

1197 WArre was renued betwene kynge Richarde of Englande, and Philip of Fraunce.

Roger Blont, } Anno. 9
Nicolas Ducket, } Bayliffes.

1198 KIng Richard toke of euery hyde land through Englande, fiue shyllynges. There was great thunder, lightnyng & rayne, suche as had neuer bene seene before, upon S. Margaretes day.

Great exa- ctions and tempest.

Constantine fitz Arnold } Anno. 10.
Robert le Beaw. } Bayliffes.

When

Richarde the first.

When truce was taken betweene
the kynges of Fraunce and Eng- 1198
land, king Richard turned his army a- Truce with the Frenche king.
ginst the Barons of Pictauia that rebel-
ed, and set their cities and Townes on
fire, spoyled their countrey, and slewe
many of his aduersaries, at the laste he
came into the dukedome of Aquitaine,
and besieged a castell of Chalne, where
one smote hym with a venemed darte, K. Richard wounded to death.
which stripe the king little regarded.
But in twelue dayes he inuaded the Castle and wan it, and put the Souldiours in pryson. Of this wounde aforesayd, he died the vi. daye of Aprill, in the
yeare of our Lorde. 1199. When he had
reigned nyne yeares & nyne monethes.
And as hee had bequeathed, his bodye
was buried at Founteuerarde, at his fathers feete, his harte at Roane, because of
the incomparable trustines and fidelitie
that he had founde in them, and his bowels with the excrementes to be buried
at the foresayde castle of Chalne, in token
of their treason and falshood.

KING IOHN.

Anno reg. 1.

IOHN brother to Richard afore named, began his reigne the first day of Aprill, in the yeare of our Lorde, 1199. Of persone he was indifferent, but of melancholy and angry complexion. He being nowe in Normandye, sayled ouer into Englande, and was crowned at Westminster vpon the Ascention day.

Philip kyng of Fraunce (in the quarel of Arthur, the sonne of Gefferey, Johns elder brother, duke of Britaine, whome certayne of the Lordes had named king of Englande) made warre vpon kyng John, inuaded Normandy, and tooke from him diuers castels and townes.

Arnold fitz Arnold } Baylifes.
Richard fitz Bartilmew.

1200 Kinge John assembled a counsayle, wherein was graunted to hym three shillinges of euery plough land through Englande, beside the subsidie of the spirituall landes: he sayled into Normandy, where he spent the tyme to his losse and dishonour, & a truce was concluded.

Three shilling of euery plough land

This yeare was a diuorce betweene

King

ng John & his wife Hawisia the Earle of Glocesters daughter, because of nere nesse of blood: and after he was maried Isabell the daughter of the Erle of Engolesme in Fraunce: by whome he had sonnes, Henry & Richard, and thre daughters, Isabell, Elianor, and Jane. K. John diuorced. Wife of king John.

In October, appeared fiue Moones, the first in the North, the second in the South, the third in the West, the fourth in the East, and the fifth in the middest of them, which went compassing the other by the space of one houre.

oger Dorset } Anno. 3
mes Barrimew } Bayliffes.

This yeare was horrible thunders & lightninges, haile, and great floudes. 1202
Raynolphe Erle of Chester, left his wife named Constance, and wedded one Clemens.

Walter fitz Alis. } Anno 4.
Symon de Aldermanbury } Bayliffes.

Philip of Fraunce, inuaded Normandie, and tooke dyuers Castels and Townes, which he gaue to Arthur, Nephew to kyng John, and Duke of Britayne. But shortly after, the same Arthur with many noble men, were taken by Kyng John, and ledde to Roan, the whiche Arthur was there shortlye 1203 dispatched, fewe men can tell howe.

[illegible] in the citie chosen. This yere were chosen 35. of the most substantiall and wysest men of the citie of London, to maintaine and keepe the assises of the same, of the whiche yearely the Bayliffes were chosen, and as of the Mayor and Shiriffes were taken.

Norman Blondell } Anno. 4.
John de Ely. } Bayliffes.

[illegible] Tempests in England. This yeare fell exceading lightning, thunders, stormes of wynde & rayne, with haile of the bignes of hennes egges, which perished fruite and corne, houses and young cattel. Also spirites wer sene in the aire, in likenes of foules, bearing fire in their billes, which fire fel on diuers houses. Philip of Fraunce made warre upon the Duchie of Normandye, till at the last he subdued the same to his dominion, with the prouinces of Guyen, Poyters and Britaine, whiche before pertayned to the crowne of England.

Walter Browne } Anno 5.
William Chamberlaine } Bayliffes.

1204 King John maried his bastard daughter to Lewlyn Prince of Wales, and gaue with her the castle and Lordship of Kyngsmore, beynge in the Marches of Southwales.

Thomas

Thomas Hauerill } Anno. 6
Hamond Bronde } Bayliffes.

IN the moneth of Januarye, began a great frost, which cōtinued till March so that the groundes could not be tylde, wherof it came to passe that in Sommer followynge, a quarter of Wheate was solde for xiiii. shillinges. 1205

John Walgraue } Anno. 7
Richard de Winchester. } Bayliffes.

King John with a great army arryued at Rochell, subdued a great part of ỳ countrey, and came at the last to the noble castle Mount Albon, which he wan. 1206

John Hollande } Anno. 8.
Edmond fitz Gerrard } Bayliffes.

King John toke the xiii. part of all the moueable & unmoueable goodes, both of Laye and Religious, throughout all Englande. Beinge muche strife about the election of an archebyshop of Caunterbury, the Monkes of Caunterburye chose Stephen Laughton. Who after was consecrated at Rome by the Pope. This beinge done, the Pope sente letters to king John, exhorting hym humbly and deuoutly to receyue Stephen Langhron, to be Archebyshop, beyng therunto canonically elected: the rather because he was an Englysheman borne, and a doctor 1207

of De-of Deuinitie. &c. When kynge John had receyued these letters, he was greatly offended at the promoting of the sayd Stephen Langhton. And foorthwith sent men in armour to expell the Monkes of Caunterbury out of the realme, the goodes and landes of their church were confiscate. Then Kynge John sent threatenynge letters to the Pope, whereunto the Pope sent a large aunswere.

Roger Winchester } Anno. 9.
Edmond Hardell } Bayliffes.

1208 The morrowe after Candelmas day, there was an horrible Eclipse of the Moone, first like bloud, and the of most ill fauoured colours. Certayne bishops in Englande, by the Popes commaundement, executed the interdictio upon the whole Realme, and they ceased throughout al England, from ministring of ecclesiastical sacraments, sauing only confession and the sacrament, to them that were in perill of death, & Baptisme of children. The king set all the bishopriks and abbayes, in the custody of lay men, and commaunded all Ecclesiasticall reuenues to be confiscate.

England interdited.

First Mayor of London. This yeare was graunted to the citizens of London, by the kinges letters patentes,

kentes, that they should yearely chose themselues a Maior, & two Sheriffes, the Sheriffes do enter on ẏ. xxviii daye of September: the Mayor doth entre on xxviii. of Octob next folowing. An. 10

Peter Duke, Thomas Neale 28. of Septeb. Sherifes.

Henry fitz Alwyne. The. 28. of October. Mayor.

1209

By the procurement of Stephen Langhtõ archbishop of Caunterbury, licence was graunted to the conuentuall churches in Englande, to celebrate deuine seruice ones in a weake.

The Exchequer was remoued to Northampton, for displeasure the king had taken with the Lõdoners. King John gathered a great army & went towardes Scotland. The king of Scottes fearing his fury, came to him & treated a peace, in the whiche he gaue 11000. markes of siluer, & deliuered his two daughters in a pledge. After this he toke homage of all free holders in England, and did sweare all men to his allegiaunce, from xii yeare olde vp wardes. This yeare was the archis of Londõ bridge begon to be builded of stone, by ẏ worthy marchauntes, Serle Mercer, & William Almã, & Bennit Bote wrigth. Also about ẏ same time, began the reparation of the priory of S. Mary ouery in Southwarke.

The Exchequer remoued.

Peace with Scottes.

Lõdõ bridge builded of stone.

Sherifes. Peter le Iosue, William Blund. 28. Septẽb.
Mayor. Henry fitz Alwyne. The. 28. of October.
1210 The king commaunded all the Jewes both men and women, to be imprisoned, because he woulde haue all their money, amongest whome there was one whiche woulde not raunsome himself. Wherfore the kyng commaunded to pull out euery daye one of his teethe, vntyll he dyd paye. 10000. markes of syluer, and when by the space of seuen dayes, they had pulled out seuen of his great teeth, the Jewe payde the foresayde summe, to the ende they should pull out no more.

Jewes raunsomed.

Irelande subdued. The kyng subdued Irelande, caused the lawes of Englande to be executed there, and mony to be coyned accordyng to the wayte of the Englishe mony. When he came to London, he caused a conuocation to be had, whereunto came the Abbottes, Priors, Templers, Hospitalers &c. All whiche he compelled to paye such a raunsome, that the summe of the mony came to 100000. pounde sterling, and also the whyte Monkes were constrained to 40000. pounde,

A mynte in Irelande.

Anno. 12

Sherifes. Adam Whetley, Stephen le grase. 28. Sep.
Mayor. Henry fitz Alwyne. The. 28. of October.
1211 The kinge went into Wales, with great force subdued all the princes & nobles,

lles, toke xxviii. pledges for their sub
ion, and then returned, whē he came
Northampton, there met him messen-
s from the Pope, Pandolfe, and Durā-
which came to make an unitie be-
ixt the king, and the bishop of Caun-
bury, with the Monkes which were
nished out of England, the king wil-
gly graunted their retourne to their
sessions, but would not make amen-
for their losse, nor restore their goo-
which he had confiscated, whereu-
the Popes Ambassadours went a-
ne into Fraunce and made no ende.
er this, ye king toke of every knighte
ich was not with him in his army in
les, twoo markes of silver of every
ld. Anno. 13.

Pādolfe and Durande.

A gret take

n fitz Pet. Iohn Garlond. 28. Septemb. Sherifes.
ry fitz Alwyn, The 28. of October. Mayor.

1212

e Welchemen with great force toke
ivers castels of ye king of Englād,
of the heades of all the souldiours
found, burned many townes, and
h a great spoyle returned. The king
ered an innumerable army, utterly
estroy all the coastes of Wales, and
en he came to Notingham, he caused y^e
iii. young men who he had taken for
ges of the Welche men to be hāged.

The Welshmen invaded England.

xxviii. yong men hanged

An the-

Pierce of Pomfret.

An Heremite in Yorkeshire, nam Peter, prophecied openly of king Joh and sid vpon the Ascention day next c ming, there should be no king, but crowne should be transposed to an oth this Peter was cast in prison.

Southwarke and London bridge on fyre.

The tenth day of Iulij at night, a m uellous & terrible chaunce happened, the citie of London vpon the south si the ryuer of Thames with ÿ church our lady in Southwarke being on fi and an exceading great multitude of p ple passing the bridge, some to quenc & some to gase, beholde sodainly ÿ no part, by the blowing of the south wyn was also set on fyre, & the people wh were euen nowe passing the bridge, p ceiuing the same would haue retourn were stopped by fire, & it came to pass that as they staied or protracted time, other end of the bridge also, namely t South end was fired, so the people thro ging themselues betwixt the two fires, did nothing els expect or looke for, th death. Then came there to succour & a thē many ships, into the which, ÿ mult tude so vnaduisedly pressed ÿ the shipp being drowned, they also perished. Thu the people greuously perishing, it wa said through the fire & the ship wrake t

them

were destroied about 3000. persons.

Anno. 14.

Rodolphe Eilād, Cōstantine Iosue. 2. Sherifes. Hery fitz Alwyne. The. 28. of October. Mayor. Pandolphe the legate, came to ȳ king ad- 1213 monishing him to receiue Stephē Langh. Pandolphe to his sea of Canterb. & the monkes Legate. to their abbey, ȳ king calling to mind manifold dangers ȳ he was in, both his own realme & also in Normādy, he promise by othe to be obedient to ȳ court of Rome. Al things being prepa- The kinges red, K. Iohn & Pandolphe, with ȳ nobles othe. ȳ realme, came together at Douer vpō Ascention euen, where ȳ king according sentēce was geuē at Rome, did resigne crown with ȳ realmes of Englād & Irland, into the Popes hands. When ȳ The kyng Ascention daye was past, Peter of Pom- resigned his fret and his sonne were hanged vppon crowne. gibbet. Stephen Langhton archbishoppe Peter hāged Canterb. & al the other ȳ were ban- S. Langhton ished, arriued at Douer, & went to Winche- restored ster to the king, who met thē in ȳ waye, and when he sawe the archbishop he fell flat vpon the earth before their feete, the teares gusshing out, he beseched them to take pitie of hym and of the Realme of England, the archbishop & the byshops seeing this great humilitie of the kyng,

with

with teares toke him vp frō the groū & brought him into ẏ cathedral churc with the Psalme of Miserere, & absol

The king absolued.

him. This yere Richard prior of Bermōdsey, did builde the hospital of Conuē in Southwarcke, in ẏ honor of S. Thoma

Ditche of London.

And this yere was begon the ditch wi out the walles of London, of 200. fo. brode. Adno. 15.

Sherifes. Martin fitz Alis, Peter Bate. 28. Septem

Mayor. Roger fitz Alwyne The. 28. of October.

1214 Pope Innocentius sent Nicolas bishop Tusculane, to release the interdiction,

Interdiction released.

which had continued fiue yeares, th moneths, and fiftene dayes. Anno. 16.

Sherifes. Salomon Basing, Hugh Basing. 28. Septe

Mayor. Saerle Mercer. The. 28. of October.

1215 The king met with the Barones in a medow, betwixt Stanes and Wynso, where he graunted the liberties of england The Charter wherof is dated, Geuen by our hand in Runingmede, betwin Stanes and Windsor, the. xvi. day of Jun Anno of our raigne 16. vnto the which all the whole realme were sworne.

Magna carta.

The king sent Pandolphe the Legate with other to Rome, to the ende that by the Apostolike authoritie, they migh make frustrate the purpose of the Barones, [illegible] sent vnto ẏ realmes beyond the sea next adioyning for the help of warre, promisinge unto them large possessions: Byþ meanes of Pandolphe, the Pope bothe disanulled the forsaide Charter and libertyes graunted, & also excommunicated the Barons. By the other messengers were procured a great nomber of men of warre, which landing at Douer, the Kinge forthwith besieged the Castell of Rochester and toke it.

The Char- disanulled.

The barons excommu- nicated.

Anno.17.

John Trauers. Andrew Newlande.28. Sep. William Hardel. The 28.of October

Sheriffes. Maior. 1216.

The Kinge take all þ Castels & strõg holds from the Barons, and dispo- sed their goodes at his pleasure. And þ Pope excommunicated theym by theyr peculiar names, at lengthe the Barons concluded to erect Lodowike þ Frenche kings sonne, and to make him kinge ouer them. About this busines they sente S. Earle of Winchester and other, ear- nestly requyringe Philip of Fraunce, to send his sonne Lodowike, which thinge the Frenche King refused to do, till the Barons had sent him xxiiii. pledges of the best and noblest of the Realme. Thē Lodowike sent ayde to the Barons.

The Barons send for Lo- dowike.

Ayde sent to the Ba- rons.

Walo who was sente from the Pope into Fraunce, to forbid the going of Lo- dowike

wike into England. But his per[...] ons nothinge preuaylinge, hee charged them vppon paine of excommunicatiō. This notwithstanding Lodowike, with a great armye arriued in ẏ Ile of Tenet. King John beeing then at Douer fled to Gilford, & so to Winchester. Lodowike subdued the whole countrye of Kente, saue the Castle of Douer, and then hee went to London, where hee was of the Barons ioyfully receiued.

Lodowike arriueth in England.

Kinge John with greate force passed through Northfolke and Suffolke, till he came at Linne, where hee was receyued with great ioye, and taking his iorneye Northwarde, he dyed of the Flixe at Newarke, and was boweled at Croxton, and buryed at Worcester. He founded Bewley, Ferendon, & Halis in Shropshyre. He builded Godstowe, and began the Chappel of Knatisboroughe. He deceased in the yere of our Lord 1216, the 19. of October, when he had raigned 17 yeares, 6. monethes and od dayes.

The Kinge dyeth.

Bewley. Ferendon. Hales. Goddow. Knarisburgh.

Henry

HENRY THE thirde.

HENRY the sonne of Iohn of the age of ix. yeres, began his reigne the 19. day of October, in the yeare of our Lord 1216. On Simon & Iudes day he was crowned at Gloucester, by Peter bishoppe of Winchester, in presence of Wallo the Legate. he remayned in the custody of W. Earle of Pembroke, highe Marshal. Anno reg. 1

...et Seintauer. W. Blanttiners. 28. of Sep. Sheriffes.
...nes Alderman. The 28. of October. Mayor.

The Barons who toke part with Lodowike, were ouerthrowen at Lincolne, and Lodowike being in London, concluded a peace, for the performance whereof othe being taken, he toke of the Citizens 5000. pounde, and departed to Fraunce. 1217. The barons ouerthrowen. Anno. 2.

...o. Bokerel. Raphe Ellonde. 28. of Sep. Sheriffes
...le Mercer. The 28. of October. Mayor.

Ranulphe Earle of Chester, Saer Erle of Winchester, William Earle of Arundel, with the Barons, Robert fitz Walter 1218.

John Constable of Chester, and William Harcourt with a great traine, toke theyr iourneye towardes Hierusalem.

Anno. 3.

Sherifes. John Vyell. John le Spycer. 28, of Sep.

Mayor. Serle mercer. The 28, of October.

1219. VVIlliam Earle Marshal gouernor of the Kinges person, and of the whole Realme dyed, and was honourable buryed at London in the newe Temple. After whose death the king remained in the gouernment of Peter bishop of Winchester. Anno. 4.

Sherifes. Richard Wimbledon. I. Vieil. 28, of Sep.

Mayor. Serle Mercer. The 28, of October.

1220. KInge Henry was crowned againe at Westminster, by Stephen Archbishop of Canterburye. Anno. 5.

Sherifes. Richard Renger John Viel. 28. of Sep.

Mayor. Serle Mercer The 28. of October.

1221. KInge Henry subdued the Welshemen whiche rebelled, and then the noble men graunted him twoe markes of silver of euery hyde of lande. William de Albeneto Earle of Arundell died, & was buryed at Wimondham a Priorie, whiche he had founded.

Straungers banished. A Proclamation made that al straungers should auoide the Realme, excepte suche as came with marchandise, and to make

make sale of them vnder the kings safe conduct.

Ranulphe, the thirde of yͤ name Earle of Chester, came out of the holy lande, & began to build the Castels of Chartley, and of Beston, and yͤ abbey of Delacresse. Chartley, Beston and Delacresse.

Anno 6.

Richard Renger. Tho. Lambert. 28. of Sep. Sherifes.
Serle Mercer. the 28. of October. Maior.

1222.

There was taken a man whiche had in his syde, hands & feete, woundes, as of the Crosse, counterfaytinge himselfe to be Christe. There was also another taken that was both man and woman, that is to say an Hermofrodite, disguised by the same subteltie that the other was, they were punished together in the counsel holden by Stephen Archebishop of Canterburye, and beinge conuicted and openly confessing their faulte, was punished by the Censure of the Churche. A counterfaite Christ.

The Citizens of London falling out with the bayliue of Westminster and the men of the subberbes at a game of Defence, and wrastlinge, made a great tumulte agaynst the Abbot of Westminster, for the whiche their Captaine, named Constantine Alophe, with his cosine, and one Galfride were hanged, & Fray at the wrestling.

 then

Then the Justicers entred ẏ Cittye with a great armye of men, and caused to bee taken and put in prison, so many as hee vnderstoode to be culpable, whose feete and handes he caused to be cut of. &c.

Anno. 7.

Sherifes. Richard Renger Tho. Lambert. 28. of Sep

Mayor. Serle Mercer. The 28 of October.

1223. IOhn Kinge of Hierusalem, a maister of the brethrene of Hierusalem, came into Englād and required ayde to win again Hierusalem, but he returned with small comforte.

Anno. 8.

Sherifes. Iohn Trauers. Andrew Bokerel. 28. of Sep.

Mayor. Richard Renger. The 28 of October.

1224. THis yere the friers Minors first arriued at Douer, 9. in nomber, 5. of them remayned at Canterburye, and did there builde the first couente of Friers Minors that euer was in Englande, the other 4. came to London, and hyred an house in Cornehill, of Iohn Trauers, frō thence they were by the Cittizens remoued to a place in S. Nicholas shambles, which Iohn Iwin appropriated vnto the commonaltye of the Cittye, to the vse of the Friers, the whole Churche was at that time builded by diuers of ẏ Cittizens.

Gray Friers in London.

Anno. 9.

hn Trauers. Andrew Bokerel. 28. of Sep. Sherifes.
ichard Renger. The 28. of October. Mayor.
T He xv. part of all the mouable goo- 1225.
des in the Realme, as well of the
lergye as of the Leity, was graunted
the Kinge, vppon condition that hee
ould graunt the liberties, which they
long time had sued for. This yeare
e King graunted to the commonaltye
the City of London, that they might
ue a common seale. An. 10.

Common seale graunted to the Cittye of London.

ger Duke. Martin fitz Willia. 28. of Sep Sherifes.
chard Renger. The 28. of October. Mayor.
This yeare was graunted to the She- 1226.
rifes of London, the Sherifewike of
iddlesex, for the summe of 300. pound
yeare. It was also graunted to the
ittye free warren, that is, free liberty
hunte a certaine circuite aboute the
ittye: And also that the Cittizens of
ndon should passe tolle free through
t all England, and that all weres in
e Thames should be plucked vp and
stroyed for euer.

Citizens of London toll free.

Anno. 11.

ger Duke. Martin fitz William. 28. Sep. Sherifes.
chard Renger. The 28. of October. Mayor.
The King made al the Charters of the 1227.
liberties of ỹ Realme, & the Forest

to be frustrate, alleging that they were graunted while he was in Wardshipp, thus it followed, that who woulde enioye the libertyes afore graunted, must renue theyr Charters of the Kings new seale, with such a price as the Iustices awarded them. Anno. 12.

Sherifes. Stephen Bockerel. H Cobham. 28. Sep.

Mayor. Roger Duke, The 28. of October.

1228. The king corrected the measures and waightes, and ordayned punishmēt for the transgressors thereof.

Anno. 13.

Sherifes. Stephen Bockerel. H Cobham. 28. of Sep.

Mayor. Roger Duke. The 28. of October.

1229. Robert Kinghā bishop of Salisbury, by the kinges helpe prosecuted the building of the newe Church at Salisburye, which his predecessor Richarde did translate. This yere was ordained by the Maior and rulers of the City of London, that no Shyriffe of that City, shoulde continue longer in office then one yeare. Anno. 14.

Sherifes. W. Winchester Robert Fitz Iohn. 28. Sep.

Meyor. Roger Duke. The 28. of October.

1230. Vpon the day of S. Paules conuersion, when Roger Niger bishop of London, was at Masse at the highe Alter in the Cathedral Churche of Saint

Paule

Paule, a great multitude of people being there, sodainlye the weather waxed darke, and an horrible thonder clappe lighted on the Churche, that the same was shaken as it would haue fallen, also out of a darke cloud came such lightening, that al the Church seemed to bee on fire with such a stenche, that al men thought they should haue dyed. Thousandes of men and wemen ranne out of the Church, and being astonied, fel vpon the ground voyde of al vnderstandinge, none of al the multitude taried, saue onlye the bishop and one Deacon, which stoode still at the highe Alter, abyding after the will of God. Darkenes and stenche in S. Paules Churche.

Anno. 15.

Ri. fitz Walter. Iohn of Woborne. 28. Sep. Sherifes.
Roger Duke. The 28. of October. Mayor.

The king gaue his sister Elianor Countesse of Glocester, to William Marshall Earle of Pembroke and the bridal beinge scantlye finished, the saide Earle William dyed, and was buried in the new Temple at London, by his father. 1231.

Anno. 16

Michel of Elena. Walter de buffele. 28. S. Sherifes.
Andrew Bokerel Peperar. 28. of October. Mayor.

The morrow after S. Martins day, began thonders very horrible, which 1232.

lasted

lasted xv. dayes, and there followed an earthquake at Huntington. Anno.17.

Sherifes. Henry of Edmonto. Gerard Bat. 28. of Sep.
Mayor. Andrewe Bokerel Peperer. 28. of October.

1233. The seuenth of April, about one of ÿ clocke of the daye, ther appeared 4. Sunnes besides the naturall Sunne, of a read colour, and a great Circle of Christall colour.

Likenes of fiue sunnes.

Robert and Roger Bacō friers.

The King being at Oxeforde, Robert Bacon, openlye preached against Peter bishop of Winchester, for that he euillye counsayled ÿ king to spoile his Realme with Pictauians. And also Roger Bacon both earnestly and pithely perswaded ÿ king to leaue the counsaile of the sayd Peter.

House of conuertes.

The house of conuertes, where now the Rols is kepte in Chauncerye lane, was builded by K. Henry. He also builded the Hospitall of S. Iohn without the East gate of Oxeforde, for sicke folke and strangers, to be releeued & kept in. Anno.18.

Hospital at Oxford.

Sherifes. Simon fitz Marie. Roger Blunt 28. of S
Mayor. Andrew Bokerel Peperar. The 28. of

1234. Richarde Earle Marshall, and Le Prince of Northwales, wyth a g force inuaded the kinges landes, & stroyed the same with fyre and sw ord from the coastes of Wales, vnto Salis

which towne also they set on fyre. | Salisburye brent.
us yere was great honger, dearth, | Famine and
estilence, so that poore muste dyed | pestilence.
ant of vituals, and the richemen
strike with couetousnes, that they
de not releue theym. Amongest
is to be noted Walter Greye Arch- | A couetous
p of Yorke, whose corne beinge b. | bishop.
olde, (doubting the same to be de-
d by vermine) commaunded to de-
it to the husbandmen that dwelte
manors, vppon condition to pay
th newe corne after harueste, and
de giue none to ye poore for Gods
And it fortuned that when menne
to a great stacke of Corne, night to
oune of Ripon, belonging to ye said
, there appeared in the sheues all
he heads of wormes, serpentes & | Anotbie ex
, and a voice was heard out of ye | ample.
mow, saying: Laye no handes on
ne, for both the Archbishop, and
t he hath is ye deuils. To be short
ayliffes was forced to builde an
wall rounde about the corne, than
t on fyre. Anno. 19.
Ashwe. Iohn Norman. 28. of Sept. | Sherifes.
w Bokerel Peperar. 28. of October. | Maior.
n Iewes which at Norwiche had | 1235.
n a boy, cyrcumcised him, minding

of

at Easter to haue crucifyed hym.

S. Mary Spitale. Walter Brune Citizen of London, and Rosia his wyfe founded the Hospitall of our Ladye in the Subberbes of London withoute Bishoppes gate, whyche now is called S. Mary Spittle.

Anno 20.

Sherifes. Gerard Bat. Robert Herdel. 28. Septēber.

Mayor. Andrew Bokerel Peperar. 28. of October.

1236. The riuer of Thames came ouer the bankes, so that men did row in wheris, in the middest of the hall at Westminster, and they roode on horsbacke to their Chambers.

Statute of Merton. K. Henry held his Parliamēt at Marton. K. Henry maryed Elianor doughter of Raimond Earle of Prouince. This Elianor afterwarde became the first founder of the Hospital of S. Katherins, by y Tower of Lōdon. S. Katherins by the tower. In the North parties of Englande, appeared a battaile of armed men of horsebacke, they seemed to come out of the earth, and to be swallowed againe into the same. Straunge appearances.

Anno. 21.

Sherifes Henry Cobham. Iordā of Couētre. 28. Se.

Mayor, Andrew Bokerel Peperar, 28. of Octobe

1237. OCtobon a Cardenal, came into England as Legate from y Pope. This yeare passed on Normye, and trouble-

some

me in the weather, very vnhealthful, that no man coulde remember ye euer many folkes were sicke of the ague.

Anno. 22.

hn Tolason. Geruas the Cordwener. 28. S Sherifes.
ndrewe Bokerel Peperer. 28 of October Mayor.
Crobon being lodged in the Abbey of Osney, the Scolers of Oxford see- nge occasion against his seruauntes, we his maister Cooke, who was the gates brother, whereat the Legat be- g amased, gate him into a steple of the hurch, and there hid him till ye kings ficers comming from Abingdon, con- ed him to Walingford, where he ac- ed the misdoers. 1238.

The Legate put to his shiftes.

A learned souldiour fayning himselfe ad, enterprised to haue slaine ye kinge his Chamber at Wodstocke: but hee as taken, and after longe impreson- ent, plucked in peeces with horses at uentrie.

K. Henry like to haue ben murde- red.

Anno. 23.

hn Gondres. Iohn of Wilhale. 28. Sep. Sherifes
charde Renger. The 28. of October. Mayor.
The King gaue the Erledome of Lei- cester vnto Simon de Montifortie. 1239.

he Tower of London was fortified. hich the Citizens feared, least it were ne for their detriment.

The tower of London repayred.

Anno. 24.

Raymond

Sherifes Raymōd Bongye. Raphe Ashwye. 28. Sep.
Mayor. William Ioyner. The 28. of October.

1240. A Stone gate which the king had builded harde by the tower of London, fel downe, which the kinge commaunded to be built vp againe.

Buildinge neare the tower of London fell downe.

Monstrous fishes. Many gret fishes came a shore, wher of xi. were sea bulles, and one of huge bignes, passed throughe the Arches o London bridge vnhurt, till she came farre as the kinges house at Mortlake, where at length she was killed.

First Aldermen in London. This yeare were Aldermen first chosen in London, which then had the rule of the wardes of the Cittye, but were euery yeare changed. Anno. 25.

Sherifes. Iohn Gysors. Michael Tonye. 28. of Sep.
Mayor. Richarde Fat. The 28. of October.

1241. The Iewes were constrayned to pay 20000. markes at two termes in the yere, or els to be banished or put in perpetual prison.

Bulwarkes about the tower againe fel downe. This yeare againe, the walles and Bulwarkes that were newly builded about the Tower (in the building wherof the king had bestowed more then xii. thousand markes) were vnrecouerable throwen downe, as it were with an earthquake.

Anno. 26.

Iohn

ohn Viell. Thomas Duresme. 28. of Sep. Sherifes.
emond Bongye. The 28, of October. Meyor.

Kyng Henry with a great army sayled 1242.
ouer into Normandye, purposinge to recouer Poyters, Guines, and other countries, but after manye bickeringes to the losse of Englishmen, he treated a peace.

Anno. 27.

n fitz Iohn. Raphe Ashwye. 28. of Sep. Sherifes.
emond Bongey. The 28. of October. Mayor.

The Thames ouerflowed the bankes 1243.
toward Lambeth, and drowned houses and feldes, the space of vi. myles, & in the greate hall at Westminster, men toke their horsebacke. Anno. 28.

Great flodes.

Hughe Blunt. Adam Basinge. 28. of Sep. Sherifes.
Raphe Ashwye Peperar. The 28 of Octob. Mayor.

Griffin the eldest son of Leolin Prince 1244.
of Northwales, whiche was kepte prisoner in the Tower of London, deuised subtilly how to escape the warde he was in, wherfore one night hauing deceaued the watch, made of the hanginges, sheetes, towels and tableclothes, a long line, & put himselfe plum downeward from the top of the tower, & as he was slyding a good pace, with weight of his body, the rope brake, and he fell & brake his necke. Richard Earle of Cornewal, the kings brother, founded Hayles in the

The miserable death of Griffin Prince of Northwales.

Countye

County of Gloucester. Anno 29.

Sherifes. Ralphe Foster. Nicholas Bat. 28. of Sep.

Mayor. Michael Toney. The 28. of October.

1245. The kinge to enlarge the Courche of Saint Peter in Westminster, pulled downe the olde walles and steeple, and caused them to be made more comlye.

S. Peters at Westminster.

Anno 30.

Sherifes. Robert of Cornhil Adā of Bentley. 28. Se.

Mayor. Iohn Gisors Peperer. The 28. of October.

1246. In the Dioces of Lincolne, there was a woman, whiche did beare children her selfe, did also get another gentlewoman with childe, and begat thre sonnes of her, one after another, or euer it was knowen. Anno. 31.

One bodye man and woman mōstrous.

Sherifes. Simō fitz megre. Laurence Frewike. 28. S.

Mayor. Iohn Gisors Peperar. The 28. of October.

1247. A Great earthquake uppon S. Valentines euē, in many places of Englād, especiallye at London about the ban of the Thames. Anno. 32.

An earthquake.

Sherifes. Iohn Viel. Nicholas Bat. 28. of Septem

Mayor. Peter fitz alline. The 28. of October.

1248. The towne of Newcastel uppon T was burned, the bridge and al, w a greuous & unquenchable fyre. T yeare was a straunge earthquake, so the toppes of houses were throw downe and stoones pluckte from t pla

Newcastell burned.

Earthquake

[p]laces, and walles did cleaue the heads [o]f chimneis and towers were shaken, [b]ut the bodies and foundations did not [s]tir, which is contrarye to the nature of [a]n Earthquake.

Anno. 33.

Nico. fitz Iosey. Gef. of Winchester. 28. Se. — Sherifes.

Michael Tonnye. The 28. of October. — Mayor.

The kinge made fayres at Westminster, to last xv. dayes, and commaunded straightlye that all trade of occupying and marchandise, should cease in ye Citye, the space of those xv. dayes. — 1249. A mart at Westminster.

Anno. 34.

Rich. Hardel. Iohn Thollason. 28. of Sep. — Sherifes.

Roger fitz Roger. The 28. of October. — Mayor.

The sea passed his accustomed bounes, flowing twyse withoute ebbes, and made so horrible noise, that it was hard a great way into the lande. Besydes this in a darke nighte, the sea seemed to be a light fyre, and the waues to fight one with another. At Winchelsey, beside Cotages for salt, and fisher mens houses, bridges and milles, aboue three hundreth houses in that towne, wyth certain Churches: through the violente rising of the sea, were drowned. — 1250. Three hundreth houses drowned in Winchelcye.

On S. Lucis day, there happened a great earthquake at S. Albons. — Earthquake

Anno. 35.

Sherifes. Humfrey Baas, wil. fitz Richard. 28. of Sep
Mayor. Iohn Norman. The 28. of October.

1251. Maior of London sworn in the Eschequer.

This yere was graunted by the King, that where before this time the Citizens of London did present their Mayor before the King wheresoever he were and so to be admitted, nowe he shoulde come only before the Barons of the Escheker, and they should admit him, and giue him his oth. Anno. 36.

Sherifes. Laurēce Frowike. Nicholas Bat. 28. of Sep.
Mayor. Adam Basinge. The 28 of October.

1252. Shepherds assembled.

The sheepheardes of Fraunce and England, toke their iourney towardes ye holy land, to the nōber of 30000 but their nōber vanished in short time. Anno. 37.

Sherifes. William Durham Tho. of Winborn. 28. Se
Mayor. Thomas Tolason. The 28. of October.

1253. Liberties of London seised.

The liberties of London was seysed by the meane of Richarde Earle of Cornewall, whoe charged the Maior ye he looked not to the Bakers for theyr syses of breade, so that ye Citty was forst to please the Earle with 600. markes. Anno. 38.

Sherifes. Iohn Northāpton. Ri. Pickard. 28. of Sep.
Mayor. Richard Hardel Draper. The 28. of Octob.

1254. Roberte Grostede bishop of Lincol in Greeke, Latine, and manye other languis

languages, did by an Epistle reprous. Edward
Pope Innocentius. Anno,39. Grostede.

Raphe Ashewie. Robert of Linco. 28. Sep. Sherifes.
Rich. Hardel draper. The 28. of October. Maior.

This yere were brought 142. Jewes 1255.
from Lincolne, whiche were accused Jewes exe-
of the crucifying of a childe, they were cuted.
sente to the Tower of London, xviii. of
them were hāged, and the other remained long in prison. Anno. 40.

Stephen Do. Henry walmonde. 28. of Sep. Sherifes
Rich. Hardel Draper The 28. of October. Mayor.

The Maior of Londō and diuers Al- 1256.
dermen and Shireffes, were depri- The maior
ued of their offices, and the gouernāce of London
of the Cittye committed to other. depriued.

Anno. 41.

Michael Bokerel. Iohn the minor, 28. Sep. Sherifes.
Rich. Hardel draper. The 28. of October. Mayor.

Hughe Bygot Justice, & Roger Turke- 1257.
leye, kept their courts in the Guild
hall of London, and punished the Bakers vpon the Tombrel. They did manye other thinges against the Lawes of
the Cittye. Anno. 42.

Rich. Owel, William Ashewye. 28. of Sep. Sherifes.
Rich. Hardel draper. The 28. of October. Maior.

For so muche as the king had oftenti- 1258.
mes promised the restitution of certaine auncient lawes, but neuer per-

foucined the same, the Lords held a Parliament at Oxeforde, where was chosen xii. Peeres, which had authoritie to correct the breakers of those ordinaunces, the king, his brethern, the Barons and noble men, takinge their othe to see the same obserued.

Twelue peeres in England.

A Jewe at Teukesburye fel into a priuye vpon the Saterday, and woulde not for reuerence of his Sabboth daye bee plucked out, wherfore Richard of Clare Earle of Gloncester, kept him there till mondaye, at which season he was foūde dead. Anno.43.

Iewe drowned in a priuye.

Sherifes. Tho.fitz Richard.Robert Cateloger.28.S.

Mayor. Richard Hardel Draper. 28 of October.

1259. The king commaunded the Mayre, ỹ he shoulde cause to be sworne before his Aldermē, euery stripling of xii.yeares of age and vpward, to be true to the king, and his heyres kings of Englād: and that the gates of the Cittye shoul be kept with harnessed mē.

Othe to the king.

Anno.44.

Sherifes. Iohn Adrian.Robert Cornehil.28,of Sep

Mayor, Iohn Gisors. The 28.of October.

1260. Reignolde de mount Earle of Somerset and Lord of Donstere, founded Newham. Anno.45.

Newham.

A

dam Browning. Henry Couētrie. 28. Sep. Sherifes.
William fitz Richard. The 28. of October. Mayor.

Kinge Henry published at Paules Crosse, the Popes absolutiō for him and al his that were sworne to maintayne the articles made in the Parliament at Oxeforde. Anno. 46. 1261. K. Henrye absolued of his othe

ohn Northāptō. Rich. Pickard. 28. of Sep. Sherifes.
William fitz Richard. The 28. of October, Mayor.

The Barons robbed alliauntes, and suche as they knewe to be againste their purpose: especially they slewe the Iewes in all places. Anno. 47. 1262. The Barons iarn out.

ohn Tayler. Richarde Walbroke. 28. Sep. Sherifes.
Thomas fitz Thomas. The 28. of October. Meyor.

There was slaine at London to the nomber of 700. Iewes, the rest were spoyled and their sinagoge defaced, because they would haue forced a Christian to paye more then twoe pence for the vsury of xx. shillinges a weeke. 1263. Iewes slaine

Northampton was taken, and the people slaine, because they had prepared wyld fyre to borne the Citty of Lōdon. Northampton spoiled.

The towne of Glouceſter wyth the Castell, was oftentymes taken by the Barons, and againe by the king, wherby they were both (as it were) vtterlye spoyled. The Cittizens of London forsyfyed the Cittye, with yron chaynes Glouceſter spoiled.

drawen ouerthwart their streates.

Anno. 48.

Sherifes. Rob. monpiled. Osbert of suffolk. 28. Sep.
Mayor. Tho. fitz Thomas. The 28. of October.

1264. ON S Pancras daye, was a battaile at Lewes, betwene king Henry and the Barons, in whiche battaile the kinge with his sonne Edwarde, and Richarde Earle of Cornewall, with manye other Lordes were taken by Simon of Mounteforde, Earle of Leicester & the Barons.

Battaile at Lewes.
The kinge, his sonne, and his brother taken prisoners.

Anno. 49.

Sherifes. Gregory Rokesley, Tho. of Lafford. 28 S.
Mayor. Tho fitz Thomas. The 28 of October.

1265. PRince Edward being now at liberty, allied him with the Earle of Glo ster, gatheringe to him a great power warred so freshly vpon Simon of Leice ster, that at the end he with many oth er his nobles, were slaine in the battel at Euisham in Worcestershyre. The sa yere was holden a Parliament at Win chester. wher at the Statutes made fore at Oxeforde, were disanulled an abrogate.

The battell of Euisham.

London was in gret daunger to ha beene destroyed by the King, for disple sure that hee had conceyued againste it because of the forenamed commotion.

Londō like to haue ben spoiled.

The king gaue vnto Prince Edward the Maior and foure Aldermē, and manye other were committed to seuerall prisons. An. 50.

Edward Blount, Peter Aunger. 28. of Sep. Sheriffes,

Thomas fitz Thomas, the 28. of October Meyor.

1266.

The king gaue diuers Citizens of London to his seruauntes.

The Kinge gaue vnto diuers of his housholde seruantes, vpon 60. housholds and houses within the Cittye, so that the owners were compelled to agre and redeeme their houses & housholde, with all their goodes or els to auoide. And thenne hee made Custos or Gardein of the Cittye, sir Othon Constable of the Tower. After this the king toke pledges of the beste mens sonnes of the Cittye, that his peace should be surelye kept in ye same. Lastly it was agreed for xx.M. markes to be payd by the Cittye of al trāsgressors and offences by them done: certaine persons excepted. Which the king had giuen his sonne.

Battaile at Chesterfield.

The xv. day of May, was the battaile of Chesterfielde against them that were disherited, where manye of them were slaine. The olde liberties of London were confirmed by a Parliamente at Northampton. Where also manye noble men that had taken parte with the Barons, were disherited.

Parliament at Northampton.

Waightes and measures. This yeare was made the statute of waightes and measure, that is to saye, that two and thirty graynes of wheate drye and rounde, and taken in the middest of the eare, shoulde way a sterlinge peny, and that xx. of those pence should make an ounce, and xii. ounces make a pound troy, and eight pound troy shold waye a gallon of wyne, and eighte gallons of wyne should make a bushell of London, which is the eighte parte of a quarter. Also thre barlye cornes drye & rounde, shoulde make an inche, xii. inches a foote, three foote a yarde, fiue yardes and an halfe to a pearch or pole, and xl. pole in length, & foure in bredth to an acre, Anno. 51.

Sherifes. Iohn Hind. Iohn Walrauen. 28. of Septem.

Mayor. 1267. William Richard. The 28. of October.

Gilbert de Clare Earle of Gloucester, for unknowen displeasure, alleinge himselfe with the exiled gentlemē and other nobles of England, rose against ẏ king, and with his armye entred into ẏ Cittye of London, building there bulwarkes, and cast ditches and trenches in diuers places of the Citty & Southwarke. After this the kinge with 109. ensignes, came towardes London, & Stratforde he pitched his tentes, and

The kinge besieged London.

cīti

ded there the space of one moneth, when many entreated to make peace: At last ẏ Erle of Gloucester in peaceable maner, rendred the Citty unto the king againe, and thenne manye that were disherited, were recōciled at the instāce of the Legate & the said Earle. Foure that ware the cognisaunce of the Earle of Darby, were put in sackes and cast into the Thames. Anno, 52.

John Adrian. Lucas Batecort. 28. of Sep. Sherifes.

Alon Suche. The 28. of October. Mayor.

Variaunce fell betweene the fellowships of Goldsmithes and Tailers of London, which caused great cuffling in the Citty, and many men to be slain. For which riot xiii. of the chiefe Captaynes were hanged. 1268. A riot in London.

The disherited gentlemen were reconcile to the kings fauour. And the v. Citizens which had remayned prisoners in the tower of Windsore, which ẏ kinge had geuen to his sonne Edwarde, when they had made their ende, with greate summes of moneye were deliuered. Anno. 53

Walter Haruy.
William Duresme. } Bayliffes.

The riuer of Thames was soe harde frosen from the feast of S. Andrew to Candelmas, 1269.

Candelmas, that mẽ and beastes passed
ouer on foote frõ Lambeth to Westminster. The marchandises was caried frõ
Sandwiche, and other hauẽs vnto Lõdon by lande, and after ŷ thaw ŷ Thames rose soe highe ŷ it drowned manye
sellers, and muche marchandise aboute
Londõ. About this time, Edmonde the
sonne of Richarde kinge of Almaine and
Earle of Cornewal, brother to king Hen
Afferyge. rye founded a Colledge at Afferige.

Anno. 54.

Sherifes. Thomas Basing, Rob. Cornehil. 28. of Sep.
Mayor. Hughe fitz Thomas, The 28. of October.
1270. The nobles of England assembled at
Alan Such London to entreate of diuers mat-
slaine. ters, wherin ther arose discord betwix
John Earle of Warren, and Alane de la
Suche, before the benche, wher the said
Alan Suche was woũded to death. And
this yere the steple of Bowe Church in
Cheape fell downe, & slewe many peo-
ple both men and women.

Anno. 55.

Sherifes. Walter Potter, Philip taylor. 28. of Sept.
Mayor. Iohn Adriã Vintener, The 28. of October.
1271. Richard king of Almaine and Earle of
Cornewal, brother to the king, deceased and was buried at Hayles, an abbey
by him builded. Anno. 56.

Gregory Rokesley, Hen. Waleis. 28. of Sep. Sherifes.
John Adrian Vintenor. The 28. of October Mayor.

In June began a great riot in the Citye of Northwich, where through the Monastery of the Trinity was burned. 1272. Riot in Norwich.
The kinge rode downe, and made enquirye for the chiefe doers therof, where xxx. yong mé were condempned, drawen, hanged and brent. Anno. 57.

Richard Paris, Iohn Bedill, 28 of Septem. Sherifes.
Sir Walter Haruy, the 28. of October. Mayor.

Kinge Henry dyed the xvi. of Nouember, in the yeare of our Lorde 1272. when he had raigned lvi. yeres, and 18. daies!, hee was buried at Westminster vpon the North side of Saint Edward. He builded a greate parte of the same Church.

EDVVARD surnamed longe shanke.

EDVVARD the first after the cōquest, & sonne to Henry ye thyrde, surnamed Longshanke, begā hys raigne ouer this Realme of England, the xvi. daye of Nouember in the yere 1272. he being in the partes beyond the Seas. Anno reg. 1

Iohn

Sherifes. John Horne. Walter Porter. 28. of Sep.
Mayor. sir Walter Haruy knight. The 28. of Octo.

1274. A fraye at Oxeforde. This yeare fel a variance at Oxeford betwene the Northern & Irishmen, wherein many Irishmen were slaine.

Anno. 2.

Sherifes. Nicholas winchester. H. Couentrie. 28. Sep
Mayor. Henry Walleis. The 28. of October.

1275. Coronation. King Edward came from the holy land and was on the xv daye of August, crowned at Westminster.

An earthquake. A Comet. Ther was great earthquakes, lightnings and thonder, a huge Dragon, and a blasing star, which made the English men afearde.

Usurye forbidden to the Iewes. Usury was forbidden to the Iewes, and ye they might be knowen from Christians, the Kinge commaunded them to weare a table the breadth of a palme, upon their outmost garmentes.

Great rot of sheepe, A richman of Fraunce, brought into Northumberlande a Spanish Ewe as bigge as a calfe of two yeares, which Ewe being rotten, infected so the countrie, that it spred ouer al the Realme, & this plague of moren, cōtinued 28. yeres afore it ended.

Anno. 3.

Sherifes. Lucas Batencourt. Henry Frowike. 28. Se
Mayor. Gregory Rokesle. The 28. of October.

Kinge

Kinge Edwarde builded the Castell of Flint, and strengthened the Castel of Rutland, and other against the Welshemē. There was a general earthquake, by force whereof, the Church of S. Michaell of the mount without Glastenburye, fell downe. Anno. 4. — 1276. Castels of Flint and Rutland. Earthquake.

John Horn. Raphe Blunt. 28. of Septēber. — Sherifes.

Gregory Rockeslye. The 28. of October. — Maior.

The statute of Mortmain was enacted by kinge Edwarde. Michael Tonye was drawen, hanged, and quartered. — 1277. Mortmaine. Execution.

Anno. 5.

Robert de Aras. Raphe Fenour. 28. of Sep. — Sherifes.

Gregorye Rockesly. the 28. of October. — Mayor.

King Edward gaue vnto Dauid brother to Lewlin Prince of Wales, ye Lordship of Froddesham. Anno. 6. — 1278.

John Adrian. Walter Langly. 28. of Sep. — Sherifes

Gregory Rockesley. The 28. of October. — Mayor.

Michaelmas Terme was kepte at Shrewesbury. Anno. 7 — 1279.

Robert Basinge. Wil. Maserer. 28. of Sep. — Sherifes.

Gregorye Rockesley. the 28 of October — Mayor.

Reformation was made for clipping of the kinges coyne, for which offēce 297. Jewes were put to execution. In this yeare began the foundation of the Church of Frier Preachers by Ludgate, and also Castell Baynarde. — 1280. Execution of Iewes. Blacke Friers builded.

Anno

Anno 8

Sherifes. Thomas Boxe, Raphe at More. 28, of Sep.

Mayor. Gregorye Rockesley, the 28. of October.

1281. Pence, halfe pence, and farthinges first coined round.

WHere the peny was wont to haue a double crosse with a crest, in such sort, that it might be easely broken in the middest, or into foure quarters, & so to make halfe pence and farthinges, it was now ordayned that pence, halfe pens and farthinges, shoulde bee made rounde. Anno. 9

Sherifes. Wil. Farindon, Nicho Winchester 28. sep.

Mayor. Gregory Rokesley. the 28. of October.

1282. Arches bora down.

THere was such frost, that v. Arches of London bridge were born downe through the violence of the Ise. Anno 10.

Sherifes Wil. Mazarer, Rich. Chekewel. 28 of sep.

Mayor. Henry Waleys, the 28 of october.

1283.

KIng Edward sent a company of souldiours into Wales, vnder the guiding of the Earles of Northumberland and Surrey. Of which company many were slaine, and sir Roger Cliffordc taken prisoner. Anno. 11.

Sherifes Raphe Blunte, Haukin Betwel, 28 of sep.

Mayor. Henry Waleis, the 28. of october.

1284.

EDwarde the firste remoued the abbeye of Abertowne to another place, an there builded a strong castel against the Welshemen. Anno 12

Iordan

Iorden goodchepe, Martin Boxe. 28 of sep. Sherifes
Henry Waleis, the 28. of october. Mayor.

Laurence Ducket Goldsmith and Citizen of London, greuously wounded one Raphe Crepin in Weste cheape, and then fled into Bowe Church, after that certaine euil disposed persons, frendes to the said Raphe, entred the Church in ye night time, and slew the saide Laurence lying in the steple, and hanged him vp. Wherefore a woman, whoe was chiefe causer of the said mischiefe, and xvi. mē with her were then put in prison, & afterwarde moe, who all were drawne & hanged, and the woman burnt. 1285. Laurence Ducket hāged in Bow Church. Execution.

Great Conduite in Cheape was first begonne. Anno 13. Great conduite.

Stephen Cornehil, Rob. Rokesley. 28 sep. Sherifes
Gregorye Rokesley, the 28. of october. Mayor.

The liberties of London was seised into the Kinges handes, and the Maior discharged for taking brybes of the bakers. W. Walleis Citizen of London, caused to bee erected in the highest part of the City, a house called ye Ton, to be a prison, it is now the Conduit in Cornehill. Iustis were proclaimed at Boston in ye faire time, whereof one parte came in ye habite of mōks, & the other in the sute 1286. Liberties of Londō seised. Boston burned.

fate of Chanons, they had couenaunted; that after the iustis, they shoulde fall to the spoile of the fayre. For the atchiuing of their purpose, they fyred ÿ towne in three places. Anno.14.

Sherifes. Walter blunt. Iohn Wade. the 28. of Sep.
Mayor. Raphe Sandwiche. the 28 of October.
1287. This yeare was enacted the statutes called Additamenta Glocestriæ.

Anno.15.

Sherifes Thomas Grosse, Walter Auden 28 of Sep.
Custos, Sir Iohn Briton. the 28. of October.
1288. This Sommer was so exceding hot, that many men dyed through the extremity therof: And yet wheat was sold at London for three shillinges iiij. d. a quarter. Anno.16

A hot sommer and cheape of corne.

Sherifes Wil. Herford, Thomas Staynes. 28. of Sep
Custos, Raphe Sandwiche the 28. of October
1289. Great hayle fel in Englande, and after ensued so continuall raine, that yere folowing wheat was sold for 16 d. a bushel: and and so encreased yerel till it was sold for xl. s: a quarter.

Anno.17

Sherifes W. Betaine, Iohn of Cauntor. 28. of Se
Custos, Raphe Sandwiche: the 28 of October.
1290. Rice ap Meridock, a Welshman rebelling, was by the Earle of Cornew in the kinges absence taken, drawen

Rebellion.

hang

hanged and quartered at Yorke. An. 18.

Fulk of S.Edmōd, Salomō Lāgford. 28. Sep. Sherifes,

Rafe Sandwiche. The. 28. of October. Custos,

The transgression of diuers Justices was tried out, and punished accordingly, some had all their goodes confiscate and then banyshed, some as well of the benche as of the assises, were sent to the tower. Anno. 19 — 1291 Justices corrected.

Thomas Romaine, Willīā de Lyre. 28. Sep. Sherifes,

Rafe Sandwiche. The. 28. of October. Custos,

The Staple of woll was ordeyned to be kept at Sandwiche. And the Jewes were banished the land Anno. 20. — 1292 Wolle staple.

Rafe Blont, Hammond Boxe. 28. Septemb. Sherifes,

Rafe Sandwiche. The 28. of October. Custos,

This yeare died Queene Elianor, the kings wife in Lincolnshire, & as she was brought towarde Westminster, there was made at euery place where she staied, a costly crosse with ye queenes image upon it, she was buried at Westminster, in the chappell of S. Edward. This yeare also died Elianour wife unto Henry the thirde, and mother to this Edwarde. — 1293 Queene Elianor deceased

The goodes, as well temporall as spirituall, of all Religious people in England were taxed, to paye the tenth part to the kyng. Anno. 21.

Sherifes. Henry Belle, Elis Russell, 28, of September
Mayor, John Breton. The 28, of October.

1294 Three men had their right handes smitten of in Westchepe for rescuyng a prysoner, rested by an officer of the citie of London. Anno. 22.

Sherifes, Robert Rockesley, Martin Aubrey 28. Sep.
Custos, Rafe Sandwiche. The 28. of October.

1295 The water of Thames did so much ouerflowe his accustomed boundes, y^t it made a great breache at Rotherheth, and the lowe ground about Bermondsey and Tothill, were ouerflowed, ascending to ye tentes of occupiers in the faire of Westminster. Anno 23.

[B]reatch at [R]otherheth.

Sherifes, Henry Boxe, Richard Glocester. 28. of Sep.
Custos, Sir John Bryton. The 28. of October.

1296 Madock with the Welchemen rebellyng the King, made against them, and ouercame them. The Frenchmen arriued at Douer, spoyled the towne, and brent a part of it. Anno. 24.

[D]ouer spoyled.

Sherifes, Iohn Dunstable, Adā Harlingbery. 28. Sep.
Custos Sir John Breton. The 28. of October.

1297 John Bayloll, was by King Edward admitted to be kyng of Scottes, and he for the same did homage, and sware fealtie. Madock capitaine of the rebelles in Wales; was drawn and hanged at London. Anno. 25.

[R]ebellion in [W]ales.

Thomas Sulfe, Adam de Fulham, 28, of sep Sherifes.
Sir Iohn Bryton the 28. of October. Custos.

John Bayl[i]el king of Scottes, rebelled, 1298
wherfore king Edwarde hailed hym Barwike won
thether. He wan from hym the castels of
Barwike and Dunbare. He slewe of the
Scottes 25. M. He conquered also Edinbrough, where he founde ẏ regal ensigns
of Scotland: that is to write, the crown,
the scepter and cloth of estate. Anno. 26

John de Storford, Wil. de Storford, 28. sep Sherifes.
Henry Wall the 28, of October. Custos.

A fire being kindled in the lesser hall 1299
of the Palayce at Westminster, the
flame therof being driuen with wynde,
fyred the buyldinge of the Monastery adioyning, whiche with the pallayce were
both consumed. Anno. 27

Richard Resham, Thomas Sely. 28, of sept. Sherifes.
Henry Walleis, the 28, of October. Mayor.

This realme was corrupted with fals 1300
mony, called Crokedon and Polard, Crokedon
which was clouen in two, and was ac- and Pollard.
cepted but halfe the value, ẏ same money was forbiddon through al Englãd,
and after called in. Anno. 28

[illegible] Darmanciars, Henry Fingrie. 28 sept. Mayor.
[illegible] Rossell, the 28 of October. Sherifes.

King Edward hearing of the rebellion 1301
of ẏ Scots, made a vyage against thẽ,

wherein he subdued a great part of the lande, and tooke the castle of Estriueline, with other, and made the lordes sweare to him fealtie. Anno 29.

Sherifes. Luke haueryng, Richard Champeis. 28. Sep.

Mayor. Elis Russel. The. 28. of October.

1302 The king gaue unto Edward his sonne the princedome of Wales, the Dukedome of Cornewale, and the Earledome of Chester. Anno. 30.

Sherifes, Robert Caller, Peter Bosenho. 28. Septemb.

Custos, John Blunt. The 28. of October.

1303 The king helde a great parliament at Caunterbury. Anno. 31.

Sherifes, Hugh Pourt, Symon Paris. 28. September.

Custos, John Blunt The. 28. of October.

1304 This yeare died Richarde Grauesende bishop of London, who is reported to haue purchased the charter and liberties of the citie of London, in the yeare of our lorde 1392. in the sixtene yeare of kyng Richarde the seconde, 89. yeares after the sayde Richarde Grauesende was buried: whiche could not be. Anno. 32.

A great and common errour reproued.

Sherifes, Wil. Cōbmartein, John de Burford. 28. Sep.

Custos, John Blunt. The. 28. of October.

1305 This yeare came out a newe wryt, called Troyllebaston, against intruders into other mens landes. Certayne theues perceiuing that the substaunce of

Troillebastō

a knight

night was hidden in the whyte Fri: A frier a
[illegible] church at London by the consent of Iudas.
das that was amongest the Friers,
y came and toke away 400 poundes
siluer, and cruelly bound the handes
the Prior and all the rest of the friers.

Anno. 33.

ger Paris, Iohn Lincolne. 28. September. Sheriffes.
m Blunt. The. 28. of October. Custos.

William Waleis, whiche had done so 1305
many displeasures to king Edward Parliament
Scotlande, was taken, drawen, hang at the newe
d, and quartered at London. The no temple.
e of Scotland in a parliament at the
we Temple in London, were sworne
be true to the king of England.

This yeare the newe great churche of Gray friers
Gray friers in London, was begon churche in
be buylded by the Lady Margarete London.
ueene, wyfe to Edwarde the firste.
hn of Bryton Earle of Richemond,
ylded the body of the churche, the re
ue was finished by Mary Countesse
Penbroke, Gilbert de Clare, Earle of
loucester, Margarete, Countesse of Glo
ter: Eleanor le spencer, Elizabeth Brughe,
ters to Gilbert de Clare &c.

King Edward deceased the seuenth of
ly, in the yeare 1307. He raigned 34.
res, vii. monethes, and xxi. dayes.

Anno. 14.

Sherifes, Williā Cawson Raynold Thūderle. 28 Sep.
Custos, John Blunt. the 28. of October.
1307 ROBart le Bruse, assembled the lordes of Scotland, and caused himselfe to be crowned. When king Edward heard of this treason, he wēt with hast into Scotlande, where he chased Robert le Bruse, and all the power of Scotland, & tooke many of the noble men prysoners.

King Edward deceased the 7. of July in the yeare 1307. He raigned 34. yeres 7. moneths and 21. dayes. His body was buried at Westminster.

EDVVARD OF Carnaruan.

Anno reg 1. EDward the seconde, sonne of the first Edward, borne at Carnaruan, began his raigne the vij. day of July, in the yeare of our Lorde 1307. He was faire of body, but unstedfast of maners, and disposed to lightnes, he refused the company of his Lordes, and men of honour.

Sherifes, Nicolas Pigot, Nigellus Drery, 28 of sept.
Mayor, Sir John Blunt, the 28. of October.
1308 KIng Edwarde gaue to Pierce Gaueston an Italian borne, the Earledom of Cornw

f Cornewale, and the lordship of Wal- | The king
ingforde. He toke to wife Isabel daugh- | maried.
er to Philip of Fraunce, and was maried | Pierce of
at Bolen. And shortly after Pierce of Ga- | Gaueston.
uestone, was by the nobilitie exiled the
Realme. An. 20.

W. Basing, James Botener, the 28. of Sept. Sherifes,
Nicolas Faringdon Goldsmith the 28 Octo. Maior.

The king calling to mynd the displea- 1309
sure done to his familiar Pierce of Gauestone, by the byshop of Chester, commaunded him to the tower of London,
wher he was straightly kept many days
af ter. Anno. 3

James of S. Edmond, Roger Palmer 28. Sep. Sherifes,
Thomas Romain, the 28. of October. Mayor.

This yeare was a prouinciall councel 13 0
at London against the Templers vp- | The Teplers
pon heresie and other filthy and wicked | put downe.
articles, wherin they were accused, and
therefore condemned to perpetuall penaunce, euery one of them thrust into seuerall monasteries. Anno. 4

Simon Crop, Peter Blackney. 28. of septeb. Sherifes,
Richard Rotham Vintener. the 28. of Oct. Mayor,

Piers of Gauestone had the custody of al 1311
the kinges iewels and treasure, of the | Treasures co
whiche hee conueyed manye out of the | ueyde out of
lande. He also brought the king to ma- | Englande,
nifold vices, as adultery & such other.

Wherefore the Lordes againe banished him out of Englande. Anno,5.

Sherifes, Symon Merwode, Rich. Wilford. 28. Sept.
Mayor, Iohn Gisors Pepperer. the 28, of October.

1312 Piers of Gauestone, was againe by the king called out of Flaunders. Wherfore the lordes being confederate, besieged hym in the Castle of Scarborough. where they toke him, and brought hym to Gauerside beside Warwike, and smote of his head.

Piers of Gauestone executed.

The knightes of ye order of S. Iohn Baptist called S. Iohn of Hierusalem, by knightly manhode, put out of the Isle of Rhodes, the Turkes and infidels that to that day had occupied the sayd Ile. Anno 6.

Rhodes won by the Christians.

Shirifes, Iohn Lambyn, Adam Lutekin. 28. Septẽb.
Maior, Iohn Gisors Peperer. The. 28. of October.

1313 This yeare was manye good lawes made in the Parliament at London, whereunto the king and his lordes, were sworne. Anno. 7.

Sherifes, Rob. Burdeint, Hugh Garton. 28. Septemb.
Mayor, Nicolas Faringdon, Goldsmith. 28 October.

1314 The Englyshemen encountred with Robert le Bruse and his Scottes, at Estriualen, where was fought a stronge battayle. In the ende whereof, the Englishemen were discomfited, & so egerly pursued by the Scottes, that many of ye noble

The battaile of Estriuelin

oble men were slayne: as Gilbert de
Clare, Earle of Glocester, Sir Robert
Clifforde, with other Lordes, and Barones, to the number of xlii. Knightes &
Barons, lxvii. beside xxii. men of name,
which were taken prysoners. And ten
thousand cōmon souldioures slayne. An. 8
...e. of Abingdō, Hamōd Chickwel. 28. Sep. Sherifes.
...ohn Gisors Pepperer. The 28. of October. Mayor.
A Tanners sonne of Excester, in dy- 1315
uers places, named him selfe sonne A Tanners
of Edward the first, and sayde that by a sonne clay-
false nourse he was stolen out of his cra- med the
dell, and Edwarde that was now kyng crowne.
put in his place, but shortlye after, hee
was conuict of his vntruthe, and drawē
and hanged at Northampton, Anno. 9
Hamōd goodchepe. Wil. Bodleigh. 28. Sep. Sherifes.
Stephen Abingdon. The 28. of October. Mayor.
This yeare arriued in England twoo 1316
Cardinals, to make peace betwixte Two Cardi-
the Realmes of Englande & Scotland, nals robbed
and to reconcile vnto the King, Thomas in England.
Earle of Lancaster, and as they went
through the North neare to the towne of
Darlington, certain robbers (Gilbert Middleton, and Walter Selby, being cheefe)
sodainly sette vppon the familie of the
Cardinals, and robbed them of their
treasure, but the Cardinals came to Der

ham.

ham, where they taried a fewe dayes for the aunswere of the Scottes, and so vnder the kinges conduit returned. Gilbert Middleton after many robberies to men in that countrey, was taken, and with his brother drawen & hanged at London.

Theues in Friers apparell.

Sir Gosselin Deinuile, and his brother Robart, with two hundred in habite of Friers, going about as outlawes, dyd many great and notable robberies, for the whiche they were after hanged at Yorke. Anno. 10.

Sherifes, William Caston, Rafe Balancer. 28. Septemb.

Mayor, John Wengraue. The 28. of October.

1317 The Scottes entered the borders of Northumberlande, and moste cruelly robbed and spoyled the coūtrey, sparing neither man, woman, nor childe. Wheat was solde for xl. S. the quarter, poore men did eate their children, dogs, cats, and pigeons donge, and there was so great a mortalitie that there wanted almost to them that were dying. Anno, 11

Famine and pestilence.

Sherifes, John Prior, William Furner. 28. of Septē.

Mayor, John Wengraue. the 28. of October.

1318 Edward le Bruse, the kinge of Scottes brother, who by the space of iij. yeares had assaulted Ireland, and without right or title had crowned himself kinge, was taken by the kinges subiectes,

Edward le bruse beheaded.

s beheaded at Dundalke. In that bat-
le was slayn 29. Batchelers of Scot
d, and 5800. others. Anno. 12

n Poyntel, Iohn Dallyng. 28. of septeb. Sherifs. 50
n Wengraue, the 28. of october. Mayor.

his yeare was a great morreyne of 1319
kyne, which were so mortally infec- Morreine of
that Dogges and Rauens eating of of kyne.
carren of the kyne, did swell with
poyson, and fell downe dead. An. 13.

. Abingdō, Iohn Preston, 28. of septēb. Sherifes.
mond Chikwel Pepperer. the 28. octob Mayor.

he king being at Yorke, the Scottes 1320
ntred into England, came thither & Scots burne
nt the suburbes of the citie, and toke the suburbes
Lorde Iohn of Britaine, Earle of Ri- of Yorke.
mond, prysoner with many other.

Many herdsmen and certaine wome Herdmē go
England, gathered themselues toge- towards Ie-
, and would go seke the holy lande, rusalem.
kill the enemies of Christe as they
, and because they could not passe o-
the great sea, they slew many Iewes
he partes of Tholosa and Aquitaine,
erefore many of them were taken &
the same sentence executed vppon
m. Anno, 14

nold at cundit, Wil, Prodhā. 28. of sept. Sherifes,
. Farendon Goldsmith. the 28. of octob. Mayor.

Tho-

1321 Thomas Earle of Lancaster, with many Erles and Barons, came to Sherburne, and from thence with displaied banners to Saint Albons, where they taried thre daies, and sent messengers to London to the kynge, demaundyng that hee woulde banyshe the twoo Hughe Spencers, & that he would graunt his letters patentes to saue harmelesse the Barons, and al other that had taken armour against the said Spencers, which when the king would not graunt, ye Barons came to London, but at the last the kinge graunted their petition, so that Hugh Spencer the elder was banyshed, but the yonger Hugh hidde him selfe and could not be taken.

The Barons in armes.

Spencer banished.

Certayne Lepars, who had made couenaunt with the Iewes to poyson all Christians in Europe, layde poyson in welles, springes, pittes, and all other waters: for the whiche there were many conuict in Fraunce and other prouinces, who were burnt, and the Iewes were apprehended layde in pryson, and executed. Anno. 15

Iewes and Lepers poysoned wells.

Sherifes, Ric. Constantin, Ric. of Hakeny. 28. Sep.

Mayor, Hamond Chickwell Pepperer. the 28. Oct.

1322 Certaine of the Barons forsaking the othe that they had made among them

-de their submission to the king, of -hich the chiefest was Roger Mortimer, -d when the kinges army, and the ar- -y of the Barons, met nere unto Burtō -pon Trent, Thomas Earle of Lanca- -r, seing the kynges army to be muche -onger then his, fled with shame, the -ng pursued them to Burghbrige, where -homas of Lancaster was takē by An- -ewe of Herkle, keper of Carlile. This -rle of Lācaster was beheaded at Pouït- -t. Anno. 16 — Earle of Lācaster taken

-hn Granthā, Richard of Ely. 28. Septēb. — She[illegible]
-mōd Chikwell Pepperer. the 28. of Oct. — Maio.
-ndrew Herkley, who was made knight — 132[illegible]
and Earle of Carlile, became a tray- — [illegible]e elder
-ur, and ioyned him selfe to the Scots. — [illegible]cuted.
-thony Lucie, layde wayte for the for- -yde Andrewe Herkley, tooke him and -ought him bounde in chaynes to Lō- -n, where he was condemned, hanged, -aded, and quartered. Anno. 17 — Sir [illegible] king Hern. disgraking Kyl.

-lā of Salis. John of Oxford. 28 Septēb. — Sherifes.
-ic Farendon, Goldsmith. the 28 of Octob. — Mayor.
Roger Mortimer, who lay imprysoned — 1324
in the tower, gaue his keper a sleepe -inke, and escaped through all the wat- -es. Anno. 18 — Mortimer escaped.

-net of Fulham, Iohn Causton. 28 of Sep. — Sherifes.
-mond Chikwel Pepperer, the 28 of Oct. — Mayor.

The

1325 The kinges counsel determined to send the Queene to her brother the French king, to establishe the peace, who went ouer with a small company. By her mediation the peace was finished. And so Edward the kinges sonne, went ouer with a competent housholde.

Whyles the Queene remayned in Fraunce with her sonne, longer then the kinges pleasure was, and would not come agayne without the Lorde Roger Mortimer, and other nobles that were fled out of England: The kynge banished backe the Queene and his owne sonne, and all other of his realme that tooke their partes. Anno. 19

Gilbert Mordon, Iohn Cotton. 28. of Sep. Richard Betain Goldsmith. the 28 of Oct.

[...]warde [...]shed his [...] and his [...]s, [...]or, [...]eene [...]g in- [...]gland, Nobles [...]ed with her.

Isabel the Queene, with Edward her sonne and Edmund of Woodstocke Earle of Kent the kinges brother, Roger Mortimer, and many other noble men that were fled out of Englande, arriued at Harwich, & immediatly the Earle Marshall, the Earle of Leicester, and the Bishops of Lincolne, Herford, Dublne, and Ely, came to her, who beyng ioyned to the Queene, made a great army, the citizens of London apprehended one of their own Citizens named Iohn Marshall, and beheaded

aded him, they toke also Water staple-
n, byshop of Exceter, & beheaded him,
nd twoo of his houshold servauntes,
cause he had gathered a great army to
withstande the Queene. Anno. 20
ich. Rothing, Roger Chäteclere. 28. sep.
ichard Britayne Goldsmith. the 28. octo.
This Richard Rothing Shirife, before
named, united the parishe church of
S. James at Garlike hithe in London.
The Queene besieged the towne and
castell of Bristow, which was sone ren-
red, and the morow after her comming
Hugh Spencer the elder, was drawen &
hanged in his armour upõ the common
gallowes. The king determined to flye
into Irelande, but being in great daunger on the see, he arrived in Wales, and
was shortly after taken. There was taken also Hugh Spencer the yonger, Robert Baldoke, and Symon of Reding, the
king was committed to Henry Earle of
Lancaster his kinsman, who broughte
him to Killingworth castle. Hugh Spē-
cer was condemned at Herford, where
he was drawen, hanged, and quartered.
Symon Reding, was drawen & hanged
on the same galowes. Robert Baldoke,
died in prisõ with tormẽts, These things
being done, the Queene with her sonne,
Roger

The citizens of London beheaded the bishop of Exceter.

Sherifes.

Mayor.

S. James at Garlike hithe

The queene besieged Bristowe.

Hugh Spencer the elder executed.

The king taken.

The king sent to Kyllingworth.

Hugh Spencer the yonger executed.

Roger Mortimer and other, went to Wallingford castell. After Christmas the queene with her sonne, came to London and were ioyfully receiued, and the morowe after helde a parliament, where by common decree they deposed the kyng, and elected Edwarde his eldest sonne. He was thus deposed from his kyngdome, when he had raigned xix. yeares vi. monethes, and xviii. dayes.

Edward was deposed.

EDVVARDE the thirde.

Anno reg. 1.

EDwarde the third, being of the age of fourtene yeares, began his reigne the xxv. daye of January, Anno. 1326. In feates of armes he was very expert. At the beginning of his reigne he was chiefly ordered by his mother Isabel, and the Lorde Mortimer. He confirmed the liberties of the citie of London, and ordeined that the Maior shoulde sitte in all places of iudgement within the liberties of ye same for chief iustice, the kinges persone only excepted, and that euery Alderman that had bene Maior, should be Justice of peace in al

The liberties of London confirmed.

in all London and Middlesex, and eue-ry Alderman that had not bene Maior, shoulde be Justice of peace within his owne warde.

1327.

About the xxi. daye of September, kyng Edwarde the seconde, was cruel-ly murdred in the castle of Barkley, by ỹ practise of the Queene his wife, the lord Mortimer, and the byshop of Hereforde. He was buried at Glocester.

K. Edwarde the seconde murdered.

S. Edmondes Bery, was besieged by the commons of Bery, the gates fyred, and all their goodes, as corne, catteil, gold, siluer, bookes, ornamentes, charters, & other wrytinges with the assay of their coyne, stampes, & all other thinges per-tainyng to their mint, was caried away: and all their manors burnt, wherby the saide abbay was endamaged an C. xl. thousand poundes.

The abbey of Bery spoyled.

Henry Darcy, Iohn Hawuen. 28. Septemb. Sheriffes.
Hamond Chickwell Grocer, 28. of Octob. Mayor.

1328

A Parliament was holden at Northamp-ton, in whiche a peace was made be-twixt the Englishmen & the Scottes, so that Dauid the sonne of Robert le Bruse, maried the kyng of Englandes sister. And the kyng of Englande with his mother, made the Scottes charters, the tenor wherof was not knowē to the English-

Parliament at Northampton.

men The Scottes made many times against the Englishmen for the fond disguised apparel by thē at ỳ time worn.

Scottes rannes.

Long beardes hartlesse,
Paynted hoodes witlesse,
Gay coates gracelesse,
Makes England thriftlesse.

Anno. 2.

Sherifes, Simō Frācis, Henry Combmartin. 28. of Sep.
Mayor, Iohn Grantham Grocer the 28. of october.

1329 Earle of Kēt beheaded

BY ỳ procurement of ỳ queene & Roger Mortimer Edmōd of Woodstock Earle of Kent the kinges uncle was beheaded, who was ỳ lesse lamented because he had an euel family, which afflicted ỳ commons.

Anno. 3.

Mayor, Richard Lazar. Henry Gisours. 28. of sept.
Sherifes. Iohn Swanlond. The 28. of October.

1330 Roger Mortimer executed.

ROger Mortimer, was taken by ỳ Lord Williā Mountecute, & sent to London, where he was condemned & hanged.

Iustinge in Chepe.

About ỳ feast of Michaelmas, ỳ king caused a solempne iusting & rūning at ỳ tilt to be made, that the like was neuer sene before, of all his secure Earles, Barons, & other nobles of englād in Chepside in London, betwixt the condutte & the great Crosse, nigh soperlane, which lasted three dayes.

Anno. 4.

Sherifes, Robert of Ely, Tho. Worwod, 28. Septē.
Mayor, Iohn Poultney Draper the 28. of octob.

Henry Earle of Lancaster, and of Leicester, hight the Stewarde of Englande, founded the newe hospitall by the castel of Leicester, wherein were an hundred impotent persones, prouided for with al thinges necessary. Anno, 5 — 1331 New hospital at Leycester.

John Mocking, Andrew Aubery. 28. of sep. — Sherifes,

John Pountney Draper the 28. of October. — Mayor,

Edward the Bayloll, sonne to Iohn Baylol was crowned king of Scottes. — 1332 Bayloll king of Scottes.

Sir Iohn Norwiche knight, founded a Colleage at Rauenyngham. Anno. 6. — Rauenynghā

Nicolas Pike, Iohn Husband. 28 of Sep. — Sherifes,

Iohn Preston Draper. the 28. of october. — Mayor,

The Scottes came with great multitudes, entending to dissolue the siege of Barwike, whome ye King couragiously met, and slue of them viii. Earles 1300. horsemen, & of the common sort [illegible]. whiche thing when the townes men of Barwike saw, they yelded to the kyng of England both the castel and the towne. The king setting garrisons in the towne and castel, sent Edward Bayloll and other nobles to kepe the realme of Scotland. — 1333 A battayle at Halidon. K. Edwarde wonne Barwike.

Anno, 7

Iohn Hamond, William Hansard. 28. of sep. — Sherifes,

Iohn Pountney Draper, the 28 of October — Mayor,

This yere king Edward and Henry the sonne of Hēry Erle of Lancaster, went — 1334 with a great army beyond the hilles of Scotland, and spoyled meny myles.

Anno.8.

Sherifes, John Kingston, Walter Turke 28 of Sep.

Mayor, Reignold at condit Vintener. 28. of Octob.

1335 Part of the Uniuersitie of Oxford went to Stamforde, because of variaunce that fell betweene the Northerne and Southerne scholers.

[illegible]ghwaters The sea bankes brake in throughout al England, but specially in y Thames, so that al the cattaile & beastes nere therunto were drowned & the land made vnfruitful by salte waters. Anno.9

Sherifes, Walter Mordon, Richard Vpton, 28. Sep.

Mayor, Reignold at condit Vintener, 28. of Octob

1336 In a parliament at Londō, K. Edward made his eldest sonne Edward, Earle of Chester, and Duke of Cornewale. He made also vi. Earles, Henry of Lancaster, sonne to Henry Earle of Lancaster, Earle of Darby. Hugh Audley Earle of Glocester. William Bohowne, Earle of Northampton. William Mountague, Earle of Salisbury. Robert Vfford, Earle Suffolke. William Clinton, Earle of Huntington. And the same day he made xx. knights whose names for breuity I leaue out of this place.

[illegible]les crea[illegible]d.

In the same parliamēt it was enacted, that no wol growing in Englād, shald

be con-

be conueyed out of the realme. An. 10
Iohn Clerke, William Curteis. 28. Septemb. Sherifes,
Iohn Poulteney Draper. The, 28. of October. Mayor.

The towne of Southampton was bur- 1337
ned down by the Frenche kinges Ga- Southampt
leis, and great discord arose betwext the barned.
two kinges of England and of Fraunce:
In a parliament at Notingham. It was Priuileges
enacted that whatsoeuer Clothworker to Clothe-
of Flaunders, or of other coūtreis, wold workers.
dwel and inhabite in Englande, they
should come quietly and peaceably, and
the moste conuenient places should be
assigned to them with great liberties &
priuileges. It was enacted ŷ none shuld
weare any cloth made without ŷ realme
the king, queene, and their children only excepted, also that none should weare
any furres that came from beyonde the
sea, except he might dispende a hundred
pounde by yeare.

The king caused to confiscate all the The good
goodes of the Lombardes, and also of ŷ of Monke
monkes of the order of Cluny & Cisteaux, confiscate.
throughout the whole realme.

The churche of England gaue ŷ tenth
for the space of three yeare. Anno. 11
Walter Neale, Nicolas Crane, 28. Septemb. Sherifes,
Henry Darcy. The. 28. of October. Mayor.

Two Cardinals which came to make 1338

Archebishop preached a-gainst the cardinals. peace betwene the kinges of England & Fraunce, fauouring more yͤ Frēch king then the king of England, as appeared in a sermō by one of thē made. The arch bishop of Caunterbury, stode vp & prea ched openly, that the Cardinals assertiōs were frivolous and vayne.

Armes of England and Fraunce ioyned. King Edward ioyned yͤ armes of Frāce with the armes of Englande, and spoy led all the North partes of Fraunce vn to Torney, appointing him selfe to be cal led king of England and Fraunce.

Anno. 12.

Shirifes, William of Pōfret, Hugh Marberol. 28. sep.
Maior, Henry Darcy. the 28. of october.

1339 The king commaunded the Englysshe men to geue him the fifth part of their goodes, & toke into his handes yͤ wolles of all his subiectes at a small price, and appointed all the corne and glebe lādes to serue for his warres. He confirmed the great Charter, and the Charter of fo rest. And tooke his passage towardes Brabant.

Wolles to the king. Charter con firmed.

Anno. 13

Shirifes. William Torney, Roger Frosham. 28. Sep.
Maior. Andrew Aubery Grocer the 28. of october

1340 The king gathered a nauy of 200. or more, and sailed towardes Flaunders where he fought with his enemies a moste cruell battayle by sea, in yͤ which the

battayle on the sea.

the

he Frenchemen & Normans were ouercome, there were slayne of the enemies [illegible] men of armes, whereof many did [illegible]ape into þ sea. There was taken, 200. [s]hips, and the rest fled. By the assistance [o]f the Duke of Brabant, and the Earle [o]f Heinald, with them of Gaunt & Ipres, [h]e entred againe into the North partes [o]f Fraunce, and beseiged the citie of Tornay. In þ meane season the Earle of Henald, sir Walter Manie, & [illegible] Cobham burnt [illegible] townes [illegible] land, taking prayes and spoyles. An. 14. The king besieged Torney.

Adam Lucas, Barth. Mar[illegible] the [illegible] of septēb. Sherifes.

Andrew Aub[illegible] Grocer. the 28. of Octob. Mayor. 1341

Two Cardinals were sent frō the Pope to king Edward, which demaunded a thre yeres truce betwene þ said kinges in which space the title that the kyng of England pretended, might be discussed to the full, and as the king returned out of little Britain, he sustained great losse by tempest upon the sea. Anno. 15. Peace for thre yeares.

Rich. of Barking. Iohn of Rokesley 28. sep. Sherifes.

Iohn of Oxforde Vintener. 28. of October. Mayor 1342

When king Edward had taken homage for the Dukedome of Britaine of Iohn Montforte, brother of Iohn sometime Duke of Britaine. He sailed ouer into Britain, wher he obtained the

K. Edwarde made a lease in Brytayne.

good wil of many great men, and with strong hand tooke many townes and castels, he besieged the towne of Vanes, & there by the mediation of the two Cardinals, truce was taken. Anno. 16

Shiriffes, John Lonkin, Richard Killingbery. 28. Sep.
Maior, Simon Fraunces Mercer. The. 28. of October.

1343 Title to Fraunce handeled at Rome.

The king of England sent to Rome, Henry of Lancaster, Earle of Darby, with many other noble men, to entreate and handle before the Pope of his title to the realme of Fraunce.

Coin of gold

The kinge commaunded Florences of golde to be made, that is to say, the peny of the value of vi.s. viii.d. the halfpeny and farthing after that rate.

William Mountacute Earle of Salisbury conquered the Ile of man from the Scottes, which Ile Edwarde the third gaue to the same Earle, and caused him to be called and crowned king of Man.

King of man

Anno. 17.

Sheriffes, John Steward, John Aylesham. 28. Septemb.
Mayor, John Hamond. The. 28. of October.

1344 Order of the Garter,

This yeare king Edwarde helde a solemne feast at his castle of Windsore, where he deuised and also established in the same castle the moste honourable order of the garter, to the number of 26. knightes, which were then chosen of the

most

other noble & valiant persones of this realme. He made in his larger [illegible] he augmented the chappell, which his progenitours kinges of Englande, had before erected within [illegible] in the castell of Windsor, adding a Deane and [illegible] Chanons more, & xxiiii. poore knightes with other ministers. Anno 26.

The chappel at Windsor augmented. xxiiii poore knightes.

Geffrey Wichingham, Tho. Legge. 26. of Sep. John Hamond the 28 of October.

Sheriffes, Maior, 1.4.5

A Sarasin came to Erle Waren, desiring leave to take a serpent in ƿ coaste of Wales, belonging to his Lordship, & whe he had taken ŷ serpent, he seid ƿ nere vnto the den, ŷ the serpent had kepte, there was great quantitie of treasure, whereby the Earle (as some say) gate no small gain.

A serpent taken in wales.

Thomas of Hatfield the kinges secretary, by medeation of the kynges letters to the Pope, was admitted Byshoppe of Derham, and when certayn Cardinals, sayde that the sayd Thomas was a light man and a lay man, the Pope aunswered and sayde, truly if the kyng at this tyme had made his requeste for an Asse, hee should haue obtayned it.

Aunswer of the Pope.

The Scottes to the number of 30000. William Douglas being their leader, entred into Westmerland, and burnt Carlil & Penrethe with many other townes

The Scottes inuade Westmerlande.

where

wherefore the bishop with a smal number copassed them in the night seasons, and with lightes and noyse so disquieted them, that they neither durst go out for victualles, nor geue their bodye to slepe but understanding of the coming of the Lorde Percy and Lord Neuill, fled for feare. Anno. 19

Sherifes, Edmond Hemenhal, Io. of Glocester. 28 sep.

Mayor. Richard Lacer, the. 28. of October.

1346 The king tooke shipping and arriued at Hogges in Normandy. The spoyled Cane to the bare walles, and toke there many prysoners. He tooke his iourney towardes Caleis, & spoiled all the cuntrey, and then besieged Caleis.

The Scottes inuade the North, During this siege of Caleis, Dauid king of Scottes, came into Northumberland, with an army of. lx. thousande, but William Souch archbishop of Yorke, the Lordes Percy, Mombray, Neuill, with other, gathered together at Beethmonde. And came to Derham, where when they had fought a great battayle, the enemies were ouercome and slayne for the moste part. Dauid king of Scottes was taken. Anno. 20.

K. of Scottes taken.

Sherifes, Iohn Croydon, William Clopton 28, of sep.

Mayor, Geffrey Wichingham. The. 28. of October.

1347 About this tyme Walter Manny, sonned

d þ Charterhouse besyde Londō, nere
to Smithefielde, & was afterwardes
ere buried.

When king Edward had a long tyme
sieged Caleis, the Frenche kyng came
breake the siege if he coulde, but when
saie he could not fulfill his desire,
set fyre on his tentes and went his
aye, which when the men of Caleis
ceyued, they yelded vp the towne and
ell, and submitted themselues to the
nges pleasure, this beyng thus brought
passe, by intercession of two Cardi-
ls, truce was taken. K. Edward wan Caleis.

This peace beyng made, it semed tho-
ghout all Englande, as a new sonne
r had folowed, because of the plety of
inges. For there was almost no wo-
but she had some of þ prises of Cane
d Caleis, wherof the matrones of Eng
d being proude, did bragge in Frēch
atrones apparell. Anno [illegible]. Commodities of peace

am Brapton, Richard Bas. 28. of Septem. Sherifes,
mas Legge. The 28. of October. Mayor,

The pestilence began in Englande a-
bout Lammas Anno. 1348, so that ma 1348
which wer whole & sound in þ morn
g, died before noone. In one day there
e xx. xl. lx. & many times more dead
ies buried in one pit. Abou the feaste The great pestilence.

of all

of all Saincles, it came to London, and slewe many, & encreased so muche, that fro Candelmas untill Easter, in a churche yarde which was then new made neare Smithfield, more then 200. dead corps, besides the bodies that wer buried in other churche yardes, wer there every day buried. About Whitsontide it ceased, first at London, & so towardes the North, in which parts it ceased about Michelmas in Anno. 1349. Anno 22.

Charterhous churchyarde.

Sherifes, Henry Picard, Simō Dolseby. 28. Septem.
Mayor. John Loukin Fishmonger. the 28. of Octo.

1349 Women disguised.

About this time tilltinges being used in every place: Ladies & gentlewomen disguised in mens apparel of party colours, resorted with daggers at their studded silke or silver girdels with wel barbed horses, & by such meanes wasted their goodes, dishonested their good fame, brake the knot of mariage.

A straunge kind of whippers of theselues.

About the feast of S. Michaell, more then 120. persons of Seland & Holland comming through Flaunders unto London, sometime in the churche of S. Paule, some time in other places of the citie, twise in the daye in sight of the people, from the loynes unto the heles covered in linnen cloth, all the reste of their bodies being bare, hauing on their heades hattes

tles with red crosses before & behind, and
euery one in their right hand a whip
with iii. cordes, eche corde hauing a knot
the midst, but the feete on their bare
oudy bodies going in procession, and
ele singing in their owne language,
the other aunswering them. Anno. 23
am of Bury, Rafe of Linne. 28. Septemb. Sherifes.
lliam Turke Fishemonger. the 28. Oct. Mayor.
Oxfordshire nere to Chepingnorton 1350
as founde a serpent hauing ii. heades A serpent
wo faces like women, one face attiret with two
the new fashion of womens attire, ye heades.
er like the old array of women, & had
nges like a backe or flyinder mouse.
King Edward had a great & notable Battayle on
tory vpon the sea by Winchelsey at the the sea.
rcey, againste ye Spaniardes. An. 24
n Notte, William Worcester. 28. Septeb. Sherifes.
hard Killingbury. The. 28. of October. Mayor.
William Edingdon, B. of Winchester, 1351
and treasurer of England, caused Grotes and
ew coyne called a groat, & halfe grote halfe grotes.
ee coyned, but these were of lesse
yghte then the Easterlynges, by rea-
wherof, victualles and marchaun-
became the dearer through y whole
alme. Anno. 25
n Wroth, Gilbert Steinesthorp. 28. Sep. Sherifes.
rew Aubery Grocer. The. 28. of Octob. Mayor.

The

1352 The castel of Guines was yelded vnto the Englishmen, dwelling in Caleis, by treason of a Frenche man. Anno, 26

Sherifes John Peache, John Stotley. 28. of Septemb.

Mayer, Adam Francis Mercer. The 28. of Octobe.

1353 S. Stephens at westminster builded. King Edwarde altered the chappell, whiche his progenitours had founded of S. Stephen at Westminster, into a Colledge of xij. secular Chanons, & xij. Vicars and other ministers accordingly, and indued it with reuenues to the summe of 500. poundes by yeare.

Dry sommer This Sommer was called the dry sommer. Anno. 27.

Sherifes. William Wolde, Iohn Litle the 28. of Sept.

Mayor, Adam Francis Mercer. The 28. of Octobe.

1354 VVolle staples. The Staple of wolle was remoued from Flaunders, and was establishe in sundry places in England, to wete: Westminster, Caunterburie, Chichester, Bristowe, Lincolne, and Hull. Anno. 28

Sherifes, Wil Totingham, Richard Smelt. 28, of Sep.

Mayor, Thomas Leggy Skinner, the 28, of Octobe

1355 Frier Augustines. The house of the Friers Augustines in London, was reedified by syr Humfrey, Bohune Earle of Hertforde and Essex.

Dissention in Oxforde. Great dissention in Oxforde happened betwene a Scoller & a Vintoner, for a quarte of wyne, so ẏ the Scoller powred

he wyne vpon the vyntoners head, and
rake his head with the pot, by reason
wherof a great conflicte was made be=
wixt the scoliars of the Vniuersitie &
e laye people of the towne. as ye may
reade in my large sommary. Anno. 29
homas Foster, Thomas Brandon. 28. sept. Sherifes,
ymond Francis Mercer. the 28. of October Maior,
Edward prince of Wales, nie to the ci- 1356
tie of Poitiers, ioyned battayle with The Frēche
ing John of Fraunce, of whome the king taken
rince by his merciall policie, wanne prisoner,
noble victorie. In this conflicte kyng
ohn was taken with his younge sonne
Philippe, and many of his nobles, and
ought into England. Anno. 30
ich. Notingham, Thomas Dosel. 28. sep. Sherifes,
enricus Picard Vintener, the 28. of Octo. Mayor,
Great and royall iustice was holden 1357
in Smithfelde before the kinge of Iustis in
nglande, the Frenche kyng, and the Smithfield
ing of Scottes. Dauid le Bruse kyng of Dauid king
cottes, was deliuered from the long of Scottes
prisonment he had bene in, in the Ca= releaced.
tell of Odiham. Anno. 31
tephen Candish, Bartho. Frosting 28 Sep. Sherifes,
ir Iohn Stody Vintner, the 28 of October. Mayor,
This syr Iohn Stody Lord Mayor, be= 1358
fore named, gaue vnto the Vinteners
London, all the quadrant wherin the

Vin

Winteres house now standeth with the tenementes rounde about, frō the lane yet called Fosters lane to the lane now called Anker lane, where is founded .13. houses for .13. poore people, whiche hetherto are there kept of charitie euer free. Anno .32.

Sherifes, John Barnes, John Burys. 28. of Septemb.

Mayor. John Louekin Fishmonger. 28. of October.

1359 K. Edwarde sailed to Calleis. Edwarde with a nauye of xi. hundred shippes, passed the sea & came to Caleis, hee deuided his armye into three partes, one company vnto Henry Duke of Lancaster, an other vnto Prince Edward, and the thirde to him selfe, and so passed into Burgundy.

Frenchemen arriued at Winchelsey. In the meane season ŷ Normans with a small nauy of shippes, arriued at Winchelsey, partly brent the towne, & slewe suche as did withstand them, wherfore the Prelates of Englande assembling from all partes in armour, the Frenchemen laughed them to scorne and went their waye. Anno .33.

Sherifes, Symō of Beningtō, John Chichester. 28. sep.

Mayor, Symon of Dalsey Grocer. 28. of Octobe.

1360 A Finall peace was concluded betwene the kynges of Englande and of Fraunce, on this condition, that king Edward should haue to his possession,

the coun

the countreies of Gascoyne, Gayen, Powters, Limosin, Baleuile, Exantes, Calleis, Guines, with diuers other Lordships, Castels, Townes, and all the lands to them belonging. This peace being cōfirmed, kinge Edwarde came to the Tower to see the Frenche king whiche he appointed his raunsome to be three millions of Florens, and so deliuered him of all imprisonment. — ii Florens was 6 shillinges 8 pence.

Anno. 34.

John Denis, Walter Berney. 28. of Sept. — Sherifes.
John wroth fishmonger, the 28. of Octob. — Meyor.

Men and beastes perished in England with thonder and lightninge: fends in mens likenes spake vnto mē as they trauayled by the waye. — 1361.

Anno. 35.

Wil. Holbeche, Iames Tame. 28. of Sep. — Sherifes
John Peche fishmonger. The 28. of Octob. — Mayor.

This yeare was greate death and pestilence in England, which was called the second mortalitye: in which dyed Henry Duke of Lancaster. And then was Iohn of Gaunte the kinges thirde sonne, whiche had maryed the Dukes daughter, made Duke of Lancaster. — 1362. The second pestilence. John of Gaunt.

At this tyme was graunted vnto the kinge for three yeares xxvi. shillinges, viii. pence, of euery sacke of woll.

O Anno

Anno. 36

Sherifes. Io. of S. Albons, Iames Andrew. 28. of Sep.
Mayor. Stephen Candishe Draper. 28. of October.
1363 SIr Iohn Cobham knight, founded the
Cobham College. College of Cobham in Kent.
Great wind. Great winde in Englande, wherewyth many towers were ouerthrowē.
Thre kings came into England. This yeare came into Englande, the French kinge, the kinge of Cypres, and the kinge of Scottes, to see and speake with the king of England. The kings of Cypres and Scotlande, shortly after returned home, but the Frenche kinge fell sicke at London, whereof he dyed.
Frost. This yeare was a great frost, from ye midst of September, to the moneth of Aprill

Anno. 37.

Sherifes. Richard Croiden, Iohn Hiltoft 28. of Sep.
Mayor. Iohn Notte Peperar. The 28. of October
1364. THe Lombarde merchauntes were accused of greate falshoode that they did to the kinge in theyr wares, wherefore manye of them were committed to the towre, tyl they had fyned at the kinges pleasure.

An. 38.

Sherifes Simon Morde, Iohn of Metford. 28. of Sep.
Mayor. Adam of Bury skinner. The 28. of October
1365. THis yeare Ingrame Lorde of Coucie, maryed the Lady Isabell the kinges daughter at Windsore.

Anno 39.

John Bukilsworth, John Ireland. 28 of Sep. Sherifes.
John Loukin fishmonger, the 28. of Octo. Meyor.

THe kinge commaunded that Peter pence should be no more bee gathered nor paid to Rome. 1366.

The thirde daye of Aprill, was borne at Burdeaux, Richard the seconde sonne to Edward the blacke Prince, who was after king of England, by the name of Richard the second.

Anno. 40

Tho Atteley, John Warde. 28. of Septem. Sherifes.
John Loukin fishmonger. The 28. of Oc. Mayor.

EDward Prince of Wales, taking compassio upon Peter king of Spaine, who was driuen out of his kingdome by Henrye his bastarde brother, entred Spaine with a great puissance, and in a battaile of Nazers, put to flight the foresaid bastarde, and restored the said Peter to his former dignitye. But not long after, Henry the bastarde, whiles kinge Peter sate at table, traiterously thrust him through with a speare, and then inuaded the Realme by treason, which by open warre he could not do. 1367.

The [illegible] [illegible] the [illegible] [illegible] [illegible] [illegible] [illegible]

Anno. 41.

John Torgold. Wil. Dickman. 28. of Sep. Sherifes
James Andrew Draper. The 28. of Octob. Mayor.

1368. The Frenchmen toke diuers townes, castels, and holdes in Poytow, that belonged to the King of Englande, and slew many of his men. Anno. 42.

Sherifes. Adā Winbingham, Rob. girdler. 26. of Sep

Mayor. Simō Mordon stokefishmonger. 28. Oct.

1369. Queene Philippe wyfe to Edwarde the third dyed, and was buryed at Westminster. This yeare was the thirde pestilence. Anno 43.

Sherifes. Iohn Pyel, Hugh holditch, the 28. of Sep.

Mayor. Io. Chichester goldsmith, the 26 of Octob.

1370. A Great part of Gascoyne fell from ŷ Prince, because of the straunge exactions he layde uppon them, and also sicknes increasing uppon him, and moneye faylinge, he returned into Englād with his wyfe. Anno. 44

Sherifes. Wil. Walworth, Robert Gayton. 28. Sep.

Mayor. Iohn Barnes Mercer, The 26. of October.

1371. Chest in Guildehall. This Iohn Barnes Maior of London gaue a chest with 1000. markes, to be lent to yong men uppon sufficiente gage. The chest standeth in the Chamber of London, without eyther moneye or pledges.

Great subsidy, &c. The king demaunded of the clergye and communaltie, a subsidy of 50000. li. The bishops were remoued from ŷ offices of Chaunceler, of Treasurer, & of of the priuye seale, and laye men put in their steedes. Anno 45.

Robert Hatfild. Adam staple. 28 of Sept. Sherifs.
Iohn Barnes Mercer. The 28 of October. Maior.

IOhn Duke of Lancaster, and Edmond Earle of Cambridge, returned oute of Gascoyne, and brought with them two daughters of Peter late king of Spaine whom afterwardes they toke to be their wyues. 1372.

The Frenchmen besieged Rochel, to the remouing wherof was sent y Lorde Hastinge Earle of Penbroke with a nomber of men of armes, vpon whom fell the Spanishe nauye in the hauen of Rochell, who slewe and toke the Englishmen, and burnt their nauye. The Earle and many noble men, were caryed into Spaine. Anno 46. Battaile on the sea.

Iohn Philpot, Nicho. Brember. 28 of Sept. Sherifes.
Iohn Piel Mercer, The 28. of October. Mayor.

IOhn duke of Lancaster entered Fraunce with a stronge power, but passinge throughe the desertes and mountaines of Aluerne, for lacke of victuals manye of his army dyed, from thence he went into Aquitaine and Burdeaux, & brought scantlye 40. horses aliue with him, it was commõly talked, he lost xxx. thousand horses in that vnluckye vyage. 1373.

Anno. 47

Sheriffes. Iohn Aubery, Iohn Fished. 28. of Septemb.
Mayor. Adam of Bury skinner. the 28. of October

1374. IOan Duke of Lancaster, Simon Sudberye, Archbishop of Caunterburye and other, assembled at Brudges to treate of peace betweene the Realmes of Englād and Fraunce, whiche treatye continued almost two yeares, and ended without conclusion of peace, but onely a truce.

Anno. 48.

Sheriffes. Richard Lions. Wil. Wodhouse. 28. of Sep.
Mayor. Wil. Walworth fishmonger. The 28. Oct.

1375. LOrde Iohn Hastinges Earle of Pembroke comming into England, after hee had raunsomed himselfe for a greate masse of moneye, which he neuer payd, dyed. Anno. 49.

Shreifes. Iohn Halle, William Newport. 28. of Sep.
Mayor. Iohn ward Grocer. The 28. of October.

1376. RIcharde Lions, and Adam Burye, Citizens of London, were accused by ÿ commons of diuers fraudes and deceites, whiche they had done to the kinge. Richarde Lions, for moneye did wiselye compounde and escaped, the other conueyed himselfe into Flaunders.

[Ac]tion of Bu[rye] [illegible] ma-[yor] [illegible] Richard Li-ons [illegible] thi-[illegible] a gold-smith.

Anno. 50.

Sheriffes. Iohn Northāpton, Robert Launde. 28. Sep.
Mayor. Adam Staple Mercer. The 28. of October.

Prince

Prince Edwarde departed out of this life and was buryed at Caunterbury, then king Edward created Richard sonne of Prince Edward Erle of Chester, Duke of Cornewall and Prince of Wales and because the King waxed feble and sicke=ly, he betoke the rule of the land to John of Gaunt Duke of Lancaster. 1377

Kinge Edwarde ended his life at his manor of Shene the xxi. day of June in ye yeare of oure Lorde 1377. After hee had reigned 50. yeares, foure monethes and 26. dayes, whose bodye was buryed at Westminster.

RICHARD of Burdeaux.

RYCHARD the seconde, sonne of Prince Edwarde, beinge but eleuen yeare of age, began his raigne the xxi. day of June, in ye yere of oure Lorde 1377. In bountye and liberalitye hee farre passed all his progenitours, but for that hee was yong, he was most ruled by yong counsaile, and regarded nothing the ad=uertisemente of the sage and wyse men Anno reg. 1.

of his Realme, which thing turned this lande to greate trouble, and himselfe to extreeme miserye.

Verses of I. Gower.

When this king first began to raigne,
the lawes neglected were,
Wherfore good fortune him forsoke,
and thearth did quake for feare.
The people also whom he pold,
against him did rebell,
The time doth yet bewaile the woes,
that Chronicles do of tell,
The foolishe counsell of the lewde,
and yonge he did receiue:
And graue aduice of aged heades,
he did reiect and leaue.
And then for greedy thirst of coyne,
some subiectes hee accusde,
To gaine their goodes into his handes,
thus he the Realme abusde.

Rye spoiled. The French men arriued at the towne of Rie, and spoyled and burnt it.

Hastinges burnt. Not longe after the Frenchmen assaulted the towne of Winchelsey, and were expulsed, but they burnt ye towne of Hastinges.

Sherifes. Andrew Pickmã. Nico. twyford. 28. Sep.
Mayor. Nicho. Erembar Grocer, the 28. of Octob.

1378. The Frenchmen came vp into Sussex nere to the towne of Rotingdõ, wher the e Prior of Lewes with a smal compa- ye met theim, and was taken prisoner y them, and two knightes with him. | The Prior of Lewes taken by the Frenchmen.

Anno. 2.

ohn Boseham, Tho. Cornewalis. 28. Sep. | Sherifes.

ohn Philpot Grocer, the 28 of October. | Mayor.

This Iohn Philpot Maior of London | 1379.

gaue to the same Citye certaine te- nementes, for the whiche the Chamber- ine payeth yerely to xiii. poore people, ery of them iiii.d. the weeke for euer, d as any of these xiii. persons dyeth, e Maior appointeth one, & the recorr en other.

Anno 3.

hn Heylindon, Williā Barret. 28. of Sep. | Sherifes.

hn Hadley Grocer, the 28. of October. | Mayor.

The Frenche Kinges Gall[eys] to take y towne of Winchelsey, but the ab[b]ot Battel to flight, and tooke one of his ... | 1380.

Anno. 4.

al Ducket, Williā Knighthode. 28. Sep. | Sherifes

ill. Walworth fishmonger. 28. of Octob. | Mayor.

This yeare the makinge of Gunnes | 1381.

was first found in Almaine. | Gonnes inuented.

was ordayned that euery person be- g of the age of xiiii. yeres, should pay re pence to the king. By meane of s payment, the commons of Kent and ex, sodenly rebelled, and assembled to ther on blacke Heath, to the nomber

of

VVat tyler, iack strawe and other.

of 60000. which had to their captaines Wat tyler, Iacke straw, Iacke shepehard, Tom Miller, Hob Carter, Raphe Ruge, & such other, who destroyed many goodly places of the nobles, as the Sauoy, saint Johns in Smithfelde, and the manor of Highbery. They fetch out of the Tower of London, Simond Sudbery Archebishop of Canterburye, Roberte Halles Prior of S. Johns, William Appelton a Fryer Minor, and beheaded them at the tower hill. They beheaded many Flemminges, and let forth al prisoners, they spoyled all the bookes of Lawe in the Innes of Courte, the Recordes of the Counters and other places. They set ẏ King forth of the Tower of London, compelling him to graunt all bondmē freedom, and that hee shoulde neuer demaund tribute or taxe of his commons and also requiered Wat Tyler and Iacke Straw, to bee made Dukes of Essex and Kent, and gouernors of the Kings person, which thinge he graunted: for hee durst in no point denye them. But W. Walworth Maior of London beinge in Smithfielde neare vnto the Kings person, rested Wat Tyler on ẏ head, that hee amased him therwith, and by and by o-ther thrust him in, & despatched him. the

The Sauoye burnt, and S. Johns in Smithfielde spoiled.

The maior of London rested Wat tyler.

the Maior with a nomber of armed men, (sir Robert Knols being their Captaine) brought the kyng into the Castle. The rude company was dispersed & sleade. Shortly after Iacke Strawe was taken, hanged, and quartered, his heade set on London bridge, his confession at ỹ gallowes I leaue for breuitye. Wil. Walworth and fiue Aldermenne were made knightes. Anno. 5.

Iohn Rote, Iohn Hinde. 28. of September, Sheriffes.
Io. Northampton Draper. 28. of October. Maior.

KIng Richard maried Anne ỹ daughter of Veselaus the Emperour. The Marchauntes did graunt to the kynge, 4. yeares customes of Wolles. 1382.

In Englande was a generall earthquake the xxi. of May, by meane wherof much harme happened. And the Saturday after, was a water shaking, that made the shippes in the hauens to totter and brose themselues. Anno. 6. Earthquake. Water quake.

Adam Bawme, Iohn Selle. 28, of Septemb. Sheriffes
Iohn Northamptõ Draper. 28. of October. Mayor.

IOhn Ball was taken at Couentry, who had encouraged the people to those insurrections which was made by Watte Tyler, & Iack Straw, he was brought to S. Albõs, & there was drawen & quartered, Iohn Wraw priest, Captaine of ỹ rebels which did ryse at Meldẽhal in Suffolk, by 1383.

petition of the commons, was drawen and hanged. Anno. 7.

Sherifes Simon Winchcombe, Io. More. 28 of Sep.

Mayor. Nicolas Brember Grocer. The 28. of Oct.

1384. IOhn Northamptō, other wise Comberton, late maior of London, began to make a newe sedition in the Citye, oftetimes setting vpon the new chosen maior with great multitudes, which whē the maior prepared to resist, a certain taylor ÿ for his estimation mighte haue beene maior, openly requyred ayde of ÿ commōs. But to auoyde the mischiefe whiche might haue folowed, he was by the counsell of sir Robert Knols, drawen out of his house & headed, which dede for the tyme suppressed the commotion of the people, who was sayde to haue conspired the death of the maior, and many other of the wealthiest sort. Afterwardes John Northampton was conuict at Readinge, and condempned to perpetuall prison in the Castell of Tintagell in the borders of Cornewall, and his goods confiscate. Anno. 8

Sedition in London.

Sherifes. Nicho. Exton, Iohn French. 28. of Septem.

Mayor. Nicho. Brember Grocer, the 28. of Octob.

1385. The third day of May was an Earthquake. The king with a great armye entered Scotlande, but the enne-

Earthquake

myes

myes woulde neither fighte, nor shewe themselues, wherfore he burnt the countreye and returned. The xviii. of Julye was an other earthquake.

Anno 9.

Iohn Organ, Iohn Churchman. 28, of Sep. Sherifes

Nicholas Brember Grocer, the 28 of Octo. Mayor.

The Duke of Lancaster, went wyth a great armye into Spayne, to claime the kingdom of Castile, which was due to him in the righte of his wyfe Ladye Constance, doughter and heyre to Peter late king of Castile. 1386.

Anno. 10

Wil. london, Wiliam More. 28. of Sept. Sherifes.

Nicolas Exton fishmonger, the 28. of Oct. Mayor.

Richarde Earle of Arundel, and Thomas Earle of Notingham, encountred with a fleete of Flemmynges, laden with Rochel wyne, & toke an 100. shippes and more, the which contayned 19. thousand tonnes of wyne, and brought them to diuers portes of Englande, wherby wyne was sold for xiii. s. 4. d. a tonne. 1387. Chepenes of Wyne

Anno. 11

Wil Venour, Hughe Follalse. 28 of Sept. Sherifes

Sir Nicho Exton fishmonger. 28. of Octob. Mayor.

Likenes of fyre, appeared in the night time, in many places of England, & went with men as they went, and staid as they did, somtime like a wheele, & in 1388. Likenes of fyre.

time

time like a barell, sometime like a long timber logge.

Thomas of Wodstocke Duke of Glocester, the Earles of Arundell, Warwike, Darby, and of Notingham, considering howe this land was misgouerned by a fewe persons about the king, entending reformation of the same, assembled at Ricot bridge, wher they toke their counsel, and with a power of 40000. came to London, and pitched in the fieldes neare to the tower, where the king kept his Christmas. And shortly after they caused the king to call a Parliament, wherof fearing Alexander Nevel Archbishop of Yorke, Robert Vere Duke of Ireland, and Michael de la Poole Chancelor and Earle of Suffolke fled yͤ lande, and dyed in straunge countryes. The kinge by counsaile of the aboue named Lordes, caused to be take sir Robert Tresilian chiefe iustice of England, sir Nicolas Brember late Maior of London, sir John Salisburye knight of Household, sir John Beauchampe, Steward of yͤ kings house, sir Simon Burleye, Lord Chamberlaine, sir James Barnes, and a sergeant at Armes named John Vske, the which by authoritye of the saide Parliament, were conuict of treason & put to death.

Execution.

And

And Robert Belkrape, Iohn Holt, Iohn Locton, Richard Graye, William Burghe, and Robert Fulthorpe Iustices, with the Lordes whiche before had voyded the land, were exiled for euer. Anno. 12.

Thomas Austen, Adā Carlehol. 28. of Sep. Sherifes
sir Nicho. Twiford Goldesmith, 28. of Oct. Mayor.

The kinge kept a general Iustis in Smithfielde for all straungers that woulde come, which continued .xiii. dayes. This yere was the battayle of Otterborne, betwene sir Henry Percye, and the Earle Douglas, where the Earle Douglas of Scotland was slaine, sir Henrye and Raphe Percye, was taken by the Earle of Donbare. Anno 13.

1389. Iustes in Smithfield. Battaile at Otterborne.

Iohn Walcot, Iohn Louey. 28. of Sep. Sherifes.
sir Wil. Vennour Grocer, the 28. of Octob. Mayor.

Variaunce arose in Oxforde, for the Welshe scholers, by the confederacye of the Southerne Scollers, assaulted the Northerne, and many murders were done on eyther syde. Anno 14.

1390. Variaunce at Oxeford.

Iohn Francis, Tho. Vinent. 28. of Septemb. Sherifes.
Adam Bawme Goldsmith, the 28. of Octo. Mayor.

In a Parliament at London it was enacted ẏ none should go ouer sea to purchase prouisiōs at ẏ Popes handes. It was graūted to ẏ K. xl. s. of euery sacke of wolle, & of ẏ poūd, 6. d. A great dearth was through

1391. Sute to the Pope forbidden. S. Wedye. Dearth.

through al Englande, not so muche for lacke of corne, as for neede of moneye.

A strannge murther. The goodman of ye Cocke in Chepe against the little condite, was murthered by night in his bed by a theefe yt came in by a gutter windowe, as it was knowen longe after by the same theefe, but his wyfe was burnte therfore, and three of his men hanged wrongfullye, whiche was great ruthe. Anno. 15.

Sherifes. John Chadworth, H. Vamer. 28. of Septe

Mayor. sir John Hind Draper. The 28. of October,

1392. A Dolphine. VPon Christmas daye, a Dolphen came vp to London bridge, foreshewing the tempestes that followed shortlye after, or els the disturbaunce of the Citizens, whiche throught the Kinges displeasure they came into. For because

The Maior of London imprisoned, and the liberties of London seased. the Londoners had denied the lendinge of a M. li. which the king demaunded of them, he caused the Maior, Sheriffes, and Aldermen of the Citye, to bee sommoned to Notingham. And there arested, and imprisoned the Maior, and the chiefest of them, and disanulled all their liberties, and made sir Edward Dalingrige Warden of London, but because he fauoured the Londoners, he was remoued, and Baldwine Radington was constitute in hys place.

Anno.

Anno. 16.

Gilb. Mansfield. Tho. Newingtó. 28. of Sep. Sherifes

sir Williã Stonden Grocer, the 28. of Oct. Mayor.

When the king saw that the Lon- 1393.
doners sore repented their tres- The kinge
passes, hee toke pittye uppon them and receiued into London.
came to Londō, wher the Citizens re-
ceyued him with soe greate glorye, as
might seeme to receiue an Emperour in
his triumph, and with such great giftes
did honour him, that the worth thereof
could not be easely esteemed.

By this meanes the Kinge became more tractable to graunte them their liberties againe: and thē the kings bench from Yorke, and the Chauncerye from Notingham, was returned to Londō.

Liberties of London restored.

Anno. 17

Drew Barentine, Ric. whittingtó. 28. Sep. Sherifes.

sir Iohn Hadley Grocer. The 28. of Octob. Mayor.

This yeare dyed Queene Anne wyfe 1394.
to K. Richarde, and lyeth buryed at
Westminster. Thomas the sonne of K. Colledge of
Edwarde the third, Duke of Glocester, Plecy.
Earle of Essex and of Buckingham, and
Constable of England, founded the Col
ledge of Plecye.

Anno. 18.

Wil. Branton, Thomas Knolles. 28. of Sep. Sherifes.

sir Iohn Froyshe Mercer, the 28. of Octob. Mayor.

1395. King Richard made a voyage into Ireland, more chargeable then honou-
A voyage in- rable. Anno. 19.
to Irelande.

Sherifes. Robert Elis, Wil. Sheringham, 28. of Sep.
Mayor. sir Wil. More Vintener, the 28. of Octob.

1396. The Kings of England & of Fraunce, met beside Calaies, and there conclu-
ding a peace, they toke a corporal othe, to performe the same. And K. Richarde toke to wyfe Isabel, the Frenche kinges Daughter. Anno. 20.

Sherifes. Tho. wilford, william Parker. 28. of Sep.
Mayor. sir Adam Baine goldsmith, the 28. of Oct.

1397 The Duke of Gloucester Kynge Ri-
chards uncle, was murthered at Ca-
Duke of leis, the Earle of Arundel and many o-
Glocester ther, was put to cruel death, for so much
murthered. as they rebuked the kinge in certaine matters somewhat liberallye.

Anno. 21.

Sherifes Wil. Askam, John Wodcocke. 28. of Sep.
Mayor, sir Rich. Wittington Mercer. 28. of Octo.

1398. Thomas Arundel Archbishop of Can-
Archbishop terburye, was banished the Realme.
of Canter- The K. caused the greate hall at West-
bury exiled. minster, to be repayred, both y walles,
Westmin- windowes & roofe with a marvelous
ster hal re- costlye worke. Henry Duke of Hereford
payred. accused Thomas Mowbreye Duke of
The Duke Northfolke, of certaine wordes by him
spo-

poken, tendinge to the reproche of the kinges person, which the Duke of Northfolke vtterlye denied: Whereuppon a combate was graunted them, but the K. taking vp ÿ quarel, banished the Duke of Hereforde for tenne yeares, and the Duke of Northfolke for euer. Anno 22.

of Herefords accused the Duke of Northfolke and both banished.

Iohn Wade, Iohn Warner. 28. of Septemb. Sherifes.
Drew Barentin goldsmith. 28. of Octob. Mayor.

About Candelmas dyed Iohn of Gaunt Duke of Lancaster, at the Castell of Leicester, & was honourablye buried in Paules Church at London. The king exacted great sommes of moneye of the shyres of the Realme, and layde to theyr charges that they had beene against him with the Duke of Glocester, the Earles of Arundel and Warwike. Wherefore hee sente his letters to all the shyres of the Realme, & brought al his people spiritual & tẽporal, to sweare vnto customs & lawes, and to ratifye those othes vnder their handes & seales. Moreouer he cõpelled them to set their seales to blãks. About Whitsontyde the king sayled into Ireland. In the meane season Henry Duke of Herford takinge his banishmẽt greuously, returned into Englãd to demaũd the inheritance ÿ was due to him. The same tyme met him Th. Arundel, late

Duke of Lancaster dyed.

1399.

Blanke Charters.

Archb. of Canterbury, and his nephew þ sonne and heyre of the Erle of Arundel, with other, who with hym toke the sea, not all to the nomber of 15. speares, hee arriued in Yorkeshyre, and there came to heim Henry Percye Earle of Northumberlande, and Henry his sonne, & Raphe Neuel Earle of Westmerland, and many other Lordes with their powers, and went to Bristow and besieged the Castel, where they toke W. Scrope treasurer, Io. Bushe & Thomas Grene, whoe straighte way were beheaded, & W. Bagot & Iohn Russell fled. K. Richarde being in Irelande, and hearing of the Dukes arriuing, forthwith toke shipping with his power, and arriued at Milforde hauen, but when he understode what preparation the Duke had made, he sought places to hyde himselfe, the Duke with his armye followyng hym. At last the king hauing placed himselfe in the Castel of Conoway, he desired to talke with Tho. Arundel late Archbishop of Canterbury, and with the Earle of Northumberland, which being graunted, hee came to the Castel of Flint, where after he had had a briefe communication wyth the Duke of Lancaster, they toke horse, and that nighte came to the Castell of Chester, & from

Duke of Lācaster arriued in York shyre.

K Richarde arriued at Milford hauen.

om thence to Westminster, and see by ater to the Tower, where hee remay= d till the next Parliament, at which ne K. Richarde yelded vp and resig- d to the said Henry, al his power and ngly title to the Crowne of Englande d Fraunce, knowledging that he wor- ily was deposed for his demerites, & isgouerning the common weale, whe had raigned 22. yeares, iii. monethes d odde dayes. K. Richarde in the tower.

HENRY OF Bolynbroke.

Henry the fourthe, sonne of Iohn Duke of Lancaster, was ordained K. of Englande, more by force then by lawfull succession or election: hee began his raigne ẏ . of September, in the yeare of oure D. 1399. He made Henry his sonne ince of Wales, Duke of Cornewall, rle of Chester, & heyre apparante to ẏ owne. Anno reg. 1

il. Waldern, Wil Hyde. 28. of Septemb. Sherifes.
Tho. Knolles Grocer, The 18. of Octob. Mayor.

The

Blancke Charters brent.

The K. caused the blanke Charters to be burnt at the Standarde in Chepe, the 6 of February,

1400.

Conspiracy.

John Hollande Duke of Excester, and Earle of Huntingdon, Thomas Hollande Duke of Surreye and Earle of Kent, Edwarde Duke of Awmarle, and Earle of Rutlande, Sonne to the Duke of Yorke, John Mountague Erle of Salisbury, Hugh Spencer Erle of Glocester, sir Raphe Lumleye sir Thomas Blunt, sir Benedicke Celie knightes, with other that fauoured Richard of Burdeaux, conspired against K. Henry, and appointed priuilye to murther him at a feast, which should be holden at Windsore: but their treason was disclosed, and they al put to death.

Death of K. Richard.

K. Richard beinge in Pomfret Castell, dyed on S. Valentines daye, and then hys body was brought to the tower of London, and so through the Cittye to Paules Church bare faced, and there stode thre dayes for all beholders, from thence he was caried to Langley, and there buried in the Church of the preachinge friers. He was since remoued by Henry ẏ fift, and lyeth at Westminster.

Verses.

O mirrour for the worlde mete,
which shouldst in Gold be bette

y which al wise men, by foresight,
their prudent wittes may whet.
o. God doth hate such rulers as,
here viciously do liue:
nd none ought rule, that by their life,
do ill example giue.
As this King Richard witnesseth well,
his e de this plaine doth showe,
For God allotted him such ende,
and sent him so great woe,
As such a life deserude: as by,
the Chronicles thou mayst know.

The Welshemen began to rebel, by the setting on of Owen Glendouerdew, wher of the King being certifyed, wente into Wales, but the Welshmen fled. An. 2. Owen Glen douerdewe.

Iohn Wakel, William Ebot 18. of Sep. Sherifes.

sir Io Fraunces goldsmith. The 28 of Octo Mayor.

There was founde in the Kings bedclothes, an Iron made like a Calthrope, hauing three sharpe prickes standing vpright, that when the King shold haue layde him downe, hee might haue thrust himselfe vppon them. 1401. The K. escaped a great daunger.

At this time was vsed exceedinge gret pride in garmēts, especially of gownes with depe & brode sleues, whereof some hing downe to the feete, and at the least to the knees, full of cuttes and iagges. Sleues of garmentes as mōstrous then, as breches of hose be now.

¶ Wher vpon a Merritian said,

Verses.

Now hath this land litle neede of broumes,
To swepe away the filth out of the strete:
Sen side sleues of penilesse gromes,
wil it vp licke, be it drie or wete,
O England stand vpright on thy feete,
so foule a wast, in so simple a degree,
Banish, or it shal sore repent thee.

Anno. 3.

Sheriffes. Wil Venour. John Fremingham. 28. of Sep
Mayor. sir John Chadworth Mercer, 28. of Octob.

1401.
Conduite in Cornehil.

This yere the Conduite standing vpon Cornehil in London was begō to be made.

Conspiracy.

Certaine men conspiring the kinges death, said K. Richard was aliue, and þ he should shortly shewe himselfe openlye, for the which a priest was taken at Warwicke, who was drawen hanged & quartered. And Walter waldocke Prior of Lannde, was likewyse hanged & headed.

Execution.

Also certaine gray Friers was taken, of the which one Richarde Frisebye doctoure of Deuinitye, was asked what he would do if K. Richard was present,

stout
yer.

who aunswered stoutly, that he would fight in his quarel against anye man euen til the death wherfore he was drawen and hanged.

The deuill appeared at Danberye in

Esse

sex, in li[illegible] of a gr[illegible] [illegible], who entring the Ch[illegible] [illegible] [illegible] [illegible]lye, whereby the [illegible] were maruei[illegible] [illegible], & same h[illegible] with a tempest of [illegible] and [illegible], the top of the steple [illegible] [illegible] downe, and halfe the Chauncell scattered abroade. Shortlye after, sir Roger Clarendon knighte, his Esquyer, and a yeoman were headed, and eyght of the gray fryers, were hanged and headed at London, and two at Leycester, all which had published King Richarde to be aliue. — *The deuil [illegible] [illegible] of a frier.* — *Execution.*

Owen Glendouerdewe wyth a companye of Welshmen, prouoked almost al ÿ chiualry of ÿ shyres that bordered nere vnto hym. The kinge went with a great power into Wales, where hee profited nothinge, for the Welshemen conueyed themselues into vnknowen places. — *Owen Glendouerdewe.* — *Armye to Wales.*

The Scottes came into this Realme with warlike force, & were ouerthrowē by the Earle of Northumberland, ÿ Erle Douglas was taken, & many other, there were drowned in the Riuer of Tweede about 500. — *Scottes ouerthrowe.*

Anno. 4.

Rich. Marlow, Rob. Chicheley. 28. of Sep. — *Sherifes.*

sir Iohn Walcot Draper, the 23 of Octob. — *Mayor.*

A great

1403. Battaile at Shrewsbury A Great battaile at Shrowesburye begõ by sir Henry Percye the yonger, vnto whom ioyned Thomas Percye Earle of Worcester, vncle to the sayde Henry and other against the king, wher sir Thomas Percye was taken and headed, and sir Hearye Percye slaine, wyth manye noble men.

Plimouth spoiled. The towne of Plimouth was burnte by the Britaines. The Frenchmen would haue landed at the Ile of Wight, but by comming of greate ayde they were constrayned to flye. Anno. 5.

Ile of wight robbed.

Sherifes Thomas Fawconer, Tho. Poole. 28 of Sep.

Mayor. sir Wil. Askam fishmonger, the 28. of Oct.

1404 THe Frenchmen came to the Ile of Wighte, to aske tribute in the name of K Richarde and Isabell hys wyfe, but those of the Ile rising against them they were glad to depart.

Dartmouth inuaded. The same yeare the Lord of Casels in Britaine, arriued at Dertmouthe wyth a great nauye, and of the rusticall people her was slaine, and xviii. shyppes were taken fraught with wynes, and a great nomber of prisoners. An. 6.

Sherifes. Wil. Louth, Stephen Spilman. 28 of Sep.

Mayor. sir Iohn Hind Draper, the 28. of October.

1405. THe son of Owen Glendouerdew was taken, and xv. hundreth with him were

[we]re taken and slaine.
Richard Scrope Archbishop of Yorke, [and] Thomas Mowbraye Earle Marshal [m]agened diuers articles against the [ki]ng, because he had put downe kynge [Ri]chard, offring themselues for them to [liu]e and dye, and caused great people to [res]ort to them. But by Iohn Duke of Bed[for]de the kings sonne, and the Earle of [W]esmerland, they were taken and pre[se]nted to the king at Yorke, where they [we]re both beheaded. Anno 7.

Archbishop of Yorke and other.

[Joh]n Barton, Wil. Crowmer. 28 of Sept. Sherifes
[Sir] Io. Wodcock Mercer. The 28. of Octo. Mayor.

[Ja]mes the sonne of Roberte Kinge of Scottes, being but nine yeares olde, [sai]ling toward Fraūce to learn Frēch, [wa]s by tempeste driuen uppon the coa[st]s of England, where being taken, he [wa]s presented to the Kinge, and see re[ta]ined prisoner till the second yeare of [He]nry the fift. Anno 8.

1406

K. Of Scottes sonne taken.

[T]ho Wotton, Geffrey Broke, 28 of Sep. Sherifes.
Richard whittingtō Mercer. 28. of Oct. Maior.

This Richarde Whittington, builded Whittington Colledge in London, & [g]reat part of the Hospitall of S. Bar[tho]lomewe in Smithfield, hee builded [the] liberary of the Gray fryers and the [ea]st ende of the Guild hall of London

1407.

Vvhittingtō colledge builded.

with smal Cōduites, commonly called bosses. And after his decease, of his goodes was builded the Westegate of London called Newgate.

sir Roberte Knolles Rochester bridge.

The yere 1407. dyed sir Robert Knolles Knight, whoe builded the bridge of Rochester, hee reedifyed the bodye of the Church of the White Fryers in London, and was there buryed.

Verses.

O Robert Knols most worthy of fame,
By thy prowesse Fraunce was made tame:
Thy manhod made the Frenchmē to yeld,
By dent of sword in towne and field.

Anno. 9.

Sherifes. Henry Pomfret, Henry Halton. 28. of Sep:

Mayor. sir Wil. Stonden Grocer, the 28 of octobe

1408. Rebellion.

A Frost lasted fiftene weekes, Henrye Earle of Northumberlande, and the Lorde Bardolphe, came into Englande with a great companye, pretending by proclamatiōs, to deliuer the people frō the great oppressions that the Englishmen were burthened wyth, where vppō much people resorted to him, but by the valiantnes of sir Thomas Rokebye Sheriffe of Yorkeshyre, hee was encountred at Bramham Moore, and there slayne valiantelye fightinge, the Lord Bardolphe was wounded to death.

Anno. 10.

The

The Duke, William Norton, 28. of Sept. Sherifes
sir Drew Barent n goldsmith, 28 of Octob. Mayor.

This yeare was a great play at Skin- 1409
ners well, which lasted eight dayes, and forthwith began a royal Iustice in Smithfield, betweene the Henowayes & our English Lords. Anno 11

John Law, William Chichley e, 28 of Sep. Sherifes.
sir Rich Marlow Iremonger, the 28. of octo. Maior.

Vpon the euen of S. John Baptiste, 1410.
John the kinges sonne being in Est- The kinges
chepe at Supper, after midnight a great sonnes bea-
debate happened betweene his meinie, ten.
and men of the Courte, till the Maior and Sherifes with other Citizens sea sed the same.

K. Henry founded a Colledge at Bat- Battlefield.
telfelde, in the country of Shrewesbury, where he ouercame sir Henry Percye and other. Anno. 12.

John Penne, Thomas Pyke, 28 of Septem. Sherifes.
sir Tho. Knols Grocer. The 28. of October. Mayor.

The Guild hall in London, was be- 1411.
gon to be made new, by the foresaid Guild hal in
Maior and Aldermen. Also the Stockes London.
market was begon by the maisters of ye bridge of London.

A Squire of Wales named Rice ap Dee, which had long time rebelled, was brought to London, and there hanged and

and quartered. Anno. 13

Sherifes John Reinwel, Wil. Cotton. 28. of Septemb

Mayor. sir Ro. Chicheley Grocer. The 28. of Oct.

1412. The King caused a new coine of nobles to be made, which were of lesse value then the olde, by foure pence in a noble. K. Henry founded the College o. Frodringhaye in Northamptonshyre.

Coine altered.

Frodringhey.

Anno. 14

Sherifes. Raph Leuinhind, Wil. Seuenoke 28 of sep.

Mayor. sir W. Waldren Mercer, the 28. of Octob.

After the great & fortunate chaunces happened to K. Henrye, beinge deliuered of al ciuil deuision and descention, hee was taken with sicknes, duringe which sicknes, som euil disposed people laboured to make dissention betwen the kynge and the Prince his sonne, by reason wherof, and by thactes of youth, which he exercised more then meanly, and for the great recourse of people vnto him, of whom his court was at al times more aboundante then the Kynge his fathers. The king suspected that he would presume to vsurpe the Crowne, he being aliue, which suspicious ielousye was occasion that hee in part withdrew his affection and singuler loue from the Prince. But when this noble Prince was aduertised of his fathers

ielousy,

ielousy, he disguised himself in a gowne of blew sattin made ful of smal oilet holes, & at euery oylet hole þ nedle wherewith it was made hanging stil by a thred of silke. And about his arme he ware a dogs coller set ful of S.S. of Gold, & the tirets of the same also of fine gold. And thus apparelled wyth a great company of Lords & other noble mē of his Court he came to the king his father, who at þ time lay at Westminster, where at hys comminge (by his owne commaundement) not one of his companye durst aduaunce himselfe further then by the fire in the hall, notwithstandinge that they were greatly and oft desired to the contrary by the Lords and great estates of the Kings court: but he himselfe onelye accōpanyed of the Kinges house, passed forth to the king his father, to whom after due salutation, he desired to shew þ intent of his mind in secrete manner.

Prince Henrye being disguised, commeth to his father.

Then the Kinge caused himselfe to bee borne in his chayre into his secret chamber, wher in the presēce of thre or foure persons, in whom the king had most cōfidence, he commaunded the Prince to shew the effect of his minde. Then the Prince kneling down before his father said: Most redoubted Lorde, & father, I

Submission of the Price to his father.

am

am this time come to your presence as your liegeman & as your sonne natural in al thinges to obey your grace as my soveraigne Lord and father. And where as I understand yee have me in suspect of my behaviour against youre grace, & ye feare I would usurp your Crown against the pleasure of your highnes, of my conversation, your grace knoweth that if ye were in feare of any man within your Realme, of what estate so ever he were, my duty were to the endaungering of my lyfe to punishe that person, therby to rase that sore from your hart. And then how much rather ought I to suffer death to bring your grace from ye feare that yee have of mee, that am your natural sonne, and your liegeman. And to that entent I have this day prepared my selfe. And therefore most redoubted Lorde & Father, I beseeche you in the honour of God, for the easinge of your hart heretofore your knees to slay me with this dagger. And at that word with all reverence hee delivered to the Kinge his dagger, sayinge: My Lorde and father, my life is not so desirous to me that I would live one day ye shoulde be to your displeasure, nor I covet not so much my lyfe, as I do your pleasure n welfare. And in youre thus doinge e in the presence of these Lordes and ore God at the daye of Judgement, J arely forgeue you my death. At these ordes of the prince, the kinge taken th compunctiō of harte cast from him Dagger, and embracing the Prince sed him, and with effusion of teares d unto hym: My right deare & harte= beloued sonne, it is of trothe that J you partly suspect, & as J now per= ue vndeserued on your party, but se= this your humilitie and faithfulnes al neither slea you, and from hence= th any more haue you in mistrust for report that shall be made unto me, & eof J assure you vpon myne honor, & s by his great wisedome was the ongfull imagination of his fathers te vtterly auoyded, and him selfe re= ed to the kings former grace and fa= r. After many moste notable coūcels ē by the king to the prince his sonne h due thankes and supplications ge to God, he gaue the Prince his be= iction, and after yelded to God his rite the xx. daye of Marche in ȳ yeare ur Lord 1412. When he had raigned yeares vi monethes and odde days, was buried at Cantorbury.

The Prince restored to his fathers grace and fa uour.

HENRY OF MONmouth.

Anno reg. 1.

HENRY the fifthe beganne his raigne the xx. daye of Marche, in the yeare of our Lorde 1412. This prince exceaded the meane stature of men, he was beautifull of visage, his necke long, his body slender & leane, and his bones small: Neverthelesse he was of marveilous great strength and passing swifte in running: he called unto hym all those younge Lordes and gentlemen that were the followers of his yong actes, to every one of whom he gave ryche giftes. And then commaunded that as many as woulde not chaunge their manners as he intended to doe, shoulde never after come in his presence.

Description of Henry the fifth.

1413

Sir John olde Castle, at that tyme Lord of Cobham, for divers pointes touching the Sacrament, before the archebyshop of Caunterbury, the byshops of London, Winchester and other, was convict and committed to the Tower of London, out of the whiche he brake on the feaste of Symon and Jude.

John

ohn Stutton, Iohn Micheil. 28. of sep. tem. Sherifes.
ir William Cromer Draper. 28. of october Mayor.

King Richardes bones were taken up and brought from Langley to Westminster.

Certayne adherentes of sir John oldecastell, assembled them in Thickets field nere unto the citie of London. But the king being warned, toke the field afore them, and toke of them so many that all the prysons about London were fylled, whereof many were after executed. 1414

Iohn Nianser Esquier, with nyne of his meine slewe Iohn Tibbey Clarke, chaunceloure with the Queene, for the whiche dede the foresayde Squier and foure of his men fledde to Saint Annes church within Aldersgate, and after forswore the Kinges lande. Anno. 2. Men forsweare the lād for murder.

Iohn Michell, Thomas Allyn 28. of septem. Sherifes,
Sir Thomas Fauconer Mercer. 28. of octob. Mayor,

The king rode toward Southamptō, where he abiding for his retenue and stuffe longing to his warres, there was discouered a perelous cōspiracie against hym by the Earle of Cambridge, sir Henry Grey, & the lorde Scrope. These with other were executed at Southampton. The King entred the sea with 1000. sayles, and the third night after arriued at 1415 Conspiracie discouered.

 Kedes

Kedecaut in Normandy.

Harflew wō. The king laid siege to Harflew, whiche was yelded to him, he fought the battail of Agincourt, where he had a marueilous victory. The same daye the new Mayor should take his charge at Westminster, early in ŷ morning came tidings to Lōdon of the victory in the battayle afore said, for whiche Te Deum was song, and all the orders of religious mē of the Citie, went a procession from Saynct Paules vnto Westminster, with the new Maior, his aldermen & the crafts, and the Queene with all her Lordes, & then the Mayor tooke his charge, and euery man came ryding home. An. 3

The battaile of Agincourt.

Sheriffes. Will. Cambidge, Allen Euerarde. 28. Sep.

Maior. Sir Nicholas Wotton Draper. 28. of Octob.

1416. The king re-turneth. The king arriued at Douer, and the Mayor & Aldermen with the crafts of London, roade euery man in redde, with hoodes redde and whyte, and met the king on the blacke heath.

The halfe-pence. Galley halfpence were put downe by Parliament. Anno 4

Sheriffes. Rob. Widington, Iohn Couentry. 28. of Sep.

Maior. Sir Henry Barton Skinner. 28. of October.

1417 On Easter daye was a great fraye in S. Dunstones church in the East part of London, the beginners whereof was

the

the Lorde Straunge, and sir Iohn Trussell knight, through the quarell of their wyues, in the whiche fray many people were sore wounded, & one Thomas Petwardine fyshemonger, slayne: wherefore both the Frayers were brought to the Counter in the Poultrye, and the Lorde Straunge for beginning the fray was the next Sunday accursed at Paules Crosse.

A fray in S. Donstone churche.

The king with all his host, sailed into Fraunce, & shortly he gate Cane, Beyoux, & many other townes and castels.

Anno. 5.

Henry Reade, Iohn Gedney. 28. of septemb. Sherifes.
Sir Richard Marlow Ironmonger. 28. Octo. Mayor. 1418

Sir Iohn Oldcastell, was sent vnto London by the Lord Powes out of Wales, the whiche sir Iohn was conuicte, and drawen to Saint Giles field, where he was hanged, & after cōsumed with fyre.

The Parson of Wrotham in Northfolk, which had haunted Newmarketh heath, and there robbed and spoyled manye of the kinges subiectes, was with his concubine brought vp to Newgate, where he died.

The perso[n] of Wroth[am] with his co[n]cubine.

Anno. 6

Raphe Barton, Iohn Parnesse. 28. septemb. Sherifes,
William Seuenoke Grocer. 28. of October. Mayor,

1419 The king besieged the Citie of Roan, the whiche siege dured halfe a yeare and more, it was yelded to him the xix. of January, there died within the towne for default of victuals during that siege mo then xxx. thousand. Anno.7

Sherifes, Richard Whittinghā, James Butler. 28. sep.

Mayor, Richard Whittington Mercer. 28. of Octo.

1420 The king was made regent of Fraunce and wedded lady Katherine ŷ kings daughter of Fraunce at Troye in Champanie, the feast and solempnitie being finished, the king besieged and wan many townes in Fraunce. Anno.8.

Shirifes, John Butler, John Welles. 28 of Septemb.

Maior, William Cambridge Grocer. 28. of octob.

The king and Queene came into England, & the xxxi. day of February, the Queene was crowned at Westminster.

1421 The king suppressed the French houses of religious Monkes and Fryers, and suche lyke in Englande. About Whitsontide, the king sailed over to Caleis, and so foorthe into Fraunce, with 30000. men. Anno.9.

Abbies and other houses suppressed.

Sherifes Rich. Gosselyng, William Weston. 28. Sep.

Mayer, Sir Ro. Chichely Grocer. The. 28. of Octo.

The sixt day of December was Henry the kinges sonne borne at Wynsore.

1422 The citie of Mewes in Britain, which long

tyme

yne had bene besieged, was yelded to the kynge. The Queene shypped at Hampton, and sayled ouer into Fraunce to king Henry, where was a ioyful meeting, but after folowed sorrowe, for the king being at Boys in Vincent, he waxed sicke and died, the last day of August, in the yeare of our Lorde 1422. When hee had reigned ix. yeares, fiue monethes, & ten dayes: and was buried at Westminster. He did edifie his royall maner that then was called Shine, and nowe Richemount. He also founded two monasteries vpon the Thames (not far from his said royall maner) the one of the religion of ŷ Chartusiers, and that he named Bethelem, the other of Religious men and women of S. Brigit, and that hee named Syon: both which houses he endued with great reuenues. Shene, Be- lem, and

HENRY OF VVindsore.

Henry the sixt being an infant of a moneth of age, began his reigne ouer this Realme of England, the last day of August, in ŷ yere of our Lord 1422. Continuing ŷ time of Anno re his youth the gouernaũce of his realme was cõmitted to ȳ duke of Gloucester, and the garde of his person to ȳ Duke of Exceter to the Duke of Bedforde, was geuen the gouernment of Fraunce, who right nobly ruled the same, so long as it pleased God to geue him life.

The xxi. of October, died king Charles of Fraunce, by reason wherof the kingdom of Fraunce should come vnto king Henry, and the nobles of Fraunce (except a fewe that helde with the Dolphin) deliuered the possession therof vnto the duke of Bedford regẽt of Fraũce, to the vse of king Henry.

Shersfes, Will, Eastfield, Rich. Tattarsale. 28. of Sept.

Mayor, Sir William Walderne Mercer. 28. of Oct.

1423 A Subsedye was graunted for three yeares, fiue nobles of euery sacke of woole that should passe out of the land.

The Westgate of London, now called Newgate, was newly builded by the executoures of Richard Whittington, late Maior of London. Anno, 2

[Ne]wgate [bu]ylded.

Sherifes, Nicholas Iames, Tho. Wadford. 28. of Sept.

Mayor, Sir William Crowmar Draper. 28, of Octo.

1424 Iames king of Scottes, who was take in the eight yeare of king Henry the fourth, and had remayned in England prysoner till this tyme, whiche was about

beat xviii. yeares was nowe delivered, The king of
and he maried in Saint Mary Overis in Scottes re-
Southwarke, the lady Jane, daughter leased.
to the Earle of Somerset, cosyn to king
Henry.

The battayle of Vernole in Perch, betwene the Duke of Bedford and the ar-
maneks with the Scottes, but the Englishe men prevayled. Anno.3

Symon Seman. John Bywater. 28. of Sept. Sheriffes
Sir John Michel Fishmonger. 28. of Octob. Mayor.

This yeare was graunted to the kyng 1425
for three yeares, to helpe him in his First custom
warres, a subsidie of xii. pence in the payde.
pounde, of all marchaundises brought
in, or caried out of the realme, and three
shillinges of every tonne of wyne, the
whiche was then called tonnage & poun-
dage, but since it hathe bene renued at
sundry parliamentes, and nowe is called custome. Furthermore, it was enac- Marchaunt
ted that all marchaunt straungers shuld straungers.
be lodged within an Englishe host with
in xv. dayes of their comming to their
port sale, & to make no sale of any marchaundise or they were so lodged, and
then within xl. dayes following, to
make sale of all they brought, & if any
remayned to be forfayte to the kyng.

Anno.4.

Sherifes, Wil. Milrede, Iohn Frokle. 28. of Septem
Mayor, sir Iohn Couentrie Mercer. 28. of Octo-
1426 The morrow after Simon & Iudes day at night, was stiring & great watch
and the morrowe next following, much people of the citie arayed them to stand
by the Duke of Gloucester protector, &
Duke of Glocester, and the bishop of Winchester. the Maior in defence of the citie against the bishop of Winchester, and the peop
of Lancaster and Chester, but the matte was appeased by the regent of Fraunce
The xxviij. day of September, was
Earthquake. terrible earthquake, the space of two houres. Anno. 5.

Sherifes, Iohn Arnold, Iohn Higham. 28. of Septem
Mayor, sir Iohn Raynewell Fishmonger. 28 of Oc
1427 This Iohn Reinewell Maior of Lon don, gaue certaine tenementes to the
Wardes discharged of fifteenes. Citie of London, for the which the sam citie is bounde to pay for euer, all such fifteenes as shall be graunted to the ki (so that it passe not three fifteenes in o yeares) for three wardes of the same, th is to say Dougate, Billingsgate, and Alga warde.

The Tower on London bridge was begonne, and the Mayor of London la the first stone. Anno. 6

Sherifes. Henry Frowick, Robert Otley. 28. of Se
Mayor, sir Iohn Gidney Draper. the 28. of Octo

fi

From the beginning of Aprill to Mar- 1428
tinmasse, was a continual rayne. An. 7
Thomas Duthous Iohn Abbot. 28. of Sept. Sherifes,
Sir Henry Barton Skinner. the 28. of Octo. Mayor,
The Duke of Northfolke was like to
haue bene drowned, passing through
London bridge, his Barge being set vpon the piles whelmed ouer, so that he
and very few escaped, being drawen vp
with ropes. There were drowned xxx.
persones.

A Britaine murdered a wydow with- 1429
out Algate, and bare away all that she Murder
had, and after he tooke succour of quite with
the churche at S. Georges in South- murder.
warke, and at the last forsweare the land,
but as he happened to come by the place
where he had done that dede, the women
of that parishe with stones and kenill
dunge, made an ende of him, so that he
went no further. An. 8.
William Russe, Rafe Hollande. 28. Septem. Sherifes,
Sir William Estfelde Mercer. 28. of Octo. Mayor,
Before the Towne of Champaine was 1430
taken a woman armed, with many o- La pucel de
ther Captaynes, the Frenchmen called Deu,
this woman La pucel de Deu, through
whom the Dolphin and al our aduersaries trusted to haue conquered agayne
al Fraunce. Anno, 9.

wal

Sherifes, Wal. Chertsey, Robert Large, 28. of Sept.
Mayor, Sir Nicholas Wotton Draper. 28. of Octo.
1431 AT Abington, began an insurrection of certaine light persons, that entended to haue wrought much mischief, but they were quieted by the lord protector, and the chiefe authour being Bayly of the towne named William Maundeuill, a weauer with other were put to death.

A comotion at Abington

Anno. 10.

Sherifes, Iohn Ardirlee, Stephen Browne. 28. of Sep.
Mayor, Sir Iohn Welles Grocer. The. 28. of Octob.
1432 This Iohn Wels of his goodes caused the Conduct named the Stādard in cheape to be buylded.

Standard in Cheape.

King Henry was crowned at Paris in Fraunce, and shortly after returned into England, and came into London, where he was royally receiued, all the craftes riding in white gownes and redde hoodes embrodered richly. Anno

King Henry Crowned at Paris.

Sherifes, Iohn Olner, Iohn Paddesley. 28. Septemb.
Mayor, ir Iohn Parncis Fishmonger. 28. of Octob.
1433 The xi. of Iune, were foure souldiours of Caleis beheaded, and 110. banished and before that time was banished. 110.

Anno. 12.

Sherifes, Thomas Chalton, Iohn King. 28. Septemb.
Mayor, Iohn Brokley Draper. the. 28. of October.

Th

he Earle of Huntington, was sent 1434
with a company of Souldiours into
rance, where he atchieued many great
es. Anno.13.

o Barawell, Symond Eyre. 28. Septemb. Sherifes.
Roger Otley Grocer. the. 28. of Octob. Mayor,

This yeare was a great Froste, that 1435
suche marchaundise as came to the Great frost,
hames mouth, was caried to London
lande. Anno.14.

o Catworth, Rob. Clepton. 28. Septẽb. Sherifes,
Henry Frowick Mercer. the 28. of Oct. Mayor,

harles of Fraunce, recouered the ci- 1436
tie of Paris, and wanne by force the
towne of Meulan, and of saint Denis, ex-
illing and murdering the Englishmen
great number. Anno.15

homas Morsted, Will. Gregory. 28. sept. Sherifes,
John Michel Fishmonger, 28. of Octob. Mayor,

he gate on London bridge with the 1437
tower vpõ it next to Southwarke, A part of Lõ
ll downe, and twoo of the furthest ar- don bridge
es of the sayde bridge, but as God fel downe.
ould no man perished. Anno.16

illiam Chapman, Wil Hallis. 28. septẽb. Sherifes,
William Eastfield Mercer. 28. of Octo. Mayor,

wen Tewther, brake out of Newgate, 1438
but was againe taken afterward, this
wen had priuely maried Queene Ka-
rine late wife to Henry the fifth, and
had

had foure children by her, whiche was not knowen to the common people tyll she was dead and buried. Anno.17.

Sherifes. Hugh Diker, Nicholas Yoo. the.28 of Sep:
Mayor, sir Stephen Brown Grocer. 28.of October.

Great winds

The 25. of Nouember fel a great winde that did much harme in many places, in London it bare much leade of ÿ Gray Friers church, and almoste blewe down the one side of the olde Chaunge, so that it was faine to be underset with tymber.

Three men slayne.

On Newyeeres day, a stack of woode fel down at Baynardes castel, & killed 3. men out of hand, & many more wer sore hurt.

1419

18. Persons murdered.

Also by fal of a staire at Bedford where the shere day was kept 18. persons were slaine, and many moe hurt.

Conduite in Fletestrete buylded.

This yeare the conduite in Fletestreate was begon to be made by sir William Eastfielde late Mayor, and it was finished of his owne coastes.

R. Chicheley his charitie.

This yeare died Robert Chicheley Grocer, who willed in his Testament, that upon his Mynde day, a good competent dinner should be ordeined for 2400 poore men, housholders of the citie, and xx. li. in money distributed amongst them, which was to euery man ij.d. Anno.18.

Sherifes, Robert Marshal, Phillip Malpas. 29. of Sep.
Mayor, sir Ro. Large Mercer. The.28. of October.

Sir

Sir Richard Wiche, vicar of Hermits worth in Essex, was burned on the tower hyll the .xvij. daye of June. After whose death was great murmour among the people, for some sayde he was a good man, and an holy, and put to death by malyce, and some sayde the contrary, So that many men and women, went by nyght to the place where hee was brent and offered there, money and Images of waxe, and made their prayers knelyng, and kyssed the grounde, and bare alwaye with them the asshes of his bodye for relyques, and this endured eight dayes, tyll the Maior and Aldermen, ordayned men of armes for to restrayne the people. Many were therefore taken and ledde to pryson. Among other was take the Vicar of Berkynge churche, besyde the tower of London, in whose paryshe all this was done, and who receyued the offering of the simple people, and for to excite and styrre them to offre the more feruently, and to fulfyll and satisfie his false couetyse. Hee tooke asshes & medled the with powdre of spices, & strowed the in y place where the said priest was brent, & so the simple people was deceiued, wening y swete flauour

A priest brēt on tower hil

Logardeman of a priest.

clauour had come of the ashis of ye dead preest. For all this, the syde Uicare of Berkingchurche confessed afterwardes in pryson.. This haue I noted to the reprofe of him, who hath writte the Vicare of Berking church, at that tyme to be burnt which is false: for hee was not brente, thoughe hee beter deserued then the oth

Posterne sonke.

The posterne gate of London by East Smithfield, against the tower of London sanke by night more then vii. foote into the earth, the xviii. of July.

An order taken for strāgers.

It was ordayned that all marchauntes straungers should go to hoste with Englishmen, to sell their marchaundise, and to bye agayne within viii. monethes after their comming, and to go agayne within the sayde terme, and in case that any of their marchandise remayne vnsolde at their departing, they to haue it with thē without any custome paying, and the goodes that they bye or sell, they shall geue to their hostesse for euery xx.s. worth, two pence, except the Easterlinges. Also it was ordeyned that euery housholde of Dutche people shall pay to the king by yeare xv.d. and euery seruaunt of them vi.d.

Anno. 19.

Iohn

n Sutton VV. wetinghale. 28. Septēb. Sherifes.
John Paddisley Goldsmith, 28. of octob. Mayor.
This yeare was a combate fought at 1441
Totchill betweene two theues thap- A combate
at and defendaunt, the appeler had fought by ij.
field of the defendaunt within thre theues at
yes. Roger Bolingbroke, for sorcery Totchill.
inst the kinge was put in the tower
London, and after stoode vpon a scaf-
de afore Poules crosse, being arrayed
his garments pertaining to that arte.
ortly after the Duches of Gloucester Roger Bo-
ared afore the king & his lordes spi- lingbroke
uall and temporall, where she was and Eliano
mined of diuers pointes of witche- Cobham.
fte, the whiche shee knowledged that
had vsed through the counsell of the
tche of Eye. The which witche was
nt in Smithfielde. Anno. 20
lliam Combis, Richard Riche. 28. Sept. Sherifes.
g, Clopton Draper. The. 28. of October. Mayor
the Duchesse of Glocester being ioy- 1442
ned to penaunce by the Clergie, on the Eliano Cob-
onday next folowyng came frō West- ham.
inster by water, and landed at the tem
bridge, from whence with a taper of
ace in her hande, shee went thorough
eteſtrete to Paules. On wednisday e
t, she landed at the Swane in Tha-
s strete, & went to Cristchurch by Al-

K gate,

gate. On Friday she landed at Quene hithe, and so went to saint Michaels in Cornhill. And after sent to ye Ile of Man, there to remaine during her life. On the [illegible] day of November, Roger Bollingbroke,

Execution. was drawen from the Tower to Tyborne, and there hanged, headed, & quartered.

Anno. 28.

[illegible] Thomas Bewmõt, Richard Nordõ. 28, sep.

Maior. John Hatherle Iremonger. 28, of October.

[illegible] The citizens of Norwich rose against the Prior of Christchurch in the same citie, & would haue fired ye Priorie, & [illegible] the towne by strong hande against the Duke of Norfolke and all his power. [illegible] the which [illegible] thither the duke [illegible] called Folkew, with the Earle of [illegible], and the Earle of Huntingdon, [illegible] many citizens & the [illegible].

Anno. 22.

[illegible] Nicholas Wilford, John Normã. 28 of sep.

Maior. Thomas Catworth Grocer 28. of October.

[illegible] An [illegible] was made by the common counsell of London, ye vpon sonday should no market bee kepte, nor any thing [illegible] or solde within the liberties of the citie.

Anno. 23.

[illegible] Stephen Foster, Hugh Wiche, 28, of septem.

Maior. Sir Henry Frowike Mercer, 28, of October.

On

On Candlemas euen, S. Paules stee- 1444
ple at London, was on fire by tempest Paules ste-
thunder and lightning at Euensong ple on fire.
time, by the great labour of people, it
was quenched, and no man perished.

Queene Margarete daughter to þ king
Cicele, came to Englande, and was The king
receiued at the Blackheath by the citize- maried.
ns of London, riding on horsebacke all
in blue gownes with redde hoodes.

An. 24.

John Derby, Godfrey Filding. 28. of Sept. Sherifes.
Symond Eire, Draper the. 28. of Octob. Mayor.

This Symond Eire builded the Leaden 1445
hal in London, and also a beautifull
chappell in the East ende of the same: o-
uer the gate wherof was written, as foloweth: Dextera Domini exaltauit me.
The Lordes right hand hath exalted me. A notable
Whereby he doing so notable a worke for example.
the common weale, also left a notable example to other Citizens.

Anno. 25.

Robert Horne, Godfrey Bolein. 28 of sep. Sherifes.
John Olney Mercer. the 28. of October. Mayor.

In a Parleament at Bery, Humfrey duke
of Glocester, was accused of high treas- 1447
on, his men voyded frõ him, & sone af- Parliament
ter he was found dead in his chãber, & at Bery.

then the parliament ended. He was buried at Saint Albons. Anno.26.

Sheriffes, Will. Abraham, Thomas Scotte 28 of Sept.

Mayor. sir Iohn Gidney Draper. 28. of October.

1448 This yeare was taken the towne of Fogers, from the Englishmen, which was the cause that all Normandy was lost afterwarde. Anno.27

Sheriffes, Wil. Catlow, Wil. Marrow. 28. of Septem.

Mayor, sir Stephen Browne Grocer. 28. of Octob.

1449 ROan was yelded to the Frenche king.
Roan yelded. Anno.28.

Sheriffes, Williã Hulyn, Thomas Caninges. 28. of Sep.

Mayor, sir Thomas Chalton Mercer. 28. of Octo.

Iacke Blewbearde, who was taken besides
Blew beard. Canterbury, for raising a rebellion was drawen, hanged, and quartered, in February.

1450 The Marques of Suffolke was banished ye land for v. yeares, for the death
A murder. of the Duke of Glocester, who sayling toward Fraunce, was met on the sea by a ship of warre, & there presently beheaded, & his dead corps cast up at Dover.

The commons of Kent, in great num-
A commotion in Kent by Iacke Cade. ber assembled on Blackheath, having their captain Iacke Cade, naming hymselfe Mortimer. Against whome the king sent a great army; but by the slyte Captaine and rebels, they were discomfited.

Syr

r Humfrey Stafford, and William
s brother, with many other slayne. At
this victory, the captaine and rebels
me to London, who entring the citie,
oke his sworde on London stone and
d: Now is Mortimer Lord of this ci-
. He caused ỹ lord Saye to be brought
the Guylde halle of London, there to
arreigned. Which before the kynges
stices, desired to be tried by his pie-
s, but the Captaine by force tooke him
m the officers, and at the standarde in
ape smote of his head. He also behea
d Sir Iames Cromer at the Myles
de. And pitching these twoo heades
twoo poles, entred the citie, and in
pite caused them (being borne before
m) in euery streate to kisse together.
ter this murder, succeded open robbe-
within the citie. But the Maior & o-
r sage magistrates, perceiuing them
ues neither to be sure of goodes nor
e, determined to expulse this ungraci
s cōpany, & sent to the Lord Scales, ke
r of the Towre, who promysed his
de, with shoting of ordinaunce: & Ma-
ew Gough was appointed to assiste the
Maior, so the captaines of the city toke
on thē in the night to kepe the bridge,
ohibiting ỹ Kentishmen to passe. The

Tyranny of the rebels.

 rebelles

rebelles hearing the bridge to be kepte, ranne with great force to open that passage, where betwene both partes was a fierce encounter. The rebelles draue the citizens from the stoulpes at the bridge foote to the drawe bridge, and set fire in diuers houses. In conclusion, the rebels gate the drawe bridge, and drowned and slue many. This conflicte endured till nyne of the clocke in the morninge, in doubtfull chaunce, so that both partes agreed to desiste from fight till the next daye, vpon condition, that neither Londoners should passe into Southwarke, nor the Kentishemen into London. Then the archebishop of Caunterbury, beyng Chaunceler, with the bysshop of Wynchester, passed into Southwarke, where they shewed a generall pardon, vnder the kynges great seale, whereupon the whole multitude retired home. The captaine fledde through the weilde into Sussex, and was slayne at Hothfelde, and brought to London in a carte, and there quartered, then the kynge roade into Kent, wher many were drawen & hanged.

Iacke Cade slayne.

The bishop of Saresbury was murdered by the commons of the Weste countrey. Anno. 29

Bishop of Sarisbury murde.ed.

Shreifes, Iohn Middleton, William Dere. 28. of sept.

Nicolas Wifold Grocer, the 28. of Octo. Mayor,
This yeare was a [illegible] by the [illegible] 1453
against the Mayor of London, for that
he tooke his charge at Westminster.
The whole Duchy of Normandy was
ceded to the French king, by meanes
of the Queene, and the Duke of Somerset. Anno. 30.
Mathew Philip, Christ. Warton. 28. of Sept. Sherifes,
sir William Gregory, Skinner. 28. of octob. Mayor,
A Commotion begun by the Duke of 14[illegible]
Yorke and other which was appeased Commotion
in a space. Anno. 31.
Richard Lee, Richard Alley. 28. of Septem. Sherifes,
sir Godfrey Felding Mercer. 28. of Octob. Mayor,
The king made his two brethren of the 1453
mothers side, the elder of them named States crea-
Edmond, Earle of Richmond, and the ted.
yonger named Jasper, Erle of Pembroke.
The Queene was delivered of a Prince
called Edwarde. Anno. 32.
John Walderne, Thom. Cooke. 28. of Sep. Sherifes,
sir John Norman Draper. The 28. of Octob. Mayor,
Before this Mayors yeare, the Mayor 1454
sherifes, & commons, were wont to Mayor of
ryde to Westminster, when the Mayor London ro-
should take his charge, but this Mayor wed to We-
was rowed thither by water. stminster.
Betweene the king and the Duke of

Yorke, with his alies at S. Albons, a cruell battail was fought. In the end wherof, the victorie fell to the Duke of Yorke. And on the kings party was slayne the Duke of Somerset, the Earle of Northumberlande, the Lorde Clifforde, with many other. After which time y Duke brought the king from Saint Albons to London. Where by a Parliament hee was made Protectour of the Realme. Anno.33

Sherifes, John field, William Tayler. 28. September.
Mayor, sir Stephen Foster Fishmonger. 28. of Oct.

1455 AT Saint Martins le grande, sanctuary men, issued foorth and hurte diuers citizens, but it was appeased by the Mayor and other. Anno, 34

Fray by sanctuary men.

Sherifes, John Yong, Thomas Oulgraue. 28. of Sept.
Mayor, sir William Marrowe Grocer. 28. of Octo.

1456 BY meanes of the Queene and other Lordes, the Duke of Yorke was discharged of his Protectorship.

Riot against Lobards

A great riote in London against the Lombardes and Italians, because a Mercers seruaunt was cast in prison for striking an Italian. Anno 35.

Sherifes, John Steward, Rafe Verney, 28. of Septeb.
Mayor, sir Thomas Canings Grocer. 28. of Octob.

1457 AT Erith within the limites of London, were taken foure wonderfull fishes, whereof one was called Mors Marina,

Monstrous fishes.

the

he second a swoorde fyshe, the other two were Whales.

A fleete of Frenchmen landed at Sandwiche, and spoyled the towne with great crueltie. Sandwich spoyled.

The prysoners of Newgate brake out of their wardes, & toke the leades of the gate, & defended it a long whyle against the Sherifes and all their officers, in so much y they were forced to cal for more ayde of the citizens, by whose ayde they finally subdued them. Anno. 36 Prisoners of Newgate.

William Edward, Thomas Reiner. 28. Sep. Sherifes,

Godfrey Bolein Mercer. 28. of October. Maior,

A fained agreement was made betwene the king, the Queene, and the Duke of Yorke, for ioy wherof the xxv. day of Marche, a general procession was celebrated in S. Paules at London. Where the king in habite royall, and his Diademe on his head, kept his state in procession: before whom went hand in hād, the Duke of Somerset, the Earle of Salisbury, the Duke of Exceter, and the Earle of Warwike, & so one of the one factiō, and other of the other sect. And behynde the king, the Duke of Yorke led y Queene with great familiaritie to al mēs sightes. 1458 Fained ag[r]eement.

A great fray was in Fletestreate betwene men of the court and the inhabitantes

The queenes attourney slayne. fauntes of the same Greate, in which af-
fray the Queenes attourney was slaine.
For this fact the King committed the
principall gouernours of Furniuall, Clif-
fordes, and Barnardes Innes to prison, in Herford castell. William Taylour Alderman
of that warde, with many other were
sent to Windsor castell. Anno, 37.

Sherifes, Rafe Iosselyn, Rich. Nedham 28, of Sept.
Mayor, sir Thomas Scot Draper. the 28 of Octob.

1459. The noble Science of Printing was
Science of printing. founde in Germany at Magunce, by
one Iohn Cuthenbergus a knight, William
Caxton Mercer of London brought it
into Englande, about the yeare of our
Lorde 1471. and first practised the same
in the Abbey of Saint Peter in Westminster.

The Duke of Yorke, & Earles of Salisbury & Warwike, with a great hoste
met the King & other Lordes of Englande
Blorehethe fielde. vpon Blorehearh, where because Andrew
Trollop, a captaine of Caleis, the night
before the battaile should haue bene, fled
with a company of the best souldiors to
the kinges part. The Duke of Yorke, the
Earles of Marche, Salisbury & Warwike, mistrusting themselues to bee to
weake, departed with a priuy company.
Anno, 38.

Iohn

John Plummer, Iohn Stocker. 28. of septemb. — Sherifes 39

Sir William Hulin Fishmonger 29. of Octo. — Mayor.

The three Earles with a great army, met king Henry at Northampton, & gaue him strong battaile. In the ende whereof the victory fel to the Lordes, the kinges host was discomfited, and many slayne, and the king taken in the fielde.

A battaile at Northampton

The Duke of Yorke made such claime to the crowne, that by consent of a parliament, he was proclaimed heire apparant.

The Duke of Yorke clay-meth the crowne.

Margaret the Queene hath gathered a company of Northern men, and neare to Wakefield, in a cruell fight discomfited and slewe the Duke of Yorke, with his sonne the Earle of Rutlande.

A battell at Wakefield.

Anno. 39

Richard Fleming, Ioh. Lambard. 28. of Sep. — Sherifes.

Sir Richard Lee Grocer. the 28. of Octob. — Mayor.

The Queene with her retinue neare saint Albons, discomfited the Erle of Warwike & the Duke of Norfolke, and rescued king Henry her husbande.

The second battayle at saint Albons

Edward Earle of March, at that time was in wales, and had a great battayle against the Earles of Pembroke & Wiltshire, at Mortimers crosse vpon Candlemas day, and put them to flight & slew many of their people. That daye he

Battayle at Mortimers crosse

se Wil-

sene thre Sunnes, euery one shewing a seuerall light, whiche afterward closed all together in one. The Earle of Warwike fled from S. Albons to the Earle of Marche, and almost all the people of the South countries fell to hym, and king Henry vnderstanding that the Erle of March with a great power was commyng toward London, he with ẏ quene withdrewe them toward Yorke.

The Earle of Warwike fled.

The K. and Queene fled

Then the Earle of Marche came vp to London with a myghtye power of Marchemen, accompanied with the Earle of Warwyke, where he was ioyfully receyued. Thus king Henry lost his kingdome, when he had raigned .38. yeares, sixe monethes, and foure dayes.

EDVVARD EARLE of Marche.

Anno reg. 1.

Edwarde the fourthe, was proclaymed kyng of England, the fourth daye of Marche, in the yeare of our Lorde 1460.

On the xii. day of March, one Walter Walker Grocer, for woordes spoken ... ing kyng Edwarde, was beheaded in [illegible] in Smithfielde.

The xiii. day of Marche, king Edward tooke his iourney towarde the North, and betweene Shirborne and Totcastre, all the North parte mette with him, and on Palme Sonday, the xxix. of March, Anno. 1461. there was as great a mortall battaile as euer was seene in Englande. In whiche battaile were slaine the Earle of Northumberland, the Lorde Clifforde, the Lord Neuile, the Lorde Welles, and many mo of bothe partes, to the nomber of xxxvi. thousand vii. hundred lxxvi. persones. But king Edwarde got the fielde, and the Duke of Excester, the Duke of Somerset, the lord Roos, the Lorde Hungerforde, and many other [illegible] of their felowship, fled to Yorke to Henry [illegible] kinge, and then fled with the Queene and her sonne [illegible] towarde Scotlande, and came to Barwike, and from thence to Edinbrough. — A battayl on Palme sonday. 1461 — King Henry with his Queene fled into Scotland.

John Locke, George Ireland, [illegible] Sheriffes,
sir Hugh Wiche Mercer, [illegible] Mayor. 1462

The kynge sent the Earle of Kent, called Lorde Fauconbridge, and other into Britayne, [illegible] wonne the towne of Conquet, and the Ile of Rothe. Anno. 2

Sherifes. Will. Hampton, Bartho. James. 28. of Sept.
Mayor, sir Thomas Coke Draper. the 28. of Octo.

1463 Margarete the Queene, and wyfe to Henry the sixt, landed in Englande, but hauing small succour and euill fortune: was fayne to take the seas agayne, and by tempest of weather, was dryuen into Scotlande. Anno. 3.

Sherifes, Robert Basset, Thomas Muschãp. 28. Sep.
Mayor, sir Mathew Philip Goldsmith. 28. of Octob.

1464 The xv. day of May, king Henries power being at Hexam, the lordes Montague with a power came thether early, and enclosed them round about, there were takẽ and slaine many of the lordes that were with king Henry, but he him selfe was fled foure dayes before with Sir Richard Tunstall, maister Thomas Manning, and Doctor Bedon, into Lancashire.

The battell of Hexam.

K. Edwarde maried.

King Edwarde toke to wife Elizabeth daughter to Iaquet duchesse of Bedforde, sister to the Earle of saint Paules, late wife of Syr Iohn Gray.

Coyne inhãsed.

The king chaunging his coyne, ordeined that the groate weyed scantly iii pence, and the Noble that was afore at vi. shillinges eight pence, should go for viii. shillinges iiii. pence &c.

Pestilence.

A great Pestilence, with a drie Somme-

mer,

r, & a hard wynter, ye Thames was
ut frozen.

In Michelmas terme were made vii.
Sergeantes at lawe, T. Yong, N. Geny, Ri.
Nele, T. Brian, Ri. Pigot, I. Grenfield, I. Ca-
tesby, & Guy Fairfax. Which held their feast
at the bishop of Ely his place in Holborne, to ye which feast, ye Mayor of London with the Aldermen, Shireffes & comons of diuers craftes being boden, repaired, but when ye Maior looked to be
set to kepe the state in the hall, as it had
bene vsed in al places of ye citie & liberties, out of ye kinges presence (vnknowen
to ye Sergeantes & against their will as
they said) the lord Grey Ruthin, then treasurer of England was there placed, wherupon the Maior, Aldermen, & comons,
departed home, & the Maior made al the
Aldermen to dine with him, howbeit he
and all the city was greatly displeased
that he was so delt with, & the new Sergeantes & other, were right sory thereof, & had leuer then much good it had not
happed. This was then, as my recorde
mentioneth more at large, recorded in the
Guylde hal, at ye request of ye comons to
be in minde a president in time to come. 4
John Tate. Iohn Stone, the 28. of Septemb. Sherifes.
Rauf Ioselyn Draper, 28. of October. Mayor.

The

1465 New coyne. The Kynge made a Noble at tenne shillinges, the halfe noble v. shillings and the farthing at two shillinges and vi. d. and ordeyned an Angelot at vi. s. and viii. pence, and the halfe therof at iii. shillinges and foure pence.

King Henry taken. King Henry was taken besydes the Abbey of Saly in Lancashire, and arested by the Earle of Warwike, Doctor Manning sometyme deane of Wyndsore, doctor Bedle, and yong Elerton, beyng in company, were all brought to the Tower of London.

Shepe transported. This yeare was graunted a licence to passe over certaine cotte wolde shepe into Spayne, which haue there multiplied greatly. Anno. 5.

Sherifes, sir Hen. Weuer, Will. Constantine. 28. sep.
Mayor, sir Raufe Verney Mercer. 28. of Octob.

1466 The Queene was delivered of a doughter, which was named Elizabeth.

Anno. 6.

Sherifes, John Brown, Hen. Bricele, Io. Stokton. 28. sep.
Mayor, sir John Yong Grocer. the 28. of october.

1467 Iustis in Smithfielde. The Lorde Scales iusted in Smithfielde with the bastarde of Burgoyne, and had the victory.

Anno. 7

Sherifes, Tho. Stalbroke, Humfrey Hayford. 28. sept.
Mayor, Thomas Olgraue skinner, 28. of Octobe

Sir

SIr Thomas Cooke Alderman of London, was accused of treason, and arreigned of the same, and found not giltye: but yet he was detayned in prison, & could not be delivered vntill hee had agreed with the Kinge for 8000. poundes which he payd. Anno 8. 1468

Simon Smith, W. Hariot. 28. of Septemb. Sherifes.
sir William Tayler Grocer. 28. of Octob. Mayor.

THis Wiliam Tayler gaue certaine tenementes, for the whiche the Cittye is bond to pay for euer, at euery fiftene to be graunted to the kinge, for al such people as shall dwell in Cordwayners streate warde, sessed at xii.d. the peece or vnder. 1469

Fiftenes discharged.

The Erle of Warwike adioyned with the Duke of Clarence the kinges brother, stirred so the Northren men, that they diuers times rebelled, and turned the king and the Realme to much trouble. But shortlye the rebels were suppressed. Anno.9.

Battaile at Danberye.

Rich.Gardiner, Robert Drope. 28. of Sep. Sherifes.
sir Rich. Lee Grocer. The 28. of October Mayor.

GEorge Duke of Clarence, Iasper Erle of Penbroke, Richard Erle of Warwicke, and the Erle of Oxeforde with other arriued at Plimouth, and an other parte at Dertmouth, which all toke theyr 1470.

voyage toward Excetour, & then Northwarde, the .xxix. of September kynge Edward fled from his hoast then beinge beside Notingham, and he wyth ÿ Lorde Riuers, the Lord Chamberlaine, & other toke shippyng at Linne, and sayled into Flaunders.

K. Edwarde fled.

The 6. daye of October, the Duke of Clarence, the Earle of Warwike, ÿ Archbishop of Yorke, the Lorde Saint Iohn wyth other Lords, spiritual and temporall entered the Tower of London, and K. Henry beinge there prisoner nigh the space of 9. yeares, they elected him to be their lawful King: and forthwith rode wyth him through London to the Bishops pallas, wher he rested till the 13. of October, and then wente on Procession, crowned in Poules.

K. Henry restored to the crowne.

Anno. 10.

Sherifes. John Crosby, Iohn Ward. 28. of Septemb.

Mayor. sir Iohn Stockton Mercer. The 28. of Oct.

1471. Queene Elizabeth wyfe to Edwarde ÿ fourth, beinge in the Saintuarye of Westminster, was deliuered of a Prince, who afterward was Edward the fith.

Prince born in Saintuary

Edwarde the fourth landed in Holdernes, in the countie of Yorke, with a very small companye of souldiours: but by meanes ÿ he vsed, & through his moth[illegible]

the

the Duke of Clarence, who turned now to his part, he came so puissantly to Londõ, & he entred the Citye the xi. day of April, and toke kinge Henry in the Bysshops Palles, and then went againste ỹ Earle of Warwicke, whom he vanquished and slewe, with his brother Marques Montague, on Gladesmore heath nere Barnet, tenne miles from London. And the fourth day of Maye, besyde Teukesburye, he overthrewe Queene Margaret, the wyfe of K. Henry. In which battaile was taken, the saide Margarete wyth Edward the Prince her sonne, the Duke of Somerset, and divers other.

Barnet field on Easter daye.

Battaile at Teukesbury.

Thomas the Bastarde of Fauconbridge, that unto him gathered a vicious company of Essex and Kent, came to the Citye of London, and fyred Bishops gate, and Algate, and fought so fiercely, that they wanne the Bulwarkes at Algate: But the citizens withstode the rebels and chased them unto the farther Stratford, and slew and toke many of them.

Thomas the Bastard lyveth by the spoyle of innocents.

Suburbes of Algate and Bishops gate set on fyre.

Henry the sixte was murdered in the Tower of London, and buryed at Chertsey, and after removed to Windsore.

K Henrye murdered.

K. Edwarde rode towarde Kente, and there caused inquirye to be made of the unthriftes of the foresayde riotte, the

Maior of Canterburye wyth eyght other were beheaded. The heades of Spling & Quintin, two captaynes under the bastard were set on Algate. But the kinge pardoned the Bastard, and dubbed him knight. In September the sayd bastard was take at Southampton and beheaded, his head was set on London bridge.

the Bastarde made knight.

The bastard lost his head.

Anno. 11.

Sherifes. John Allein John Shelley. 28. of Septemb.

Mayor. sir W Edward Grocer. The 28. of October

1472. The Earle of Oxforde, and his Ladye. The Erle of Oxeford was sent prisoner unto Guines, where he remained so long as Edward the fourth raigned, in al whiche time the Ladye his wyfe, mighte neuer come to him, nor had any thinge to liue vpon, but what people of their charityes woulde geue her, or what she got by her nedle.

Anno. 12.

Sherifes. John Browne, Thomas Bedlow. 28. of Sep.

Mayor. sir W. Hampton fishmonger. 28. of Octo.

1473 Strompets punished. This Maior punished manye strompets and harlots, and caused them to ryde with ray hoods, & made a payre of Stockes to be set in euerye ward.

Anno. 13.

Sherifes William Stocker, Rob. Billisdō 28. of Sep.

Mayor. Sir Iohn Tate Mercer. The 28 of October.

Thomas

Thomas Burdet was put to death for a word speaking, after this sort. He had a white bucke in his parcke at Arrow, which kinge Edward comminge thether to hunt killed. Thomas Burdet hearinge therof, wyshed the buckes head in his belly, that had moued the kinge to kill the said bucke: but this tale was told ye kyng, and the same Thomas Burdet was apprehended and accused of treason, for wishyng the buckes head, hornes and all in the kinges belly, and [illegible] of London, [illegible] and lost his head. 1474. Thomas Burdet Esquire of Warwikeshire beheaded for a word speaking.

Anno. 14.

Edmond Shaw, Thomas Hill. 28. of Sept. Sheriffes.
& Robert Drope. Draper. 28. of October. Mayor.

This Robert Drope buylded the East ende of the Conduite in Cornhill. 1475. Conduite in Cornhil.

K. Edward sayled into Fraunce with a great armye, to ayde the Duke of Burgoine: but by sute of the French kyng, a peace was concluded. Anno. 15.

Hughe Prince, Rob. Colwiche. 28. of Sep. Sheriffes.
& Robert Bassit Salter. the 28. of Octob. Mayor.

This Maior did sharpe correction vpon Bakers, for makinge of light bread, he set diuers of them on the pillorie. Also Agnes Deintie, was there punished for sellinge of mingled butter. 1476. Agnes deintye.

Anno. 16

Sherifes. Richarde Rawson Wil Horne. 28 of Sept.
Mayor. sir Raphe Iosselin Draper The 28 of Oct.
147[illegible]. By the diligence of this Maior the
London new wall of London, from Creple-
wall. gate to Bishoppes gate, was made: the Maior with his companye, made all
part betweene All hallowes Church and
Bishops gate, of their owne proper costes. and the other companyes made the other parte. Anno. 17

Sherifes. Henry Collet. Iohn Stocker. 28 of Sept.
Mayor sir Humfrey Heyford Goldsmith. 28. Oct.
14[illegible]. George Duke of Clarence in ŷ towr
The Duke of London, made his end in a rondlet
of Clarence of Malmesey, & was buryed at Tukes-
murdered, bury by his wyfe, doughter to the Erle of Warwicke, which being wyth chyld, dyed of poyson, but a litle before hym.

Anno. 18

Sherifes. Robert Hardyng, Robert Bifielde. 28. of S.
Mayor. Richard Gardiner Mercer. The 28. of Oct.
1479. This yeare was a greate death, and
Great pestilence. also a great death at London, and in diuers other partes of this Realme.

Anno. 19.

Sherifes Thomas Ilam, Iohn Warde. 28 of Septem.
Mayor. sir Bartho. Iames Draper. The 28. of Octo.
1480. This Thomas Ilam Sherifes newly buylded the great conduicte in Chepe of his owne proper coastes.

T

The xxii. day of Februarye, three thee- | Execution.
were drawen, hanged, and brent, &
er two were pressed to death, because
y had robbed S. Martins the great, and
er places. An. 20.

I. Daniel, william B[illegible]con. 28. of Septem. Sherifes.
ohn Browne Mercer, the 28. of Octo. Mayor, 1481.

The King requested great summes of
money to be lente him of the Citti-
s of London, who graunted to lende
5000. markes, which was repayed
ine. Anno. 21.

b Tate, Wil. Wyking, Ri. Chawry. 28 S. Sherifes.
lliam Harlote Draper. The 28. of Octo. Mayor. 1482.

This yeare the Scottes beganne to
stirre, against whom K. Edward sente
Duke of Gloucester, and diuers o-
r, which returned againe wythoute
notable battayle.

Anno. 22

White, Iohn Mathewe 28. of Sept. Sherifes
Edmonde Shaw Goldsmith, 28. of Oct. Mayor. 1483.

This Edmonde Shawe builded Creple
gate at London. Creplegate.

Kinge Edwarde makyng great prouisi-
n for warre in Fraunce, ended hys
the ix. of April in the yeare of oure
rde 1483. When he had raigned xxii.
res, i. moneth & fiue dayes. Hee was
ryed at Windsore, leauinge after hym

two sonnes, Edwarde the Prince, and Richard Duke of Yorke, wyth v. daughters as Elizabeth that after was queene (and wyfe to Kinge Henry the seventh) Cycelie, Anne, Katherine and Bridget.

EDVVARD the fith.

Anno.reg.

EDwarde the fifth of the age of xi. yeares, begã his raigne ouer this realme of Englande the ix. of Aprel, in the yeare of oure Lorde 1483. Which yonge Prince raigned a small space, eyther in pleasure or libertye, for hys uncle Richard Duke of Glocester wythin three monethes, depriued hym, not onlye of hys Crowne, but also of his lyfe. This Edwarde raigned two monethes and xi. dayes.

RICHARDE Duke of Glocester.

Richard

Richarde the thirde, brother to Edwarde the 4. thorowe manye cruell dedes, lastly obtayned ỹ Crowne of Englãd, the 22. daye of June, in the yeare 1483. He put ...th those noble menne, whiche hee ...ught would not cõsent to hys mind. ...onge the which were the Lorde R... ...the Lorde Richard Graye the Quee... ...sonne, sir Thomas Vahan, and sir Ri... ...d Hawte at Pomfret: And the Lorde ...ynges, in the tower of London al on ...daye. The other he corrupted with ...e giftes, then hee ... from the ...ene Elizabeth, (beyng in Sainctuary) her yongest sonne, and brother to ỹ ...ince. Thirdly he caused to be publi... ...d at Paules Crosse, by one doctoure ...we, that Edwarde the fourth his elder ...ther was not rightlye begotten by ...mother, but by aduoutry: And ther... ...that neyther hee nor his children, ... righte to the Crowne, but that of ...ht pertayned vnto hym. Fourthly, ... caused the Duke of Buckingham, ... Guild hall of London, by an eloquẽt ...tion, to perswade ỹ people to chuse ...kyng, and to crye K. Richarde, &c.

Anno reg. 1

Queene Elizabeth toke Saintuarye.

Hee

Hee with his wife Queene Anne, were both crowned at Westminster on the 7. day of July. At which time was taken for rebels against the king, Robert Russe, sergeant of London, Wil. Davye pardoner of Hornslow, John smith grome of K. Edwardes stirrope, and Stephen Irelande Wardroper in the Tower, with many other, who were charged ÿ they had sent writinges into Britaine to ÿ Erles of Richmont and of Pembroke &c. And also mente to have stolne out of ÿ Tower of London, Prince Edwarde & his brother the Duke of Yorke &c. For ÿ which they were drawen from Westminster to the Tower hill, and there all 4. beheaded. And shortly after Prince Edward with Richarde Duke of Yorke his brother, were smouthered in theyr beds by the handes of Myles Forest, and John Dighton.

dward the fth mur- ered. (Edward the fifth murdered.)

Sherifes. Tho. Norland, Wil. Martin. 28. of Sept.

Mayor. sir Rob. Balisdon Haberdasher. 28. of Oct.

1484. Grudge began betweene K. Richarde and his nere frend the Duke of Buckingham, in so much that the Duke with diuers other noble menne, intended to bring into the land, Henry Erle of Richmont as right heyre to the Crowne. For this conspiracye the Duke was taken

uke of uckinghã eheaded.

and

and beheaded at Salisburye the 2. daye of Nouember: many other Knightes and gentlemē were executed in December.

The 12. day of December was a great fyre at Leaden hall in London, where was burnte much housinge, and all the stockes for Gunnes, and other prouision belonging to the Citye.

This yeare K. Richard began ŷ highe Tower at Westminster.

The vii. of August, K. Henry the sixte was remoued from Chertseye to Windsore. Anno. 2.

Rich Chester, Tho. Britain, Raphe Astri. Sherifes.
sir Thomas Hill Grocer. The 28. of Octob. Mayors,
William Stocker Draper, the 24. of Septe.
Iohn Warde Grocer, the 8. of October.

Collingborne Esquier, was drawne frō Westminster through the Citty of Londō to the Tower hill, and there hanged, headed, and quartered.

Queene Anne dyed in Lent, and was buryed at Westminster. sir Roger Clifforde Knight, & one Foskewe, were drawen through London, and at S. Martins sir Roger Clifforde woulde haue broken from the Shirifes, & haue taken Saintuarye, but the Sheriffes tooke hym agayne, and had him to the Tower hyll, and 1485.

and there cut of his heade, and Foskewe had his Charter.

Henry Earle of Richmond, the Earle of Pembroke his brother, the Earle of Oxforde, the bishop of Excester, wyth manye other Knightes and Esquiers, wyth a small companye of Frenchmen, landed at Milford hauen nere vnto Pembroke the 7. daye of Auguste. Whose commynge when it was hearde of, dyuers noble menne wyth theyr retenue forsakinge Kinge Richarde, gathered to him in great noumber: so that his strẽgth in short space greatly encreasinge. At a village neare to Leicester, called Bosworth, hee met wyth hys ennemyes the xxii. of August: where betweene them two houres and more, was foughten a sharpe battaile. In conclusion K. Richarde wyth diuers other was slaine, & Henrye obtayned a noble victorye: After which conquest, he was by the Lord Stanley, immediatlye Crowned Kyng of England in the field, wyth ẏ Crown which was taken frõ K Richardes head. K. Richarde was broughte to Leicester, & there buryed at the Graye Fryers, whẽ he had vsurped the Crowne two yeres and two Monethes.

A battaile at Bosworth

HENRY EARLE of Richmond.

Anno. reg. 1.

HEnry the seuenth began to raigne ouer thys Realm of Englande § xxii. daye of Auguste in the yeare of oure Lorde 1485. He was a Prince of maruayleus wysdome, policye, Iustice, temperaunce, & grauitye. Hee so behaued him in the time of his reigne, that notwithstanding many and greate occasions of trouble, vnquietnes and warre, hee kepte his Realme in right good rule and order. On § foresaid xxii. day of August, was a great fyre in Bredstreete of London, & in the same fyre, was burnte the parson of S. Mildreds, and an other man in the parsonage. &c.

Parson of S. Mildreds brent.

This yeare the greate Conduite in Chepe was newe made, of the goodes of maister Thomas Ilam, Alderman of London, and marchant of the Staple.

Great Conduite in Chepe builded.

This yeare first began the sweating sicknes, the 21. day of September, and continued vntill the ende of October: of

Sweatinge sickenes.

the

the which a wonderful multitude dyed: and in London besides other, Thomas Hill Maior dyed on ye xxvi. day of September, in whose place was chosen sir William Stocker Draper, who receyued his othe at the vtter gate of the Tower of London, but he likewyse deceased about seuen dayes after: in the whiche seuen dayes departed other foure Aldermen, as Thomas Ilam, Richarde Rawson, Thomas Norland, and Iohn Stocker: And then was chosen for Maior, Iohn Warde Grocer, who continued that office the full of Thomas Hilles yere, that is to say, till the feast of Simon and Iude.

Two maiors and 6. Aldermen deceased in 7. dayes.

Thre maiors in one yeare.

Sherifes. Iohn Tate, Iohn Swan. The 28. of Septemb.

Mayor. sir Hughe Brice Goldsmith. 28. of Octob.

Yeomen of the guard. The xxx. day of October ye king was crowned at Westminster, hee ordained a nomber of chosen Archers to giue daily attendance on his person, whom he named Yeomen of his Guarde.

A preste. 1486. The King sent vnto the Lord Maior of London, requiring him and his Citizens of a preste of vi. M. Markes. Wherfore the Maior with his brethren and common counsell of the Citye assembled, and graunted a prest of 2. thousand pound, which was repayde againe the next yeare following.

Wheat

Wheate was at three shillinges the bushell: Bay salt at [illegible] and [illegible] pens three shillinges the bushell. Anno reg. 2.

This yere the Crosse in Cheape was new builded, towarde the buildinge thereof, Thomas Fisher Mercer, gaue a thousand markes. Crosse in Cheape.

Anno. 3.

[illegible] Perciuall, Hughe Clopton. 28 of sep. Sherifes.

Henrye Colet Mercer, the 28. of Oct. Mayor.

The xviii. of January, the King was maried with Elizabeth, eldeste daughter of Edward the fourth: by which meanes the two families of Yorke and Lancaster, was knit together in one. K. Henry maryed.

[illegible] Fran[illegible]cis Louel, and Humfrey Stafforde, rebelled in the North, wyth them was Martin Swarte. Which commotion was appeased by the Duke of Bedforde. There was slaine Iohn Earle of Lincolne, the lord Louel, Martin Swart, and other, about foure Thousande. This battaile was fought on the [illegible] day of June, nigh to a village called Stoke. 1487. Martin Swart. A battaile at Stoke.

In the moneth of September, the Quene was deliuered of her first sonne named Arthure. Anno reg. 3. Prince Arthure.

Anno. 3.

Iohn Fenkill, W. Remington. 28. of sept. Sherifes

Wil. Horne Salter. the [illegible] of October. Mayor.

In

1488. IN Julye was an other preste for the King, made in the Cittie of London of 4. Thousande pound, which was leuied on ẏ craftes shortly after was the thirde prest of two Thousand pounde, which were both repaied the next yeare
An. reg. 4. following. Those sommes of moneye with many mo, was to aide ẏ Archduke of Burgoine, against ẏ Duke of Britaine.

Iohn Ashleye, ẏ sonne of sir Iohn Ashley Knight, with two other, were drawē from Westminster to the tower hil, and there beheaded. Anno. 4.

Sherifes William Isake, Raphe Tinley. 28. of Sept.
Mayor. sir Robert Tate Mercer, the 28 of Octob.
1489. THis yeare was a talke of the tenth
Anno reg. 5 peny of al mens goodes and lands: through whiche the commons of the
Erle of Northumberland slaine. North slew the Erle of Northumberland, wherefore Iohn of Chamber theyr Captaine with other were hanged at Yorke.

Anno. 5.

Sherifes William Capell, Iohn Brooke. 28. of Sept.
Mayor. sir William white Draper. The 28. of Octo.
1490. ROger [illegible] dwellinge wythin
Desperatiõ. Ludgate [illegible] a shoppe wel stored
Anno reg. 6 wyth drapery, slew himselfe. For whiche goods was much busines betwene the kings Almoner and the Sherife.

Anno. 6.

Henrye

H Coote, Ro, Reuel, Hugh Pemberto. 28. S | Sherifes.
John Mathew Mercer. The 28. of Octob. | Mayor.

SIr Robert Chamberlaine Knighte, was beheaded. The king required a beneuolence, towarde his iourneye into Fraunce. | 1491. Execution.

Creplegate of London, was new builded, at the charges of sir Edmonde Shaw Goldsmith, late Mayor. | Creplegate.

Henry the kings second sonne, borne at Grenewiche the xxii. of June. | Henry the kings son.

This yeare the Condnite in Gracious streate, was begon to be builded of the goodes, and by y Executours of sir Thomas Hill Grocer. | Anno reg. 7. Condnite in Gracious streate.

Wheate was sold at London, for xx.d the bushel, which was compted a great death. Anno 7. | Death of corne.

Thomas Woode, W. Browne, 28. of Sept. | Sherifes.
sir Hughe Clopton Mercer and Bacheler. | Mayor.

THis Hughe Clopton Mayor of London, and during his life a batcheler, builded a stone bridge of 18. Arches at Stratforde vppon Auon, and also a waye of foure miles long, &c. | Stratforde vppon Auo.

K Henry toke his voyage into Fraunce with a greate armye, to ayde the Britaynes against the Frenche king. | 1492. An reg. 8.

Anno. 8.

Sherifes W. Purchas W. Welbecke, 28. of Septem.
Mayor ſir W. [illegible] Martin ſkinner. 28. of October

1493. PEace concluded betwene the kings of Englãd and Fraunce, king Henry returned into England.

Pillory pardoners. Two pardoners were ſet on the pillorye thre market dayes, for forging of falſe pardons, wherewith they had deceyued many people, and for that one of them had fayned himſelfe to be a prieſt: he was ſent to Newgate wher he dyed, and the other was driuen out of ẏ Citye with ſhame enough.

Anno reg. 9. Fray againſt the Stilliard. A fray was made againſt the Stilyerde men, by Mercers ſeruants, & other: for the which diuers of them were ſore puniſhed, and the chiefe authors were kept long in priſon. An. 9.

Sherifes. Robart Fabian, Iohn Winger. 28 of ſept.
Mayor. Raphe Aſtry fiſhmonger. 28. of October.

1494. Saintuarye men executed. FOure Saintuary men of S. Martins le grande, were taken out of the ſaide Saintuarye for forginge of ſeditious bils, for the which, and for other treaſons, thre were iudged to dye, who with two other, the one a Flemminge, the other a Yeoman of the Crown, were executed at Tyborne.

Anno. 10. Wheate was ſolde for ſixe pence the buſhell, Baye ſalte at three pence halfe-

penye

nyce the bushell, Nantwiche salte at 6. pence the bushel, white herringe at 5. shillings the barrell, red herringe at 3. shillings the cade, red sprottes, 6. d. the cade. And Gascoine wyne at 6. pounde the tonne. Wheate, salt, and wine.

Anno. 10.

Nicholas Alwin. John Warner. 28. of sep. Sherifes

Richard Chaury salter. The 28. of Oct. Mayor. 1495.

Sir William Stanley was beheaded at the Tower hill.

Anno, 11.

White herring sold at xl. pence a barrell being good.

Parkin Warbecke, naminge hymselfe Richarde of Yorke, K. Edwards seconde sonne, arriued at Dele in Kent, where he was driuen backe by the uplandishmen, and other of the inhabitantes of the countrye, with the losse of diuers of his men. And shortlye after were hanged, an hundred and three score persons of the forenamed rebels, in diuers and sondry places of England. Parkin Warbecke.

Anno. 11.

Iho Kneisworth. Henry Semer, 28 of Sep. Sherifes.

Henry Colet Mercer. The 28. of Octo. Mayor.

The xvi. of Nouember, the sergeants feast was kept at the bishop of Elies place in Holborne, where the kinge and Queene were present.

The Scottes brake into the North partes of Englande, by the settinge on 1496.

of Perkin Werbecke, & did much harme to the borderers. Anno. 12.

Sherifes. John Shawe, Rich. Haddon. 28. of Septem.

Mayor. John Tate Mercer. The 28 of October.

S. Anthonis in London builded. This John Tate, new buylded and enlarged S. Anthonis Church in London, a goodly foundation with a free schole, and a certaine nomber of Bedemē now displaced.

1497. By meanes of a parlamente that was graunted to the king, a new commotiō was made by the commons of Cornewall, which vnder the leadinge of James Tucher of Audleye, Lord Audeley, with

Blackheath field. Michaell Iosephe the Blacksmith, and diuers other, came to blackheath, where the kinge met with them, & discomfited the rebelles and toke theyr Captaynes, which were shortly after drawen, han-

Execution. ged and quartered. The Lord Audeley was beheaded at the tower hil, the 28. day of June.

An. reg. 13. The King sente an armye into Scotlande, vnder the guidinge of the Earle of Surreye & the Lord Neuel, who made sharpe warre vpon the Scottes.

Great hail. In Bedfordshire at the towne of S. Nedes, fel hailestones that were measured 18. inches about. A mariage was concluded betwene Prince Arthure & Lad

Kathe

atherine the Kings daughter of Spaine. | Pillory pardoner.
A false pardoner named Simond Lolly, was set on the pillorye in Cornehil, for gathering money by a fayned pardon.

Perkin Werbecke landed at Whitsonne in Cornewall, & assaulted & to wne Exceter and other places, but finally he toke the Saintuary of Beaudley, and was after pardoned his life. 13. | Perkin Werbecke.

Barthol. Rede. Tho. Windough. 28 of Sep. | Sheriffes
William Purchas Mercer. The 28. of Oct. | Mayor.

Perkin Werbecke endeuoured to steale secretely out of the land, but he was taken againe, and by the kinges commaundement taken the tower of London: after, hee was shewed in Westminster, and in Cheape on Scaffoldes, and stocked. Anno 14. | 1498.

Tho Bradbery. Stephen Iennins. 28 of Sep. | Sheriffes.
John Perciual Marchant Tailer. 28. Oct. | Mayors.

A Shomakers sonne borne at the bull in bishoppes gate streat of London, was hanged at S. Thomas Waterings on shroue tuesday, who had named him selfe Edwarde Earle of Warwicke, and sonne of George Duke of Clarence, which George since the beginning of king Henries raigne, was kept secretely in the Tower of London.

Good Gascoine wyne was solde at | 1499

London for fortye shillings a Tonne; Wheate for foure shillinges a quarter, and Bay salt for foure pence a bushell.

Anno. 15.

Sherifes. James Wilford. Richard Brond. 28. of Sep.
Mayor. sir Nicholas Alwin Mercer. The 28. of Oct.
1500. Perkin Warbecke. Perkin Warbecke, and John a Water, Mayor of Corke, were executed at Tiborne. Edwarde Plantagenet Earle of Warwicke put to deathe at the tower hill. And shortlye after Blewet and Atwoode were hanged at Tiborne.

Anno. 16.

Sherifes John Hawes. Willia Steale. 28. of Sept.
Mayor, sir Wil. Remingto fishmonger 28. Octob.
150 . Richmont. The king builded new his manour at Shene and named it Richmonte, for many notable & rich iewels were there brent not long before, he builded newe Baynardes Castell, and repayred Greenewiche.

Anno. 17.

Sherifes, sir Laurence Ailmer, Hery Hede. 28. of Sep.
Mayor, sir John Shaw Goldsmith. The 28. of Octo.
First maiers feast at Guild hall. This sir John Shaw Mayor of Londo, caused the kitchens and other houses of office to be builded at the Guild hal and since that time the Mayors feast hath bene there kept, wheras before they were kept eyther at the Grocers or marchant Taylers hall.

The xiiii.day of Nouember, Prince Arthure being xiiii.yeares olde and two monethes, was maryed in S. Paules Church at Lōdon, vnto Katherin doughter to Ferdinando king of Spaine. Which Arthur the second of April, departed this mortal life at Ludiowe, and was buried at Worcester. Prince Arthur maried

The ditches of the Cittye of London called Turnmilbroke, wyth all the course of Fleetdyke and other, was so scoured downe to the Thames, that barges and boates might come to Holborne bridge with fish and fewel, and they kept their markets as they had done of old tyme. 1502. The ditches of London new cleansed

Anno. 18.

Henry Kebel. Nicholas Nines. 28 of Sept. Sherifes.
Bartholo. Rede Goldsmith. 28. of Octo. Mayor.

This yere began the new worke of the kings Chappel at Westminster. And Elizabeth Queene of England, died in childbed, & was buried at Westminster. Chappel at Westminster.

The fellowship of Taylers in London, purchased of the king to be called Marchant Taylers. 1503. Marchant Taylers.

The Priour of the Charterhouse of Shene, was miserably murthered in his cell in a Cell of the same house, by meanes of one Goodwine a Monke of the same Cloister. The king of Scottes maryed Murder at Shene.

Margaret

Margarete the daughter of K. Henry y 7.

Anno. 19.

Sheriffes. Christ. Hawes, Rob. Watton. Tho. Grange.

Maior. sir Willia Capel Draper. the 28. of Octob.

1504. New coine. A New coine of siluer, of grotes and halfe grotes, with halfe faces.

Anno. 20.

Sheriffes. Roger Achilley, Wil. Browne. 28. of Sept.

Maior. sir Iohn winger Grocer. The 28. of Octob.

1505. Prison broken. The prisoners of the Marshalsey in Southwarke, brake out and many of them beyng shortly after taken, were put to execution, specially those which had layne for felonye or treason.

Anno. 21.

Sheriffes. Richarde shore, Roger Grone. 28. of Sept.

Maior. sir Tho. Kneisworth fishmonger. 28. Octob.

Conduite at Bishops gate builded. This Thomas Kneisworth builded the Conduite at Bishops gate, he gaue to the company of the fishmongers, tenementes, for the which they be bounde to finde foure scholers: two at Oxford, and two at Cambridge. They be bound also to giue to sixe aged poore people of their companye, to euery of them at Bartholomew tyde, a winter garment for euer. And also to giue to the prisoners of Newgate, euery yeare xl. s.

1506. The K. of Castile. Through a great tempest of wind, Philippe king of Castile and his wife, were

we-

[illegible] driuen into Englande, as they were passinge towarde Spaine, whose were honourably receyued by the Erle of Arundel. This tempest was straunge to many men, because the violence of ỹ winde had blowen downe the Egle of brasse from the Spire of Paules Church, and in the falling the same Egle brake, and battered the signe of the black Egle in Paules Churchyarde, that time being but for houses, where now is the stole of 4. houses. Anno 22. Weathercocke of Poules.

W. Copinger. Tho. Iohnson, W. fitz Wil. Sherifes.

Richard Haddon Mercer, the 28 of oct. Mayor.

Allen the king of his goodnes deliuered oute all prisoners in London, which lay for foure shillings & vnder. 1507 Prisoners deliuered.

Anno. 23

W. Butler, Iohn Kirkeby, 28 of Septemb. Sherifes

W. Browne Mercer, Laurēce Aylemer. Dra. Mayor.

In the ende of Aprill dyed William Browne Maior, and for him was chosen Laurence Aylemer Draper. 1508.

The Citye of Norwiche was nere consumed with fyre, at Easter and Whitsuntyde. Anno 24. Norwicke a fryer.

Io. Exmew. Rich. Smith. 28. of Septemb. Sherifes

Ste. Genings Marchant Tailer, 28. Oct. Mayor.

This yeare was finished the goodly hospitall of the Sauoye, neare vnto 1509.

Cha-

Hospitall of the Sauoy builded.

Charing Crosse, which was a notable foundation, done by king Henry the seuenth, vnto the which he purchased landes, for the releuing of 100. poore people. Hee also builded three houses of Franciscan Fryers, which are called Obseruauntes, at Richmont, at Grenewiche, and at Newarke, and three other, which are called Couentuals, at Canterbury, newe Castell and Southampton.

The yere 1509. dyed king Henrye the seuenth at Richmont the xxii. of April, when he had raigned xxiii. yeres and 8. monethes, & was buried at Westminster in the newe Chappel, which he had caused to be builded, and left behinde him Henry Prince of Wales, Lady Margaret Queene of Scots, and Ladye Mary promised to Charles King of Castile.

HENRY THE eyght.

Anno 1509.

HEnry the eight, being 18. yeres of age, began his raigne the 22. dey of April, in the yeare of our Lord 1509. Of personage he was tal & mighty, in wit and memo-

rye

excellent.

In the month of June King Henry ma- ryed the Lady Katherine his first wyfe, who had beene late the wyfe of Prince Arthure deceased. On Midsommer day the King and Queene were crowned at Westminster. The kinge maryed and crowned.

George Monox. John Ducket. 28. of Sept. Sherifes.

Tho. Bradbury Mercer. W Capel Draper. Mayors.

About ye beginning of January, died the aforesaid Thomas Bradbury Ma- or, and for him was chosen sir William Capell Draper.

Sir Richarde Empson knight, and Ed- munde Dudley Esquire, who had beene great counsailers, to the late K Henry the seuenth, were beheaded at the tower hill the 17. day of August. 1510. Anno 2.

Doctor Colet Deane of Poules, erected a free schole in Poules Churchyard at London, and committed the ouersight thereof, to the maisters and wardeins of the company of Mercers, because him- selfe was borne in London, and sonne of Henry Colet, who was a Mercer, & Maior of London. Paules schole buil- ded.

John Milborne. John Rest. the 28 of sept, Sherifes.

Henry Keibel Mercer, the 28 of October. Mayor.

Henry, the first sonne of K Henrye the eyghte, was borne on Newe yeares 1511.

daye

Anno.reg.3. day, and on S. Mathewes day following the childe dyed.

Sherifes. Nicholas Shelton. Tho. Mirfin. 28. of Sept.
Mayor. sir Roger Achuley Draper. 28. of Octob.

THe nauies of England and Fraunce,
meeting at Britaine Baye, fought a
1512. cruel battaile, in the which the Regent
Battaile on of England, and a Caricke of Fraunce
the sea. being coupled together were burned, &
An. reg. 4. their Captaines with their men al drowned. The Englishe Captaine was sir
Thomas Kneuet, who had with him 700
men. In the French Caricke, was sir
Piers Morgan with 900. men.

Sherifes Rob Holdernes, Rob. Fenrother. 28. of Se.
Mayor W. Copinger fishmonger Ri Haddō Mer.

1513. WIlliam Copinger deceased, and Richard Haddon mercer, was chosen
Mayor.

Bowe ste- This yeare was finished the beauti-
ple builded. full steeple, with the lanterne of Bowe
church in Cheape.

There was graunted to the king, two
Anno reg. 5 fiftenes, & 4. dismes and head mony.
Great pay- In Maye the king ordayned a great
ment. army & went into Fraunce, where hauing vnder his banner the Emperour
Maximilian, and all the nobilitye of Brabant, Flaunders and Holland, discomfited
the whole power of Fraunce, and conquered

...ted Turwine the 22. of Auguste, and ...ly after toke the Cittye of Turneye ...ppoyntment the 19. of September. Turney and Turwin.

The kinge of Scottes invaded this ...de wyth a mighty armye, but by the ...ligence of the Queene, and the man... ...re of the Earle of Surrey, the kinges ...ueteraunt, he was himselfe slaine at ...m...ne, wyth three bishoppes, thre ...ots, xii. Earles, xvii. Lordes, besi... knightes and Gentlemen, and xviii... ...sand Scottes slaine in the fielde, ... the ordinaunce and stuffe taken, the ...f August. Anno. 5. Scots fielde at Bramston hill.

...n Dawes, Io. Pridges, Roger Basford. Sherifes.

...V. Browne Mercer. Io. Tate Mercer. Mayors.

...r William Browne deceased, and for ...im was chosen Iohn Tate Mercer. 1514.

...d Iohn Dawes deceased, and for him ...s chosen Roger Basford.

...n a Parlyament was graunted to y ...g, the greate subsedye of vi. pence y ...unde of euery mans goodes. Subsedye.

...i August a peace was made betwene ...kinges of England and of Fraunce, du... ...g both theyr liues: And in October a ...riage was made betwene the French ...g, and the Lady Mary the kings sister. Anno. 5. Mariage of the kings sister.

...es Yarford, Iohn Mundy, 28. of Sept. Sherifes.

...eor. Monoxe Draper. ...of October. Mayor.

Richard

Richard Hunne. Richard Hunne a marchant Tayler of S. Margarets parishe in Bregestreate, who for denying to giue a mortuary for his child beinge buryed, had beene put in the Lowers towre aboute the ende of October, was nowe the v. of December found hanged in the said towre, and after burned in Smithfield.

1515. On Newe yeres euen dyed the French king. And the 9. of Aprill a newe peace was concluded betweene the kinge of

Anno 7. England, and the new French kyng.

The Duke of Suffolke maried. The next moneth Charles Duke of Suffolke wedded the Lady Mary, the kings sister, late Queene of Fraunce.

Sherifes. Henry Worley. Richard Grey. W. Bailye.

Mayor. sir William Butler Grocer, the 28. of Oct.

Ladye Mary, K. Henries doughter, was borne at Grenewich on the eyght day of Februarye.

1516. Margaret Quene of Scottes, K. Hen-

Anno. 8. ries eldest sister, who had maryed Archibald Duglasse, Earle of Anguise, fled into England, & laye at Harbottel, where she was deliuered of a child, called Margarete. In Maye she came to London, where shee taryed a whole yeare before she returned.

Sherifes. Thomas Seimer. Richard Thurston. 28. sep.

Major. sir Iohn Rest Grocer. The 28. of October.

This

This yeare was such a froste, that all men with cartes might passe betwene Westminster and Lambeth. Great frost.

This yeare on Maye euen, was an insurrection of yong persons and prentises of London againste aliens, of the which diuers were put to execution, with their Captain Iohn Lincolne a broker, the residue to the nomber of 400. and xl. wome tyed in ropes al along, one after another in theire shertes, came to West. hall, with roopes aboute theyr neckes & were pardoned. The Queene of Scottes returned into her country, to the Erle of Anguishe her husband. 1517. Anno 9. Euil May daye. Queene of Scots.

Io. Baldry. Richard Symon. 28 of Septe. Sherifes.

Tho. Exmew Goldsmith. 28. of Octob. Mayor.

Many dyed in England of the sweatinge sicknes, and in especiallye at London, wherfore Trenity Terme was one day at Oxeford, & adiourned againe to Westminster. The City of Turney was deliuered to the Frenche king. 1518. Sweatinge sickenes. Anno 10. Turney yelded Frēche.

Iohn Allein James Spencer, the 28. of sep. Sherifes.

Tho Mirfin Skinner. The 28. of Octob. Maior.

The Earle of Surreye was sente into Ireland as deputy, & the Earle of Kildare was of his office discharged. 1519. Anno. 11.

In July Cardinal Campaius came into England, from the Pope, to exhort K. Henry to make war on the Turkes. Cardinal Campaius.

Sherifes John Wilkinson, Nic. Partrige. 28. of Sept.
Mayor. sir James Yarford Mercer The 28. of Oct.

1520. Anno, 12. A S K. Henrye was at Caunterburye wyth the Quene, in redines to haue passed the sea, he heard of the Emperors comming, with whom he met at Douer, and accompanyed him to Canterburye, wher after the Emperour had salut þ Quene his aunt, he toke shipping into Flaunders: the last daye of May kynge Henrye passed ouer to Calleis, and met wyth Fraunces the Frenche kynge, at the Campe betwene Arde and Guisneis. Immediatly after he met wyth þ Emperor, wyth whom hee wente to Grauelin, and þ Emperour returned wyth hym to Caleis, after which time they departed, and K. Henry returned into this Realme.

Sherifes. Io. Skeuingtō, Io. Kemble. The 28. of Sept.
Maior. sir Io. Bruges Draper. The 28. of October.

1521. Anno. 13. Duke of Buckingham. The xvii. day of May, was Edwarde Stafford Duke of Buckingham behedded at London.

A greate pestilence in London, and other places.

Sherifes. Io Britaine, Tho Pargetor. 28. of Septem.
Maior. sir Iohn Milborne, Draper, the 28. of Oct.

Alme, houses bulded. This sir Iohn Milborne builded certaine almes houses, adioyninge to þ Crouched Friers Churche in London, where wherein be placed xiij. aged poore people, who hauing their dwellinges rent free, and also twoo shillinges and sixe pence the piece, payde to them the first daye of euery moneth for euer.

The first of March, the French kyng attached all Englishemens goodes at Bardeaux, and therfore al Frenchemens bodies and goodes were attached in London, and they were cast in prison. Frenchmen attached.

The xx. day of May Cardinal Wolsey rode through London to Douer, to mete with ŷ Emperour of Rome, who came into England, and was honourably receiued into London, by the Mayor, Aldermen, and commons of the citie, the first of June, the king him selfe accompanying him: from thence hee wente to Windsore, and sate in the stall of the garter. After great feastes, iustes, and honorable entertaynement, hee departed to Hampton, and sayled from thence into Spayne. During this tyme, the Earle of Surrey Lorde Admirall, brent Morles in Brytaine, and then returned into the Realme: not long after, he passed ouer to Calleis and entred Picardy, and brent diuers townes and Castels. Hee besieged Hesding, but because Wynter drewe nere, he raysed his siege, and re- 1522 Anno, 14. The Emperours coming to London.

turned home.

The Duke of Albeny entered this lande with a great army, but hearing ÿ the Earle of Shrewsbury was comming he toke a truce for sixe moneths.

Sherifes. John Rudston, Iohn Champneis. 28. of sep.

Mayor. sir Iohn Mondie Goldsmith. 28 of Octob.

The Lorde Rosse and lord Dacres of ÿ North, burned the towne of Kelley in Scotland, with foure score Villages, & also did ouerthrow 18. towers of stone, with all their bulwarkes.

The Emperour, king Henry of England, Ferdinando, Duke of Austrige, the bishop of Rome, the citie of Venice, and diuers other in Italy, were confederate against the Frenchemen. The

The Rhodes taken by the Turkes. Turkes besieged the Rhodes, and on Christmas daye tooke it, to the great rebuke of Christen men.

The Earle of Surrey burned xxxvii. villages in Scotland, and despoiled the countrey frō the east marches to ÿ west.

1523 This yeare the xv. of April, began a Parliament at the blacke Friers in London, wherin was grāted a great subsidy

Christierne king of Denmarke and his Queene, arriued at Douer, and the xvi day of June, they came to London, and lay at the byshop of Bathes place.

The

The Duke of Suffolke with many o- Anno re. 15.
ther lordes and knightes, were sent in-
Fraunce with an army of 10000. men,
who passing the water of Some without
battaile, toke diuers townes & Castels,
and destroyed the countrey.

ichael English, Nicholas Ienings. 28. sep. Sherifes,
Thomas Baldrie Mercer. 28. of October. Mayer,

In December, at the citie of Couentry, Conspiracy at Couentry
one Francis Philip, scholemaster to the
inges henchmen Christopher Pickering,
larke of the Larder, and Anthony Mani-
ile gentleman, entended to haue taken ye
inges treasure of his subsidie, as the
ollectors of the same came toward Lon-
on, and there with to areysed men and
aken the castel of Killingworth, and then
o haue made battaile against the king:
or the whiche they were drawen, hanged, and quartered at Tyborne the xi.
daye of Februarye. The rest that were taken were executed at Couentry.

This yeare the Earle of Surrey brent 1524
Iedworth in Scotlande, and toke dy- Anno 16.
uers holdes.

The souldiours of Guines, toke a great
booty at a fayre in the towne of Morguy-
son, and sir Robert Ierningham, with di-
milances of Callees, toke diuers French
prisoners.

Sheriffes, Rafe Dodmer. William Roche. 28. of Sept.
Mayor, sir William Bailie Draper. 28. of October.

The .xi. of Marche was great triumph in Englande for the takynge of the Frenche kyng by the Emperour, before the citie of Pauie.

1525 Abbayes, The Cardinall suppressed Priories. This yeare the Cardinall obteyned licence of the Bishoppe of Rome, to suppresse certaine small Priories to the intent to erect two Colleges, one at Oxforde, an other at Ipswiche, and to indue them with landes.

King Henry in ieopardy. King Henry was like to haue bene drowned by leaping ouer a ditche in folowing his hauke.

The tilte was set vp at Grenewich.

A truce betwene England & Fraunce for a certayne space.

Sheriffes, John Caston, Christ. Askew. 28. of septẽb.
Mayor, sir Iohn Allen Mercer, the 28. of October.

The .xi. of February, doctor Barnes of Cambridge, bare a fagot at Paules, there was present the Cardinall with .xi. byshops, ỹ bishop of Rochester made the Sermon agaynst Martin Luther.

Sheriffes, Stephen Pecocke, Nicho. Lambert. 28. Sep.
Mayor, sir Thomas Seymer Mercer. 28. of October.

1526 Anno. 18 A Proclamation for golde, the Frenche crowne was valued at iiij.s.vi.d. ỹ Angel at vii.s.vi.d. ỹ riall at xi.s.iii.d.

and so

and so euery peece after that value.
In Nouember, December, and Ianuary, fell suche rayne that thereof ensued great floudes, which destroyed corn
fieldes and pastures, and drowned many
sheepe and beastes, then was it dry tyll y
end of Aprill, and from thence it rayned
euery day or night, til the third of Iune. 1527 Anno. 19
Harman was drawen to Tyborne,
and there hanged for coynynge of false
gold.
This yere was such scarcitie of bread Scarcitie of bread.
in London, & all Englande, that many
people dyed for defaulte thereof. the kyng
of his goodnes sent to the Citie of hys
owne prouision vi C. quarters, or els
for one weeke there had bene litle bread.
The bread cartes comming from Stratforde to London, were mette at Myles
ende by the Citizens, y the Lord Mayor
and Sheriffes, were fayne to go and rescue the same, and see them brought to
the markets apointed. The wheate was
at xv.s. the quarter. Shortly after, the
Marchauntes of the Stillarde brought
from Danske and other places beyonde
the seas suche store of wheate and rie,
that it was better cheape at London thē
in any other place of the whole realme.
Iohn Hardy, William Hallis. 28. September Sherifes.

Mayor. Sir Iames Spencer Vintner. The 28. of Oct.

GEnerall peace proclaymed betweene King Henry of Englande and Frances the French king, during their liues.

Peace proclaymed. 1528 Anno 20. A ship chased.

A Frenche Crayer of xxx. tunne, being manned with xxxviij. Frenchmen, and a Flemishe Crayer of xxvij. tonne and 24. Flemmings meting at Margate the one chased ŷ other alonge ŷ ryuer of Thames to ŷ towre wharfe of Lōdō, where sir Edmund Wallingham lieutenaunt of the Tower staied them both, & tooke both their captaines and their men.

Sweating sicknes.

The 17. day of June, the terme was adiorned to Michaelmas after, because of the sweating sicknesse that then raigned in London, and there was no suche watche at Midsomer, as before tyme had bene accustomed.

Sherifes. Rafe Warren, Iohn Long. the 28. septemb.

Legate from Rome.

The 7. day of October, came to London a Legate frō Rome called Cardinal Campegius, who afterward with Cardinall Wolsey sate at the blacke Friers.

Mayor, 1529 sir Iohn Rudstone Draper, the 28. of Octob.

A Prisoner seeming so weake that hee was brought out of Newgate in a basket, brake from the sessions that when the sessions was done, and ran through the presse of people to ŷ gray friars church

within

went to Calleis and to Bologne, where he met with the Frenche King.
S. Stephen Pecocke Haberdasher. 28 Oct. Maior.

The fyftene day of December, was a great fyre at the byshop of Lincolnes place in Holborne. Fire at Holborne.

The xii. daye of Aprill, being Easter eve, the lady Anne Bulleine, was proclaimed Queene of England. 1533

The twelfe daye of Maye, one Paker, the towne Clarke of London, heng him selfe. An. 25.

On Whitsonday was the Lady Anne Bulleine solempnely and honourablye crowned at Westminster. Queene Anne.

The fourth of July, Iohn Frithe, and a yong man named Andrew Hewet, a tailers seruant, were brent in Smithfeld. Iohn Frith.

The v. of July, Queene Katherine was proclaimed prince Arthurs wydowe. Prince Arthurs widow

The xvii. day of July, were two marchauntes slaine on the water of Thaines towardes Westminster, by one Wolfe & his wyfe. Murder.

This yeare it was enacted, that all butchers should sell their biefe, mutton and other flesh by weight, that is to say, biefe for an halfpeny the pound, & mutton for thre farthinges, &c. At that tyme Biefe and mutton solde by weight.

fatte

fatte Oxen were sold for xxvi. shillings & viii eight pence the piece, fat weathers for three shillinges and foure pence, fat calues for the lyke pryce, a lambe for xii pence, and at the Butchers in London was solde peny pieces of biefe for the reliefe of the poore, euery piece ii. pound, and two pounde and a halfe, and some tyme in the yeare three pounde for a peny, and xiii. of the same pieces for xii. and xiiii for xii. pence. Mutton at viii. pence and xx. pence the quarter, and a hundred weight of biefe for foure shyllinges and eight pence.

Lady Elizabeth borne. The seuenth day of September, was the Lady Elizabeth daughter to king Henry, borne at Grenewiche, and there Christened at the Friers churche.

Sherifes, William Forman, Thomas Kitson 28. Sept.

The fifth day of October was a great fere at Baynardes Castell.

Mayor sir Christofer Askew Draper. 28. of octob.

The xxiii. of Nouember being sonday, on a scaffolde before the crosse at Paules, there stoode a Nunne named Anne Barton of Courtopstreete beside Caunterbury, and two obseruaunt friers, and Goulde, parson of Aldermary in London, with an other priest confessor to the sayde Nunne, and two laye men

the byshop of Bangor preaching, shewed their offences, from whence they were sent to the tower.

The xxvii. daye of January, was a great fyshe taken at Blackwall, called a Whale, and was brought up to Westminster to the king to see, & so brought down to broken wharfe, & there cut out. A great fish taken.

The first daye of Aprill, were Wolfe and his wife hanged on twoo gibettes, at Lambeth Marshe, for murdering of the twoo marchaunt straungers afore named. 1534 Wolfe and his wife.

The xx. day of Aprill, two Monkes of Caunterbury, two obseruant friers, the parsone of Aldermary in London, and the Nunne, called the holy maide of Canterbury in Kent. Al these were drawen from the Tower of London unto Tyburne, and there hanged and beheaded, their heades set on London bridge, and other gates of the citie, and their bodies buried. Execution. The same daye all the craftes & companies in London, were sworne to the king, Queene Anne, & their heires. Othe to the king and to queene Anne About that tyme al the priestes throughout England, were called to be sworne before the archbishop of Caunterbury & other byshops, and al men through England, were sworne in their shieres and Anno. 26

townes

townes where they dwelled. For refusall whereof, Doctor Fisher bishop of Rochester, sir Thomas Moore late lord Chauncelor, were sent to the tower of London, and diuers other priestes, religious, & laymen, were sent to other prisons.

The xv. day of May, was a great fire at Salters hall in Breadstrete.

The v. day of June, were al seruauntes and Prentices in London, of the age of twenty yeares, sworne to the kyng and Queene.

Lord Dacres — The ninth day of July, was the Lord Dacres of the North, arraigned at Westminster of highe treason, where he was founde by his piers not gilty.

Friers houses suppressed. — The xi. day of August, was al the places of the Obseruaunt Friers, as Grenewiche, Caunterbury, Richemount, Newewarke, and Newe Castell put downe.

The xiiij. day of August, was a great fire at Temple barre, and muche hurte done, and certain persons burned. The 16. day of August was burned the kings stable at Charing crosse, called ye Mewes

The kinges stable brent. — wherein was burned many great horses, and great store of hay.

Sherifes, Nico. Leuson, Wil. Denham, 28. of septem.

Cromwel. — Maister Thomas Cromwel sworne master of the Roules, the xx. day of October

ohn Champneis Skinner. 28. of Octob. Mayor
Nouember was held a parliament
herin ye bishop of Rome with al his
thoritie was cleane banyshed thys
me, and commaundemẽt geuen, that
should no more be called Pope, but
hop of Rome, & that the kyng should
reputed as Supreme heade of the
rch of England, hauing ful authori-
to reforme all errours, heresies, and
ses in the same. Also the first fruites The first
tenthes of all spirituall dignities & fruites.
motions were grãted to king Hẽ-
with a subsidie of the layetie of 12.d.
the li. and a fiftene with a tenth.
The xxix. daye of April, the Prior of 1535
Charter house of London, the Prior Anno.27.
Beual, the Prior of Exham, and a bro-
r of Syon called maister Reignoldes,
a priest called Maister Iohn Hayle, Execution
car of Thistilworth were all iudged at at Tiborne.
minster to be drawen, hanged and
artered at Tyborne, who were there
cuted the fourth daye of Maye, and
ir heades and quarters set on the ga-
of the citie, and one quarter was set
the Charter house.
The 8. day of May, the king comaun-
all about his Court to polle theyr
des, and to geue them ensample, hee
caused

Polid heads, caused his owne head to be polled.

Hollanders. The xxv. day of May was at Saint Paules in London, examined xix. men and vi. women borne in Holland, xiiii. of them were condemned, a man and a woman were burnt in Smithfielde, the other xii. were sente into diuers good townes there to be executed.

Execution. The xviii. of June were iii. Monkes of the Charterhouse, named Exmewe, Mydlemore, and Nudigate drawen to Tiborne, and there hanged and quartered.

Byshop of Rochester The xxii. day of June, was doctor Fisher byshop of Rochester, beheaded at Tower hyll.

Sir Thomas Moore. The vi. day of July sir Thomas Moore was beheaded at the Tower hill for denyall of the kinges supremacie.

Sherifes, Humfrey Monmouth, Iohn Cotes. 28. sep.

Abbeis visited. In October the king sent doctor Lee, to visit the abbeis, priories, and nounceries in England, & to put out all religious persons that would go, and all that were vnder the age of 24. yeares.

Mayor, sir Iohn Allein Mercer. the 28. of October.

The xi of Nouember was a great procession at London for ioy the French king was recouered of his health.

Lady K deceased. The viii. day of January, died Ladye Katherine Dowager at Kymbalton, & was buried

buried at Peterborowe.

A parliament beginning in February granted to the king & his heires to the augmentation of the crowne, all religious houses in the realme, of the value of 200. pounde and under, with all landes and goodes belonging to the said houses. Smal houses suppressed.

This yeare, on Mayday king Henry being at a Justes at Grenewiche, sodenly departed to Westminster, hauing onely with him vi. persones. The next daye Lady Anne Bulleine Queene was had to the Tower, and there for things layd to her charge, was beheaded the xix. day of May, her body with the head was buried in the Tower church. The Lorde Rochforde, brother to the sayd Queene, Henry Norris, Marke Smeton, William Brierton, and Francis Weston, all of the kynges priuie chaumber, about matters touching the Queene, were put to death the xvii. day of May. 1536 Anno. 28 Execution.

The xx. day of May, the kyng maried Lady Jane daughter to Sir John Seymor knight, which at Whitsontide was openly shewed as Queene. And on tuesday in Whitsonweke, sir Edward Seymor was created Vicount of Beachampe, and sir Walter Hungerford, was made Lorde Hungerforde. King maried.

A parliamēt. The viii. of June, the king began his parliament. And the bishops with the clergy, helde a conuocation at Paules church in London, where after muche disputing, they published a booke of religion, entituled: Articles deuised by the kinges highnes.

On S. Peters day, the king helde a great iusting and triumphe at Westminster.

States created. Maister Thomas Cromwel secretary to the king, & maister of the Rolles, was made lord keper of the priuy seale. The lord Fitzwarren, was created Earle of Bathe, and the morrow after, maister Thomas Cromwel was made lord Cromwel and also high Vicar general ouer the spiritualtie vnder the king, & sate diuers times in the conuocation house amonge the bishops as head ouer them. The xx. of July, Henry Duke of Richemount and Somerset, and Earle of Northampton, a bastard sonne of king Henry died at S. James, and was buried at Thetford.

Vicar generall.

Duke of Richemount.

The pater noster, Crede, and Commaūdemētes

Thomas Lorde Cromwell, Lorde priuy seale, and vicegerent, sent out vnder the kinges spiritual seale certaine iniunctions to the prelates and clergie of this realme, charging the Curates to preache to their parishoners, and to teache them their Pater noster, Aue, and Crede, the C[ommaun-]

maunmaintenaunces in Englishe.

Richard paget, William Bowyr. 28. of Sept. Sheriffes.

In the beginning of October, at a sise for the kinges subsidy, kept in Lincolne shire, the people made an insurrection, and gathered nie xx. thousand persons, against these the king did send the Duke of Suffolke, the Earle of Shrowesbury, and the Earle of Rutland, with a strong power, whereof when the rebels had knowledge, they desired pardon, brake up their armie, and departed everye man home, but their captaynes were apprehended and executed.

Commotion in Lincolneshire.

The ninth of October, a priest and a Butcher were hanged at Windsore, for woordes speaking in the behalfe of the Lincolneshire men.

Execution at Wynsor.

The men of Lincolnshire being pacified, within sixe dayes after, began a newe insurrection in Yorkeshyre, for ye same cause, the people gathered to the number of xl. thousande, and tooke the Archebyshop of Yorke, and the Lorde Darcy, and caused them to be sworne to their party. Against these rebelles the kyng sent the Duke of Northfolke, the Duke of Southfolke, ye Earle of Shrowesbury, & the markes of Exceter, with a great army, with whom a battail was

Commotion in Yorkshire.

 appointed

appointed to haue ben fought on the euen of Symond & Iude thapostles, but as God would, there fell such a rayne the night afore, that ye two armies could not come together: wherupon at the request of the Duke of Northfolke, they desired him to sue to the king for their pardō, & that they might haue their liberties. Which the Duke promised, & rode in post to the King, then lying at Windsor, to know his pleasure, & so appeased them. Aske that was chiefe of this rebellion, in December folowing came to London, & was not only pardoned but rewarded with great giftes.

Commotion appeased.

Mayor, Sir Rafe Warreine Mercer. 28. of October.

The xii. of Nouember, sir Thomas Newman, bare a Faggotte at Paules crosse, for singing masse with good ale.

Penance.

The xiii. daye of Nouember, maister Robert Pagington, a Mercer of London, was slaine with a gunne, as he was going to masse at S. Thomas of Akers.

Robert Pagingtō slain.

The xxii. of December, the Thames being ouerfrosen, the King and Queene rode through London to Grenewiche.

The thirde of February was Thomas Fitzgarret late Earle of Kyldare, and fiue of his vncles, drawen, hanged, & quartered at Tyborne for treason.

Execution.

In

In February, Nicholas Musgraue, Thomas Gilbie, and other, stirred a newe rebellion, and besieged the citie of Carlile, from whence they were driuen, & many of them taken and put to death. A new com motion in Yorkeshire

In the same moneth of February, Sir Frances Bigot, sir Robert Constable, and other began an other conspiracie. An other c spiracy.

The 2[illegible]. day of Marche, were xii. men of Lincolnshire drawen frō newgate to Tyborne, & were hanged & quartered: fiue were priestes, and seuen laye men. 1537 Executi

In April certaine commissions were sent into Somersetshire to take vp corne, whereupon the people began to make an insurrection, which was by meanes of younge Maister Paulet and other alayed, the beginners to the number of lx. were taken and condemned, whereof xiiii. were hanged and quartered, one beyng a woman. Anno. 2

In Iune the lord Darcy, the lorde Hussey, sir Robert Constable, sir Thomas Percy, sir Frances Bigot, sir Stephen Hamelton sir Iohn Bulmer and his wife, William Lomley, Nicolas Tempest, the Abbots of Ierney and Riuers, and Robert Aske, were all put to death: sir Robert Constable, was hanged at Hul, ouer the gate comonly called Beuerley gate, for that is Executio leadeth toward Beuerley. Aske was hanged in chains on a tower at Yorke. Margaret Cheyne, other wise lady Bulmer, burned in Smithfield, the lord Darcy beheaded at tower hill, the lord Hussey at Lincolne, & the other suffered at Tyborne.

Cromwell. The xxvi. of August the lorde Cromwell was made knight of the Garter.

Sherifes. John Gresham, Thomas Lewen. 28. Septem.

The x. of October, on saint Edwards eue, was borne at Hampton courte, the noble prince Edward, and Queene Jane left her life the xiiii. day of October.

Mayor. Sir Richard Gresham Mercer. 28. of Octo.

The viii. day of Nouember the corps of ye queene was caried to Wyndsore, and buried with great solempnitie.

Execution. The xviii. of February a seruaunt of the lady Pargetours was drawen, hanged and quartered for clipping of golde.

The xxv. day of February, sir Allyn a priest, and a gentleman, were drawen to Tyborne, and there hanged and quartered for treason.

The xxi. day of Marche, Henry Harfam Customer of Plymmouthe, and one Thomas Ewell, was hanged and quartered at Tyborne.

1538 Anno. 30. The xxii. daye of May, Frier Forest was hanged and brent in Smithfelde

for

denying the kinges supremacie, with
m was brente the Image of Darvell Execution.
atherne of Wales.
The 27. day of May was a great fire Fire in Ro-
saint Margaret Pattens, called Roode de lane.
ne, where were many houses burned:
d nine persons were there burned to
ath.
In July, was Edmunde Conningsbie Execution.
tainted of treason, for counterfaitinge
the kinges signe manuel. And in Aust, was Edwarde Clifford for the same
use attainted, and both put to executiō
Tyborne.
The sunday after Bartholomew faire Hangman
as one Cratwell hangman of London, hanged.
d twoo parsones more, hanged at the
restling place on the backside of Cler-
enwell, for robbing of a Bouth in Bar-
lmew fayre. In September by the mo-
on of y Lord Cromwell, all the notable Images tak
mages, unto the which were made any downe.
ilgrimages and offeringes, were ut-
rly taken away, as the Images of our
ady at Walsingham, Ipswiche, Worcester
nd of Wilsdon, with many other, and
ikewyse all shrynes.
Vil. Wilkinson. Nic. Gibson. 28. of septem. Sherifes.
ir William Forman Haberdasher. 28. octo. Mayor.

This Nicolas Gibson shirife and Grocer of London afore named, builded a free schole at Ratcliffe nere vnto Londō, appoynting to the same schole for the instruction of lx. poore mens children, a scholemaister and Vsher, with a stipend of ten pound by the yere to the maister, and vi pound xiii. shillings iiii. pence to the Vsher. He also builded certayne almes houses, adioyninge to the sayde schole, for xiiii. poore and aged persons, which quarterly do receiue vi. shillinges viii. pence a piece for euer.

Free schole at Ratcliffe.

Almes houses at Ratcliffe.

The fifth of Nouember, were Henry Marques of Excester, and Earle of Deuonshire, Sir Henry Pole knight, lord Mountague, and sir Edward Neuel, sent to the Towre. The two lordes were arraigned the last of December at Westminster, the third day after was arraigned sir Edward Neuel, sir Geifrey Pole, & two priestes, Croftes, and Collins, & Holland a mariner, and al attainted. The ix. day of January, were the two Lordes & sir Edward Neuell beheaded at the tower hil: the two priestes and Holland, were drawen to Tyborne, and there hāged and quartered, & sir Geffrey Pole was pardoned.

Execution.

The xvi. daye of Nouember, was the

blacke

blacke friers in London suppressed, the next day the Whyte fryers, the next day the Gray fryers, and the Monkes of the Charterhouse, and so all the other immediatly. Fryers suppressed.

The xxii. day of Nouember, John Nicholson otherwise Lambert, was burnt in Smithfielde.

On Ashwednesday, were John Johns John Potter, & William Mannering, hanged on ẏ southside of Paules church yarde, for killing of Roger Cholmeley Esquyre en the same place. Execution in Paule churcheyarde.

The thyrd of Marche was sir Nicholas Carew of Bedington in Surrey, knight of the Garter, and maister of the kinges horse, beheaded at the Tower hill. Execution.

The ix. of Marche, the king created sir William Pawlet knight, treasorer of his housholde, Lorde Saint Iohn. And sir Iohn Russel controller of his housholde Lorde Russell. Sir William Par, Lorde Par. States created.

The xxviii. of Aprill, began a parliament at Westminster: in the which Margarete Countesse of Saresbury, Gertrude wife to the Marques of Excester, Reynold Pole, Syr Adrian Foskewe, and Thomas Dingley, knight of saint Johns, and diuers other were attainted of treason: 1539 Anno. 39

Foskew

Foskew and Dingley were beheaded the the x. daye of July. And al the religious houses in Englande suppressed and not suppressed, was graunted to the king for euer. The 8. daye of May the citizens of London mustered at the Myles ende all in bright harnes, with coates of white sylke and cloth, and cheynes of Golde, in three great battailes, the number was xv. thousande, beside wifflers and other wayters: who in goodly order passed through London to Westminster, and so through the sayntuary, and round about the parke of S. James, through ẏ field, and came home through Holborne.

Religious houses.

Great musters at London.

The viii. day of July Grifith Clerke, vicar of Wandsworthe, with his Chaplayn and his seruant, and frier Waire, were al foure drawen from ẏ Marshalsey vnto saint Thomas a Wateringes, and there hanged and quartered.

Execution.

Sherifes Tho. Fevre, Thomas Huntlow. 28 of septēb.

Mayor, Sir William Hollis Mercer. 28. of October.

This Thom. Huntlow sherife, gaue to ẏ Haberdashers certaine tenementes, for the which they be bound to geue to x. poore almes people of the same company euery one of them viii. d. euery sonday for euer. And also at euery quarter dinner to be kept by the maisters of the same

Charitable deedes.

[illegible] company to be geuen to euery one [illegible] those x. poore people before named, a [illegible] loafe of breade, a pottle of ale, a [illegible] of biefe, worth 4. d. in a platter, [illegible] porrage & foure pence in money.

The 14. daye of Nouember Hugh Fe- [illegible] Abbot of Reading, and three [illegible]: the one called Rug, and the [illegible] Onion, were attainted of hyghe [illegible], for denying the king to bee su[illegible] head of the Churche, they were [illegible] henged, and quartered at Rea[illegible]. The same daye was Richard [illegible], Abbot of Glastenbury, han[illegible] and quartered on Tarre hill, beside [illegible] monastery, for the same cause. Execution at Reding. Execution at the Tar hill.

The firste of Decemb[er], was John [illegible], Abbot of Colchester, put to exe[illegible] for the like offence.

[illegible] December, were apointed to waite [illegible] the kinges highnes 50. yonge Gent[illegible] called Pencioners. Pencioners.

The thirde of January, was the Lady [illegible] of Cleue, receiued at Black heath, [illegible] brought to Grenewiche with great [illegible]: and the sixt daye of the same [illegible], she was maried to K. Henry. Lady Anne of Cleue.

The xiii. daye of Aprill, was Tho[illegible] Lorde Cromwell, created Earle of [illegible], and made great Chamberlayn of Eng- 1540 Cromwell.

England. And also Gregory Cromwell his sonne made Lorde Cromwell.

In a parliament which began ỹ xvi[illegible] day of April, there was graunted to the king iiii. fifteenes, and a subsidie of two shillinges of landes, and xii. pence of goodes, towardes the charge of Bulwarkes. The Religiõ of saint Johns in Englãd, which of most men was named ỹ Knightes of the Rhodes, was dissolued.

Anno. 32.

Order of Rhodes.

In May, was sent to the tower, doctor Wilson & Doctor Sampson, Byshop of Chichester, for releuing certaine prysoners, which denied the kinges supremacie: and for the same offence, was one Richard Farmer Grocer of London, a rich and a welthy man, and of good estimation, committed to the Marshalsey, and after in Westminster haule arraygned and attainted in the Premunire, and lost all his goodes.

Richard Fermer.

The ix. of July, Thomas Lord Cromwell, Earle of Essex, being in the counsayle chamber, was sodainly apprehended, and committed to the Tower. The xix. day of the same moneth, he was by parliament attainted of heresie, hyghe treason, felony, and extortion, and neuer came to his aunswere. And the xxviii. of July beheaded at the tower hill, with the

Cromwel beheaded.

...me Walter Hungerforde of Hey...
...ry.

...ng Henry by authoritie of Par... ...nt and conuocation, was deuor... ...om the Lady Anne of Cleve.

Anne of Cleue deuorced.

...e xxx. of July, Robert Barnes, Tho... ...errard, William Ierome, priestes, ...burned in Smithfielde. The same ...Thomas Abell, Edwarde Powell, and ...de Fetherstone, were drawen, hang... ...nd quartered, for denying the kyng ...supreme head of the Churche.

Execution in Smithfielde, and at Tyborne.

...e fourthe daye of Auguste, were ...n from the Tower to Tyborne ...persones, and one ledde betwene ...and there hanged, and quartered: ...as the Priour of Dancaster, an... ...illiam Horne, a lay Brother of ...harter house of London, Gyles ...n Gentleman, a Monke of W... ...re, Clement Philpot, and Iames ...e, and a fryer.

Execution

...e ditches about London were cast.

...e viii. of August was the lady Ka... ...e Hawarde shewed openlye as ...ne, at Hampton court.

Kyng Henry maried.

...e xi. of September was hanged in ...fielde afore Bethlehem bridge a ...ner, named Iames Rynacian, who ...layne one Capon a Florentine in a

Harlottes cause many murders,

gardine, for his harlot.

A great drought. The latter end of this yere was great death of hote burning agues and fixes, and such a drought, that welles & small ryuers were dried up, and many cattell died for lacke of water: the salte water flowed aboue London bridge.

Shiriffes, William Laxton, Martin Bowes. 28. of Sep.

Maior, Syr William Roche Draper. 28. of Octo.

The xxii. of December, was Rauf Egerton, and Thomas Harman, put to death for counterfaytyng the kynges great seale.

1541 Anno, 33. Commotion in Yorkshire. In April certaine persones began a newe rebellion in Yorkeshire, which were shortly taken, and sent to executi in diuers places, of which Leigh, Tatersale, and Thornton, were put to death at London the xxviii. daye of May, and sir

Execution. John Neuill knight, and x. person more was executed at Yorke. The same daye the Countesse of Sarisbury was beheaded in the Tower of London.

Execution. The ix. daye of June, were Damport and Chapman, twoo of the kinges garde hanged at Grenewiche for robbery.

The xxviii. daye of June, the Lorde Leonard Gray, deputie of Irelande, was beheaded at the Tower hill. The same day were hāged at saint Thomas a wa-

terings

brings Mantel, Royden & Frowdes, gentlemen, for a spoyle and murder that they had done in one of the kinges parkes vpon May morning, the Lorde Dacres of the South, beeing in company with thē: and on the morowe which was S. Peters day, the Lorde Dacres was led from the tower a foote betwene the two sherifes, through the Citie to Tiborne, and there put to death for the same offence.

In August, the king toke his progresse to Yorke. — Progresse to Yorke.

The first day of July, was a Welsheman drawen, hanged, and quartered, for prophecying the kinges death. — Execution.

Sir Rouland Hill, Henry Suckley. 28. sept. — Sherifes,

Sir Michel Dormer Mercer 28. of Octob. — Mayor,

On Christmas euen at vii. of ẏ clocke at night, began a great fyre in the house late called Elsing spitle, neghe to Creplegate in London, whiche at that tyme was the house of syr Iohn Williams maister of the kinges Iewels, whiche fyre did muche harme to the kinges Iewels, and many of thē were embesiled. — Fyre at Elsing spitle.

The Lady Katherine Hawarde, whome the king had maried, for her vnchaste liuing committed with Thomas Culpeper and Fraunces Dercham, was by parliament attainted, Culpeper and Dercham were — Execution at Tyborne.

put to

put to death at Tyborne the tenth daye of December.

K. Henry K. of Irelande. The xxiii. day of January, the king was proclaymed kyng of Irelande.

Q. Katherine beheaded. The xiii daye of February, were beheaded within the tower, the Lady Haward other wyse called Queene Katherine, and the Lady Rocheford.

A mayde boyled. The xvii. of March, Margarete Davy a mayde, was boyled in Smithfielde, for poysoninge three housholdes that shee had dwelled in. The xx. of March, Clement Dyar a Vintoner, was drawen to Tyborne, and there hanged & quartred.

Execution.

1542 Anno reg. 34 In May, king Henry toke a loane of money of all such as were above the value of fifty pounde and upwarde.

The fourth day of July, the Scottes began to invade the borders.

The Earle of Desmond. In Auguste, the Earle of Desmond of Irelande came and submitted him selfe to the king, and so returned.

Sherifes. Hēry Hubblethorn, Hēry Hācottes. 28. sep.

The great Oncle. The first of October, the great Oncle of Ireland, was created Earle of Tyron, and his sonne Lorde Duncane.

The Duke of Norfolke entred Scotlande the xxi. day of October, burning & wasting all the Marches, and there taried without any battayle profered by the

the Scottes, untill the middest of Nouember.

Iohn Coates Salter. The 28. of October. Mayor.

After the departure of our armye from Scotland, the king of Scottes made a roode into Englande, and did muche harme, but at the last sir Thomas Wharton & sir William Musgraue, with a fewe of the borderers, met wyth the Scottes the xxiiii of Nouember, where they being in nõber 15000. were ouercome, in which conflicte was taken the Lorde Maxwell, the Earles of Glencarne and Cassiles, with all the Captaynes of the armye. And on S. Thomas euen the Apostle, they were broughte to the Tower of London, where they laye that night, þ next day followyng, they were by þ kings charges apparelled in silke and rode through the City to Westminster, where they were sworne to be true prisonners, and then were deliuered to the custodye of diuers noble mē, which honorably entertayned them. At newe yeares tyde they were sent home agayne agreeing to certaine articles. Scottes taken prisoners.

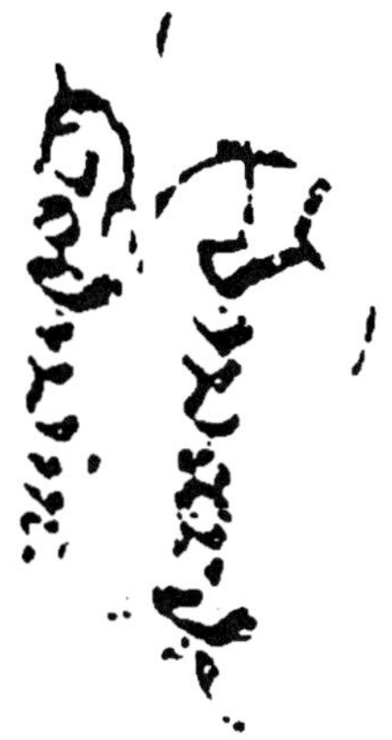

The thirde day of Iune, the Abrine a Lord in Irelād, and diuers of the wilde Irish, submitted them to K. Henry. The said Abrine was created Earle of Clanricarde. 1543. Anno, 35.

reade.

The kinge maryed. The 12. of Julye K. Henry maryed the Ladye Katherine, late wyfe to the Lorde Latimer, and sister to the Marquesse of Northampton, at Hampton Courte.

Going to Landerley. In July K. Henry sent ouer 6000. men to Landerseve, whyther also came the Emperour in proper personne wyth a great army, & shortly after came downe the French kyng in proper person with a great army, & offered to giue battaile to the Emperour, by reason whereof the siege was raised.

Execution. The 18. daye of July, Anthony Person, Roberte Testwoode, and Henry Filmer, were brent at Wyndsor.

Great pestilence. A great death in London of the pestilence: & therefore Michaelmas Terme was adiourneyed to S. Albons.

Sherifes. John Toules, Richard Dobbes. 28. of Sept.
Mayor. sir W. Bower Draper. sir Raph waren Ma.

This sir William Bower deceased the xiii. day of Aprill, being Easter day, and sir Raphe Warren, serued the residue of that yeare.

At Al hallontide a roade was made in to Scotland by the garrison there: who burned 60. villages, and toke greate prayes.

This yere chaunsed foure Ecclipses, one

one of the Sonne the xxiii.day of January, and three of the Moone.

Fowre Eclipsis in one yeare,

Lorde Edward Seymer Earle of Hereforde, was made Liefetenaunte of the North partes, and sent thether with an armye, for the defence of that countreye.

The vii. of March Germine Gerdiner, Lake person of Chelsey besyde London, & Singleton, were executed at Tiborne, for denying ỳ king to be supreme head, and shortlye one Ashbye was likewyse executed for the same.

Execution.

The fourth of Apryl a gonne poulder house called the blacke Swan, standing upon East Smithfield, was blowen vp wyth other houses nigh adioyning: and therein were burned fiue men, a boye, and a woman.

1544

Houses blowen vp.

Vppon May day, a nauy sent by the Lorde Admiral, toke their voyage into Scotland from Tinmouth, with whō was the Lorde Edward Seymer, Earle of Hereforde, the kinges Lieuetenaunte & general captaine of the armye, which ỳ fourth day of May arriued at Lyth, the hauen of Edenboroughe, and tooke the towne of Lyth and spoyled it. After which they made toward Edenborough, where at a certaine bridge the Scottes had layde their ordinaunce, but by the

Anno 36.

Lyth and Edenbrough taken,

polli-

pollicye and manhoode of our Captaynes and souldioures, the Scottes ordinaunce was won, and discharged agaynst themselues, and thereby were put to flight. After this the towne of Edenboroughe sent vnto the armye, pretending to deliuer the towne vpon certaine cōditions, to the behoofe of oure kinge: but when the army entred, they were inuaded by them: for which cause the towne was destroyed.

Coines enhaunced.

The xvi. of Maye, a proclamation was made for the enhaunsing of Golde to the rate of xlviii. shillinges, & siluer to iiii. shillinges the ounce. This time the kyng caused to be coyned base Moneys, which was since that time called downe, the fifth yere of Edward the sixt, and called in, the second yeare of Quene Elizabeth.

Base money coined.

After the Whitson holye dayes, the Duke of Northfolke, and the Lorde priuy Seale, with a great army toke their voyage into Fraunce, and besieged Muttercl, where they laye vntill the kinge had won Bologne: Not longe after the Duke of Suffolke with many other noble men passed the seas, and encamped before Bologne on the East syde.

Armye into Fraunce.

The xiiii. day of July K. Henry himselfe

selfe with a goodlye companye, passed from Douer to Calaice, and the 26. daye encamped on ẏ Northsyde of Bologne: after whose comminge the towne was so battered with gonneshotte, and certaine of their towers beinge undermined so shaken with force of Gonnepouder, that after a monethes siege, the Captaine sente woorde to the king, that hee would yelde the towne to his behoofe, uppon condition that all, which were within, mighte departe with bagge and baggage, which conditions king Henry graunted, and the Bolleyners departed one and other, to the nomber of 4454. K. Henrye went to Bolome. Boloine wonne.

The xxv. daye of September, the king with his Nobilitye, entred into highe Bologne, and afterward returning frõ thence, landed at Douer the first daye of October

John Wilford. Andrew Judde. 28. of Sept. Sherifes.
sir William Layton Grocer. 28. October. Maior.

This yeare was taken by the kinges shippes of the West country, and of the Englishe coast, to ẏ nomber of 300. frenche shippes and more, so that the Grayfryers Churche in London, was layd full of wyne, and the Austen fryers and blacke Fryers, were layde full of Heringes and other fishe, that was taken Prises taken.

ken going into Fraunce.

A beneuolence. The King demaunded a beneuolence of all his subiectes, both spirituall and temporall, toward his wars in Fraunce and Scotland, and the 12. of Januarye, the Lord Chauncelour, the Duke of Suffolke with other of the Kings counsel, beganne to sit at Baynardes Castell, for the Cittye of London, callinge before them, first the Maior and Aldermen &c.

M. Richard Rede Alderman. And because M. Richard Rede Alderman would not agree to pay as they set him, hee was commaunded in paine of death forthwith to serue the king in his warres in Scotland: who departed fro London the 23. of Januarye. Also sir

Sir William Roche. William Roche Knighte, and Alderman, for wordes of displeasure taken by the kinges counsel, was by them sent from Baynardes Castell to the Fleete the 26. of January, where he remayned tyl passion Sonday followinge.

A rode into Scotland. In the beginning of Marche a Rode was made into Scotlande towarde the towne of Gedworth by the Englishmen, where at the first gate greate prayes, but they were so greedye and wente so farre that a greate army of Scottes beset the wyth iii. battayles, so that the Englishmen for the most parte were slaine and take,

taken, amonge whom sir Rafe Euars, M. Rede
Lord Euars and warden of the Marches Alderman
was slaine, and maister Rede Aldermā taken priso-
of London, wyth other taken prisoners ner.
by the Scottes.

In May Trinity terme was adiour- 1545.
ned because of the warres.

The xxv. of July, the French kinges Anno 37.
nauye commynge oute of Newhauen and
Depe, arriued in Sussex afore Brighthamp
stede, where they set certaine of theyr
souldiours a lande to burne, but ÿ Be- Frenchmē
cons were fyred, & the mē came so thicke arriued in
so thicke, that the Frenchmen fled, and Sussex.
did litle hurt.

The xix. of July by misfortune of shotinge a gonne in one of the Hedgehoges The Hedge-
a shippe afore Westminster, a firken of hoge.
gunne pouder fyred, and slue vii. men,
and the viii. leaped into the Thames &
was drowned. The xx day of Julye ÿ
Kinge beinge at Portsmouth, a goodlye
ship of England, called the Mary Rose,
wyth sir George Carrew the Captayne, Mary Rose
and many other Gentlemen were drow drowned.
ned in the middest of the Hauen by great
negligence.

The xxi. of Julye the French Galleis
and nauy came afore Portsmouth Hauē,
and landed certaine of theyr armye in

the Ile of Wight at S. Helens point, and there burned and encamped about .ii. M. men, but they were soone driuen away wyth losse of their Captayne and many souldiours. The Earle of Hereforde, was sent into Scotland, with an armye of xii. Thousande men, where he destroyed diuers townes.

Frenchmen at the Ile of Wight.

The [illegible] of September, sir Iohn Dudley knight, Lorde Lisle, Lorde Admirall of England, landed with [illegible] men at Treporte in Normandie, and there burnt the towne and Abbeye, wyth certaine houses about it, and [illegible] shippes, & a Barke that lay in the hauen.

Treport.

The [illegible] of September the Churche of saint Gyles without Creplegate was burnt.

S. Giles Churche.

George Barnes. Raphe Allein The 28. Sep. Sherifes.
Sir Martin Bowes Goldsmith the [illegible] of Octob. Mayor.

The [illegible] day of Nouember, a Parliament began at Westminster, where was graunted to the kinge, a subsidye of two shillinges of the pounde of moueable goodes, and [illegible] shillinges the pound in landes to be paid in two yeres, and all Colledges, Chauntries, and Hospitals, were committed to the kinges order, during his life, to alter and transpose.

Chauntries giuen to the king.

The 26. day of February should a woman

Pardon at the stake

1546

n haue bene burned in Smithfield, clippinge of golde but the kinges don came, she beinge at the stake.

Stewes put downe.

Anno 38

Aboute Easter the Stewes was put wne by the kings commaundement.

In May the kinges shippes toke one the Frenche kings Galleis with gret les.

A generall procession.

The xiii. day of June being Whitson-e, a continuall peace was proclay-d in the Citie of London, betwene kynge of England and the Frenche g, wyth a generall Procession at ẏ e of Proclamation.

Execution.

The xvi. daye of Julye were burned Smithfield for the Sacramēt, Anne ewe, otherwyse Anne Kime Gentle-man, John Lassels gentleman, Nicho- Otterden priest, John Adlam Taylor: Doctour Shaxton somtime bishoppe alisburye, who had beene of the same ion, preached at the same fyer, and nted, perswading them to do ẏ like.

The Admiral of Frāce

he xxi. daye of Auguste, came into gland, Mounsier Deneball highe Ad-al of Fraunce, wyth great triumph brought wyth him ẏ Sacre of Depe iii. Galees well beseene in deuers ts, and landed at London at the to- r harfe, where he was honourably

re-

receyued wyth many nobles and piers of this Realme, wyth great shooting of Gonnes, & so broughte to the bish.op of Londons Palles, and leye there tho nights. On Monday he rode to Hampton Court, where the King laye: and before hee came there, Prince Edwarde receyued hym wyth a companye of fiue hundreth coates of veluet, and the princes lyuerye were wyth sleues of cloth of Golde, and halfe the coate embrauderded wyth golde. And there were to the nomber of eight hundred horses, royally apparelled, which brought him to the Mannour of Hampton Courte.

Conduite in Lothbery.

In September the water of Finsbery was brought to the Conduites of London wall, at S. Stephens in Colmanstreat, and to a newe conduite at S. Margaretes in Lothberye.

Sherifes. Rich. Ieruis. Thomas Curtise. 28 of Sept.

Mayor. H. Hoblethorn Marchant tayler. 28. Octo.

Duke of Northfolke and Erle of Surreye.

The xii. of December Thomas Duke of Northfolke, and the Earle of Surrey his sonne, was sente to the Tower of London prisoners, the one by water and the other by land.

Execution.

The 20. of December William Harpin was drawen from Newgate to the Tower hill, and there hanged for coyning.

The

The iii. of January the Church of the ... Gray Fryers in London, was ope... and that daye preached at Poules ... the bishop of Rochester, who de... ared the kinges gifte to the Cittye of ... ondon for the releuinge of the poore ... ople, which gift (by Paten vnder the ... eat seale) was S. Barthilmewes spittle, ... Churche of the sayd Gray Fryers, & ... urch of S. Nicholas fleshambles, & ... Church of S. Ewens, to be made one ... rish Church within ÿ Gray Friers, ... d in landes for the mainteyning of ÿ ... me, 500. markes by yeare for euer.

K. Henry his gift.

The Lord Henry Haward Erle of Sur... y was araigned at the Guilde hall in ... ndon on the 13. day of January, & be... aded at the tower hil the 19. of Janu... ye. These thinges beinge done, the ... of January, K. Henry departed of this ... appointing his first heyre to be his ... nne Prince Edwarde, the second Lady ... arye, by his first wyfe Quene Kathe... ne, and ÿ third Ladye Elizabeth by his ... cond wyfe Anne Bulleine. Whe he had ... igned 37 yeares 9. moneths and dv... ... yes, he was buried at Windsour.

Execution.

Edwarde

EDVVARD
the sixte.

Anno reg. 1

EDward the sixt, begã his raigne the 28. daye of January, in the yeare 1546. when hee was but nyne yeares olde.

K. Henrye his father by his will, had appointed for his priuye counsel, the Archbishop of Canterbury, the Lord Chauncelour, the bishop of Durham with other, to the nomber of .16.

The first of Februarye, the Earle of Hereforde was elected (by the executors of K. Henry) to be Protectour of the kings person.

Protector.

The 6. of February, the Earle of Hereforde, Lord Protectour in the Tower of London, endued K. Edward wyth the order of Knighthoode, and then Immediatly the King standing up, Henry Hublethorne Lord Mayor of London was called forth, who kneelinge afore the Kinge, the Kinges Maiestye toke the sworde of the Lord Protectoure, & made him knight.

The Kinge made knighte.

Lord maior made knight.

The 17. of February, was sir Edward Seymer Earle of Hereford & Lord Protectour

States created.

mour, created Duke of Somerset, the Lord Parre Earle of Essex, created Marques of Northampton. Sir Iohn Dudley, Lord Lisle, & admiral, created Earle of Warwicke, and Lorde Chamberlaine of Englande. Sir Thomas Writhsley and Lorde Chauncelloure, created Earle of Southampton. Sir Thomas Seymer made Lord Seymer, Lord of Sidewell and high Admirall of Englande. Sir Richarde Riche made Lorde Riche. Sir William Willoughby made Lorde Willoughby. Sir Edmonde Shieffielde made Lorde Sheffielde.

The 20. day of Februarye, K. Edward was crowned at Westminster, with gret solempnitye. The kinge crowned.

The 6. of Marche the greate seale of Englande, was taken from sir Thomas Wrethsleye Earle of Southampton, and delivered to the Lord Protector, and on the morrow it was delivered to the Lord Saint Iohn Lord great maister.

This yeare 1547. the xv. of Maye, Doctoure Smithe recanted at Poules crosse. 1547 Doctour Smith.

The Lorde Protectoure with the reste of the counsayle, sente Commissioners unto all partes of the Realme, willing them to take all Images oute of their Churches Images taken downe.

Churches for the avoyding of Idolatry wyth them were sent diuers preachers, to perswade the people from their beades, and such like Ceremonyes. At the same time, Procession was commaunded to be no more vsed.

Procession forbidden.

In August, the Duke of Somerset, and the Erle of Warwicke, wyth a noble armye, were sent into Scotland: and nere to Edenboroughe, at a place called Muskelboroughe, the Englishmen and Scottes met, where betweene them on the x. of September was foughten a sharpe battaile: The victorye fell to the Englishmen, and of the Scottes were slain 14. Thousand, and taken prisoners xv. hundreth. whereof many were gentlemen, and not aboue lx. Englishmenne slaine.

Muskelborough field.

Sherifes Tho. Whyte. Ro. Chertsey. 28. of Septemb.

The 23. of October sir Richarde Riche, lord Rich, was chosen lorde Chauncellour.

Mayor. sir Iohn Gresham Mercer. 28. of October

The 4. of Nouember the Parliament begon at Westminster, the morrowe after begā the conuocation at Poules.

A parliamēt

The 16. of Nouember the kinges maiesties visitors caused the Rode wyth all the Images in Poules Church, to be taken

Visitors.

[illegible] downe, and forthwith al Images [in] euery parish Church in London, and [th]orowoute all Englande, was pulled [d]owne and broken.

The 24. of December, the Parliamēt [wa]s proroged, in the which was gran[ted] to the king al Chaunteries, free Chap[pe]lles and brotherhodes, & an Act made [fo]r the receyuing of the communion in [bo]th kindes of brede and wyne.

Chanteries geuē to the king.

Communiō.

In the moneth of Marche, the kinges Commissioners were sente into euerye [s]hire in Englande, to suruay al Colled[ge]s, free Chappels, Chaunteryes, and [b]rotherhods, & Poules Churche with [d]iuers other parishes in London, songe [th]e seruice in the Englishe, and so forth [th]orough the whole Realme.

1548

Anno. 2.

Church seruice in Englishe.

The Watche in London at Midsom[mer], of long time before layde downe, [was] now againe vsed, both on the Eue [of S]. Iohn and S. Peter, in as comely [and] beautifull a maner, as it had beene [a]ccustomed at anye tyme before, which [W]atche was greatly beautifyed wyth ŷ [n]umber of more then thre hundreth Di[mi]lances and light horsemen, that of [la]te had beene prepared and mustred by [th]e Cittizens of the same Cittye, to bee [se]nt into Scotlande, for the rescue of ŷ towne

Watch at Midsommer.

Horsemen to Scotlād.

towne of Hadington.

Bishop of Winchester

On S. Peters daye, Stephen Gardener Bishop of Winchester, preached at Westminster in the Court afore the king and the Cousel, and on the morrow after he was for that Sermon, sente to the Tower of London, where he remayned all the kings raigne.

A priest of Cornewall executed.

The 7. of July a Priest was drawen from the tower of London into Smithfieldes, and there hanged and quartered, for that hee and other in Cornewall, had slaine one of the kinges Commissioners, the other of his societye, were put to deathe in diuers other partes of this Realme.

Doctour Cockes.

The 8. of Julye, Doctour Cockes the kinges Almoner & scholemaister, preached at Poules Crosse, where hee reade and declared the Artecles whiche the Bishoppe of Winchester had promysed to haue opened before the kinges Maiestye.

A great pestilence.

This yere in London was greet mortality by the pestilence. Wherefore commaundement was geuen to all Curates and other, hauing to do therewith, that no corps should bee buryed before 6. of the clocke in the morning, nor after 6. at night, and that ther should at the butying of euery corps be ronge one Bell at the least, the space of three quarters of an houre.

Wil. Locke. Iohn Aylephe. 28. of Septem. Sheriffes.

Sir Henry Amcottes fishmonger. 28. Oct. Mayor.

The 16. of Nouember, S. Annes church within Aldersgate was brent. Saint Annes Church.

The 16. of Ianuarye, the Lorde Thomas Seymer. Lord Admiral of England and brother to the Lord Protector was sente to the tower of London, and the xx. of Marche, he was beheaded at the tower hill. Anno. 3. Lord Admiral beheaded.

The x. of April beganne the pulling down of the cloister of Poules Church in London, with the daunce of death and other monuments, and also the Chappell in that Church yard. About that time the steple with a great parte of S. Johns Church in Smithfield was blowen vp with gunne poulder, to build ÿ Duke of Somersets house at the Strande. 1549

The 23 of April 5. houses were burned at broken Wharfe.

The 13. of May, William Pate Monier, was hanged at S. Thomas of Waterings. Execution.

In May by meanes of a Proclamation for enclosers, the Commons of Somersetshire & Lincolnshire made a commotion, Commotion in Somerset and Lincoln shire. ...ection, who brake vp certaine parkes of sir William Harbards & Lord Sturtuns, but sir William Harbarde slewe and executed many of those rebels.

In July the commons of Essex & Kent, Suffolke and Northfolke, rose against inclosers, and pulled downe diuers parkes and houses. Also the commons of Cornwal & Deuonshire, required not onlye that the inclosers might be dispatched, but also to haue their old Religiō, and acte of 6. articles restored. these besieged the Citty of Excester, which was valiantly defended. Against these rebels was sent the lord Russel, Lord priuye seale with a nomber of souldiours, who entred the Cittye of Excester the .5 of August, and slew and toke prisoners of the rebels more then 4000. and after hanged diuers of them in the towne & about the country. The Lorde Gray was also sent with a nōber of strāgers horsemen, whoe in diuers conflictes slewe many people, & spoyled the country.

Commotiō of Cornewall.

Rebels subdued.

On Mary Magdalins daye in the morning, the bailly of Rumford in Essex, was hanged on a gibbet within Algate of London, and one other of Kent was likewyse hanged at the bridge foote towardes Southwarke.

Execution at Algate.

he last of July the Lord Marques of
orthampton, entered the Citty of Nor-
iche, and that night the rebels entered
e towne, and burned parte thereof, &
ut the Lorde Marques to flight, and
lewe the Lord Schefilde.

The 2. of Auguste, the Frenche Em-
assador, gaue a defiaunce to the Lorde
Protectour, from y French king, wher-
uppon, forthwith all Frenchmen wyth
heir goodes, beinge no denisens, were
pprehended. The 16. of August one
was hanged withoute bishops gate, an
other sent to Waltham & there executed.

Frenchmen appreheded

Execution.

The 22. of August Iames Webbe Vicar of Barforde, was sent to Alesburye &
ther executed, Iohn Allein was executed
at Tiborne. Roger Baker at the Tower
hill, and Willam Gates at Totenhem.

The rebels in Northfolk and Suffolke,
encamped themselues in Saint Nicholas woode, neare vnto Norwich, against
whom sir Iohn Dudley Earle of Warwicke, wente wyth an armye, where
both hee himselfe, and a greate nomber
of Gentlemen that were with him, meeting with the rebels, were in such danger, as they thoughte al to haue dyed in
the place: but GOD broughte it so to
passe, that as well there as in all other

places, they were partly by power constrayned, partlye by promise of theyr pardon perswaded, to submit themselues. The 28. dayes of August, tidinges was brought to the Kinges maiestye, that these rebels in Northfolke were subdued, and that the Earle of Warwike had entered the City of Norwich the 27. of August, and had slaine aboue 5. Thousand of the rebelles & taken their chiefe Captaine, called Robert Kite of Windam Tanner. And the said Earle put to execution diuers of the rebelles in diuers places about Norwich.

Rebelles at Norwich subdued.

Roberte Kyte takē

The 20. of September, Edmond Bōnar bishoppe of London, was sent from Lambeth to the Marshalsey, for a Sermon which hee had preached at Poules Crosse on the first of September, & on the first of October hee was depriued of his bishopprike, and sente againe to the Marshalsey, for disobeiinge the kinges order in Religion. And shortlye after Doctoure Ridley bishoppe of Rochester was preferred to bee bishoppe of London.

Boner bishop of Lōdon depriued.

D. Ridley bishoppe of London.

Sherifes John Yorke. Richarde Turke. 28. of Sept.

The viii. of October, after a common counsell in the Guild hall, where all the Lords of the Counsell came, the

Lorde

the Chauncelloure and other, decla- diuers abuses of the Lorde Protec- , desiring the Citizens to be ayding assistaunce with them for the preser- g of the kinges Maiestye. The Le- dined at maister Yorkes house, be- one of the Sheriffes. And in the af- noone about 4. of the clocke procla- tion was made in diuers places of Citiye with two trompetters, foure roldes, and two kinges of armes, rey and Clarenceaux, in theyr coates armes, the Seruaunte of the Trem- ers, and the common cryar, maister ke sheriffe, maister Chalner one of clerkes of the counsell, which red the oclamation, wherein was contained ers articles touchinge the euill go- nment of the Lord Protector,

P[illegible] clamation [illegible] the Protec- tour.

the xiiii. of October in the after none Duke of Somerset was broughte frō ndsore, ryding through Holborne, & t Newgate, and soe to the towre of ndon, accompanyed wyth dyuers rdes, knightes and gentlemen, with horse, the Lorde maior, Syr Raphe rren, Syr Iohn Gresham, Maister re- dee, Syr William Locke, and both § riffes, named Iohn Yorke, and Richard ke, Syr Iohn Baker, Syr Richarde

Protector broughte to the Tower.

 South-

Southwel. Sir Edmond Candish, and Sir Thomas Pope, sitting on their horses against Soper lane, with al the officers of the Shereffes standing by them with halbardes, and from Holborne bridge to the Tower, certaine Aldermenne or their deputyes on horsebacke in euerye streate, wyth a nomber of housholders standing with billes as he passed through the streates to the tower hil, where hee was deliuered to the Constable of the Tower, wyth Syr Michael Stanhoppe, knight of the priuy Chamber, syr Thomas Smith Secretarye, Syr Iohn Thin knight, Wolfe of the priuye Chamber, and Grey of Reding.

The kyng dyning in Southwark. The xvii. of October, the Kinges maiesty came from Hampton Court to his place in Southwarke, & there dined, & after dinner he made maister Yorke one of the Shereffes knight. And then he rode through the Citye of London wyth his nobilitye, to Westminster.

Mayor. Sir Roulan Hill Mercer. 28. of October.

This sir Roulande Hill caused to bee made a causey, from Stone to Namwich, in length foure myles, for horse & man safely to passe, with also diuers lanes on both sides the same causey: hee caused likewyse a causey to be made fro

nchurch to Bransen in Warwikeshyre, ne then two myles of length, & gaue pound in money toward making of men bridge, three myles from Couē-e. He made the high way to Kilborne re to London, he made foure bridges o of them of stone contayning 18. ar-s in them both, the one ouer ẏ riuer Seuerne, called Acham bridge, the o-r Terne bridge, for that the water of rne runneth vnder it, the other two of mber at Stoke, and built new a good rt of Stoke Churche. Moreouer hee ilded one notable free schole at Dra- Free schole at Draton.
in Shropshyre, of continuance for er, with maister and Vsher, and suffi-ient stipends besides conuenient lod-ges for the same: and also one yeerely te, to maintayne and repayre ẏ same ole house for euer. He also purcha-a free fayre to the sayd towne, wyth ree market weekelye, and a free mar-t for cattell euery fourteene dayes. hee gaue to the hospitall of Christes Sir Rowlande Hil his gift.
urch in London, in his life time fiue ndred pound in money, and one hun-ed pound at his decease.

The xxix. of Nouember, Robert Kite, Kite and his brother executed.
d William Kite his brother, were de-liuered out of the tower to sir Edmonde

Windam

Windam knight & Sherife of Northfolke to be conuayed to Norwiche, where Robert Kite was hanged in chaynes on the toppe of Norwiche Castell, and William Kite his brother hanged on the toppe of Windam steple the seuenth of December.

Barones crea-ted.

The xix. of Januarye, sir John Russell Lord priuye seale, was created Earle of Bedforde. And Lord S. John Lorde great maister was created Erle of Wiltshire. And sir William Paget comptroler of the kinges house, was made Lord Paget.

Murder cō-mitted.

Also the xix. of Januarye at nighte, were murdered by S. Pulchers Church against the kings head without Newgate, two Captaynes that had serued ye king in his warres at Bologne and elswhere, the one was called Peter Gambo, and the other Filicirga, which murder was cōmitted by Charles Gauaro a Flemminge, who came post from Barwike to London, to do that acte. On the morrowe he and thre of his companye were taken in Smithfield by the Lord Paget and sent to newgate. And the xxiiii. of Januarye, the said foure persons called Charles Gauaro, Balthasar Gauaro, Nicholas Desalueron, & Fraunces Deualasco were had in a cart from Newgate to Smithfield, & by the waye as they went, at the

Execution.

place

te where the [illegible] Char-
Gararo [illegible]
ye head [illegible]
[illegible] Smithfield [illegible]
ed. The [illegible] of January [illegible]
ndel Esquier, Thomas [illegible] [illegible] executed.
[illegible] Bery, [illegible] Captaynes of the
ts in Deuonshyre, were drawen fro
Towere to Tyborne, and there han-
and quartered.

On Candlemas day, Lord Saint John
le of Wiltshire Lord great maister, Anno .4.
president of the counsel, was made
high treasurer of England. And
John Dudley Earle of Warwike, Newe officers made.
de great Chamberlaine: was made
d great maister of the kinges house-
d, and the Lord William Parre Mar-
s of Northampton, was made Lorde
at Chamberlaine of houshold.

e Earle of Arundel late Lord Cham-
laine, and the Earle of Southamptõ,
re banished from the counsell & com
unded to keepe their houses.

The sixte of Februarye, the Duke of Duke of Sõmerset deliuered.
merset kynge Edwardes uncle, was
uered out of the Tower, & the same
ht he supped with the Earle of Warke, at the sheriffes house called mai-
Yorke.

The

Execution. The tenth day of February, one Bell a Suffolke man, was drawen from the Tower to Tiborne, and there hanged and quartered, for mouing a newe rebelliō in Suffolke and Essex.

1550. Peace proclaymed. The last day of March a generall peace was proclaymed betweene the kinges of England and Fraunce, and in ẏ same peace were included the Emperour & ẏ Scottes.

Southwarke purchased. This month of March, the Lord maior of London, and the Aldermen, purchased all the liberties of Southwarke by the kinges letters patent.

Bolloigne yelded. The xxv. day of Aprill, the towne of Bolloigne was yelded vp to the French kyng.

Ioane Butcher. The second day of Maye, one Ioane Knel, otherwyse called Ioane Butcher, or Ioane of Kent, was burned in Smithfeeld for heresye.

Execution. Certaine lewde persons attempted a new rebellion in some part of Kent, but they were sone repressed, and certaine of the chiefe, as Richarde Lion, Goddard Gortan, and Richarde Irelande, were apprehended and put to death the xiiii. day of May.

Trinitye Terme was reiourned to Mychaelmas, for that the Gentlemen shoulde

and kepe ẏ common people in quiet.

...gustine Hind. Iohn Lyon. 28. of Sept. Sherifes.

...Andrew Iudde Skinner. 28. of October. Maior.

...his sir Andrew Iudd erected a no-table schole at Tunbridge in Kente, wherin be brought uppe and nourished ...good learning, greate store of youth, ...wel bred in the shyre as brought fro ...her countryes adioyning. Free schole at Tūbridge

The 17. of December, the Thames be-...th the bridge did ebbe and flowe 3. ...mes within 12 houres.

This yeare on S. Valentines daye at ...ersham in Kent, one Arden a Gentle-...n, was killed by the consente of hys ...ne wyfe. For this acte the wyfe her ...fe was burned at Canterbury the xiiii. ...y of Marche, the same daye two other ...re hanged in chaines at Feuersham, & ...woman brente: Mosby and hys sister, ...re hanged in Smithfield at London. ...d Blacke Will the ruffian that was ...ed to do the acte, after his first scape ...s apprehended and burnte on a scaf-...de at Flushing in Sealande. Anno reg. 5. Murder at Feuersham.

The 14. day of February, Stephen Gar-...er bishop of Winchester, was depri-...d of his bishoprike, and so committed ...the tower again. Into his place was ...nslated Doctour Poynet who before was Bishop of Winchester depriued.

was bishop of Rochester.

1551. The 24. day of Aprill, George of Paris, a Dutchman was burned in Smithfield, which held opinion of ÿ Arians.

An Arrian burnt.

The 25. daye of May, betwene ÿ houres of eleuen and one of the clocke at after none, was an earthquake of a quarter of an houre longe, at Blechingleye, at Godstone, Tytsey, Rygate, Croydon, Beningron, Albery, and dyuers other places in Southery.

Earthquake

The 9. of Julye proclamation was made in London, for the abatemente of the coine, the shillinge to ix.d. and the grote to iiii.d. which toke effecte imme- diatly after ÿ proclamation was made. Which said proclamation was so soden ly set forth, that the Lord maior of Lon don see it not til it was proclaimed.

The first fal of the moneye.

The infeccious sweating sicknes be gan at London the viii. daye of Julye, whiche was so terrible, that people beyng in best health, were sodainly take, and dead in xxiiii. houres, or xii. or lesse for lacke of skill in guardinge them in their sweat. And it is to be noted, that this mortalitye fell chiefelye or rather onelye on men, & those also of the best age, as betwene xxx. & xl. yeres of age. Also it followed Englishmen as well

Sweatinge sickenes.

with

within the Realme as in strange countreis: wherfore this nation was much afrayde of it, and for the tyme began to repent, and remember God, from whō the plague might well seeme to be sent. But as the disease in time relented, so our devotion in shorte space decayed, the first weke there dyed in London 800. persons and then it ceased.

The 17. day of August was proclamation made, that the shillinge which of late was called downe to ix. d. shoulde be curraunte for vi. d. the groate ii. d. the halfe groate, i. d. a peny, a ob. &c.

Second fall of the monye.

John Lambart. John Coper. 28. of Sept.

Sherifes

The xi. day of October, ỹ Lord Marques Dorset, was created Duke of Suffolke: the Earle of Warwike Duke of Northumberland: and the Earle of Wiltshire Marques of Winchester: and sir William Herbert the maister of the horse Earle of Pembroke.

Dukes and Earles created.

The xvi. day of October the Duke of Somerset was brought againe to the tower of London, and the nexte morning ỹ Duches his wyfe, was brought thither. there went also with the Duke the lord Gray of Wilton, sir Raphe Vane, sir Thomas Palmer, sir Myles Partrige, sir Michael Stanhope, sir Thomas Arundell & divers

Duke of Somerset agayne to the tower.

and divers other.

Stiliard put downe. In this moneth of October the liberties of the Stiliard was seased into the kinges handes, for divers causes forfayted contrary to their intercourse.

Mayor. Sir Richard Dobbes Skinner. 28. October.

The xxx. day of October was proclaimed a new coine of moneye, both silver and gold, soveraines of fine gold at xxx. s. Angels of fine gold at x. s. & divers other pieces of golde of lesser value: A piece of silver of v s. & a piece of ii s. vi. d. the sterling shilling xii. d. and sondry other smaller pieces of money.

New coine.

The 6. daye of November the olde Queene of Scottes rode through London, wyth a great company of English men wayting on her, after she had laine foure dayes in ÿ bishops place besydes Poules Church.

The queene of Scottes.

Duke of Somerset araigned. The first day of December, the Duke of Somerset was araigned at Westminster hall, and there acquited of treason, but condempned of felony.

Muster of horsemen. The 7. day of December, was a generall muster of the horsemen which were in the wages of ÿ nobles of the Realme and for the which the kinges Maiestye allowed yearely for everye man xx. li. the which muster was made uppon the

causy

cawsey ouer agaynste the kinges Pallas at S. James, the nomber of horse was esteemed to be a thousand.

The xx. of December, the greate seale was taken from the Lorde Riche Lorde Chauncellour of England, and deliuered to doctour Goodrike bishop of Elye.

At Christmas the Kings maiestye kept hall at Grenewiche, and there passed the tyme wyth greate myrth. George Ferris gentleman of Lincolnes Inne, and one of the kinges maiestyes seruauntes, being Lorde of the merye disportes, who so pleasauntlye behaued himselfe, that the kinges Maiestye had great delighte in his pastimes.

The xxii. daye of Januarye, Edwarde Duke of Somerset, K. Edwardes vncle, before mencioned, was beheaded at the tower hill. Execution.

The 26. day of Febiuary, Syr Raphe Vane, and Syr Miles Partrige, were hanged at tower hill, & Syr Michael Stanhope, wyth Syr Thomas Arundel, were beheaded, which foure knightes were condemned as accessary to the Duke. Anno 6. 4. knightes executed.

This yeare the Sea brake in at Sandwiche, and did ouerflowe all the Marshes there about, it ouerflowed the marshes besyde Wolwiche and beyonde S. Katherins. Highe waters.

Katherines.

The last day of Aprill, through negligence of the gunne powder makers, a certaine house with thre last of powder, was blowen vp & burnt the said gunne powder makers, beinge xv. in number, were al slaine at the tower hill, a little from the Minoris beside London.

1552. Touse blowen vp.

Muster of horsemen.

The 16, of May, the king called to muster al the men of armes, which he lately had made to be vnder the banners of certaine Lords and nobles of ye Realm, his maiestye then lyeing at Grenewiche, which bandes appeared in the parke in most goodlye araye.

A monster.

The third day of August, at Middleton xi. miles from Oxforde, a woman brought forth a childe, which had two perfecte bodyes from the nauel vpwarde, and were so ioyned together at the nauel, that when they were layd in length, the one head and body was East, and ye other Weste, the legges for both the bodyes grewe oute at the midst where the bodyes ioyned: & had but one issue for the excremente of both the bodyes, they liued xviii. dayes, and when they were opened, it appeared they were both women children.

The eyght day of August, were take

about Quinborough three great fishes called Dolphins, and the weeke folowing at Blackwall, were fire more taken and brought to London, the lest of them was greater then any horse. | Great fishes taken.

The month of August, begon the great prouision for the poore in London, towardes the whiche euery man was contributory, & gaue certain money in hand and promised to geue a certain weekely. The first house was begon, at Gray friers in Newgate market.

William Garret, Iohn Mainard. 28, of sep. Sheriffes,

The vii. of October, were two great fishes taken at Grauesende, which were called Whirlepooles, they were afterward drawen vp aboue the bridge. Great fishes taken.

Sir George Barnes Haberdasher. 28. of Oct. Mayor,

This sir George Barnes, gaue one windmill in Finsbury field, to the company of the Haberdashers of London, ye profites therof to be distributed to the poore almose people of the same company. Also he gaue to be distributed to the poore of the parishe of S. Bartholomewe the little xviii. pence in bread euery sunday for euer. Charitable dedes of G. Barnes.

The xxiii day of Nouember the first children were taken in to the hospital at the Gray friers called Christes hospi- Christes Hospitall.

pitall, to the number of almoste foure hundred.

Anno.7 The x. of Aprill the kinges maiestie gaue to be a worke house for the poore

1553 and idle persons of the citie of London, his place of Bridewell, and seuen hundred marke lande of the Sauoy rentes, with all the beddes and bedding of the hospitall of the Sauoye towardes the maintenaunce of the said worke house.

Voyage into Moscouia. The xx. day of May by the encouragement of one Sebastian Cabota, three great shippes well furnished, were set forth for the aduenture of the unknowen viage to Moscouia, and twoo other shippes were sent forth to like aduentures.

Great thunder. The xxii. of June, about xii. of the clocke at noone, by a terryble clappe of thunder one dore of S. Denise in London, was driuen open.

K. Edward deceased. King Edward being about the age of xvi. yeares, was long sicke of a consumption of the lightes, and the sixte daye of July ended his lyfe when he had raigned vi. yeares v. monethes & odde days, and lieth at Westminster.

The Lady Jane. The x. of July in the after noone, about thre of the clocke, the Lady Iane daughter of the lady Fraunces the duches of Suffolke (which lady Jane was ma-

rie

red unto the Lorde Gilford Dudley, the fourth sonne unto the Duke of Northumberlande) was conueyed by water to the Tower of London, and there receyued as Queene. After fiue of the clocke the same after noone, was proclamation made with a trumpetter, and two of the Haroldes kynges at armes, and one of the Shiriffes, of the death of kyng Edwarde the sixt, and howe he had ordayned by his letters patentes, bearing date the xxi. of June last past, that the sayde Lady Jane should be heyre to the crown of Englande, and the heyre males of her body. &c.

Lady Jane proclaymed Queene.

The xi. of Jul. Gilbert Potte, drawer to Ninion Sandes Vintener, dwellyng at S. Johns head within Ludgate, was set on the pilory in chepe, with both his eares nayled & cleane cut of, for wordes speaking at the time of the proclamation of lady Jane. The same daye at after noone, Ninion Sanders the maister of the sayde Gilbert Potte, and one John Gwen a Gunner, shooting London bridge towarde the blacke Friers, were bothe drowned.

Execution in chepe.

Misfortune.

The Lady Mary fled to Fremingham castell in Suffolke, where the people of ỹ countrey almoste wholly resorted unto her,

The Lady Mary fled. Framingham.

ker, and in Oxforde sir John Williams, in Buckyngham shiere, sir Edmond Peckham, and in diuers other places, manye men of worship, offering them selues as guides to the common people, gathered great powers, & with all spede made to warde Suffolke, wher lady Mary was. In the meane time the xiiii day of July, by appointment of the counsell, the Duke of Northumberlande, the Earle of Huntington, the lorde Gray of Wilton, and dyuers other, with a great number of men of armes, wente to fetche her by force, and was on their waye as farre as [illegible] the [illegible] day of [illegible]ly being sunday, doctor Ridley bishop [illegible] London, by commaundement of the counsell, preached at Paules crosse, perswading the people in the title of lady Jane late proclaimed Queene, and denying the title of Lady Mary. But the [illegible] day of July, ye counsell partly moued with the right of her [illegible], partly considering that the moste of the Realme was wholy bent on her side, changed their mindes, and assembled them selues at Baynardes castel, & there commoned with the Earle of Pembroke, & immediatly with the Mayor of London certaine Aldermen, the Sherifes, Garter, king of armes and a trumpet,

pet,

et, came into Cheape. where they pro- Lady Mary
laimed ŷ lady Mary daughter to king proclaimed
enry the eight, & Queene Katherine, Queene.
ueene of Englande, Fraunce, & Ire-
ande, defendor of the faith &c. The same
ight the Earle of Arundell & the lorde
aget, rode in post to the Queene.

The xx. daye of July, John Duke of
orthumberland, being at S. Edmonds
ery, returned backe agayne to Cam-
ridge, and about v. of the clocke in the
uening, he with such other of the nobilitie as were in his company, caused the
lady Mary to be likewise proclaymed
ueene of England. But shortly after
e was arested in the kinges colledge
y one maister Slege sergeant at armes,
nd the xxv. of Julye being S. James day
e with other were brought up to the
ower of London, under the conduction
f the Earle of Arundel. Thus was the
matter ended without bloudshed,
which men feared woulde
haue brought the death
of many thou-
sandes.

QVEENE
Mary.

Anno re. 1

MARY the eldest daughter of king Henry the eight, began her raigne ouer this Realme of Englande, the sixt day of July, in the yere of our Lorde 1553. Shee was proclaimed Queene at London the xix. day of July, and the xx. day at the castell of Framingham, and at Cambridge as is aforesaid. And afterward being accompanied with a goodly band of noble men, gentlemen, and commoners, gathered out of all partes of the Realme, came to London, and entred the tower the third day of August. Where Thomas Duke of Norfolke, Doctor Gardener late bishop of Winchester, and Edward Courtney, sonne and heire to Henry Marques of Excester prisoners in the tower, kneled on yͤ hill within the same tower, askyng pardon, whom she gently saluted, bidding them ryse, on the morrowe they receyued the Queenes pardon, and the Duke of Norfolke and Doctor Gardiner, was sworne of the Queenes counsell.

Prysoners pardoned.

The fifth of August, Edmond Boner, late

late byshop of London, prysoner in the Marshalsie, and Cutbert Tonstal, the olde bishop of Durham, prisoner in the kings benche, had their pardons, and were restored to their seas. And shortly after, al the bishops which had bene deprived in the tyme of king Edward the sixt, were restored to their bishoprikes, & the other which were placed in K. Edwardes tyme were removed, also all beneficed men that were maried, or would not forsake their opinion, were put out of their livinges, & other knowen to be of the cõtrary part were set in ỹ same, especially if any were alive, that in the time of K. Henry or Edward, were put out of the same bishoprikes or benefices.

Bishops restored and other displaced.

The xi. of August, certain gentlemen minding to passe through Londõ bridge in a wherrie, were there overturned, & seven of them drowned.

Wherry overturned.

The xiij. day of August, maister Bourne canon of Paules preaching at Paules crosse, so offended some of the audience, that they breaking silence cried, pul him out, pul him out, and one threwe a dagger at hym, which rebounded backe againe, & then maister Bradford and John Rogers two preachers of king Edwardes time with much labour conveied the sayd

Dagger at the precher.

 maister

maister Bourne out of the audience into Paules schole. The xxii. of August, the duke of Northumberland, sir John Gates, & sir Thomas Palmer, Knightes, were beheaded at the tower hill. The 26. day of August in ŷ euening, the notablest ship in ŷ worlde, was burnt at Wolwich, called the great Harry, by the negligence of mariners, she was of burthē a thousande tonne.

Execution.

Great Harry burnt.

The 4. of Septēber was proclaymed certaine new coines of gold and syluer, that is to say, a soueraigne of fine golde of xxx. shillinges, the halfe soueraigne, called the ryall, xv. shillinges, an angell of x. shillinges, the halfe angell v. shillinges. Of siluer, the groate, halfe groate and the peny, and all base coynes to bee currant, and to go as before that proclamatiō. Also the same day, the Queene by proclamation pardoned the subsety of foure shilling the pound landes, & two shilling eight pence the pound of mouable goodes, graunted in the last parliament of king Edwarde the sixt.

New coyne of gold and siluer.

Subsidy pardoned.

Sherifes, Thomas Offley, William Hewit. 28. of Sept.

The last of September, Queene Mary rode through the citie of Londō to Westminster, the pageantes in places accustomed, most gorgeously set forth, and a

...ā on the ...her cock ...aules.

tchem m stoode on the wethercock of Paules steple, holdinge a streamer in his hande of v. yardes long, and bowed his knee when the Queene rode by: vnder him were two scaffoldes, one aboue the crosse, an other aboue the bowell of the crosse, both set with streamers & torches, which could not burne the wynde was so great. The morow the Queene was crowned at Westminster by Doctor diner byshop of Winchester. Coronation.

The fifth of October, the parliament gan at Westminster. Parliamẽt.

The 25. of October, the barge of Graues by great misfortune of a Catch running vpon her, was ouerthrowen, and ii. persones drowned, and xvi. saued swimming. Grauesend barge.

The xviii. the xxv. the xxvii. dayes of tober, were certaine disputations in the long chappell at the North doore of ules, concerning Transubstantiation, nothing throughly determined. Disputations in Paules churche.

Tho. White Marchant taylor. 28. of Oct. Mayor.

s same sir Thomas White, renewed, rather erected a college of Oxford, was in great ruine and decay, now saint Johns colledge, and before nard colledge, indowing the same landes and reuenues, to the great Charitable dedes of sir Tho. White.

pre-

preferrement of learning. He erected free
The donatiõ of sir Thomas White.
scholes at Bristow, and at Reading, &
also in his life gaue to the Citie of Bristow two thousand pound of ready money to purchase landes to the yerely value of 120. pounde, for the whiche it is
agreed that the Mayor, burgesses, & co-
minaltie of Bristow. In Anno. 1567. and
so yearely during the terme of ten yeares
then next after cause to be paide at Bristowe, one hundred pounde of lawfull
money, the firste eight hundred pounde
to be lent to xvi. poore young men Clo-
thiars and free men of the same town,
for the space of tenne yeres, fiftye poun
the piece of thẽ, putting sufficient sureties for the same, and at the ende of ten
yeres, to be lent to other xvi. at the dis-
cretiõ of the Mayor, Aldermen, & fou
of the common councell of the said citi
The other two hundred poũd, to be em
ployed for the prouision of corne for th
releefe of the poore of the same citie, f
their ready money without gaine to
taken. And after the ende of ten year
then at the marchaunt Taylors haule
London, vnto the Mayor & commin
of the citie of Yorke, or to their attou
authorised the summe of C.iiii.poun
to be sent vnto foure younge men of

fi

Queene, and the Lord Gilforde her husbande, were arraigned at the Guildhal of London, and condemned of treason.

The v. daye of December, the parliament was dissolued, in the whiche all statutes made either of Premunire, in tyme of King Henry the eight, or concerning religion and administration of the Sacramentes vnder K. Edward the sixt, were repealed, and communicatiō was had of the Queenes mariage with king Philippe the Emperours sonne.

The beginning of January, the Emperour sent a noble man called Ecmendane, and other Ambassadoures into Englande to make a certayne conclusion of the mariage betwene kyng Philip and Queene Mary.

Execution at Tyborne.

The xiii of January, one Haruy was drawen from the towre to Tyborne, and there hanged and quartered for counterfeiting the Queenes hand in a patent, & also brake out of pryson in the towre.

The queenes purpose to mary was opened.

The xv of January, the Lord Mayor and Aldermen of London, were sent for to come to the court, and to bring with thē xl. persons of ÿ hed cōmoners of citie, & when they came afore the counsell, the lord Chancellor declared to the queenes pleasure was to mary the Prince of Spayne, which should be a great strength, honour, and enriching the realme of Englande.

The purpose of this mariage was so greuously taken of diuers, that for this, and religion, they in such sort conspired against the Queene, that if the matter had not broken out before the tyme appointed, men thought it would haue brought much more trouble & daunger. Commotion in Kent.

The xxv. of January, sir John Gage, lord Chamberlain to the Queene, certified the Lord Mayor of London, that sir Thomas Wiate, with certaine Rebelles were up in Kent about Maidstone, wherupon great watch was kept that night, and the Lord Mayor rode to peruse the same, and euery night after, two Aldermen did likewise peruse the watch, and in the day tyme, the gates of the Citie were warded by substantiall citizens. Sir Thomas Wiat.

The xxvii. of January the Lord treasurer came to the Guilde hall from the counsel, to request the citizens to make out 500. foote men well harneysed to go against Wiat, which was graunted and made ready by the companies the same night, on the morrow the saide 500 men were mustered at Leaden hall, and there deliuered to their captaines, and sent by

water

water to Gravesende.

The [illegible] day of January, the Duke of Norfolke with the captain of the Garde that were sent from the Queene with souldiours and yeomen of the Garde, & the captaine and souldiours that went out of the citie, mynded to assaulte Rochester castel where Wiat with his people lay, but the captains of the citie with their souldiours fledde ouer Rochester brydge to Wiat, so that the Duke was faine to returne againe to Londo͞n. Thus

Wiat streng thened.

Wiates number being increased & much strengthened with the Queenes ordinaunce & treasure, The xxx. of January he remoued from Rochester and came to Blackeheath.

In this meane tyme Henry Duke of Suffolke father to Lady Iane lately proclaymed Queene, flying into Leicestershiere and Warwikeshiere, with a small company in diuers places, as he went, made proclamatio͞ against ye queenes mariage with ye prince of Spain, &c but people did not greatly incline vnto h[illegible]

The first day of February in the af[illegible]

The Queene came to the guild haule.

noone being Candlemas euen, all the [illegible]mons of the citie were assembled in th[illegible] liueries at the Guilde hall, whether [illegible] Queene with her lordes & ladies c[illegible] [illegible] ming from Westminster, and there af- ter vehement wordes against Wiate, de- ed that shee meant not otherwyse to rry, then the councell should thinke th honourable and commodious to y alme. And if they thoughte good that could continue unmaried, as she had ne the greatest part of her age, & there- e willed them truly to assiste her in pressing suche as contrary to their du- s rebelled.

She appointe lorde William Haward Lord Willia Haward. utenaunt of the Citie, and the Earle Pembroke generall of y field, which e preparerd all thinges necessary for t purposes, with great provision of n and artillerie.

While this provision was making, ate came neare unto the Citie, and entred into Southwarke, the third y of February, and the morrowe after ndlemasse daye, wherefore the drawe dge was broke downe, ordinance bent that part, general pardon proclaimed all them that woulde geue ouer and ue the rebels, and a great rewarde pointed to him that tooke Wiate pri- er. After Wiate had layne two dayes Southwarke, he turned his iorny to ston on Shrouetuesday in the mor- ning

ning, being the vi. of February, where he passed ouer the Thames, & purposed to haue come to London in the night: but by meanes that the cariage of his great ordinaunce brake, he was so letted that he could not come before it was faire daye. The same daye in the after noone

Execution.

were two men hanged on a gibbet in Poules churchyarde, by marshall law, one being the Duke of Suffolkes seruaunt, and had bene [illegible] of Leicester, the other was a baker. On the morrowe early in the morning being Ashwednesday, the earle of Pembroke, and diuers other were in saint James field with a great power, and their ordinaunce so bent that Wiat was faine to leaue the common waye, and with a small company came vnder saint James wall from the danger of the ordinaunce, & so went by charing crosse vnto the bell sauage right vnto Ludgate without resistence, in at which gate he thought to haue bene receyued. But perceiuing that he was deceiued of his purpose, he fled backe agayne, and by temple barre was taken and brought to

Wiat taken.

court gate, and from thence by water sent to the tower of London.

The tenth of February the Duke of Suffolke which was taken in Leice-

shire

shire, was brought to the citie of London by the Earle of Huntingdon, and one of his brethren with him, and so had to the tower. The Duke of Suffolke.

The xii. daye of February, Lady Jane the Duke of Suffolkes daughter, & her husband Lord Gilford, which hitherto had bene kept in the tower, were nowe beheaded, for feare least any other should make lyke trouble for her title, as her father had attempted. Execution.

The xiiii. and xv. of February, about the numbre of fifty of Wiates faction, were hanged on xx. payre of galowses made for the purpose in diuers places about the citie. The xvii. of February, was proclamation made that all straungers should voide the realme within 24 dayes next ensuing, vpon payne of confiscation of there goodes (all free denizons, marchauntes, Ambassadours and their seruauntes except.) Execution. Straungers voyded.

The 22. of February, certain of Wiats faction, to the numbre of foure hundred and more, were led to Westminster, couples together with halters about their neckes, and there in the tilt yarde knelyng afore the Queene, they cried for mercy, and she gaue to them pardon. Kentishmen pardoned.

The 23. of February, the duke of Suffolke

was beheaded at the tower hill.

1554. The seconde daye of April, the Parliament began at Westminster, which
aliament. should haue bene kept at Oxforde.

The x. of April, doctor Cranmer archb.
of Canterburie, Ridley of London, and
Disputation Oxford. Hugh Latimer, were conueyed from the
tower of London to Oxforde, there to
dispute with the deuines.

iat execu-ted. The xi. day of April, sir Thomas Wiat
was beheaded at Tower hill, and after
quartered, his quarters were set vp in
diuers places, & his hed on the galowes
at Hay hill, where it was soone after
stolne away.

The xxviii. of April, the lord Thomas
Gray, brother to the late Duke of Suffolke, was beheaded.

xecution at yborne. William Thomas a gentleman, and certaine other persones, were apprehended
for conspiring Queene Maries death,
the same William Thomas for that offence,
the 18. day of May, was drawen, hanged,
and quartered at Tyborne.

The x. of June beyng Sunday, doctor
Pendleton preaching at Paules crosse, a
gonne was shotte, the pellet whereof
went nere by the preacher, but the shoo-
ter could not be founde.

The xxii. daye of June, was a proclamation

tion made concerning shooting in ..gunnes.

The xv. day of July, Elizabeth Crofte, ..ench of the age of xvi. or xviij. yeres ..inge uppon a scaffolde at Paules ..all the Sermon time, confessed .. she being entised by lewde councel, .. upon the 14. day of March last past ..nterfait certain speaches in an house ..out Aldersgate in London, about .. whiche, the people of the whole citie .. wonderfully molested. Anno. 1. Spirite in a wall at London.

The xix. day of July, king Philip the ..perors sonne passing out of Spaine ..ued at Southampton: the fourth day ..er, he came to Winchester in the eue..ng, & there going to the churche, was ..ourably receiued of y bishop, and a ..at nūber of nobles, for that purpose ..ointed. The next day he met with the ..eene, with whome he had longe and ..iliar talke. The xxv. daye being S. ..es day, the mariage was solemnised ..twene hym and Queene Mary. They ..er after with a goodly cōpany brought .. London, and there with great pompe ..n receiued of the citizens the xviii. ..e of August. King Philip came to Winchester.

..nd Woolfe, William Chester. 28. sep. Sherifes.

The 26. of October a Spaniard was

 hanged

hanged at charing crosse, who had slayn an Englishman, one of sir George Giffordes seruauntes, there was offered for this Spaniarde by the straungers 300. crownes to saue his life.

Mayor, Sir John Lion Grocer the 28. of October.

The xii. of Nouember, the parliamet began at Westminster.

Cardinall Poole. The 23. of Nouember Cardinal Poole came out of Brabant into Englande, and was receiued with muche honour in all places as he passed. At the same tyme he was by parleament restored to his olde estate and dignitie that he was put from by king Henry the Queenes father: and shortly after came into the Parliament house, where the kyng, Queene, & other states were all present. Then he declaryng the cause of his legacie, firste exhorted them to returne to the comunion of the churche, and restore to the Pope, his due authoritie. Secondly he aduertised thē to geue thankes to God that had sent them so blessed a king and Queene: finally he signified, for so muche as they had with great gentlenes restored hym to his honour and dignitie, that he moste earnestly desired to see them restored to the heauenly court & unitie of the church. The next day the whole court of parlia

ment,

ment, drewe out the forme of a supplication, the summe whereof was, that they greatly repented them of that schisme that they had liued in. And therfore desired the kyng, Queene, & the Cardinall, that by their meanes they might bee restored to the bosome of the churche, and obedience of the sea of Rome. The next day the king, Queene, & Cardinall, being present, the lord Chauncellor declared what the parliamēt had determined concerning the Cardinals request, and offred vnto the king & Queene the supplication before mētioned, which being read, the Cardinal in a large oration, declared howe acceptable repentance was in the sight of God. &c.

The second daye of December, being Sondaye, Cardinall Poole came from Lambeth by water, & landed at Paules wharfe, and comminge from thence to Paules churche, he was there receiued by the lord Chauncelor with procession where he taried till the kinges cōming, who came from Westminster by land, & all his nobles before hym at xi. of the clocke, and so the kyng and the Lorde Cardinall with the Lordes of the priuie councell being present, the Lord Chauncelour entred Paules crosse, and preached a Sermon, in the whiche he decla- red that the king & Queene had restored the Pope to his supremacy, & the three estates assembled in the parliament had submitted them selues to the same.

The 27. of December, the prince of Piamount Duke of Sauoye, with other Lordes, were receiued at Grauesende, by the Lorde priuy seale and other, and so conueyed to Westminster.

The Prince of Piamont.

The ix. of January, the Prince of Orenge beyng receiued at Grauesende, was conueyed through London bridge, and landed at the Duke of Suffolkes place, neare vnto charing crosse.

Prince of Orenge.

The 4. of February M. John Rogers, vicar of saint Sepulchars, was burned in Smythfielde.

The xviii. of February, the bishop of Ely, with the Lord Mountacute and dy- uers other, rode through the citie of Lon- don towardes Rome Ambassadours fro the kyng, Queene, and counsell. It is to be noted, that against Easter, the Lorde Courtney Earle of Deuonshire came a- gayne to the court. And about x. dayes after, the Ladye Elizabeth came to the Queene, both at Hampton court, where the Queene had taken her chamber to be deliuered of childe.

Ambassadours.

At

At this tyme and long before, it was bruted through Englande, that Queene Mary was with child and great preparation was made for her deliuery, but all proued contrary, for shee neuer had childe, nor great hope to haue any. Queene bruted with childe.

On Easter day, a certayne parson named Williā Branche, alias Flower, with a wood knife wounded a priest, as he was ministring the Sacrament to the people in S. Margaretes church at Westminster: for the which offence, ẏ said Wil. Flower, the xxiiii. of Aprill had his right hande smitten of, and for opiniō in matters of religion was burned in the Sanctuarye nighe vnto S. Margaretes church yarde. 1555 Execution.

In May, the Lord Cardinal Poole, the lord Chauncelour of England, the Earle of Arundell, high Steward of England, and the Lord Paget, went ouer sea to Calais, and neare vnto Marke, treated with the Emperours and French kinges cōmissioners, for peace to be had betwene the said princes, Cardinall Poole being president there, who returned into England, about the middest of June, without any agreement making. Ambassadours.

The tenth of Maye, William Constable alias Fetherstone, a Myllers sonne, about the age of eightene yeares, whoe

A false one named to be Edward. had named himselfe to be King Edward the sixt, was takē about Eltham in Kēt, and conueyed to the Marshalsey. The xxvii. daye Maye, carted round aboute Westminster haule before al the Judges, and then whipped about the palace and so foorth till he came into Smithfielde, and there was banished into the North in which countrey he was borne, he had sometyme bene a lacaey to Sir Peter Mewtasse.

The first of July, Maister John Bradford was burned in Smithfield.

Anno.3 The xxi. of Auguste, was a terrible fight on the Sea, betwene the Duches men and Frenchmen, nere vnto Romney [illegible], whereas ii. shippes were brent & sonke, that is to say, sixe Frenche shippes, and fiue great Hulkes taken by the Frenchmen.

Monstrous fishe. About the same time was brought to Lynne a monstrous fishe of ix. foote in length.

In September, the Kyng went ouer Sée to Brusselles in Brabant to visite the Emperour his father.

Shiriffes. Thomas Leigh, John Machill, 28. of Sept.

Great water. The beginning of October fell suche rayne, that for the space of vi. dayes men might rowe with boates in S. Georges fyelde,

[...]de the water came into Westminster hall, and there stoode halfe a yeare [...]. Also vnto the palace of Westminster, and into Lambeth Church, that a man might rowe about the Church with a whirrie.

The xvi. day of October Doctor Rydley and Doctor Latymer, were burned at Oxforde.

William Garrard Haberdasher. 28. Oct. Mayor,

In October and Nouember, a parliament was holden, in the which ÿ queene gaue vp vnto the spirituall men, the first fruites and tenthes of all Ecclesiasticall liuinges. In this Parliament was granted to the king & Queene a subsedy of ÿ laytie from fiue pound to x. pound viii. pence of ÿ pound, from x. pound to xx. pound xii d. of the pound, & from xx. pound vpward xvi. pence the pound of moueable goods, & so forth of lands, & all strangers double. Also the Clergie graunted a subsedy of sixe shillinges of the pounde of their promotions.

A subsedy granted to the Queene.

Stephen Gardiner bishop of Winchester and Chauncellour of England, dyed the 9 of Nouember, & was buried at Winchest.

John Philpot was burnt in Smithfield, the xviii. day of Nouember.

On new yeres day the Queene gaue ÿ

great

Chanceler and Lorde preuy seale. great seale to doctor Heath archebishop of Yorke, and made him Lorde Chauncelour, and gaue the preuay seale to the Lorde Paget, and made hym Lord preuye seale.

One named himselfe king Edward was hanged. The 26. of February, William Constable, alias Fetherston, was arraigned at the guild haule in London, who had caused letters to be cast abroade in the citie & other places, that King Edward þ vi. was aliue, & to some simple persons shewed himselfe to be King Edward, for þ which sedicion the sayd William had ones ben whipped as is afore sayd, and nowe was condemned to be drawen, hanged, and quartered, whiche was executed accordingly the xiii. of Marche.

Archbishop of Caunterbury. The xxi. day of March, Doctor Cranmer archebishop of Caunterbury, was burned at Oxforde, Cardinall Poole, on sonday next followyng, was consecrated archebyshop of Caunterbury.

1556 And on the feaste of the Annunciation of our Lady, receiued the palle at Bowe churche in Cheape.

Newgate a fyre. On Palmesonday euen, at x. of the clocke afore noone, a parte of Newgate called Manninges haule, was brent to the grounde and no prysoners lost.

Conspiracy. A conspiracie was made, by certayne per-

persones, whose purpose was to haue robbed the Queenes Escheker, to the entent they might bee able to maynteyne warre against the Queene. This matter was uttered by one of the conspiratours: whereby Vdall, Throgmorton, Peckham, Daniell and Stanton, were apprehended for the same, and diuers other, fled into Fraunce. Sir Anthony Kingston, was apprehended and died by the waye comming up to London.

The xxviii. of April, Throghmorton, and Richarde Vdal, were drawen to Tyborne, and there hanged and quartered. Execution.

The xix. day of May, Stantō was likewyse executed at Tyborne.

The viii. day of June, Kelly, Dethicke, and Bedell, were also drawen to Tyborne, hanged and quartered.

The xviii. day of June, Sandes, a younger sonne to the Lorde Sandes was hanged at S. Thomas a Waterings, for a robberie. Executions.

The xxvii. day of June, were 13. persons brent at Stratford the Bowe.

The vii. day of July, Henry Peckham, and Iohn Daniell, were hanged and headed at the Tower hyll. Anno, 4.

In the yeare last past, began the hotte burning Feuers and other straunge diseases,

seases, whereof died many old persones; so that in Londō ther died seuen Aldermen in the space of x. monethes, whose names were Henry Herdson, who deceased the xxii. of December. in Anno 1555 Sir Richard Dobbes, late Maior. Sir Will. Laxton, late Mayor, Sir Henry Hoblethorne late Mayor, Sir Iohn Champneis, late Mayor, Sir Iohn Ailesse late Sherife, and Sir Iohn Gresham late Mayor, who deceased ỹ xxiii. of October in this yere. 1556. This Sir Iohn Gresham gaue to euery warde in London x. pound, to be distributed to the poore of the same wardes, and to ii. score poore men and women, to euery one of thē thre yardes of blacke cloth for a gowne of viii. or ix. shillinges the yarde, to be ready made to their backes. He gaue also to maydes mariages. And to the Hospitalles of London, aboue twoo hundreth poundes of ready money.

Seuen Aldermen deceased.

Sir Iohn Gresham.

Sherifes, William Haper, Iohn Whyte. 28. Septemb.

Mayor, Sir Tho Offley Marchant Taylor. 28, of Oct.

The xvi. of December, Gregory Carpenter Smythe, beinge a straunger borne, was arraigned at Newgate for making counterfeited keyes, wher with to haue opened Newgate in the night, & so to haue slayne the keper, and let forth

prysoners, at whiche tyme of his ar-
gnement, hauing a knyfe in his sleue
thruste it into the syde of one Willia
ytterentes, his felowe prysoner, who
re wytnes against hym, so that hee
as in great peryll of death thereby.
r the whiche acte he was immediatly
ken from the barre, and in the streate
fore the iustice haule, his hande being
iken of, his bodye was hanged on a
we gybet set vp for that purpose: the
me tyme, the keper of Newgate was
aned and indited for that the sayde
risoner had weapon about hym, and
s handes loose.

Executions.

The fourth of January, a shippe pas-
ng before Greenewiche (the court being
ere) shotte of her ordinaunce, and one
ece being charged with a pellet of
one, passed through the walles of the
arke and did no more harme.

The xxvii. of Februarye, an Ambas-
dour came to London from the Em-
rour of Cattay, Muscouie, and Ruslande,
ho was honourably met and receiued
Totnam, by the marchaunt venturers
London, ryding in veluet coates and
haynes of golde, and by them conduc-
d to Smithfield barres, and there re-
iued by the Lorde Mayor of London,

An ambassa dour from Muscouie.

with

with the Aldermen and Sheriffes, and so by the Lorde Mayor, Aldermen, and Marchant venturers, conueyed through the Citie, vnto Maister Dimokes place in Fanchurche streate, where he lodged vntill the twelfth of May nexte folowyng, at the whiche tyme he toke shipping at Grauesende with the Prymrose, and three other shippes to sayle to Moscouye.

Murder. The Lord Sturton with much crueltie murthered two men: & for the same was arraigned and cōdempned at Westminster, the seconde day of Marche, hee was conueyed through London to Salesbury, and there hanged with foure of his seruauntes the vi. of Marche.

King Philip, who had beene a good season in Flaunders to take the possession and gouernement of the lowe countries, in Marche retourned into England, and the xxii. day he passed through London beyng accompanied with the Queene, and the nobles of the Realme.

1557 The xxiiii daye of Aprill. Thomas Stafforde and other Englyshemen, to the nomber of xxxii. persones, comming out of Fraunce, toke the castel of Scarborough, which they enioyed two dayes, and then were taken and brought to London,

Scarbrough castell takē.

her on the 28. day of May the said
as Stafforde was beheaded at
e hyll, and vpon the morow, were
his cōpany drawen to Tyborne
ere hanged and quartered. Execution.

e first of May, Maister Thomas
of the North, was made knight
ter Lord, and the morowe after he
reated Earle of Northumberland,
e Queene gaue him all the landes
e had bene his auncetours remay-
a her handes. Earle of Northumberlād.

e seuenth of June open warre was
ymed against the French king.
e first of July, the king passed ouer
to Caleis, & so into Flaunders,
he made great prouision for war
st the Frenche king, and the same
h, the Queene sent ouer an armye
thousand horsemen, foure thou-
footmen, and twoo thousande
ers, for to ayde kynge Phylippe,
of the Earle of Pembroke was
nerall. Warre proclaymed. Englishmen sent to saint Quintins.

e xv. of July, dyed the Lady Anne
ne at Chelsey, and was buried at
inster the eight of August. Anno. 5

e xviii. daye of August, was taken
wne of Sainte Quintine by kynge
with the helpe of Englishmen, as
the

the siege whereof, the Lorde Henry Dudley, yongest sonne to the Duke of Northumberlande, was slayne with a gonne. This yeare before haruest, wheate was sold for iiii. Marke the quarter: Malte at iiii. and fortye shillinges the quarter, Beanes at. xl. shillinges the quarter, Rye at forty shillinges the quarter. And pease at xlvi. shillinges viii. pence. But after haruest, wheate was solde for v. shillinges the quarter: Malt at vi. shillinges and viii. pence, Rie at thre shillinges and iiii. pence. and in the countrey wheat was sold for foure shillings the quarter: Malte so foure shillinges and eighte pence, and in some places a bushel of Rye for a Pound of Candels whiche was four pence.

Saint Quintines won.

Dearth and plenty.

Sherifes, Richard Malarie, Iames Altam. 28 of sept.

Mayor, Sir Thomas Curteis Fishmonger 28 Octob.

Calleis lost,

The first of Ianuary, the Frenchemen came to Calleis with a great army, & layde siege thereunto, and within foure or fiue dayes were maisters thereof, and shortly after, wan all the peeces on that syde the sea. It is to be noted, that the Councell of England raysed great power to haue gone to the defence of that towne, but such tempest rose, as the like in many yeares had not bene sene, wherby the y no shippe could broke the sea.

The French king enuaded Flanders, and spoyled and brente Dunkirke, before kinge Philippe coulde come to the rescue, but before the Frenchmen returned oute of Flaunders, the Flemminges and the English shippes meeting wyth them uppon the sandes, betweene Dunkirke and Grauelin, slew of them a great number. 1558.

In Sommer great preparation was made, both on Kinge Philippe and the Frenche kings parties, and they retayned still mighty armyes, of purpose to inuade eche other: but nothinge beinge done, towardes winter brake up theyr Campes.

The seuenth of July within a mile of Notingham, was a marueylous greate tempest of thōder, & as it came through two townes, it bet downe al the houses and Churches. Also the grasse cutte of, sixe acres of medowe was taken by a storme, and seene flying in the ayre, was neuer knowen ferther where it became, the cartes were broken and cast a great way. Also betwixt these ii. townes ran the riuer of Trent, wher the tempest folowed the riuer a Thousand foote, and toke uppe the water with the myre and Anno.reg.6

wind in the bottome which was carried a quarter of a myle, and cast agaynst the trees: also the trees were pulled vp by the rootes & cast twelue score foote of, being two carte lodes a peece. And a childe was taken vp forth of a mannes handes two speares length hye, and caried a hundreth foote, and then let fall, and brake his arme, and so dyed, wyth foure or fiue other menne in the country thereabout that was slaine, and neither fleshe nor fain perished, also ther came a litle before the tempest, some hailestones that were xv. inches about. &c.

Tempest at Notingham

This Winter ẏ quartaine agues cōtinued in like maner, or more vehemently then they had don the last yere before passed, wherethrough dyed manye olde people, and speciallye priestes, so that a great nomber of parishes in diuers places were vnserued, and no curates to be gotten for moneye.

Sherifes, John Halse. Rich. Champion. 28. of Sep.
Mayor, Sir Thomas Lieg Mercer. 28. of October.

Kinge Philip beinge absent out of this Realme, & Queene Mary being dangerously sicke, ended her life, the xvii. day of Nouember, whē she had raigned fiue yeres, foure monethes and twelue dayes. The same day dyed Cardinall

Poole

Poole, & a little before two of her Phisitions, and diuers bishops and noble men, whom the Queene had esteemed greatlye.

QVEENE Elyzabeth.

ELYZABETH oure most gracious and soueraine Ladye, to the great comfort of Englande, was wyth full consente proclaymed Queene the 17. day of Nouember, in the yere 1558. Not lōg after she came frō Hatfield in Hartfordshire, vnto the Charterhouse in Londō: and went from thence to ẏ Tower, wher shee remayned vntill preparation was made for her graces Coronation. Anno. 1558.

The xiiii. day of January shee passed through the Citty to her Pallas at Westminster, shewing very comfortable and gentle countenaunce vnto the people: the next daye following, her grace was Crowned in S. Peters Churche at Westminster by Doctor Oglethorpe Bishop of Coronatiō.

of Castile.

The report of this was verye ioyfull to such as in Queene Maries tyme for religions sake fled into Germany, and other countryes, whervpon they shortly returned.

The twenty day of January beganne a Parliament at Westminster, before y States whereof in Westminster church, Doctour Cox, late come from beyonde the Seas, and sometime Scholemaister to K. Edward y sixt, made a learned Sermon. In this Parliamente, the first fruits and tenthes, were graunted to the Crowne, and also the supreme gouernment ouer y state Ecclesiasticall, likewyse the Booke of common prayer and administration of the Sacraments in our vulgare tongue was restored, to be done as in the tyme of K. Edwarde the sixt.

A Parliament.

The third day of April the Queenes maiestye appointed a conference or disputation to bee had at Westminster Church, betwext the old bishoppes and certeine learned men late com from beyond the Seas, concerning matters of Religion. but the matter came to none effecte.

1559. A conference at Westminster.

The seuenth of April was a ioyfull

peace

[illegible]eace proclaymed betwixt our soueraine [La]dy Elizabeth Queene of Englande, [a]nd Henrye the Frenche kinge. And [th]e like peace betwene her maiestye, [a]nd the king and Queene Dolphiners of [S]cotland.

Peace proclaymed.

The viii. daye of Maye the Queenes [h]ighnes rode to the Parliament house, [a]nd gaue her royal assente to al suche actes [a]s ther were made. A subsedy was grant[ed] of ii.s. viii.d. the pound of mouea[b]le goodes.

Parliament dessolued.

The xxiiii. daye of June being ÿ feast [o]f S. John Baptist, the seruice in the mo[th]er tongue was fully established and [ta]ke effeacte throughoute this Realme, & [t]he Masse wyth other latine seruice, was cleane abolished.

The seruice in Englishe.

The ii. of Julye the Citizens of Lo[n]don had a muster afore the Quenes ma[ie]stye at Grenewich in ÿ Parke, of xiiii. C. men, wherof viii. C. were wyttemen al in fine Corslets, iiii. C. Haquebuts in shyrtes of Male wyth Moryans, & ii. C. Halberts in Almanriuets, which the companyes of the Cittye of Londō found as they wer appointed by ÿ Lord Mayor and Aldermē, they had to euery C. ii. Wyfflers richlye apparelled, and xii. Wardens of the beste companyes of the

Muster at Grenewich.

the Citty ryding in Cotes of black vel-uet to conducte them, wyth Droms and Flutes, and vi. ensignes al in Ierkens of white Bridges Satten cutte, and ly-ned with black Sarsenet, with Cappes hosen & skarfes accordingly. The Cap-taines Mayster Constable and maister Saunders, brought them to battaile raye, afore the Queene, euen as they shoulde haue foughte, which made a goodly shew in the Emperours and French kin-ges Embassadoures being present wyth the Queenes Maiestye.

...hops de-
...ed,

In the moneth of July, ye olde bishops of England then being aliue, were cal-led and examined afore the Queenes ma-iestyes counsel, as Yorke, Elye & Londō, wyth other, who refusinge to take the othe touching the Queenes supremacye and other articles alledged to them, they were depriued frō theyr bishopprikes. Also diuers Archdeacons, Deanes, Persons and Vicars were depriued from their benefices, and some commit-ted to prison, in the Tower, Fleete, Marshalsey and kinges bench.

...mmissio-
...rs appoin
...t.

Commissioners were appointed for the establishing of Religiō throughout the whole Realme.

Also the houses of Religion newly er-

erected

ncred by Queene Mary, were al suppres-sed, and taken into the Queenes landes.

The Eue of S. Bartholomewe, the daye and the morowe after &c. were burned in Poules Churchyarde, in Cheape, & in diuers other streates of the Cittye of London, al the Roodes and other Images of Churches, some burned therin with all other ornaments of these Churches.

Houses sup-pressed.

Images bur-ned.

The .8. & 9. of September, a solemne obsequie was kept in Poules Church at London, for Henry the Frenche kinge who dyed of a wounde which he recey-ued at a triumphe, iusting in the Citye of Paris.

An obsequie at Poules.

Thomas Lodge. Roger Marten. 28. of Sep. Sherifes

Sir William Hewet Clothworker. 28. Oct. Mayor.

About this time many men of Warre were conueyed out of Fraunce into Scotland, whereby it was suspected that they wold sodenly inuade this Realm: whereupon the Queenes maiestye sent the Duke of Northfolke toward Scot-land as general with an army, who re-mayned at Berwicke.

Anno. 2. the 17. of No-uember.

In the moneth of April the Lord Gray of Wilton beinge Lieuetenaunte, entred Scotlād wyth an army of x. M. which were taken from Trente Northwarde, 1560.

 and

and besieged the towne of Lyth, where betwene the Frenche and English, were oftentimes skyrmishes, and many men slaine on both partes, for few were taken prisonners.

In May a noble man of Fraunce was by the Frenche king sent into England, who after he had talked wyth the Counsel (by lisence of the Queenes Maiesty) passed into Scotland to talke wyth the Dowager, and the Frenchmen, for the appeasing of the matter. At his returne agayne into Englande he obtayned such fauor of the Queene, that her grace sent sir William Cecill knighte, her maiestyes principall Secretary, together wyth Maister Doctor Wotton, to treat wyth the Frenchmen, who by theyr wysedomes so well ordered the matter, that they agreed uppon a peace, whiche was concluded in xiiii. Articles, and the Frenchmen to depart.

Houses blowen vp.

The 5. daye of July through shotinge of a gon which brake in the house of one Adrian Arten a Duchman in Croked lane and setting fyre on a fyrkin and a barrel of gunpouder, iiii. houses were cleane blowen downe, and diuers other sore scattered: there were slaine ix. persons men & women, & diuers sore hurte and brused.

On Michaelmas euen it was publi-
ed by Proclamatiō ẏ the teston of the Base money
fat, being marked with the Porte- called in,
kys, should then forthwith be taken
4.d.ob. & the second sort being mar-
d with the Greyhound for ii.d.q. the
ed and worst sort not being marked
th one of those markes aforenamed,
to be taken for anye value, the three
y piece which was coyned for 4.d.
ld be but one d.ob. the ii.d.peece for
.q. And shortly after her grace re- Newe coy-
ed vnto all her subiectes fine ster- ne.
g money, both of gold and siluer, for
t corrupt and base coyne, calling ẏ
e to her maiesties myntes, according
he rates before mentioned.
istopher Draper. Thomas Roe. 28.sep. Sheriffes.
William Chester Draper 28.of Octob. Maior.
he xxi. of Marche a notable Gram- Anno 3. the
mer schole was founded by the ma- 17. of Nou.
Wardens, & assistentes of the right
shipful company of the marchante Marchaunt
ylers of the Citty of London in the Taylers
ish of S.Laurence Pountency. schole.
The tenth daye of Aprill, was one
lliam Geffrey whipped frō the Mar- 1561.
sey in Southwarke, to Bedlem,
thoute Bishoppes gate of London,
that he professed one Iohn Moore, to

be

be Christ our Sauiour: on his heade, & about the cart were papers wrytten, as followeth: William Geffreye, a moste blasphemous heretike, denying Christe oure Sauiour in Heauen. The sayde Geffreye beinge stayde at Bedlem gate, John Moore was caused to bee brought forth: and then where as the sayde Geffreye had til this tyme for all hys sore whipping, styl professed John Moore to be Christ, now he forsoke him, and cōfessed Christ to be in Heauen. Then the sayd John Moore, beinge examened and aunsweringe them very ouerthwartlye was cōmaunded to strep himselfe, which he seemed to do verye willinglye, who was after tied to the cart, and whypt an arrowes shot from Bedlem, whereat þ last he confessed Christ to be in Heauē, and himselfe to be a sinful man.

A false Christ whipt.

Poules steple on fyre.

The .iiii. day of June being Wednesday, betwene iiii. and v. of þ clocke in the after noone, the steple of Poules in London, was fiered by lightening, and brast forth as it did seeme to the beholders, ii. or iii. yardes beneth the Crosse, and so brente rounde aboute in the same place, þ the top wyth the Crosse fel of, & lighted on the Southsyde of Poules Church, & then the spyre brent downe-

warde

made like a cresset, or a Becken to the ... the steeple and the Belles, and then downeward so terribly and vehemently, that within the space of 4. houres, the same Steeple, and the roofes of the Church, so muche as was timber or otherwyse combustible, were consumed, which was a lamentable sighte, and pitifull remembringe to the beholders thereof.

...exander Auenon. Hamfrey Baskerville. Sherifes.
...Wil.Harper Marchant tayler. 28.Octo. Maior.

The xv day of Nouember, the Queenes maiestie published a Proclamation, wherein her grace restored to the realme diuers small pieces of siluer money, as the piece of vi.d. iiii.d. iii.d. ii.d. & i.d. the halfepeny, and thre farthings. And also forbad all maner of forraine coynes to be currante wythin the same Realme: as well golde as siluer, callinge them into her maiesties myntes: excepte two sortes of crownes of golde, whereof the one was a Frenche crowne: & the other a Flemish crowne. A newe coyne.

This yere in England were manye monstrous byrthes, as in March a mare brought forth a foale wyth one body being in good proportion, and two heads, hauing as it were a lōg tayle growing out Anno 4. the 17. of No. Monstrous. 1562.

out right like a horne, betwene the same two heads. Also a sow farrowed a pigge with iiii. legges like unto the armes of a man childe, with handes and fingers, snoute and eares disfigured. &c.

Aboute Aprill a sowe farrowed a pig which had two bodies, viii. feete, & but one head, many calues and lambs were monstrous, & one calfe had a coller of skin growing about the necke, like to a double ruffe, which to the beholders semed straunge and wonderful.

A monstrous child.

The xxiiii. day of May a monstrous child was borne at Chichester in Sussex, the head armes and legges like unto an Anatomy, the breast & belly monstrous bigge, from the nauill, as it were a lōg string hanging: about the necke a great coller of flesh and skinne growing like to the Ruffe of a shert or neckerchiefe, comming up about the eares pleyting or folding. &c.

Goinge to Newhauen.

The Quenes maiesty in September addressed a bande of her subiectes to the Towne of Newhauē in Normandy: who were embarked at Portesmouth, because that hauen is most apt for transportatiō to that place. Upon whose arriuall the Townes menne and enhabitantes ioyfully surrendred themselues, and theyr

towe

one, into the possession of ẏ Queenes ...iestye. Which was kept by English... from September 1562. to the 29. of July thẽ next following, which ...s in the yere 1563. The gouernour ...hich band was the right honourable the Earle of Warwicke, who with Captaines seruing there, which were great experience and seruitours trained by them to knowledge of seruice, other with part of the old approued ...rison of Barwicke, did at that time ...manfullye defende the piece, and ...tantly encountred by sundrye skirmishes and conflictes, with the County ...graue and hys bandes: the most parte thereof were happelye atchieued to the ...te ouerthrowe of the aduersaryes ...re, and singuler commendations of ...e.

...liam Allen. R. Chamberlaine. 28. Sep. Sheriffes
Thomas Lodge Grocer. 28. of October Mayor.

On the Saturday next following, ẏ ...th day after Christmas, a great tempest of wind & thonder happened in the ...ne of Leicester, which uncouered ...shes of houses, & ouerturned ma... Anno 5. the 17. of Nouember. A tempest at Leicester.

... When the Frenchmẽ with huge ...myes assembled oute of all partes of ...nce, to recouer the place of palace, 1563.

ỹ keeping whereof, by our power, was
the double wo of their common wealth,
ther bred through the season of the yere,
and putrefaction of the ayre, a miserable
and infortunate plague amonge our
men, which maruelouslye encreased,
with the death of diuers of the best Cap
taynes and souldiours, wherewythall
there followed a cruel and quick siege,
whereat was present the yonge Kynge
hymselfe, the Queene his mother, the
Constable, and the best tryed nomber of
warlike souldiours within the whole
country, besydes an other sort of yonge
and old that cared not for life nor land,
so theyr owne aduenture might win a
gaine the cause of their distresse, lyeth
by a general ayde, the Marishes were
made passable and firme ground, whiche
by men of great experience was thought
impossible. And wyth common helpe ỹ
Cannons were placed, the Castell and
walles were battered, & sondrye brea
ches made beyond expectation. How
beit they were rewarded by our Sun
ners & made to taste the bitter fruite of
their desperate approche, to their great
terror & annoyance. The Erle of War
wicke with ỹ remnant of our Captaines
and Souldiours, in couragious order

sta

ldyng at the seuerall breaches readye
defend their assaultes, which perceiu
d by the enimies, they caused their
umpets to sound ye blast of Emparle,
t composition of eyther parte mighte
made, to auoyde ye imminent slaugh
and effusion of bloude. This offer
as not misliked, both partes con
nted, the towne was deliuered ye 29.
of July, vpon condition that ye Eng
men should depart.

This yeare as ye haue hearde, the
ague of pestilence being in the town
Newhauen, through the nomber of
ldiours that returned into Englãd,
e infection thereof spred into diuers
es of this Realme, but especially the
ty of London was so infected, that in
same whole yeare, that is to say, frõ
first of January 1562. vntil the last
December. 1563. there died in ye Citie
& liberties thereof, contayning 108.
rishes) of all diseases xx.M. iii.C.
iii. there died of ye plague, being part
the nõber aforenamed xvii.M. iiii.C.
d foure persons. And in the out paris
s adioynyng to the same City being
Parishes, dyed of all diseases in the
hole yere aforesayd iii, M. ii. C. lxxx.
viii, persons, & of them of the plague
being

Newe Hauē deliuered to the French.

Great pestilence.

A hundred and eyghte parishes in London.

A xi. oute parishes,

being part of the sayde nomber last be=fore named, ii. M. vii. C. xxxii. so that ye whole totall summe of all those ye dyed of al diseases in the whole yeare, as well wythin the Citty of London, and liber=tyes of the same as in the oute parishes nighe adioynynge, was xxiii. M. vi. C. lx. and of them of the plague (being part of the total sum before named) dyed in all xx. M. i. C. 36.

Tempest.

The viii. of Iulye in the morninge happened a great tempest of lightning and thonder, where through a woman wyth three kyne were slaine in the Co=uente Garden neare to Charinge Crosse. At the same time, in Essex a manne was torne al into peeces as he was carying haye, his Barne was borne downe, and his hay brent, both stone and trees were rent in many places marueylouslye.

This yeare the Counsell of Kinge Philip at Bruxelles, commaunded Pro=clamation to be made in Andwarpe and other places, that no Englishe shyppe wyth any clothes, should come into any place of their lowe countryes, their co=lour of this restraint, was as they said, the daunger of the Plague which was that time in London, and other places of Englande: but for oure wolles they would

uld not restrayne them: but woulde ne had them gladly. But the Queenes aiestie through the sute of our Mar= aunt adventurers woulde not suffer y Wolle to passe towardes Bruges in anders, but caused the wolle flete to discharged, and our Clothflete was t to Emden in East Frieslande about ster next folowing, being in An. 1564. For so much as the plague of Pesti= ce was hotte in the citie of London, re was no Terme kepte at Michel= as.

There was in September an Earth= ake in Lincolne and Northampton= ire and other places. Earthquake

Ward Bakes, Rouland Haiward. 28. Sep. Sherifes.

Iohn Whyte Grocer, the 28. October. Maior.

After the election of this Maior, by y Councelles letters, the Queenes ma= ties pleasure was signified to Syr o Lodge then Maior, that for so much the plague was so great at that tyme the citie the new Maior elected shold t kepe any feaste at the Guildhaule, for ubt that through the bringing toge= r of suche a multitude, the infection ght the rather increase: for the weeke t this Maior came from his house in Countrey to take the office on hym No Maiors feaste.

there died within the citie and out parishes aboue ii. M. persones, wherfore this Sir Iohn White on the xxix. daye of October, toke his othe at the vttermoste gate of the tower of London, and not past viii. Aldermen to folowe him.

Anno reg. 6 Lightning and thunder

In December from the first day to the xii. was such great lightning and thunder, and especially on the same xii. daye at night, from viii. of the clocke tyll it was past ix. that the lyke had not beene lightly seene by any man then liuing.

Monstrous fishe.

In the moneth of December was taken on the shore at Grimsby in Lincolnshyre, a great and monsterous fishe, being in length 19 yardes, his tayle xv. foote brode, and vi. yardes betwene his two eyes.

Terme at Hertford.

For that the plague was not fullye ceassed in London, Hyllarye Terme was kept at Hertforde besyde ware.

1564 Peace proclaymed.

The thre and twenty daye of Aprill, was a ioyful peace proclaimed betwene England and Fraunce.

The Plague being ceased in London bothe Easter and Mydsomer Termes were kept at Westminster.

Watch on S. Peters euen

This yeere through the earnest sute of the Armorers, there was on the Vigile of saint Peter, a watche in the Citie of

London,

London, whiche did onely stande in the hyghest streates of Cheape, Cornhyll, and so foorth towardes Algate, whiche was to the commons of the same city as chargeable as whē in times past, it was most commendably done, whereas this being to small purpose, was of as smalle number well lyked.

The fifth of August the Queenes maiestie in her progresse came to the Uniuersitie of Cambridge, and was of all the Studentes (being inuested according to the degrees which they had taken in the scholes) honourably and ioyfully receyued in ÿ Kings Colledge, where she did lie, during her cōtinuāce in Cambridge. The dayes of her abode, were paste in scholasticall exercises of Philosophy, Physicke and Diuinitie, the nightes in Comodies and Tragidies, set foorthe partlye by the whole Uniuersitie, and partly by ÿ Studētes of the kings Colledge. At ÿ breaking vp of the diuinitie act, being on Wednesday ÿ ix. of August, (on ÿ which daye shee rode through the towne, & viewed the Colledges those goodly & auciēt monumēts of kings of Englande her noble predecessors) shee made within S. Maries churche a notable oration in Latin, in the presence of the

Queenes progresse.

Dd ij whole

whole learned vniuersitie, to the Students great comfort. The next daye she went forwarde on her Progresse to Hinchinbroke by Hunungdon

[illegible]iman for [illegible] daye.

The xxx. day of August it was enacted by a common counsell of the Citie of London, that all such citezins as from thence forth should be constrayned, to sel their houshold stuffe, apparayle, leases of houses or suche lyke, should cause the same to be brought to the common outcryer appointed for the same, and he to make sale therof retaining one farthing vpon the shilling for his paynes.

[illegible]eat flods.

The xx. daye of September arose so great fluds in the Ryuer of Thames, that many marishes and medowes were drowned, to the greate losse of manye through drowning of their Cattayle.

Sherifes. Edward Iackman. Lyonell Ducket. 28. Sep.

[illegible]bsequi for [illegible]e Emperour.

The second day of October in the after noone, was a solemne obsequie kept at saint Paules church in London, for Ferdinando the Emperour, late beinge departed out of this mortal life, & likewise the morowe next after, in the forenoone.

[illegible]ierie Empressions.

In the moneth of October, many fiery impressions were sene as it were, proceding forth of the element, & specially

on the

the viii.day at night, from viii. of the clocke til somewhat past xi. al the regions of the element seemed to be couered with flames of fire, proceeding from the northeast and northwest, towardes the middest of the firmament: where for the moste part of an houre it stayed, and descended Westwarde: and all the same night being the next after the change of the Moone, seemed nigh as light as it had bene day.

Richard Malory Mercer, the 28. Octob. Maior. Anno reg. 7

The xx. day of Nouember in the morning, through negligence of a mayden with a candell, the snuffe falling in an hundred weight of Gunnepowder, three houses in Bucklarsbury, were sore blowen and shattered, the mayde died within two dayes after, if this powder had lyne in a lower part of the house, as it laye in a Garret, it had done much more harme. Houses shattered.

The xxi. day of December being S. Thomas day, began a frost whiche continued so extremely that on New yeares euen, people went ouer and a long the Thames on the yce from London bridge to westminster, and people plaid at the footeball as boldely as on the dry lande. On Newyeares daye, being Mondaye, Thames troden ouer.

 on

on Tuesdaye and Wednesdaye, dyuers gentlemen and others, set vp prickes on the Thames, and shot at the same, great numbers of people standing at either pricke to behold them. The people both men and women went on the Thames in greater numbers then in any streete of the citie. On the Wednesday it began to thawe: but men went ouer and along the Thames on Thursday al daye, but on Friday being the v. daye of January at night, was no yce to be sene, betwene London brydge and Lambeth, which sodaine thawe caused suche great floudes and hie waters, that it bare downe many bridges and houses, and drowned many people in England, especially in Yorkeshire, where Owse brydge was borne away with other. On Newyeres day proclamation was made in Londō by the queenes cōmaundement, that the restreaint before sayde betwene England and Flaunders, & other things done since y first yeare of her maiesties raigne, touching the premisses should be suspended for a time: & thereupon a Diete, by consent of both realmes was appoynted to be kept in Bruges for these matters, and diuers other griefes and complaints of the

[Margin note:] ...e bridge ...ne downe

e subiectes on both parties.

The 26. day of January at night were o Tydes in the space of two howres London, on the morowe was lyke: yse two in the morning, two at night, Monday were likewise twoo tides in e morning, and at night but one, as derly it hath bene accustomed.

Fight tides in 2 nightes and a day.

The iii. daye of February, Henry Stu- t lord Derneley, a younge man, about age of xix. yeres, eldest sonne of Ma- w Erle of Lineux, (who was gone in Scotland at Whitsontide before) ha- ng obtayned licence of the Queenes aiestie, toke his iourney to warde Scot- nd, accōpanied with v. of his fathers n: where, when he came, was honora- y receyued, and lodged in the kinges dgings: and in the summer folowing aried Mary Queene of Scotland.

Henry Stuert.

About this time for the queenes maie- e were chosen and sent in commission Bruges the honorable Lord Montague ight of the honourable order of the arter, Maister Doctor Wotton, one of e Queenes maiesties honorable coun- yle, Maister Doctor Haddon, one of e maisters of requestes to her highnes ith others in commissiō for the same: aister Doctour Aubrey was chosen for

Commissioners sent to Bruges.

the marchauntes Aduenturers of England, and they came to Bruges in Lent in the yeare 1565. and continued there tyl Michaelmas followyng, and then was the dicte prolonged tyll Marche. 1566.

1565 The xxij. daye of Aprill, the Ladye Margaret Countesse of Lineux, was commaunded to keepe her Chamber at the white hall, where she remained in that sort, vntill the 12. day of June, on which daye shee was conueyed by sir Fraunces Knolles and the Garde, prysoner to the tower of London by water.

Watche at Midsomer. On S. Peters euen at night was the like standing watch in London as was the same night xij. moneth es.

Tempest at Chelmsford. The xvj day of July, about ix. of the clocke at night, began a terrible tempest of lightening & thunder, with showres of hayle, which continued vntill iiij. of the clocke in the next morning. In the which tempest muche harme was done in and about Chelmesforde in Essex, as by destroying of v. C. acres of corne the beating doune of al ẏ glasse windowes on the east side of the sayd towne, and of the West and Southsides of the church, the beating of the tiles of their houses, throwynge downe dyuers barnes and chimneys, with the battelmentes of

these

heir churche, &c. The hayle stones be- ing measured, were founde to be vi. in- ches about. At the same time was much harme done in many other places of this realme, as at Leedes, Crambroke, at Douer in Kent &c.

Christopher, prince and Marckgraue of Baden, with Cicely his wife, sister to ye king of Swetheland, after a long & daun- gerous iourney, wherin they had trauai- led almost xi. moneths. In September landed at Douer, and the xi. daye of the same they came to London, & were lod- ged at the Erle of Bedfordes place, nere vnto Iuie bridge, where within 4 days after, yt is to say, the xv day of Septem- ber, she trauailed in childbed, and was deliuered of a man child, which childe the last of September was christened in the Queenes maiesties chappel of white haule at westminster, the queenes maie- stie in her own person being godmother the Archebishop of Caunterbury, & the duke of Northfolke godfathers: at the christening, the Queene gaue the name Edwardus fortunatus.

The Marck graue of Baden.

Iohn Riuers, Iames Hawes. the. 28. Sept. Sherifes.

Sir Richard Champion Draper. 28. Octob. Maior.

The xi. of Nouember, the right hono- rable Ambrose Erle of Warwike, A mariage. maried

maried Anne, eldest daughter to the Erle of Bedford: for the honour and celebration of which noble mariage, a goodlye challenge was made & obserued at Westminster at the tilte, at the tourney, & at barriers. At x. of the clock at nighte, the same day, a valiaunt seruisable man called Robert Thomas maister Gonner of Englād, desirous also to honour ẏ feast and mariage daye, in consideration the said Earle of Warwike, was generall of the ordenaunce within her Maiesties dominions, made three great traynes of Chambers, who at the fiering of the second was vnhappely slayne by a peece of one of the chambers.

aister gō- ... slayne.

The 28. day of December there rose a great storme and tempest of wynde, by whose rage the Thames and seas ouerwhelmed many persones, and the great gates at the West ende of saint Paules churche in London (betwene the which standeth the brasen piller) were through the force of the wynde then in the Westerne parte of the world blowen open.

...n.reg.&. ... .Nouēb.

...aules ga... s blowen ...pen.

In Januarye, Mounsier Rambuley a knight of the order in France, was sent ouer into England by the Frenche kyng Charles the ix. of that name, with the order of Saint Michael, who at Windsor

...rder of S. ...ichael.

was

as stalled in the behalfe of the sayde
renche kyng with the knighthoode of
e most honourable order of the Garter
d the xxiiii. of January in the chappel
her Maiesties pallace of White haule.
The sayde Mounsier Rambuley inuested
homas Duke of Norfolke, and Robert
arle of Leicester, with the sayd order of
int Michael.

The Marques of Baden and the Lady
icelie hys wyfe, syster to the kyng of
wethen, who came into this lande in the
oneth of September last paste as be-
re is declared, being thē by the Quee-
es speciall appointment at their arri-
all honourably receiued by the Lorde
Cobham an honourable Baron of this
ealme and the Lady his wyfe one of the
Queenes maiesties priuie Chāber, now 1566
n the moneth of Aprill departed the
me agayne, the Marques a fewe days
efore, his wyfe being bothe conducted
y a lyke personage the Lorde of Abur-
aueny to Douer.

Marques of Baden departeth.

The houses in Cornehill which were
ought at the Citezens charges and in
ebruary by the Bel man cried, and after warde solde, were in Aprill and May
next following by such as had bought
hem taken downe and caried away. Af-

ter warde

ter the grounde beyng made playne at the charges also of the citie. Possession thereof by certaine Aldermen was geuen to the right worshipfull sir Thomas Gresham knight, Agent to the Queenes highnes, in that place to builde a place for marchauntes to assemble in, at his owne proper charges, who on the vii. daye of June in the after noone, layde the firste stone of the foundation (beyng bricke) and forthwith the workemen folowed vpon the same with such diligēce that by the moneth of Nouember in Anno. 1567. the same place was couered with slate.

The royall exchaunge in Cornehil begon.

The commissioners before named apointed for the matters of Flaunders, keping their diete at Briges, agreed to refer the whole matter to the princes on both sides, and if they can not agree, thē the marchauntes to haue 40. days to repaire home with their marchandise & in the meane time al things to stand as thei were then, our commissioners departed from Bruges about the 26. of June.

The 31. of August the Queenes maiestie in her progresse came to ÿ vniuersitie of Oxforde, and was of all the Studentes, which had loked for her cōming thither 2. yeres, so honourably and ioyfully ally receiued, as either their loyalnes towardes the Queenes maiestie, or the expectation of their frendes did require. Concerning orders in disputacions, & other Academical exercises, they agreed much with those whiche the vniuersitie of Cābridge had vsed two yeres before. Comedies also and Tragedies were set forth by the vniuersitie, and playde in Christes churche, where the Queenes highnes lodged. Amongst the which, the Commodie intituled Palemon and Arcet made by maister Edwardes of ÿ queenes Chappel, had such tragicall successe, as was lamentable. For at that time by the fal of the side wal & a payre of stayres, & great prease of the multitude, three men were slayne. The v. of September after disputations, the Queenes maiestie at the humble sute of certain of her nobilitie and the king of Spaines embassadour, made a breefe Oration in Latine to the vniuersitie, but so wise and pithy as England may reioyce, that it hath so learned a Prince, the vniuersities may triumphe that they haue so noble a Patronesse, and forraine countreys may wonder to behold such excellēcy in that sexe. The 6. of September after dinner her grace cōming from Christes church

The quenes progresse.

Missfortune.

oute.

ouer Carfox, and so to saint Maries (the scollers standing in order according to their degrees euen to the East gate) certaine doctors of the vniuersitie did ryde before her in their Skarlet gownes and hoodes, and maisters of Arte in blacke gownes & hoodes: the Maior also with certayne of his brethren did ryde before her in Scarlet to the end of Magdalene bridge where their liberties ended, but the doctors and maisters went forwarde till to Shotouer, a mile and more out of Oxforde, because their liberties extended so farre, & there after orations made, her highnes with thankes to the whole Vniuersitie, bade them fare well, and rode that night to Rycote.

Sherifes. Ri Lābard Amb. Nicholas, Io. Lāgley. 28. S.

Maior. Sir Christopher Draper Iremōger. 28. Oct.

Souldiours into Ireland

The valiaunt Captaine Edward Randolfe Esquier leiutenaunt of the ordinaunce, and Coronel of a M. footemē in September last past, was with his bande imbarked at Bristow, and within few dayes after landed at Knocferyns in the North partes of Irelande, and from thence by water to a place called Derry, by which passeth the riuer of Lōghfoile, there the saide Coronell in shorte space fortified to the great annoyaunce of Iohn

Onele

ell: and by great foresight and expe-
ence guarded him selfe and his charge,
ll the sayde Onell (to hynder and di-
rbe his aboade there) the xij. of Nomber arriued with a greate armye of
erne, Galloweglasses and horsemen,
ith whom the said Captaine Randolfe
countred, and him there so discomfi-
as after that conflicte he durst neuer
proch the Queenes power, and to his
erpetuall fame, the sayde Captayne by
ason of his bolde and hardy onset, that
y lost his life.

Charles James, the firste of that name, Christning in Scotland.
one to Henry Steuert Lord of Darnley &
ary, King and Queene of Scots was
orne in Edenburgh Castell the xix. of
une last past, and the xviii. day of De- An.reg.9
mber this said yere solempnly christe-
d at Sterling, whose Godfathers at the
hristening, were Charles K. of Fraunce,
d Philibert Duke of Sauoye, and the
ueenes maiestie of England was the
odmother, who gaue a Funt of golde,
riously wrought and enameled, way-
g 333 ounces, amounting in valewe
the summe of M.xliii li.xix.s.

On Shroue monday next followyng
ing the x. of February in the mornyng
enry Steuert Lorde of Darneley before

naimed

K. of Scottes murdered. named King of Scottes, by Scottes in Scotlande was shamefully murdered, the reuenge whereof remayneth in the mightye hande of God.

The xxii. of February, the Lady Margaret Douglas Countesse of Lineaux, mother to the said King of Scots was discharged out of the Tower of London.

Seuē Aldermen deceased. Within the space of x. monethes last past died vii. Aldermen of London. The first Edward Banckes, who deceased the ix. of July Anno. 1566. Richarde Chamberlayne late Shriefe, sir Martin Bowes sir Richarde Malorie, sir William Hewet, and sir Thomas White, late Mayors, and then Richarde Lamberte one of the Sheriffes for that yeare the iiij. of Aprill Anno 1567. for him was chosen Iohn Langle, Goldsmithe who serued tyll Michaelmas that the new Shriues entred.

Owsestre burnt. The xxii. of Aprill, by great misfortune of fyre in the towne of Owsester in Wales, xii. miles from Shrewesbury to the nūber of ii. C. houses, that is to say vii. score within the walles & iii. score without in the suburbes, besides cloth, corne, cattell, and many bothe men and women were consumed, which fire cōtinued two houres, it began at two of ẏ clocke

...ke in the after noone, and endeth at ... to the great meruailing of manye, ... so great a spoyle and destruction in ... short tyme should happen.

The xxiiii. of April being thursday, the Sergeants feast was kept at Greys ... neare vnto Holborne, and there ... re at that tyme made vii. newe Ser... ntes of the lawe.

Sergeantes feast.

The xvii. day of May, by casualtie of ... in the towne of Milnall in Suffolke ... mile from Newmarket, to the num... er 37. houses besides Barnes, Sta... s and suche like, were consumed in ... space of two houres.

Mylnal burnt.

On Saint Johns euen at night being ... like standing watche in the Citie of ... ndon as on Saint Peters euen in the ... re last before passed, certayne Con... bles of euerye warde, beyng verye ... ll appointed with the handsomest of ... ir watchemen cleane armed in Cor... s, and also diuers party showes done ... the charges of youngmen in certaine ... ishes awayghted on the Lord Maior, ... ying from the Guildhaule through ... eape to Algate and backe agayne, ... iche being lyke to haue made a very ... ndsome sight, was for lack of good or... in keping their array muche defaced.

Watche at London. &c.

Coronation in Scotland.

The xxix. daye of July, Charles James the younge prince of Scotlande, after a sermon made by John Knokes, was crowned kyng of Scottes at Sterling churche, where was red certayne Commissions with the Queenes priuie seale at them, for the establishing of the same, the first for her resignatiō of the crowne, and gouernement of the younge Prince her sonne, the seconde to authoryse the Earle of Murrey to bee regent during his minoritie, the thirde to geue authoritie and power to seuen other ioynyng with the sayde Earle of Murrey, in case he should refuse to exercise the same alone, that is to say, the Duke Chatileray, the Earles of Lenox, Argile, Athell, Morton, Glencarne, and Marre, these commissions being ended, the byshop of Akeley with twoo superintendents proceaded to the coronation, ỹ Earle Morton & Lorde Hume, toke othe for the kyng, that he should rule in the faithe, feare, and loue of God, to maintayn the religion nowe preached in Scotlande, and persecute al aduersaries to the same &c. The whole ceremonie of the coronation was done in their mother tongue, and at that tyme the Queene of Scottes was prysoner at Loughleuen.

Tho-

Thomas Ramsey, William Bonde. 28. Sept. Sherifes,
Sir Roger Martin Mercer. 28. of October. Maior.

After a drye Sommer folowed a fyne Winter with suche a scarcitie of fodder and hay, that in diuers places as in Yorkeshire and the Peake, hay was sold for v.s. the stone, there folowed also a great death of cattell, especially of horses and shepe. Anno re. 10 17. of No.

The 18. of March through vehement rage & tempest of windes, many vessels in ÿ Thames, with two tiltbotes before Graues end, were sonke & drowned. 1568. Great wynd

The xxvi. of June deceassed Thomas Yonge, Archbyshop of Yorke, at the Manor of Sheafelde, and was honourably buried at Yorke.

Io. Aleph Ro harding, James Bacō. 28. Sep. Sherifes.

This yeare at the costes and charges of the citezins of London, a newe Conduite was builded at Walbroke corner nere to Dougate, which was finished in the month of October, the water wherof is conueyd out of the Thames. Conduite in Walbroke builded.

The xx. of October were taken in Suffolke at Downam bridge nere vnto Ipswiche 17. great & monstrous fishes, some of them conteyning 27. foote in lengthe, the other 24. or 21. foote a piece at the least. Monstrous fishes.

Maior. Sir Thomas Roe marchant Taylor. 28. Oct.

Anno. re. 11 The xxvi. of Nouember deceassed Robert harding Salter, one of the Shyriues of London on the morrowe next following was chosen Iames Bacon Aldermā, who succeeded till Michaelmas that the new shriues toke their charge.

Execution of coyners. The 17. of January Philip Mestrel a Frenchman and two Englishmen were drawne from Newegate to Tyborne, and there hanged, the Frenchman quartered, who had coyned golde counterfet, the Englishemen, the one had clipped syluer, the other had cast Testons of tynne.

1565 The 28. daye of Marche the Pencioners wer appointed in Armour on horsback mustered before the Queenes maiestie at S. Iames beside Westminster.

A muster of the Pencioners.

A great lotarie being holden at London in Paules churchyarde, which was begon to be drawen the xi. of January last past, continued day and night, till the vi daye of this moneth of May wherin it was fully ended.

A lotary at London.

Buriall for the dead prepared This yeare sir Thomas Roe Lorde Mayor of London caused to be inclosed with a wall of bricke, a certayne piece of ground, nere vnto Bedlem without byshops gate, containing nigh one A-

cre o

re of lande, to be a place of buriall for the dead of such parishes in London as in lacke of conuenient ground within their said parishes were accustomed to bury in Powles churchyarde.

This yere on the eue of S. John Baptist at Midsomer was onely a standing watche in euery warde of London, well armed in corslets, the constables prepared and apparelled as had bene accustomed, and sir Iohn White Alderman rode the circuite, which the Maiors of London, in tyme past had vsed to do.

The 27. of August Andree Gregoreuich: win, embassadour from Muscouie, landed at the tower wharfe, and was there receiued by the Lord Maior of London the Aldermen and Shrieues, in skarlet with the Marchauntes aduenturers in coates of blacke veluet, all on horsebacke who conueyed him riding through the citie to the Muscouie house in Seeding lane there to be lodged.

Embassadour from Muscouy.

The plague of pestilence somewhat raigning in the Citie of London, Michaelmas terme was by proclamation first adiourned vnto the third day of Nouember, then to begin at Westminster, and after by like proclamation adiourned vnto Hillary terme next folowing.

Terme adiourned.

Sheriues. Henry Bechar, William Danne, 28. Sept.

The xi. of October, Thomas Hawarde Duke of Norfolke, was brought frō Barnam beside Wynsore by lande to Westminster, and from thence by water to the tower of London prysoner, sir Henry Neuell being his keper.

D. of Norfolke sent to the tower.

Maior. Sir Alexander Auenon Iremonger. 28. Oct.

This Maior went by water to Westminster, and there tooke his othe, as hath bene accustomed, but kept no feast at the Guild haul, least through coming together of so great a multitude, infectiō of the pestilence might haue increased. That weeke, that is to saye, from the 21. vnto 28. of October, there died in the Citie and out parishes of all diseases, C lii. of the whiche nomber lt. were accompted to die of the plague.

The Earles of Northumberlande and Westmerland rebell.

Thursday the ix. of Nouember Thomas Percye Earle of Northumberlande, receiued the Queenes maiesties letters to repayre to the court, & the same night other conspiratours perceiuing him to be wauering and vnconstant of promise made to them, caused a seruaunt of his called Beckwith (after he was layde in his bedde) to bustle in, and to knocke at his chambre dore, willing him in haste to ryse and shifte for him selfe, for that

his

is enemies (whome he termed to bee
ir Oswalde Vlthrop, and master Vaghan)
eere about the parke, and had beset him
with nombers of men, whereupon he a-
rose and conuayed hym selfe alwaye to
is kepers house, in the same instant
hey caused the belles of the towne to
e rong backward, & so raised as many
s they coulde to their purpose, the next
ight the Earle departed thence to Bran-
pithe, where he met with Charles Earle
f Westmerlande, and the other confede-
ates. Then by sundry proclamations
hey abusing many the quenes subiects,
commaunded them in her highnes name
o repayre to them in warlyke maner,
or the defence and suertie of hir maie-
ties persone, some tymes affirmyng
heir doynges to be with the aduyse and
consent of the Nobilitie of this Realme, who in dede were wholy bente
as manyfestly appeared) to spende their
lyues in dutiful obedience, against the
and all other traytours: sometemes pretending for conscience sake to seke to reforme religion: sometime declaring that
hey were driuen to take this matter in
hande, least otherwyse forayne princes
might take it vppon them, to the great
perill of this Realme.

 Vpon

Upon monday the xiii. they wẽt to Derham with their banners displayed, and to get the more credit among the fauourers of the old Romishe religion, they had a crosse with a banner of the fyue woundes. As sone as they were entred Derham they went to the minster, and tare the Byble, communion bookes, and other suche as there were. The same night they went agayne to Branspethe. The xiiii. they went to Darlington, and there had masse, whiche the Earles and the reste hearde with suche deuotion as they had, then they sent their horse men to gather together suche nombers of mẽ as they could. The xv. the Earles parted, Of Northumberlande to Richemond, then to Northallerton, and so to Borowbrige, Of Westmerlande to Ripon, and after to Burowbrige, where they both met agayne. On the xviii. they went to Wetherby & there taried thre or foure days: and upon Bramham more they mustered them selues, at whiche tyme they were about two thousend horsemen and fyue thousande footemen, whiche was the greatest nomber that euer they were. From whence they entended to haue marched towardes Yorke, but theire myndes being sodainly altered, they returned

The rebels [illegible] the Byble.

Anno reg. 12. 17. Noueb.

ned, & the xxiii. beſieged Bernardes
tell, whiche caſtell was valiauntlye
ended by ſir George Bowes and ho-
Bowes his brother the ſpace of a xi.
es, and then deliuered with compo=
on to depart with armour, munitiō,
ge and baggage. In the whiche tyme,
Queenes maieſtie cauſed the ſayde
les of Northumberlande and Weſt-
lande, to be proclaymed traytours
h all their adherentes and fauourers
xxiii. of Nouēber: The Lord Scrope
dē of the Weſt marches, calling vn=
im the Earle of Cumberlande and o=
gentlemen of that countrie kept the
e of Carlyle. The Earle of Suſſex the
ueenes maieſties lieutenaunt gene=
in the North, publiſhed the like pro
mations (in effect) as had bene pu=
hed by the Queenes maieſtie againſt
ſayd rebelles, and alſo ſent out to al
he gentlemen as he knewe to be her
ieſties louinge ſubiectes vnder his
e, who came vnto him with ſuche
nber of their friendes, ſeruauntes
tenauntes, as he was able within
e dayes to make about ſiue thouſand
ſemen and footemen, and ſo being ac
panied with the Earle of Rutlande
lieutenaunt, the Lorde Hunſdon ge=
nerall

Bernardes caſtell beſieged by the rebels,

The Earles of Northūberland and Weſtmerland proclaimed traytours.

nerall of his horsemen, & sir Rause Sadler Treasurer, who came to Yorke with their seruauntes. On Sunday the fift of December, they marched from Yorke to Topclife, sir George Bowes with his power comming from Bernardes Castell (as is afore sayde) mett them at Sisay, then they went to Northalerton, and after two nightes to Croftbridge, then to Akle, then to Derham, then to Newe castell, The xx. daye to Exham, from whence the rebelles were gone the night before to Naworth, where counsayling with Edward Dakers, concerning their owne weakenes, as also howe they were pursued by the Earle of Sussex and his power of vii. thousand euen almoste at the heeles. And moreouer that the valiaunt Earle of Warwike, the Lorde Clynton Lord admiral of Englande, and the Lorde Ferrers Viscount Hereford, with a farre greater armie of xii. thousand out of the South, was not farre behinde them at Borowbridge, the next night the two Earles of Northumberland and Westmerlande, vnknowing to their assotiates, fledde to Herlawe in Scotland. The other rebels were shortly after taken without any resistaunce, The fourth and fift of January, did suffer at Derham to the nombler of 66. Constables

The Erle of Sussex with an army went agaynst the rebelles.

The Earle of Warwike with an army went against the rebelles.

The Earles of Northumberland and Westmerland fled into Scotlād.

stables and other, amongest whome the Alderman of the towne, and a priest called parson Plomtree, were the moste notable. Sir George Bowes being Marshall, finding many to be fautors in the foresaid rebellion, did se them executed in diuers places.

Rebels executed at Disham.

The xxi. of January a prentice (to the good example of other) was hanged on a gibbet at the North ende of Finck lane in London, for that he the xiii. of December, strake his maister with a knife, whereof he died.

A prentice executed at Finke lane.

The xvii. of Feb. was the first corps buried in the new churchyarde (which was the yeare last before enclosed by S. Tho Roe, nere vnto Bethlem) & on saint Mathewes day folowing, maister Molline archdeacō of Londō, in ỷ place preached a sermon, wherat the Lorde Maior, Aldermen, and Shreeues were present. &c.

The 22. of Febr. Leonard Dacre of Harlsey, in the countie of Yorke Esquire, hauing raised a nombre of people, the L. of Hunsdon & other, setting on him with a company of valiant souldiours, slewe many of his people, & forced hym to fly into Scotlande.

Leonard Dacer fled into Scotland

On good Friday, Symon Digby of As- 1570
kewe, Iohn Fulthrop of Iselbecke in the

county

Rebels executed at Yorke.

countie of Yorke Esquires, Robert Peneman of Stokesley, Thomas Bishop the yonger of Poclyngton in the same countie of Yorke gentlemen, were drawen frō the castel of Yorke to the place of execution, called Knaues myre halfe a myle without the citie of Yorke, & there hāged headed, and quartered, their foure heads were set on the foure principall gates of that citie, with foure of their quarters, the other quarters were set vp in ŷ countrey. Oscolphe Clesbe, was drawen to the galowes, and retourned agayne to the castell.

The Earle of Sussex made a iourney in to Scotland.

The xvii. of April the Earle of Sussex Lieutenaunt generall in the Northe, with the Lord Hunsdon, Lorde gouernor of Barwyke, and wardon of the East marches, with all the garrison and power of the same, began a iourney into Scotland, and the same night came to Warke xii. miles from Barwyke, and so the next morning entred into Tyuidale, and marching in warlike order, they brent, ouerthrewe, rasyd and spoyled al the castels townes, and villages of their enemies tyll they came to the castel of Mosse, standing in a strong marise belōging to the Lorde of Bucklughe, whiche lykewyse was rasyd, ouerthrowen, and brent,

so u

so marched forwarde and burnt the
le countrey before them tyll they
e to Crabing. The same daye sir Iohn
ar, wardon of the midle marches,
h the garyson and force of the same,
ed lykewyse into Tyuidale vppon
head xvi. myle from Warke, with
like order, they brent, rased, and
led the countrey before thē tyl they
e to a strong castell called Craling,
e possession of the Lorde Fernherst,
the likewyse they ouerthrewe, rased
brent, with other castels, pyles and
nes, along the countrey, tyll they
e at Cralyng, where both the armyes
, and so marched vp the Ryuer of
ice, rasing, burning and spoylyng,
ls and pyles alōg the ryuer, til they
e to Gedwurth, where they both lod
and were courteously receiued. The
day the Lorde Chesford warden of
middle marches of Scotland, cam
ith all the principall men of his
erd, to the Lorde Lieutenaunt, and
ubmitte them selues and were assu
for that they had not receyued the
lishe rebelles. The xix. they
ded into two partes, the one parte
d the Riuer of Tevit, and brent the
ll of Fernihurst, and all other castels

Sir Iohn Fostar with a garison entred Scotlād

and

and townes belonging to the Lorde of Fernilherst buryll Bedrell, and so passed to Mynt wher both tharmies met again, and so brent on both sydes that ryuer til they came to a great towne called Hawicke, where they entended to haue lodged, but the Scottes had unthatched the houses & brent the thatche in the stretes, and them selues fled with moste part of their goodes, but by the industrie of the Englishmē, the timber with the thatch was also burned, sauinge one house of stone. The xx. day tharmy marched forwards to a house of ỹ Lord of Buckluch, whiche they ouerthrewe, and then marched North to the ryuer of Trewyt, where they brent & spoyled such castels, peles and townes, as belonged to the Lorde of Bucklughe, his kinsmen & adherents, and that night returned to Gedwurth. The xxi. part of tharmy went to the ryuer of Bowbent, and ther brent and spoyled all on both sydes of that ryuer, & the other part marched to the ryuer of Call, and there wasted and brent all on both sides that ryuer, and returned to Kylsey. The xxii. the Lorde Lieutenaunt with the whole armie returned to Englande and came to Barwike. In all which time ther was neuer any shew by ỹ Scottes made

e to resist or defend their countrey.
the same time the lord Scrope war:
of y west marchis, entred Scotlād
brent & spoyled those partes almost
ountrees, and had diuers conflictes,
gaue sondry ouerthrowes and toke
y prysoners, & returned safely. Du:
all those inuasions, the marchis of
gland in all places were so garded,
he Scottes durst not once offer to
r into Englād, so that not one house
burned, nor one Cowe taken out of
glād. There wer rased, ouerthrowe &
rent in this iourney aboue 50. strōg
tls and pyles, & aboue 300. townes &
ages, so that there be very fewe in y
ntrey, that either haue receiued oure
glish rebelles, or inuaded England,
either haue castell, pyle, or house,
them selues or their inhabitauntes,
tenauntes, besydes the losse of theyr
des. The xxvi. the Lord Lieutenant a
ompanied with the Lord gouernour,
Marshal, & diuers lusty gentlemen,
taynes, & souldiours, to the nomber
000. set forwarde to Warke, and so to
rm castel, which castel they besieged.
he same was yelded, the Lord gouer:
r, the Marshal, & diuers other, toke
ssion for our soueraigne Ladye the

Queenes

Lord Scrope entred Scotlande,

Queens maiestie, & expelled the Scots that were therin, to the nomber of .lx. persones, in their aparel on their backs only, without armour, weapō, bagge or baggage, among whom there wer two Englyshemen, one Hiliard the Earle of Northumberlandes man, and a vagraunt persone named William Godswher, which both wer caried to Barwyke, & there executed the .24. of May. The lord Liuetenaunt returned to Barwike the .xxix. of Nouember. The of May, his honor sent maister Drewry Marshall with the nōber of 1000. to take Fast castel, which at the first comming was deliuered to ye Marshall, who expelled the Scottes in nōber .x. and placed .xiiii. of our English mē against al Scotland, it is so stronge a pece, and so returned to Barwyke. The .xi. of May, the Lord Lieuetenaūt made foure knightes, Viz Sir Thomas Mannors Sir George Carre, Sir William Drewry, Sir Robert Constable. And the same daye set forwarde towarde, Edenborough with diuers Scot bandes, with horse, armed pikes, and pieces of great ordinaunce, to ioyne with the Lorde Morton and other of the kynges power of Scotland, in pursuing of the Englishe rebelles & suche of the Scottes as supported them,

Rebelles executed at Barwyke.

tle. Duke Hamelton and other, who
ere in armes at Litchcoye, xii. myles
om Edenborough, to defend their cause,
e forsayde newe made knightes with
eir bandes came to Edenborough the
ii. of May, and departed from thence
Litthcoy. The 17. the foteme marched
Fankirke. vi. myles from Sterling, and
William Drewry with the horsemen,
arched to Sterling to see the kyng, whō
ey founde so perfecte in all thinges as
s age and nature could permit. The
iiii. they departed to the fote bandes,
d so together marched to Glascoye,
here the Lorde Hamelton had besieged
house of ŷ kynges, but hearing of their
mming, he fled with dishonour. The
x. the generall with other horsemen &
me shot, passed to Dunbarton, to beewe
e streytes of the castell there, being
pt by the Lorde Flemyng, the byshop
S. Andrewes and other, the rest of this
urney valiauntly atchieued I leue for
euitie.

The xxv. of May in the morning, was
und hanging at the bishop of London
s palace gate in Paules churchyarde,
Bull whyche latelye hadde beene
nt from Rome, contayninge dyuers
rible treasons against the Queenes

A bull from Rome, hanging on the gate of the bishop of London.

 maiestie,

maiestie, for the whiche one Iohn Felton, was shortly after aprehended and committed to the tower of London.

The Nortõs executed.

The xxviii. of May Thomas Norton & Christopher Norton, of Yorkeshire beinge both condemned of high treason against the Queenes maiestie, for the late rebellion in the North, were drawen from þ Tower of London to Tyborne, & there hanged, headed, and quartered.

Hameltõ in Scotlande yelded to our general

The xxvii. of May, þ castle of Hamelton in Scotlande, was yelded to sir William Drewry, general of our army, and by him presently spoyled & burnt. The 28. sir George Carre with the horsemẽ came to Lithe, wher the whole army met, this daye a very faire house with the whole towne, of Hamelton was brent. The 29. they brent an other house of the Dukes, called Kemiel and an other at Lytheo, the whole towne & diuers other faire houses, was yelded to our General, who returned to Edenborowe & so to Berwyke, the iii of June.

Conspiracy in Norfolke

A conspiracie was made, by certaine gentlemen and other in the countie of Northfolke, whose purpose was on Midsomerday, at Harlestone fayre, with sound of trompet and drome, to haue raysed a nomber, and then to proclayme their deuelishe pretence. This matter was dis

ed by one of the conspiracie, named
te, whereby, dyuers were apprehen=
d, and afterward arraigned at the citie
Norwiche, before the Lorde chiefe
ustice of Englande and other: there
ere dyuers for that facte condemned, Execution at
d three of them hanged, boweled, and Norwiche.
uartered, Iohn Throkmoorton gentle=
an, who stoode mute at his araigne=
ent, but at the galowes confessed him
lfe to be the chiefe conspiratour, and
at none had deserued to dye but he, for
at hee had procured them. With hym
as executed Thomas Brooke gentlemā,
e 30. of August, & George Redman was
kewise executed. the 2. of Septēber.
The fourth daye of August, the Duke
f Northfolke was remoued from the
Tower of London, to the Chartarhouse
eare vnto Smythfielde. The same
aye was araigned at the Guylde haule
f London, Iohn Felton, for hangyng the
Bull at the gate of the Byshop of Lon=
on his place: and also twoo young men
were lykewyse arreigned for coyning,
nd clypping of Coyne, who all were
ounde guylty of hyghe treason, and had
Iudgement to be had to Newgate, and
from thence to be drawen, and after han
ged, boweled, and quartered.

Felton executed with other,

The viii. day of August Iohn Felton, was drawẽ from newgate into Paules churcheyard, and there hanged on a gallowes newe set vp that morning before the byshops palaice gate, and being cut downe aliue, he was boweled and quartered. After this the same morning the sheryues returned to Newgate, and so to Tyborne with two young mẽ which were there hanged, boweled and quartered, for coyning and clipping, as is afore sayde.

A iourney into Scotland by the Erle of Sussex.

The xxii. of August the Earle of Sussex Lorde Lieutenaunt generall for the Queenes maiestie in the North, and the Lorde Scrope warden of the West marches, with diuers others marched from Carlile with the Queenes army as well of horsemen as footemen, into Scotlãde passing ouer the ryuers of Eske, Leum, & Sarke, which ryuer of Sarke parteth England and Scotlande, & so to Dornock woode, and then to Annonna, a stronge house of the Lorde Haries, whiche they rased and ouerthrewe with other there abouts, from thence to Hodhim, whiche they burnt and blewe vp, from thence to Kennel, a towne belonging to the lord Cowhill, whiche they brent, from thence to Domfres which they sacked and spoyled,

),of suche paltry as the fugetiues h[illegible]
t, and also rased and ouerthrewe a
mptuous house belonging to ẏ queene
Scottes, in the kepinge of the Lorde
rris, then passing the ryuer of Logher.
y brente and spoyled Cowchilles and
wtracke, and then returning to Dun-
s, and so to the towne of Banckende,
hiche they brent with an other house
rtaining to William Maxwell of ẏ Iles
d so to the castell of Carlauoracke stan
ng in a marishe iust to an arme of the
ea, whiche partith Annerdall and Gal-
vaye, whiche castell they blewe vp ⁊
urned homewarde transporting our
dinaunce ouer quicke sandes ⁊ bogs,
here neuer the like was done before,
d so came to Dornoke woode. The
viii. of August they marched towardes
rlile, where by the waye they burnt ⁊
erthrewe two houses of the Greames,
one being Arthur Greames, alias Car:
, the other Riche Gorge, twoo no:
ile theues. The same daye at night
er the Lordes comming to Carlile, le
de knightes, sir Edwarde Hastinges,
Franncis Russell, sir Valentine Browne,
William Hilton, sir Robert Stapleton,
Henry Curwen, and sir Symond Mus-
gue.

Sherifes. Frannces Bernam. Wil. Boxe the 28. Sep.

Highe waters which drowned many.

The v. of October at night, happened a moste terreble tempest of wynd and raine, both on the sea & land, by meanes wherof about midnight, ye waters ouer flowing drowned many medowes, pastors, cattel, houses & goodes, to ye vtter vndoing of a great nomber the subiectes of this Realme. Besydes the losse of manye menne, women and chyldren, some drowned in theyr beddes, some in the wayes trauayling. &c.

Maior. Sir Rouland Hayward clothworker. 28. O.

Anno re. 13 17. of No.

The 23. of January, the Queenes maiestie accompanyed with her nobilitye, came from her house at the Strand, called Somerset place, and entered the Cittye of London by Temple barre, Fletestreate, Cheape, and so by ye North syde of ye Burse, to sir Thomas Greshams in Bishops gate streate, where shee dined: After dinner her grace returninge through Cornehill, entered the Burse on the South side, and after her highnes had viewed euery part therof, aboue grounde, but especiallye the Pawne, whiche was richlye furnished wyth all sortes of the fynest wares in the whole Cittye: she caused the same Burse by an

Harolt

rald of armes and sound of Trompet be proclaymed The Royall exchaunge. The 17. of February at a place called nnaston, neare Marcleghe hyll, in the ountye of Hereforde, was seene the ounde to open, and certaine rockes yth a peece of grounde, remoued and nt forward the space of iiii. days, ma nge at the fyrst a terrible noyse as it nt on the earth, it remoued it selfe be- ene vi. of the clocke in the eueninge, vii. the next morrow, forty paces, ca ing great trees and sheepe cotes, some pe cotes wyth lx. shepe in them, som es fel into the chinckes and are swal- wed, other that grewe on the same ound, grow now as fermely on a hil, d some that stode East stand West, and se that stoode West stande Easte. The pthe of the hole where it first brake te, is thirtye foote, the breadth of the each is viii. score yardes, and in le~gth oue xx. score yardes. It ouerthrewe nnaston Chappel, also ii. highe wayes remoued nighe one hundred yardes, yth the trees of the hedge rowes. The ound in all is xxvi. acrees and where llage grounde was, there is pasture te in place: and where was pasture, ere is tyllage ground gone vppon it.

The Royal exchange.

A straunge kinde of earth mo- uinge.

Kk iiii .The

The grounde as it remoued draue the earth before it, and at the lower part ouerwhelmed the grounde, so that it is growne to a great hill of xii. fadome highe. It remoued from saturday til monday at night folowyng & so standes stil.

1571 Parliament. The seconde of Aprill, a parliament began at Westminster, wherein was graunted to the Queenes maiestie (towardes her great charges, in repressing the late rebellion in the North, and pursuing the sayde rebelles and their fautors which were fled into Scotlande) by the clergy a subsedye of vi. s. in the pounde, and by the temporalitie two fiftenes, with a subsedie of two shyllinges and viii. pence in the pounde.

Iustis at Westminster. The firste, seconde, and third of May, was holden at Westminster before the Queenes maiestie, a solempne Iustis, at the tylt, torney, and barriers, The chalengers were Edwarde Earle of Oxforde, sir Charles Hawarde, sir Henry Lee, and, Christopher Hatton Esquier, who al did very valiauntly, but the chiefe honour was geuen to the Earle of Oxford.

Execution at Tyborne. The first of June, Iohn Story a doctor of the Canon lawe, who before had ben condempned of highe treason, was drawen from the tower of London to Tyborne,

me, and there hanged, boweled, and
artered, his head set on Londō bridge
d his quarters on ÿ gates of the city.
The xviii. daye of June, & the fourth
Trinitie terme, there was a combat ap-
inted to haue bene fought for a certein
ner and demayne landes belonging
reunto, in the Ile of Harte, adioyning
he Ile of Shepey in Kent, Symon
we and John Kyme, were playntiues
o had brought a write of right against
omas Paramore, who offered to defende
right by battayle, whereuppon the
intyues aforesayde accepted to aun-
ere his chalenge, offering likewyse
defende their right to the same man-
and landes, and to proue by battail
t Paramore had no right nor good ty-
to haue the same maner and landes.
reupon the sayde Thomas Paramor
ught before the Judges of the com-
n place at Westminster, one George
rne a bygge, brode, stronge set fel-
e, and the plaintifes brought Henry
lor maister of defence, and seruaunt
he right honourable Earle of Ley-
er, a proper slender man, and not so
as the other. Thorne caste downe a
ntlet, which the Naylor tooke vp. Vpō
ounday before the battaile shoulde be
tried

A combat appointed to haue ben foughte on Tuthyll.

tried on the nexte morowe, the matter was stayed, and the parties agreed that Paramour beynge in possession shoulde haue the lande, and was bounde in 500. pounde to consyder the playntifes, as vpon hearinge the matter, the Iudges shoulde awarde. The Queenes maiestie was the taker vp of the matter, in thys wyse. It was thought good that for Paramours assuraunce, the order shoulde bee kepte touching the combate, and that the plaintifes, Lowe and Kyme, shoulde make defaulte of appearaunce, but that yet suche as were sureties for Naylor, their championš apperance should bring hym in, & likewyse those that were sureties for Thorne, should bring in the same Thorne, in discharge of their band, & that the court should sitte in Tuttell fieldes, where was prepared one plot of ground xxi. yardes square, double rayled for the combat, without the West square a stage being set vp for the Iudges, representing the court of the comon pleas. All the cõpasse without the listes, was sette with scaffoldes one aboue an other for people to stand and behold. There were behind the square where the Iudges sat, two tentes, the one for Naylor, the other for Thorne. Thorne was ther in the morning tymely,

The quarell of combat stayed.

[illegible]mely, Naylor about vii. of the clocke, [illegible]me through London, apparailed in a [illegible]ublet, & a paire of galey gascoyne bree[illegible]hes all of crimosin sattin cut and racid. [illegible]is stocks of knit crimosin silke, a hat of [illegible]lack velust with a red band and red fe[illegible]her, before him were foure drommes play[illegible]ng all the waye, the gauntlet cast down [illegible]y George Thorne, was borne before the [illegible]yd Naylor vpon a swerdes point, & his [illegible]aston (a staffe of an elle longe, made ta[illegible]er wyse tipt with horne) with his child [illegible]hard lethar was borne after him, by [illegible]skam a yeoman of the Queenes garde. [illegible]e came into the palace at Westminster, [illegible]nd stayinge not longe before the haule [illegible]ore, came back into the kinges streate, [illegible]nd so alonge through the sanctuary and [illegible]otehill strete into the fielde, where he [illegible]aied till past ix. of the clock, and then [illegible] Ierome Bowes brought hym to his [illegible]ente. Thorne beyng in his tente with [illegible] Henry Chenye longe before. About [illegible]nne of the clocke, the Court of comon [illegible]leas remoued, and came to the place [illegible]epared, when the Lorde chiefe Ju[illegible]ice with twoo other his asociates were [illegible], then Lowe was called solempnly to [illegible]ome in, or els he to lose his wryte of [illegible]ght.

Then

Then after a certayne tyme the sureties of Henry Naylor were called to bryng in the sayde Naylor champion for Symon Lowe, and shortly thereupon, sir Ierome Bowes leading Naylor by the hande, en=treth with him the listes, bringing hym downe that square by which he entred, beyng on the lefte hande of the Judges, and so about tyll hee came to the nexte square iust against the Judges, and there making curtesy, first with one legge & then with the other, passed foorth till he came to the middle of the place, and thē made the like obeysaunce, & so passing till they came to the barre, there he made the lyke curtesy, and his shild was held vp aloft ouer his head. Naylor put of his netherstockes, & so bare foted & bare legged saue his sylke scauilones to the ankles, and his doblet sleues tayed vp aboue the elbowe, and bare headed came in as afore is sayde. Then were the sure=ties of George Thorne called to bring in the same Thorne, and immediatlye sir Henry Cheyne entring at the vpper ende on the right hande of the Judges, and vsed the lyke order in comming about by his syde as Naylor had before on that other syde, and so comming to the barre with like obeysaunce, held vp his shild.

Procla=

proclamation was made that none
ould touche the barres, nor presume
come within the same, except such as
ere appointed: after all this solemp ne
der was finished. The Lorde Cheffe
stice, rehersing the maner of the brin=
ng the wryte of right by Symon Lowe,
the aunswere made thereunto by Para
re, of the proceding therein, and how
ramore had challenged to defende his
ght to the lande by battayle, by his
mpion George Thorne, and of the ac=
pting the trial that was by Low with
s champion Henry Naylor, and then
defaute in apperaunce in Lowe hee
iudged the lande to Paramore, and dis=
ssed the champions, acquiting the sur
s of their bandes. He also willed Hēry
ylor to render agayne to George
orne, his gauntlet, whereunto the said
ylor aunswered, that his Lordshippe
ight commaunde hym any thyng, but
llingly he would not render the said
untlet to Thorne except he could wyn
and further he chalenged the sayde
orne to playe with him halfe a score
lues, to showe some pastyme to the
rde chiefe Justice and the other there
embled, but Thorne aunswered, that
came to fight and would not playe.

Then

Then the lord chiefe Justice cōmending Naylor for his valiant corage, cōmaunded thē both quietly to depart ẏ field. &c

D. of Northfolk sent to the Tower.

The vii. of September, the Duke of Northfolk was remoued from the Chartarhouse, and conueyed to the Tower of London prisoner.

The xxii. of Septemb. deceased Iohn Iewel, B. of Sarisbury, in his life a moste eloquent & diligent preacher, but a farre more painful & studious wryter, as his workes remaining beareth witnes, wherby his fame shall neuer die.

B. of Sarisbury deceased.

Sherifes. Henry Myles, Iohn Branche the. 28. Sept.

Maior. Sir William Alin Mercer. 28. of October.

The Christians victorye against the Turkes.

GReat reioycing was made at London with banqueting & boene fiers, ẏ ix. of Nouember, for ioye of the late come newes, of a marueilous victory optayned by the Christiā army by sea, against the Turkes, wherein was taken & sonk of the Turkes galeys, galiots & brygātines 230. there were slayn of the Turks more then 30. thousande, besides a great nomber of prisoners taken, & about xii. thousand Christians that had ben slaues with the Turkes, were set at libertie. The Christians lost vii. galeis, & were slayne about vi. or vii. thousand.

Anno. re. 14

The. xxx. of Decemb. r, Thomas Grey

[illegible]as by the Queenes maiestie, restored [Ea]rle of Kent.

The xiii. of January deceased sir Wil. [P]eter Knight, who for his iudgement & pregnant wit, had bene secretary and of [pri]uy counsael to 4. kinges & Queenes [o]f this realme, & 7. times lord Embassa[do]ur abroade in forain landes, he great[l]y augmẽted Exceter colledge in Oxford, [&] also builded almes houses for ye poore.

Sir W. Peter deceased.

The xvi. of January, the Duke of Nor[fo]lke was araigned in Westminster hal, [a]nd there by his piers founde giltie of [h]igh treason, & had iudgmẽt accordingly

D. of Norfolk araigned.

The x of February Kenelme Barney & Edmond Mather, were drawen from the Tower of London, & Henry Rolfe from [t]he Marshalsey in Southwarke, al thre [t]o Tyborne, & there [ha]nged, [bo]weled, & [q]uartered, for treso[n] [illegible] Mather, [fo]r conspiracy, & R[olfe for] counterfey[t]ing the Queenes m[illegible] hande.

Mather and Barney executed with Rolfe.

The x. of March, d[ecea]sed sir William Pawlet knight, Lor[d S]t John. Erle [o]f Wylshire, Marques of Wynchester, [k]nyght of the honourable order of the Garter, one of the Queenes maiesties [pr]iuie counsel, & Lord high treasurer of Englande, this worthy man was borne [t]he yeare of our Lorde 1465. the fifth of

Sir W. Pawled L. Treasurer deceased.

Edward

Edwarde the fourth, and lyued one hundred yeares and sixe with more, in viii. kynges and queenes dayes, he serued vi. kynges and Queenes, Henry the seuenth Henry the eight, Edwarde the sixt, Mary the first, and Queene Elizabeth. All these he serued faithfullye, and of them was greatly fauoured. Hym selfe did see his childrens childrens children, growen to mans estate, a rare blissing geuen by God to men on these our dayes.

1572 The xxv. and xxvi. of Marche, by the commaundement of the Queenes maiestie her counsayle, the citezins of Lōdon assembling at their seuerall haules, the maisters collected and chose out the most lykelye and actiue persones of euerye their companies, to the nomber in all of three tho[illegible] whome they appointed to be pyk[illegible] shot, the pyke men were foorth[illegible] armed in fayre corslettes & other [illegible]niture, according therunto, the gon[illegible] had euery of them his Caleuer with [illegible] furniture and moryās on their heads, to these were appointed dyuers valiaunt Captaines, who to trayne them vp in warlyke feates, mustered them thryse euerye weeke, some tymes in the artylery yarde, teaching the gunnars to handle their pieces, some tyme

The citezins of London made a show at Grenewiche.

ne at the Myles ende, and in Saint
eorges fielde, teaching them to skyr=
ishe, In the which skyrmishyng, on ÿ
yles ende, the x. of April, one of the
nners of the Goldsmythes companye
as shotte in the syde wyth a pece of
skoring sticke left in one of the Cale=
ers, whereof he dyed, and was buried
e 12. of April in Poules Church yard,
the gonners marching from the My=
s ende in battaile ray, shot of their ca=
ners at his graue. On May daye they
ustered at Grenewich before ÿ Quee=
es maiestye, where they shewed many
arlike feates, but were much lynde=
d by the weather, which was all day
owringe, they returned that nyght to
ondon, and were discharged on the
ext morowe.

The fourth of May Walter Deuereyx, Ferers of Chartley Vyscount Heriford, was created Earle of Essex. And Edward ...nes, Lord Clinton, and say, Admyrall of Englande, was created Earle of Lin= colne.

Earles of Lincolne, and of Essex created.

The viii. of Maye, the Parliamente began at Westminster, and that day in ÿ Parliament, by the Queenes Maiesties writtes, sir Henrye Compton, sir Henrye Cheynie, sir Henry Norris was called Barons.

Parliament.

Barons [illegible]

Roges burnt through the eare.

In this Parliament, for so much, as the whole realme of England, was exceadingly pestered with Roges, vagabōds and sundrye beggers, by meanes whereof daily happened diuers horrible murders, thefres and other greate outrages it was enacted that all persones aboue ye age of 14. yeares, beinge taken begging, vagrant & wandering misorderly, should be apprehended, whipped, & burnt through the gristle of ye right eare, with a hot Iron.

Executiō at the wel with ii. buckets.

The xviii. of May, Martin bulloke was hanged on a gibet by the well with two buckettes in bishops gate streate of Lōdon, for robbyng and moste shamefullye murdering of a marchaunt named Arthur Hall, in the parsonage of saint Martyn by the sayde well.

Earle of Lincolne and other ambassadours into Fraunce.

About Whytsontyde the ryght honourable Earle of Lyncolne, was sent into Fraunce Ambassadoure, beinge accompanyed wyth the Lord Dacres, the Lord Ryche, the Lord Talbot, the Lord Sandes, & the lord Clynton, sir Arthur Chambernowne, syr Ierome Bowes, and syr Edwarde Hastinges knyghtes, with diuers other Gentlemen who takyng shippe at Douer, cut ouer to Bulleyne, where they were very honourablye.

ly receyued, and from thence conueyed by iourneyes to Paris, where they were lodged in a house of the Kynges, named Le chasteau de Loure, beyng attended on of the Kynges officers. Fyue dayes after, they wente to the Kynge at a house named Madryll, where the kynge wyth hys twoo brethren, the Admyrall, and the moste parte of the nobles of Fraunce mette them a distaunce from the place, and brought them into the house, where they dyned, and remayned tyll Sondaye followyng, from whence the King and hys Nobles, with the Nobles of Englande came to Paris the kynge hys twoo brethren, and oure Ambassadour, rydinge in one Couche together, and the nobles of England and Fraunce beynge so placed also in Couches came to the sayd Castell of Louure, and there dyned, After dynner the Kinge, oure Ambassadour wyth the Nobylitye of both Realmes, wente to a Churche named S. Germain, where the Frenche kinge, his brethren and nobilitye harde euensonge, the noble men of England wyth drawing them into a Chappel [illegible] song was done, were they fetched [illegible] by the nobles of Fraunce to the kynge and his brethren, that awayted there comminge, wher was construed the league, (which had bene concluded at Eloys the xix. of Aprill, deputyes beynge there for the Frenche party. Fraunces Mountmorancye, Reynolde Virago, Sebastian de Laubespine, and Pawle de Foys. And for the Queene of Englande, sir Thomas Smith, & maister Walsingham Embassadours.) This being done, they departed wythoute the walles of Paris to a gardeine of pleasure, wher they supped, after supper ye kyng departed to his place of Madrill, and the nobles of Englande to the castell of Louuer. On Mondaye, the Admirall feasted the nobles of England, on tuesday the Duke of Aniow the kynges brother, and on wednesdaye the Duke of Alanson his yonges brother, & so passed in feastinge and banquetynge, wyth riche giftes on both parties, on friday, the nobles of England toke leue of the kyng, and on sondaye came to S. Denis & after to Bolloigne where they toke shippe and returned into Englande.

Leaguewith Fraũce confirmed in Fraunce.

The second of June in the morninge betweene the houres of seuen and eight Thomas Hawarde Duke of Northfolke, was beheaded on a scaffold new set vp, on the tower hill.

Duke of Northfolke beheaded.

About the ix. of June, Fraunces Duke

of Montmorancy Marshall of Fraunce, gouernour and Lieutenaunte generall to Charles the nynth kynge of Fraunce, and Pawle de Foyes, of the priuye counsaile to the said kyng, and Bertrame de la Lige a Lorde Le Lamote, Felowe and knight of thorder of S. Mychael, Ambassadoures for the same kinge, aryued at Douer, the xiii. day they rode Londo bridge towards Sommerset house at the Strand, wher they were lodged, the xv. being sondaye, the sayd Embassadours repayred to the whyte haule, where they were honourably receyued of the Queenes Maiesty, with her Nobilitye, and there in her graces Chappell, about one of the clocke in the after noone, the articles of treatye league, or confederacy and sure frendshyppe, (concluded at Bloyes the xix. of April, as is afore shewed) betweet the Queenes maiestye and the Frenche kynge, beynge redde, the same was by her Maiestye & his Embassadoures, confirmed to be obserued and kept, without innouation or violation. &c. The rest of that day with great part of the night following, was spent in great tryumphe wyth sumptuous banquettes. The xviii. of June ye feast of S. George was holden at Windsore,

French Ambassadours.

League with Fraunce confirmed at Westmister.

S. Georges feast at Winsor.

sore where the Frenche Embassadours were royallye feasted, & Fraunces Duke Montmorancy, was stalled knight of ye most honourable order of the Garter. The xxviii day of June, the forenamed Embassadours departed from London towardes Fraunce.

Lord treasuror, L. Preuy seale, L. Chāberlain with other officers.

The xiii. daye of Julye, the Queenes Maiestye, at Whyte halle, made Syr Wylliam Cicell Lord of Burleigh, Lorde highe Treasurer of Englande. Lorde William Hawarde late Lorde Chamberlaine, Lorde priuye Seale. The Earle of Sussex Lorde Chamberlayne. And Christopher Hatton, Captayne of the Garde. &c.

Erle of Northumberlād executed.

The 22. of August, Thomas Percy Erle of Northumberland, late of Topclyffe, who had bene before attainted by Parliament of high treason, as beinge one of the principall conspiratours in the late rebellion, was beheaded at Yorke, aboute two of the clocke in the after noone, on a newe Scaffolde set vp for that purpose in the market place.

Sheriffes. Ry. Pype, Nicholas Wodroffe. 28. Septem.

Maior. Lionel Ducket Mercer. The 28. October.

Anno. 15.

The xxiiii. of Nouēber, Edward Erle of Darby, Lord Stāley & Strang of Knockyng, Lorde and gouernour of the

Isles

Illes of Man, knyght of the noble order f the Gartar, and one of the Queenes Maiesties priuie counsell deceased. His yfe and death deseruing commendatiō, nd creanynge memorye to be imitated, was such as foloweth. His fidelitie to inges & 2. Queenes in daungerous ty- mes and greate rebellions, in whiche ime and alwayes as cause serued, he ore Lieutenant of Lācashyre & Ches- hyre, and lately offered x. M. men to ŷ Queenes maiestie of his owne charge, or the suppression of the last rebellion. His Godly disposition to his tenaūts, neuer forsing any seruice at their hands ut due payment of their rente. His li- eralitye to straungers and such as she- wed thēselfe gratefull vnto him. His fa- mous house keping, & xi. score in check owle, neuer discontinuing the space of lii. yeres. His feeding especially of a- ged persons, twyse a day, lx. and od, be- ide al commers thrise a weeke appoin- ed for hes dealyng dayes, & euery good frydaye these 35. yeares one wyth ano- ther 2700. wyth meate, drincke, money, and moneye worthe. There was neuer gentleman or other, that wayted in his eruice, but had allowance from him o haue as well wages, as other wyse Erle of Dar by deceased for horse and man. His yearely portion for the dispenses of his house. 4000. li. His cunning in setting bones disioynted or broke, his Chirurgerye and desire to helpe the poore. His delivery of his George and seale to the Lorde Straunge, wyth exhortation that he might kepe it see unspotted in fidelitye to his Prince as he had, and his ioy that he dyed in ye Queenes favour. His ioyfull partinge this world, his taking leave of all his servaunts by shaking of handes, and his remembraunce to the last day.

Hall and Wilkinson executed.

The 28. of Novẽber Iohn Hall late of Battel in Sussex Gentleman, and Oswald Wylkinson, late of Yorke, and Jaylor of Yorke Castell (being before arraigned & condempned of treason) were drawen from the Tower of Lõdon to Tyborn, and there hãged, bowelled, & quartered.

Great frost.

This yeare a great and sharpe frost, almost continually lasted, from the feast of all Saintes, till after the feast of the Epiphanye of oure Lorde, wyth some tymes great and deepe snowes, and sometimes raynes which friesed as fast as ye same fell to grounde, where throughe at Wrotham in Kent and manye other places, the armes & bowes of trees beinge over charged wyth Ise brake of, and fel

feon

from the Rockes of the same trees.

The 12. of Januarye, William L. Hawarde Baron of Effingham, Lord priuye Seale, knighte of the noble order of the Garter, and one of the Queenes Maiesties priuy counsel, deceased at Hampton Court.

Lord priuy seale deceased.

Thus good Reader, I haue brought this abridged Summarye of the Chronicles of Englande, from the first comming of Brute into this Land, unto the yeare of Christe, 1573. desiringe thee to take this and other my larger trauayles in good part, like as I haue paynfullye (to my greate coste and charges) oute of many old hidden historyes, brought the same to light, and freelye for thy greate commodity, bestowed them upon thee. I wishe to be plaine & true, and I wish the Readers to trye or they truste, then shall they see whoe of late hath abused me, & deceyued them with lyes smoothlye tolde.

The conclusion.

Of smoth and flattering speache,
remember to take heede.
For truth in plaine wordes may be tolde,
of craft a lye hath neede.

¶ The age of the worlde.

THE first age from the creation of Adam to the floud of Noe, which continued yeares 1656

2. The seconde from Noe to Abraham. 292.

3 The thirde, from the birth of Abraham, til the departing of Israell out of Egipt. 503.

4 The fourth from the departing of Israel out of Egipt til the building of the temple yeares. 481

5 The fifte, from the building of the temple till the captiuitye of Babilon. 414

6 The sixth, from the captiuitye, of Babilon, till the birthe of oure Sauiour Iesus Christe 614.

7 The seuenth, beginninge at the birth of our sauiour Iesus Christ hath continued till this present yere of our Lord 1573. and shall last till the worldes ende.

The age of the world at the birth of Christ was 1961, The age of the worlde this presente yeare of oure Lorde 1573. is 5535.

Of the Uniuersityes in aglande, and Colledges in the same, with the founders, and principal benefactours, and also the time when euerye of those Colledges were founded.

Haue before tyme reioysed (sayth Erasmus Roterdam) that Englande was so well furnished wyth so manye men of excellent learning: but w I begin to enuye her felicitye, for t she so flourisheth wyth all kinde of erature, that by takinge the commendaion therof from other Regions, shee as it were marueilouslye obscure n. And yet this cõmendation is not now first due to Englãd, in ÿ which s well knowen haue beene of longe e men of great learning. The Uniityes proue this to be true, which h for their antiquity and worthines tend with the most auncient & wor Uniuersityes in the world.

Cambridge (as some learned wryters affirme) was first frequented wyth Phi- Cambridge

Philosophers and Astronomers, procured from Athens by Cantebar a Spaniarde, in the tyme of Gurguntius who was king of Britaine, before the byrth of Christ, yeres. 375.

Peter Colledge.

Peter Colledge was erected of two auncient hostels, by Hughe Balsame, sometyme subprior of Elye. 1256
This Hughe was afterward the tenthe bishop of Elye, and finished this Colledge in Anno 1284.

Clare haule

Clare haule was first builded by Richard Badow then Chauncelor of the Studentes ther, and the same was called Uniuersitye haule. 1326.
It was since that, enlarged by Gwalter Thacstede maister of the said haule, who wyth consent of the sayd Richard Badow resigned the foundation thereof, to the Ladye Elyzabeth de Burgo, doughter of Gilbert Clare Earle of Gloucester, and after Countisse and heyre of Clare, who by that name called it Clare haule.

Pembroke haule.

Pembroke haule was founded by Marye of Valentia, doughter to Gwido Erle of S Paule in Fraunce, wyfe to Adomare de Valentia Earle of Pembroke, shee obtayned of Kinge Edward the thirde, whose cosyne shee was, to founde this Colledge in her awne grounde: wyth purchasing two or thre tenements there-by, and named it Awla de Valence Marye Anno. 1343.

Corpus Christi Colledge was first begon to be bulded, by the Alderman and brethren of Corpus Christi Guild. 1342. This Colledge was brought forth, the rather by the helpe of the brethren of S. Maryes Guild and fraternity, newly adioined to þ other Guild. 1344 In the yere 1353. they did electe Henrye Earle of Darbye and Lancaster, whoe should obtaine them fauour for the purchasinge of Mortmaine, for such landes and tenementes, as after many did sell them. This Earle of Darbye in the 18. yeare of Edward the thyrd, was created the fyrst Duke of Lancaster, and then they elected him theyr Alderman, who recognised theyr statutes, not by the Dukes seale, but by the Seale of þ Alderman of that Guilde.

Corp. Christi College.

Trinitye haule, was first an Hostell purchased by John Cranden sometyme Prior of Elye, who procured it for hys brethren the monks of that house, to be studentes there, in the time of Edward the third, whych Hostel was afterward purchased by William Bateman byshop of Norwich, who bulded his Colledge

Trinity hall.

of Trinitye haule vpon the sayd grounde, beyng the first founder therof, he deceased in the yeare of Christ. 1354.

Gunuile and Caius Colledge.

Gunuile & Caius Colledge, was fyrst founded by Edmonde Gunuile sometyme parson of Terington in Northfolke, hee gaue it to name Gunuile haule, as appeareth by hys statute. 1348.

At his decease, he leauinge a good masse of money, commended the further finishyng of the same haule to William Bateman bishop of Northwiche, whoe wyth the assente of the Aldermen and brethrē of the Guilds of Corpus Christi and our Ladye, chaunged wyth theym the sayde house wyth theyr house called the stone haule, wher now Gunuile & Caius Colledge standeth. 1353.

At this day Iohn Caius Doctour in Phisicke somtyme fellow and now maister of the sayd Colledge, hath enlarged the house and now made a seconde foundation, wyth geuing certaine maners and landes to the same. 1557.

Kings Colledge.

Kinges Colledge was first foūded by Kynge Henrye the sixte, in the yeare of Christ. 1441.

The same King altered the forme of his first foūdation in ÿ yere of Christ 1443

Edward the fourth, in displeasure of ÿ

first

-t foundation, wythdrewe from that olledge so much land as the first Foū-r had geuen them, but afterward hee lo:ed them to ẏ inheritaunce of 500. arkes. After hym Henrye the seuenth ished that notable Chappell, begon Henry the 6. to the glasing, stalles, & ing with Marble, which was done King Henry the eyght

Queenes Colledge was begon by Lady -et wyfe to King Henry ẏ sixt. 1446 he procured a Mortmaine of an C. li. yere. Anno 1448. At thintercession Andrew Ducket, sometime principall Barnard Hostell, (which hostell hee to the sayd Colledge) he was par-of S. Botolphes in Cambridge, who by owne moneye and helpe of others, chased certaine tenementes, & buil-his Colledge, being the first presi-t of the same, who gaue aswel by his as by his testament diuers sūmes, parcels of lande, and also procured aine giftes of the Duke of Clarence, ycilye Dutches of Yorke, of Richard ke of Glocester, of Anne Dutches he same, of Edwarde Earle of Salis-e, Maulde Countesse of Oxford, & maduke Lumley bishop of Lyncolne h dyuers other. Elyzabeth wyfe to King Queenes Colledge.

K. Edward the 4. finished that which Queene Margaret had begonne in the yeare. 1465.

Katharine haule.

Katherine haule was founded by Robert Wodlarke doctor of diuinitie, and prouost of the kings Colledge, & Chaũcelar to the Uniuersitye, as is testifyed by the Charter of K. Henry the 6. bearing date the xxxvii. of his raigne, which was the yere of Christ. 1459.

Iesus Colledge.

Iesus Colledge, was founded by Iohn Alcocke, the 29. byshop of Ely, who did conuerte the monastrye of saynt Radygond (the abbesse lyuing a dissolute life, the monastery then destitute of gouernmente, the edyfices fallen in ruine, and in conclusion the Nonnes departinge thence, leauinge it desolate) into a Colledge of Chaplens & scholars, the yeare of Christ. 1496.

The rentes thereof hath bene more amplified by sir Robert Reade knight, doctour Elcston, Doctor Royston & Doctor Fuller.

Christes Colledge.

Christes Colledge was foũded by K. Hẽry the 6. who named it Gods house, as it was somtime a great hostel so called. K Henry the seuenth grãted his charter to Ladye Margaret hys mother, Countesse of of Richmond and Darby,

encreaſe the ſtudentes there, tranſla
ge it at her diſpoſition, ſo that from
nce forth it ſhould be called Chriſtes
lledge. 1505.

Saint Iohns Colledge, being firſt an
Cell of Religious Chanons, was e-
ted by Nigellus the ſeconde biſhop of
ye, treaſurer to Kyng Henry the firſt
yere of Chriſt. 1134 — Saint Iohns Colledge.

hoſe Chanons lyued by the name of
ſpitall and brethren of S. Iohn, untill
yeare of Chriſt. 1510. though at that
me ſo farre decayed that ther was but
Prior and two brethren, & by the di-
idacions of theyr goodes mouable &
mouable, they abaſed theyr reue-
ues, within the ſpace of x. yeres laſt
, from the ſumme of an hundreth &
tye pound, to 30. pounde &c. Where-
pon, Kyng Henry the eight, Richard
ſhoppe of Wincheſter, Iohn byſhop of
cheſter, Charles Sommerſet Lorde of
rbert, Thomas Louell, Henrye Marne,
d Iohn ſeinte Iohn Knightes, Henrye
mby and Hugh Aſhton Clarkes: exe-
tors of the Teſtament of Lady Mar-
et Counteſſe of Richmond & Darbye,
aundmother to K. Henry the eyght,
d mother to K. Henry the ſeuenth, by
n the ſuppreſſion of the ſaid Priorye.

Thee

she beinge preuented by death, leauinge behind her sufficient goodes, and committing the same to those her said frends and executours, they erected the sayde Colledge. 1511.

Magdalene Colledge.

Magdalene Colledge was first an hostill or haule inhabited by diuers monkes of sondrye Monasteryes, Edwarde Duke of Buckingham translated the same to a Colledge, naming it Buckingham Colledge, who builded vp the haule in the yeare of Christe. 1519. After him Thomas Audleye of Walden, sometime Chauncelour of Englande, toke on hym to be founder of the sayde Colledge, and going about to establishe the same, was preuented by deathe, so that what hee had begonne, he lefte vnperfite, and altogether vnfinished.

Trinitye Colledge.

Trinitye Colledge was founded by Kynge Henrye the eyghte, in the yeare of Christ. 1546. This Colledge was builded in the plat where sometyme Edwarde the thirde builded hys house called the Kinges haule, in the yeare of Christ. 1334. There was ioyned vnto this haule a Colledge called Michaell house, wyth an Hostill called Phisicke Hostell,

and

and after tha buildinge thereof beinge one of three, hee named it Trinity Colledge.

Michaell house was first founded by Haruious de stanton a priest, Chauncellour of the Eschequer to Edward the second, of whom hee obtayned lycence to erecte the sayde Colledge in the yeare of oure Sauioure Christ. 1324.

☞ And thus farre of the Uniuersitye of Cambridge, wyth the Colledges and haules in the same.

The Uniuersity of Oxforde was instituted by kinge Alfred a Saxon: after the birth of Christ. 873. yeres. And hath Colledges.

UNIVERSITY Colledge was founded in the tyme of Kynge Alfred, by sir William Archdeacon of Duresme in the yeare. 873. Vniuersitys Colledge.

Balioll Colledge was founded in the tyme.

Baliol Colledge. tyme of Edward the first, by Iohn Bayli-oll Kinge of Scotlande, in the yeare of Christ. 1263.

Mertō colledge. Merton Colledge was founded in ẏ tyme of Edwarde the first, by Walter Marton byshop of Rochester, the yeare of Christ. 1276.

Exeter Colledge. Exceter Colledge was foūded in the tyme of Edward the seconde, by Walter Stapleton bishop of Exceter. 1316. And augmēted in ẏ tyme of our Soue-raine Ladye Queene Elizabeth, by sir William Peter Knighte, in the yeare of Christ. 1566.

Oryall Colledge. Oriall Colledge was founded in the tyme of Edward the second, by sir Adā Browne Almoner of the said Kynge, the yeare of Christ. 1323.

Queenes Colledge. Queenes Colledge was founded in the tyme of Edward the third, by sir Roberd Englishfeld Chapleyne to the Lady Philippe, wyfe to the same Edwarde, the yeare of Christ. 1340.

New Colledge. Newe Colledge was founded in the tyme of Kynge Richarde the seconde, by William Wickam bishop of Winchester, the yeare of Christ. 1375.

Lincolne Colledge. Lincolne Colledge was founded in the time of Hēry ẏ fifth, by Richard Fle-

ming

The way from Barwyke to Yorke, and so to London.

From Barwyke to Belford xii.mile
From Belford to Anwyke xii.mile
From Anwyke to Morpit xii.mile
From Morpit to Newcastel xii mile
From Newcastel to Durham xii.mile
From Durham to Darington xiii.mi.
From Darlington to Northalerton xiiii.mile
From Northalerton to Toplif vii.mi.
From Toplife to Yorke xvi.mile
From Yorke to Tadcaster viii.mile
From Tadcaster to Wentbridge xii.mi.
From Wentbredge to Dancaster viii.mile
From Dancaster to Tutford xviii.mi.
From Tutford to newarke x.mile
From Newarke to Grantham x.mile
From Grantham to Stanford xvi.mi.
From Stanford to Stilton xii.mile
From Stilton to Huntington ix.mile
From Huntington to Roiston xv.mile
From Roiston to Ware xii.mile
From Ware to Waltham viii.mile
From Waltham to London xii.mile

The way from Carnarvan to Chester, and so to London.

The distaunce of Myles.

FRom Carnaruan to Conway.
xxiiii.mile

From Conway to Denbigh. xii.mile
From Denbigh to Flente xxi.mile
From Flente to Chester x.mile
From Chester to Nathe xiiii.mile
From Nathe to Stone. xv.mile
From Stone to Litchefield. xvi.mile
From Litchfild to Colsill xii.mile
From Colsill to Couentree viii.mile
And so from Couentrie to London, as hereafter followeth.

¶ The way from Cokermouth to Lancaster, and so to London.

FRom Cockermouth to Kiswik vi.mi.
From Keswike to Grocener viii.mi.
From Grocener to Kendale xiiii.mile
From Kendale to Burton vii.mile
From Burton to Lancaster viii mile
From Lancaster to Preston xx.mile
From Preston to Wygam xiiii.mile
From Wygan to Warington xx.mile
From Warington to Newcastel, xx.mi.
From Newcastel to Lichfield xx.mile
From Lichfield to Couentrie xx.mile
From Couentrie to Dauentrie xiiii.mi.
From Dauintrie to Tocester x.mile
Frō Tocester to Stony Stratford vi.mi.

From

From Stony Stratforde to Brickhill vii. mile
From Brickhill to Dunstable vii. mile
From Dunstable to S. Albons x. mile
From S. Albons to Barnet x. mile
From Barnet to London x. mile

¶ The way from Yermouth to Colchester, and so to London.

From Yermouth to Beclis viii. mile
from Beclis to Blybour viii. mile
From Blybour to Snapbridge viii. mi.
Frō Snapbridge to Woodbridge viii. mi.
From Woodbridge to Ipswiche v. mile
From Ipswiche to Colchester xii. mile
From Colchester to Eastford viii. mile
From Eastford to Chelmsford x. mile
From Chelmsford to Brentwood x. mi.
From Brentwood to London xv. mile

¶ The waye from Douer to London.

From Douer to Canterbury xii. mile
frō Caterbury to Sittingborn xii. mi
Frō Sittingborn to Rochester viii. mi.
From Rocher to Grauesend v. mile
From Grauesend to Dartford vi. mile
From Dartford to London xii. mile

¶ The waye from S. Bureine in Cornewail to London.

From

The distaunce of Miles.

FRō S. Buriens to the mount xx. mile
from the mount to Thury xii mile
from S. Thury to Bodman xx. mile
from Bodnam to Launstone xx. mile
from Launston to Ocomton xv. mile
from Ocomton to Crokehornwel x. mi.
from Crokehornewel to Excester x. mi.
from Excester to Honiton xii. mile
from Honiton to Chard x. mile
from Chard to Crokehorne vii. mi.
from Crokehorne to Shirborne x. mile
from Shirborn to Shaftsbury x. mile
from Shaftesbury to Salisbury xviii. m.
from Salisbury to Andevor xv. mile
from Andevor to Basingstocke xviii m.
from Basingstock to Hartford viii. mile
from Hartford to Bagshot viii. mile
from Bagshot to Staines viii. mile
from Staines to London xv. mile

¶ The way from Bristowe to London.

FRom Bristowe to Marsfeld x. mile
from Marsfield to Chipnam x. mile
from Chipnam to Marleborow xv. mi.
from Marleborow to Hungerford x. m.
from Hungerford to Newbery vii. mi.
from Newbery to Reading xv. mile
from Reading to Maydenhead x. mile
from Maidenhead to Colbroke vii mi.
from Colbroke to London xv. mile

The

The distaunce of Myles.

¶ The way from saint Dauids to London.

Rom S. Dauids to Arford xx. mile
from Arford to Carmarden x. mile
om Carmarden to Newton x. mile
om Newton to Lanbury x. mile
om Lanbury to Brecknoke xvi. mile
om Brecknoke to Hay x. mile
om Hay to Harford xiiii. mile
om Harford to Ross ix. mile
om Ross to Glocester xii. mile
om Glocester to Cicester xv. mile
om Cicester to Farington xvi. mile
om Farington to Habington vii. mi.
om Habington to Dorchester vii. mi.
om Dorchester to Henley xii. mile
om Henley to Maydenhead vii. mile
om Maydenhead to Colbroke vii. mi.
om Colbroke to London xv. mile

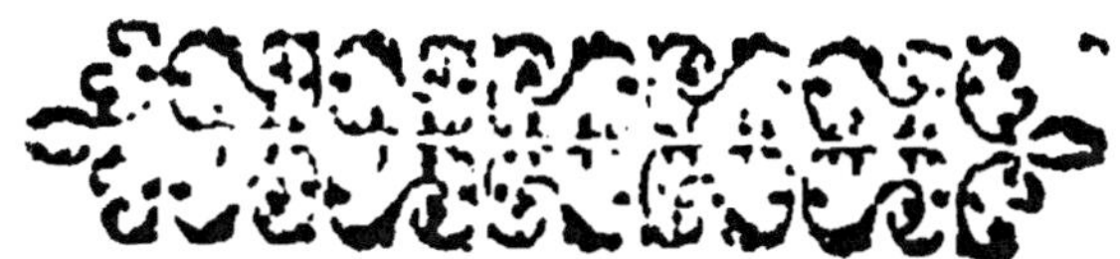

Here folowe the principall Fayres kept in Englande.

Fayres in January.

The first daye, being Twelfe daye, at Salisbury. The 25. being S. Paules day, at Bristowe, at Grauesende, at Clerchingford, at Northalerton in Yorkeshire where is kept a fayre euery wednesdaye from Christmas vntill June.

Fayres in February.

The first day at Bromley. The second at Lynne, at Bath, at Maydestone, at Bickelsworth, at Budworth. The xiiii at Feuersham. On Ash wednesday at Lichfield, at Tamworth, at Royston, at Exceter, at Abington, at Circeter. The 2 at Henly vpon Thames, at Tewkesbur

Fayres in Marche.

On saint Georges day, at Stamforde and at Sudbury. The 13. dey at My at the Mount, and at Bodmin in Cornwal. The v. sonday in Lent, at Grantham at Salisbury, On Mondaye before our Lady day in Lent, at Wisbich, at Kendal at Denbigh in Wales. On Palmsonday euen, at Pumphret. On Palmsonday, Worcester. The 20. day at Durham. On our Lady day in Lent, at Northampton, at Walden, at great Chart, at Newcastell. And all the Lady dayes at Hunting

Fay

Faires in England.

Fayres in Aprell.

He v. day at Maidingford. The 7. at
Darby, The 9. at Beckeliworth, at Bi
gworth or monday after, at Euesh[illegible]
Worcestershire. On tuesday in Easter
[illegible], at Northfleete, at Rockforde, at
[illegible]tchin. The [illegible] monday after Easter, at
[illegible]uth, The 23. at Stafford, On S. Geor
[illegible]s day, at Charing, at Ipswich, at Ta[illegible]
[illegible]rth, at Ambthil, at [illegible]mingham, at Gil[illegible]
d, at S. Pombers in Cornwall. On S.
[illegible]arkes daye at Darby, at Donmow in
[illegible]sex. The 25. at Tenderden in Kent.

Fayres in May.

A May day, at Rippon, at Perin in
Cornwall, at Chestree in Wales, at
[illegible]refield in Suffolke, at Stow the olde,
Reading, at Leicester, at Chensford,
Maydstone, at Brickhill, at Blacke[illegible]
[illegible]ne, at Cugelton. The third at Bren[illegible]
[illegible]de, at Henningham, at Elstow. The
[illegible], at Beuerley, at Newton, at Oxford,
[illegible] Ascentio day, at Newcastel, at Fern,
Brymecham, at S. Edes, at Bishopp
[illegible]ratford, at Wickham, at Midlewiche,
Stopford, at Chappel frith. On whit
[illegible]euen, at Skipton upon Crauen. On
[illegible]tsonday, at Reic hill, at Selby, and
[illegible]ry wednesday fortnight at Kingstone
on Thames, at Ratesdall, at Kirby

Stephin

Stephin in Westmerland. On mondaye in whitson weeke, at Darington, at Excester, at Bradford, at Rygate, at Burtō, at Salforth, at Whitchurch, at Cokermouth, at Appleby, at Bicklesworth, on tuesday on whitson weeke, at Lewse, at Rochford, at Caunterbury, at Ormeskyrke, at Herith. On wednisday in whitson weeke at Sandbacke. On Trinitie sunday, at Kendal, and at Rowell. On thursday after Trinitie sunday, at Prescote, at Stafford, at S. Innes, at Newbery, at Couentrie, at S. Eves, at byshop Stortforde, at Rosse. The 19. at Rochester, at Dunstable. The 27. day at Lenham. The 29. at Cranbrooke.

Fayres in Iune.

The ix. day at Maydestone. The xi. at Okingham, at Newborough, at Macclefelde, at Holt. The 23 at Shrewesbury, at saint Albons. The 24. at Horsham, at Bedel, at Strackstocke, at S. Innes, at Wakefield, at Colchester, at [illegible]ding, at Bedforde, at Barnewel, at Wolverhampton, at Cranbroke, at Glocester, at Lincolne, at Peterborough, at Winsore, at Marstone, at Lancaster, at Westchester, at Hallefaxe, at Ashborne. The 27. day at Folkestone. The 28. at Peterborne, at saint Pobes. The 29. at Woodhurst, at Mar-

kel-